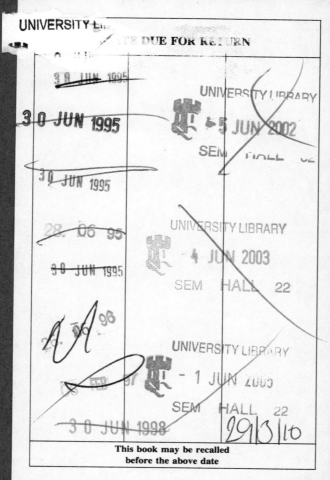

THE VICTORIAN SERIAL

VICTORIAN LITERATURE AND CULTURE SERIES

Karen Chase, Jerome J. McGann, *and* Herbert Tucker
General Editors

DANIEL ALBRIGHT
Tennyson: *The Muses' Tug-of-War*

DAVID G. RIEDE
Matthew Arnold and the Betrayal of Language

ANTHONY WINNER
Culture and Irony: *Studies in Joseph Conrad's Major Novels*

JAMES RICHARDSON
Vanishing Lives: *Style and Self in Tennyson, D. G. Rossetti, Swinburne, and Yeats*

JEROME J. MCGANN, EDITOR
Victorian Connections

ANTONY H. HARRISON
Victorian Poets and Romantic Poems: *Intertextuality and Ideology*

E. WARWICK SLINN
The Discourse of Self in Victorian Poetry

LINDA K. HUGHES and MICHAEL LUND
The Victorian Serial

THE
VICTORIAN
SERIAL

Linda K. Hughes
and
Michael Lund

UNIVERSITY PRESS OF VIRGINIA
Charlottesville and London

THE UNIVERSITY PRESS OF VIRGINIA
Copyright © 1991 by the Rector and Visitors
of the University of Virginia

First published 1991

Library of Congress Cataloging-in-Publication Data
Hughes, Linda K.
　The Victorian serial / Linda K. Hughes and Michael Lund.
　　p.　cm. — (Victorian literature and culture series)
　Includes bibliographical references (p.　) and index.
　ISBN 0-8139-1314-4 (cloth)
　　1. English literature—19th century—History and criticism.
　2. Periodicals, Publishing of—Great Britain—History—19th century.
　3. Serialized fiction—Great Britain—History and criticism.
　4. Poetry—Publishing—Great Britain—History—19th century.
　5. Books and reading—Great Britain—History—19th century.
　6. Serial publication of books—History—19th century.　I. Lund,
Michael, 1945–　.　II. Title.　III. Series.
PR468.P37H84　1991
820.9′008—dc20　　　　　　　　　　　　　　　　　90-20878
　　　　　　　　　　　　　　　　　　　　　　　　　　CIP

Printed in the United States of America

FOR
Louis and Marian Lund
A. M. and Helen Stauth

Contents

Illustrations

Preface

This study makes extensive use of reviews published in Victorian periodicals as individual installments of serial works and eventually completed volumes appeared. To conserve space, we have given in-text citation only of this extensive body of reviews. Whenever citing a review we have identified the journal title, the number or issue date, and the page number on which the relevant commentary appeared (reviews quoted from the *Critical Heritage* series are listed in our bibliography).

This study was made possible in part by an Interpretive Research grant from the Division of Research Programs of the National Endowment for the Humanities, an independent federal agency. The grant provided us with time away from teaching and funded travel for collaborative work. Travel to Collections awards from the Division of Fellowships and Seminars of the National Endowment for the Humanities allowed us to check our transcriptions from Victorian periodicals housed at the British Newspaper Library in Colindale. ACLS Grants-in-Aid provided initial support for our investigation of reviews of individual serial installments at Colindale.

We wish to thank the staff of the British Newspaper Library for their assistance during our work there. We also benefitted from the assistance of Pat Howe and Norma Taylor of Lancaster Library, Longwood College; Joyce Martindale of Mary Coutts Burnett Library, Texas Christian University; and Wilma Rife of Mabee Library, Washburn University.

THE VICTORIAN SERIAL

I

Introducing the Serial

A RECURRENT FEATURE OF Victorian literature was the tendency to look at life from within its temporal sequence, from points in the middle of life's progress, after the beginning and before the end. David Copperfield on the road from London to Dover and a loving family in Aunt Betsey and Mr. Dick, only one stage in his lifelong pilgrimage toward fame and fortune, provided a familiar point of reference for the last century.[1] Nineteenth-century images for human life, in fact, often stressed length more than shortness. And many Victorian narratives underscored the opportunities along life's path rather than its limited options: a series of recognized steps (not without danger, to be sure) marked the individual's (and the group's) long climb from infancy through maturity and on to an adulthood marked more by accomplishment than failure. The notion of the individual (and communal) life span as expansive, rich, nurturing, had underpinnings in more than the culture at large, however.[2]

This expansive vision of life is embodied in a central literary form of the era, the serial, a continuing story over an extended time with enforced interruptions.[3] Scholars have already established a great deal of the serial's history. Richard Altick's 1957 volume, *The English Common Reader,* remains the standard work on the rise of the serial as a popular form, the growing readership of the Victorian era, the means of serial literature's distribution, and its evolving format from the 1830s to the close of the nineteenth century. A number of studies have shown how individual authors designed—or modified—their work for serial issue. Others have studied the economic underpinnings of the serial form, a project that continues within newer theoretical frameworks today. Many have also begun to document the number of serials published in the Victorian era and the periodicals in which so many appeared.

Two major issues, however, have gone largely unexamined. First, though the serial has certainly been seen as an essential element in the literature of the dominant middle class, the serial's links to fundamental assumptions and values of that culture have received little attention. Yet the serial embodied a vision, a perspective on stories about life, intrinsic to Victorian culture. When we speak here of "the Victorian serial," therefore, we will be referring to a specific literary form (a continuing story over an extended time with enforced interruptions), to a body of work that appeared in the nineteenth century, and to a set of values bound up in the form and its traditions.

Second, if serialization is a well-known phenomenon, the dynamics of serial reading are far less familiar. What difference did it make that Victorians took two years (or even longer) to read a work that we customarily read in, say, two weeks today? A major concern of our study is thus to examine how reading stories a part at a time, with breaks between reading periods dictated by publishing format, affected the ways Victorian audiences first encountered sixteen major works of poetry and fiction. The results, based on accounts left by large numbers of Victorian readers, are often different from twentieth-century interpretations based on single-volume readings. These differences suggest not only that, for first readers, publication format became an essential factor in creating meaning but also that this reading process was entertwined with a vision of life no longer shared by the dominant literary culture of the twentieth century.

The first indication that the serial was an important cultural force is its pervasiveness. The impact of the serial's popularity in the wake of *Pickwick Papers* (1836–37) is evident in a sermon delivered by Thomas Arnold in Rugby Chapel in November 1839, three months after Frederick Marryat's *Phantom Ship* had completed its seventeen installments in the *New Monthly Magazine,* one month after Dickens's *Nicholas Nickleby* had completed its nineteen-month run, and during the month in which the eleventh part of Harrison Ainsworth's *Jack Sheppard* appeared in *Bentley's Miscellany* and the fifth part of William Thackeray's *Catherine* appeared in *Fraser's Magazine* (Vann 106–7, 63, 19, 133).[4] Arnold, seeking to explain the want of high seriousness among some of his students, remarked,

> (39, 41)
>
> *one cause I do find, which is certainly capable of producing such a result; a cause undoubtedly in existence now, and as certainly not in existence a few years back. . . . This cause consists in the number and character and cheapness, and peculiar mode of publication, of the works of amusement of the present day. In all these respects the change is great, and extremely recent. The works of amusement published only a very few years since were comparatively few in number; they were less exciting, and therefore less attractive; they were dearer, and therefore less accessible; and, not being published periodically, did not occupy the mind for so long a time, nor keep alive so constant an expectation; nor, by thus dwelling upon the mind, and distilling themselves into it, as it were drop by drop, did they*

possess it so largely, colouring even, in many instances, its very language,
and affording frequent matter for conversation. . . . They are of that class
which cannot be actually prohibited; nor can it be pretended that there is a
sin in reading them. They are not the more wicked for being published so
cheap, and at regular intervals; but yet these two circumstances make them
so peculiarly injurious.

If Arnold reveals that educators' complaints about the distractions of popular culture are not new, his anxiety also testifies to the excitement and impact wrought by the serial's sudden popularity. The number of serial works continued to grow throughout the century, and though not all shared the regular issuance remarked on by Arnold,[5] they became a familiar format to first readers of fiction, poetry, and prose.

That a great deal of Victorian fiction first appeared in installments is well known, though the work of documenting its extent is still under way. J. Don Vann lists just under two hundred novels in *Victorian Novels in Serial,* and space constrained him to limit his index to selected authors (none of the works of Mary Elizabeth Braddon, for example, are included, nor are the novels serialized by Joseph Conrad). An enormous number of additional novels were serialized in the magazines and newspapers in the last half of the century. And the practice was shared by other European novelists as well. The list of titles first appearing serially includes Flaubert's *Madame Bovary* (1856–57), Tolstoy's *Anna Karenina* (1875–77), Dostoevsky's *The Brothers Karamazov* (1879–80), Henry James's *The Portrait of a Lady* (1880–81), and Howells's *The Rise of Silas Lapham* (1885).

A number of prose works, too, appeared in installments, including Carlyle's *Sartor Resartus* (1833–34), Newman's *Apologia Pro Vita Sua* (1864), Arnold's *Culture and Anarchy* (1867–68),[6] Morris's *A Dream of John Ball* (1886–87), and almost all of Ruskin's major works.[7] Serialization became so prominent, in fact, that a substantial body of poetry also appeared serially. Some of these extended the tradition of poems issued a volume at a time at irregular intervals, a practice common to Samuel Butler's *Hudibras* in the seventeenth century and James Thomson's *The Seasons* in the eighteenth, as well as to Byron's *Don Juan,* Tennyson's *Idylls of the King,* and Morris's *Earthly Paradise* in the nineteenth century.[8] The Victorian serial poems issued irregularly, however, still exhibited a continuing story over extended time with enforced interruptions, and they were read by an audience attuned to a vast production of serial literature. Reviewers thus regularly spoke of individual volumes under consideration as "instalments."

In addition, many Victorian poems were serialized on a periodic basis, further indicating the serial's pervasiveness. Among the serial poems we discuss, Patmore's *The Victories of Love,* Browning's *The Ring and the Book,* and Morris's *The Pilgrims of Hope* were all published in monthly installments, two of them in periodicals. Other serial poems of the age include Bulwer Lytton's *The New Timon* (issued in four anonymous parts, December 1845–March 1846) and *St. Stephen's* (January–March 1860) in *Blackwood's;* Alexander Smith's *A Life-Drama* (1 March 1852–15 January 1853) in the *Critic;* Arthur Hugh Clough's *Amours de Voyage* (February–May 1858) in *Atlantic Monthly;* William Allingham's *Lawrence Bloomfield in Ireland* (November 1862–November 1863) in *Fraser's Magazine;* and James Thomson's *City of Dreadful Night* (22 March–17 May 1874) in the *National Reformer*—a by-no-means inclusive list.

As the reference to *Hudibras* and *The Seasons* suggests, serialization was not new to the Victorian era.[9] But that serialization became pervasive in the Victorian era, making the erudite Thomas Arnold consider it a new phenomenon in the 1830s, suggests that something in the culture of the time made it especially receptive to the serial.[10] Of course, rising literacy rates, urbanization, and growing prosperity played an essential role in making the serial a characteristic nineteenth-century form. But beyond the fact that serialization made literature more affordable to a mass audience, the serial was attuned to the assumptions of its readers.

The serial form, for example, harmonized in several respects with capitalist ideology. Norman Feltes argues that the serial novel fulfilled the middle-class desire for a "cheap luxury": the part was a thing to be had for the time being yet also promised more to come, and the richness of detail and expansion of the text over time suggested a world of plenitude (*Modes* 9, 13–14). Indeed, the confident capitalist framework during the booming years of nineteenth-century economic expansion had a kind of literary analogue in the serial form. The assumption of continuing growth and the confidence that an investment (whether of time or money) in the present would reap greater rewards in the future were shared features of middle-class capitalism and of serial reading. (The opposite process, the accumulation of debt leading to bankruptcy and ruin, simply completed the linear pattern of fiscal processes. Rags-to-riches stories were appropriately one of the most popular forms for this century.) In addition, the perseverance and delay of gratification necessary for middle-class economic success were, in a sense, echoed in serial reading, which required readers to stay with a story a long time and to postpone learning a story's outcome. Readers approaching stories within a single volume can "cheat," thumbing ahead to a mystery's solution; serial readers could not. If the original impetus behind serialization was economic, then, additional reasons for the form's appeal seem to lie in the ideological harmony between the serial form and its middle-class readership.

Involvement in an ongoing story, from its advertised commencement through a long publication to its satisfying conclusion, matched significant patterns of Victorian life in addition to capitalism. Certainly, this age subscribed to a notion of personal development running from infancy through maturity and ending in old age, as we discuss in chapter two. Though not as much as in earlier ages, many still conceived an underlying pattern in life of the Christian's journey from this world to the next, powerfully represented in *Pilgrim's Progress,* a work read by more people in England than any book except the Bible, and in the calendar for the church year, which retraced Christ's life from Advent through Pentecost. Evangelical and Utilitarian ethics also insisted on steady application over great reaches of time to achieve distant rewards.

Others elements of Victorian intellectual life would also have operated to make the serial an amenable form for the age's best literature. As Richard Altick (*Victorian* 96–97), Jerome Buckley (1–2, 6), and many others have noted, dramatic changes in conceptions of time occurred during the nineteenth century: time at once contracted and expanded. If technological innovations like the railroad and the rapid changes of a newly industrialized society helped speed up the sense of time's passage,[11] new work in geology, history, archeology, and biology acted to emphasize the immensity of time. This enlarged sense of time was conceived partly as an expanding sequence, partly as an accumulation of layers, a point given force by archaeologists' excavations and geologists' stratigraphic columns.

An analogous contraction and expansion in reading time can be observed in serial literature. If the publication of works a part at a time met the needs of increasingly rushed readers who were not free to devote continuous hours to reading, the serial dovetailed even more with the new awareness of time's extended duration. The characteristic story told in a serial is, emphatically, a long story. Just as its details are so manifold and complex that they are difficult to fit within the confines of a single volume, so the telling expands to involve weeks, months, even years. As Malcolm Bradbury and David Palmer assert, "unlike those Romantics who identified eternity in the brief moments of personal epiphanies, unlike the symbolists who struggled to rescue form from history and time-bound discourse, the Victorians responded to the sequence of time, to its motion and unfolding perspectives" (8). And this was a sensibility reinforced by the extended sequence of the serial form. The serial also had a layering effect over time, putting down first one layer of story, then another as part succeeded part. Thomas Arnold again captured the point when he spoke of serial stories "dwelling upon the mind, and distilling themselves into it, as it were drop by drop."

Another manifestation of the age's new understanding of time was its historicism, the sense that human nature was not always everywhere the same but that individual cultures began, developed, and then lapsed only to be supplanted by a new order. We discuss historicism and its relation to the serial form in greater detail in chapter three, but it is worth noting here that Victorian interest in history would also have helped make the serial a congenial Victorian form: both historicism and serial literature focused on gradual developments over time and a complicated skein of events. And insofar as historical consciousness made Victorians view their own age as an age of transition, the serial might again seem congenial, since every installment (except the first and the last) was both an event in itself and a transition from the story's past to the future. The frequent (if by no means universal) assertions of progress in the age would also have promoted the popularity of a form that depended so much on audiences' anticipation and delight in "more to come."

Victorian historicism as well as the increasingly prominent work in geology and biology embraced another central tenet of dominant Victorian ideology, uniformitarian rather than catastrophic principles, models of steady, continuous, consistent development rather than abrupt, cataclysmic, revolutionary change. In the early 1830s Charles Lyell "won the geological war against catastrophism, which enabled his belief in the uniformity of rate to become a textbook shibboleth" (Sulloway 39).[12] Nor were uniformitarian principles restricted to scientific or historical treatises. Following 1848 many British citizens congratulated themselves on the political gradualism that had saved England from the dislocations on the Continent; earlier, in 1842, Tennyson had celebrated a land in which "Freedom slowly broadens down / From precedent to precedent" ("You ask me, why, though ill at ease"). Uniformitarianism was even an element of railway travel. As Wolfgang Schivelbusch remarks, "The mechanical motion generated by steam power is characterized by regularity, uniformity, unlimited duration and acceleration"; he quotes an early promoter of the railway, who proclaimed, " 'No animal strength . . . will be able to give that uniform and regular acceleration to our commercial intercourse which may be accomplished by railway' " (9).

Within the framework of the Victorian middle class, then, scientific, political, historical, and even industrial sectors displayed a uniformitarian ethos. Uniformitarianism was also a feature of serial literature, especially serials published at regular intervals. But in any case the serial confuted the "catastrophic" notion of artistic inspiration, a kind of gigantic creative shudder that results in a single aesthetic product. The serial occurred gradually, not suddenly, and it was premised on such uniform principles that a month's hiatus in the plot was not fatal to the work's underlying coherence or continuous growth.[13]

Indeed, the serial shared with other Victorian cultural constructs an entire cluster of developmental, gradualist tendencies. Such tendencies were an essential part of work done in the life sciences. For example, nineteenth-century embryological theory (first articulated by C. F. Wolff in 1759) displaced older notions of the fetus as a miniature human being and instead viewed the origin of human life as a linear series of developmental phases leading inevitably from simpler to more complex organization of life (Chapple 2, Shuttleworth 11–12). A serial literary work also grew from simpler to more complex order, from a single initial fragment to an accreting and diversifying collocation of characters and plot lines. *Idylls of the King* excepted, serials also grew in a strict chronological sequence over a span often lasting longer than fetal development, a sequence determined by publishing schedule and reinforced by the linear narrative technique associated with literary realism.

In the culture at large, again, biblical accounts of creation as an instantaneous and full-blown event were challenged by the Darwinian theory of evolution that viewed creation as a slow unfolding of life-forms over vast amounts of time with pauses (or at least gaps in the fossil record) between developments. Serialization, analogously, fostered an approach to narrative as a gradually developing story and pattern of significance, with pauses between parts for additional reflection and speculation, rather than as a finished aesthetic product to be read and considered as a whole all at once.

As a result of the work by Darwin, the geologist Charles Lyell, and others, nature itself was historicized (Jordanova 28, Toulmin and Goodfield 232), while history consolidated its prestige by linking its work to that of science, since both examined the processes of change and development (Jann xi–xii). We should not forget that serialized works like *David Copperfield* carried the term *History* in their titles,[14] a convention inherited from the eighteenth century but one that acquired greater force because serialization imparted literal history to fiction during the many months of serial publication.

Thus, to grasp why serialization became so pervasive and agreeable a vehicle for the age's best literature, we need to see that the serial form was more than an economic strategy. It was also a literary form attuned to fundamental tendencies in the age at large. As Jordanova observes of the era, "Analogies abounded: individual life histories, the history of the earth, of nations, tribes, races and empires, cities and families, the development of a foetus, of languages themselves" (28–29)—and, we would add, of serialized literary works.

If the extended time of processes was common to many of the age's intellectual frameworks, an extended reading time was a crucial element of serial literature. While we are all familiar with the fact that Dickens issued eight of his major texts in a twenty-part, nineteen-month format, we do not always take into account how much the sheer length of time affected Victorians' understanding of major works.[15] Even readers in the last third of the century did not expect to complete their favorite novels in less than the year and a half of Trollope's *Phineas Finn* (October 1867–May 1869 in *St. Paul's Magazine*), the year of Hardy's *The Woodlanders* (*Macmillan's Magazine,* May 1886–April 1887), the eleven months of Kipling's *Kim* (*McClure's Magazine,* December 1900–October 1901), or the four years of Hardy's *The Dynasts* (1904–8). The most commonly noted effect of the serial's publication schedule is suspense and anticipation (inspired by the cliff-hanger), but suspense is only part of what happened. Because the reading time was so long, interpretation of the literature went on during the expansive middle of serial works. Readers and reviewers engaged in provisional assumptions and interpretations about the literary world, which then shaped the evolving understanding of works as they continued to unfold part by part. And a work's extended duration meant that serials could become entwined with readers' own sense of lived experience and passing time.[16] The response to and involvement in such extended works, then, was different from what modern readers experience completing entire works in a few days or weeks.

The physical books that nineteenth-century readers held in their hands and the context in which the reading experience occurred also differed from the editions or classroom texts of Victorian literature often studied by twentieth-century scholars. Reading did not occur in an enclosed realm of contemplation possible with a single-volume text; rather, Victorian literature, because of its parts structure, was engaged much more within the busy context of everyday life. It was not possible to enter into an imaginary world and remain there until the story's end; instead readers repeatedly were forced to set aside a continuing story and resume everyday life. In that space between readings, their world continued to direct a barrage of new information and intense experience at readers; and that context complicated and enriched the imagined world when the literary work was resumed.

Even within the covers of individual installments, signs of the outer world were a part of the reader's text. Novels issued in separate monthly parts were framed by advertisements for the latest medicines, clothes appropriate to the emerging, successful middle class, the most recent domestic appliances, books of travel, cheap editions of classic texts, and the latest best-sellers. Even as individual parts of poems or novels were being read in periodicals, in addition, they were surrounded by other stories—political, historical, scientific—on neighboring pages. Long poems issued in separate volumes over time also featured advertisements for succeeding parts of the same work, the author's collected editions, or the productions of other contemporary poets.

Not only did the real world intrude on individual fictional worlds, but many literary texts overlapped each other in their parts publication. For instance, *The Holy Grail and Other Poems* from Tennyson's *Idylls of the King,* volume two of Morris's *Earthly Paradise,* and the sixth monthly number of Trollope's *The Vicar of Bulhampton* all appeared in December 1869. An extended concurrent literary event involved Thackeray's *Pendennis* and Dickens's *David Copperfield,* two bildungsromans concerned with the development of an author's personality, parts of which appeared simultaneously from May 1849 through November 1850 (Lund 59–78).

In addition to individual poems and novels that provided a context for the response to other works of literature, texts from other spheres sometimes affected audiences' understanding. As Louis James has provocatively suggested, we might even view each volume of a specific periodical like the *Cornhill* (a bound annual, semiannual, or quarterly set) as a single text by a corporate author; for subscribers certainly read much in each issue of their favorite journal, linking together in their minds not just specific continuing stories but overlapping ongoing presentations tied together by editorial principles (350–52).

Just as each individual text in its separate monthly part, single volume, or periodical installment was surrounded by other stories, it was also frequently accompanied by a visual context, illustration. This too meant that for Victorian audiences the novel or poem was not always a self-contained verbal entity but a reading process embedded in a specific material framework that shaped response. Each monthly part of a Dickens or Thackeray novel began with an illustrated cover and two full-page illustrations inspired by the thirty-two pages of text, and many novels in periodicals as late as the 1890s contained drawings to heighten involvement. Even poetry was frequently illustrated, although the illustrations did not always appear with the original text. For instance, the illustrations for *Idylls of the King* (1859) by Gustave Doré were issued in four parts by Edward Moxon from 1867 to 1868. And subsequent editions of many other poets were often lavishly illustrated. Thus, the individual Victorian serial text was surrounded by other texts and pictures that inspired a more complex, multifarious response than we sometimes acknowledge in critical readings.

Similarly, individual Victorian readers existed within a community of readers whose voices in person and in print augmented understanding of literary works. This community of readers shared a number of elements in their literary experience, such as the pleasure and excitement of anticipation.[17] Letters, newspaper reports, and personal reminiscences consistently attested to the excitement of "magazine day" (the first of the month when new issues appeared in bookstalls across the country). Once they had purchased or borrowed the latest installment, Victorians might read it aloud. This practice, in a family or neighborhood, enhanced the sense that literature in nineteenth-century England was a national event, that response was public as well as private. Moreover, reactions to the latest part could be shared and intensified. The time between installments in serial literature gave people the opportunity to review events with each other, to speculate about plot and characters, and to deepen ties to their imagined world.

Word of mouth and early, short notices in newspapers spread the readership of popular serials. As the serial work progressed over time, the community of readers often increased in size as well, an analogue of Victorian growth in other spheres, as we explain in chapter four. As the audience grew, so did the sense of closeness between readers and characters. Indeed, a story's characters could come to seem a part of readers' own extended family or circle of friends. The opportunity for this acquaintance was one reason that Richard Holt Hutton preferred the serial form for certain works:

(305–6)
> *We are disposed to maintain that no story gets so well apprehended, so completely mastered in all its aspects, as one which, written as a whole, is published in parts. There is, at all events, this to be said in its favor,— that it is the only way in which human life itself, of which fiction is supposed to be the mirror, can be studied. There, you are not allowed to*

see the beginning, middle, and end at a sitting, like the springing-up,
budding, and blowing of a flower beneath the bidding of an Egyptian
conjuror, but must usually become perfectly familiar with the human
elements of a story before you see them even begin to combine into a plot.
And in the case of Middlemarch, *we are perfectly sure that, other things*
being equal, those will understand it best and value it most who have
made acquaintance slowly during the past year with all its characters, and
discussed them eagerly with their friends, in all the various stages of their
growth and fortune.

Personal appeals to authors that they provide happy resolutions to plots or
the return of favorite characters from disaster or even death underscore the
importance of the serial's creation of intimacy between reader and story.
They also remind us of readers' sense of closeness with the author. Thus,
literature in Victorian England had an immediacy and pervasiveness now
generated perhaps only by best-sellers and television; and this context,
difficult for us to recreate in classroom or formal analysis, is important to
understanding the age and its works.

We need, then, to see the serial taking place amidst many different
texts and many different voices. In fact, different versions of the same
story sometimes even appeared concurrently. Dramatizations of a Dickens
novel, for instance, were often being staged before the serial version had
run its course. His *Tale of Two Cities* appeared both as a novel in eight
monthly parts and in the pages of the weekly *All the Year Round* (30 April–
26 November 1859). Tennyson's *Idylls* were available in the separate
volumes first issued and in library or cabinet editions, which arranged the
various idylls in the chronological sequence of the kingdom rather than the
order of publication. In addition to all these interconnected texts, individual readers pursued their own ongoing lives, with their many contexts of
personal, professional, and political concerns, at the same time they assim-
ilated and reacted to the great variety of literary works available to them.

The interruptions inherent in serials naturally encouraged writers to
work in the primary mode of the Victorian age, realism. Reading one
installment, then pausing in that story, the Victorian audience turned to
their own world with much the same set of critical faculties they had used
to understand the literature. And then a week or month or more later, they
picked up again a continuing story to be apprehended in much the same
way they had been interpreting the reality presented in newspapers and
letters and by word of mouth.

The techniques of literary realism that allow such transition between literature and life might be dismissed by modern masters, and it might seem the special qualities of the individual work were muted or blurred by the many voices that surrounded it. But readers did not, in fact, express difficulty at keeping separate their multiple stories in varied formats. When contexts did mix one with another, moreover, results often revealed important ideas Victorians held about themselves and their world. Scholars have noted a number of instances of authors affected by contemporary events while composing their works. Hardy, for instance, developed his famous cliff-hanging scene in *A Pair of Blue Eyes* (September 1872–July 1873) partly in response to an article in *Fraser's* by Leslie Stephen, which placed religious doubt in the context of recent scientific discoveries. Yet we have hardly begun to explore how Hardy's readers themselves might have reacted to parts of *A Pair of Blue Eyes* in the context of what was being published at the same time in *Tinsley's Magazine*. The overlapping context of other serials and other periodicals offers additional complication, but also additional excitement, for scholars who wish to trace the creation of reputations for individual works and authors.

As we have been arguing, much of what made literature meaningful to the nineteenth century occurred during the reading of a work, before its ending had been reached, just as we all assess the importance of events in our personal lives and in the world without knowing how it will all turn out. The best source for information about such reactions remains Victorian periodicals, particularly the London weeklies.[18] In the second half of the century, inexpensive Sunday newspapers like the *Guardian, Lloyd's Weekly London Newspaper, Bell's Weekly Messenger, Reynold's Weekly Newspaper, News of the World, Sunday Times, Weekly Dispatch, Weekly Times, Illustrated London News* and others regularly reviewed monthly installments of fiction and poetry. Even though many notices were brief and their authors sometimes less distinguished than the reviewers of the more prestigious monthly and quarterly periodicals, their commentary provides a guide to Victorian middle-class reading of important literary works. Our analyses of individual texts in the chapters that follow incorporate this remarkably detailed record of audience response, while also including additional commentary from the more well-known journals included in the *Wellesley Index to Victorian Periodicals*. Though we would have liked to distinguish between male and female, urban and rural, middle-class and working-class reviewers in the weeklies, it has been impossible to do so with extant scholarly tools. Identifying this record of reader response according to cultural categories awaits future research;

meanwhile we present what we have found to be dominant reactions to major texts.

In exploring the serial reading of major Victorian texts we are not ignoring the fact that many people read volume editions in a single or a few sittings after parts publication had been completed. However, those texts and that tradition have been well documented by others. The established view of the Victorian serial, in fact, derives from a bias for these volume texts. According to the modern theory of serials the form was, for instance, necessarily sensational because each part had to contain an exciting event to retain audience interest. Further, anything that appeared in installments was fragmentary, inferior to a work that was contained within certain boundaries or was whole and complete. An installment form was also said to be so loose and undisciplined that extraneous matter, padding needed to fill out individual parts, was bound to lessen the value of a work. And when the audience voiced its opinion about the serial's content as it was appearing, the author who responded, positively or negatively, was compromised in the control of artistic material. Such charges have been aimed at poems as well as novels, specifically Tennyson's *Idylls of the King*.[19]

Such negative assertions about the serial form, however, are products of a time, the first half of this century, in which both the subjects and forms of Victorian literature were being denigrated. While in the last forty years much Victorian literature has been restored to respectability, the installment form itself remains suspect.[20] We offer here, however, a positive view of the Victorian serial both as an art form and as a set of assumptions. Implicit in our argument, for instance, is an assertion that because the serial story went on in an extended delivery or publication despite breaks, such works embodied a conviction that human activities can be sustained over considerable reaches of time and extended across gaps in their performance. That the narrative was made up of a number of parts suggests that a short form was inadequate to the task at hand and that the activity depicted required an expansive mode for its full character. And the choice of an installment mode over a single issue suggests that the audience's commitment to the story was expected to be great, for the author allowed the readers or listeners the extra time of pauses in delivery or publication to mull over, speculate about, or even challenge material presented in each part of the whole. And the author counted on the story's appeal to regain that audience's attention after a break.

Our effort here, then, is to show a generally ignored aspect of the

Victorian literary experience. Even in the cases where volume publication followed an initial serialization, the shaping influence of the installment text was often more important than has been recognized. For instance, many Victorian readers were so intrigued by the portrait of Honoria in the two anonymous volumes of *Angel in the House* published in 1854 and 1856 that they could not accept her very different but more interesting role in the 1860 *Faithful for Ever* published under Patmore's name. Meredith's *Diana of the Crossways* appearing in the *Fortnightly Review* (June–December 1884) determined later reaction to the longer, complete text published in February 1885. And we believe negative reaction to Hardy's last novel *Jude the Obscure* actually took shape months before it was published, during the serialization of this tale under the title of *Hearts Insurgent* (December 1894–November 1895).

Our approach in chapters two through five is to look at serial novels and poems that treat a central subject of the age: home, history, empire, doubt. Attempting to recreate elements of the original serial reading of these works, we explore how the principal theme was shaped by installment structure. Crossing genres to discuss novels and poems within this framework, we hope to focus on the serial form itself and the ways in which it manifested key values of the age. Our reading of each work is supported by liberal quotation from contemporary Victorian periodical reviews of individual installments and is placed within modern scholarly evaluations. In chapter six we explore how the Victorian serial mode clashed with the modernist single-volume form in significant turn-of-the-century texts, spelling an end to a form and the ideas implicit in it.

We have been moved to write by the awareness that we no longer live in the age of the literary serial, that we are governed by the mode of single-volume publication and the sets of beliefs that have traveled with it for this century. But by examining an old frame of reference from our own place in time, we hope to illuminate both landscapes.

II

Creating a Home

No magic of her voice or smile
Raised in a trice a fairy isle,
But fondness for her underwent
An unregarded increment,
Like that which lifts, through centuries,
The coral reef within the seas,
Till, lo! the land where was the wave.

Coventry
Patmore,
Angel in the
House

"Why, Mother!" said Alice Marwood, shaking
her ragged skirts to detach the old woman from
them: "there are two sides to that. There have
been years for me as well as you, and there has
been wretchedness for me as well as you."

Charles
Dickens,
Dombey and
Son

. . . a novelist must go on with his heroine, as a
man with his wife, for better or worse, and to the
end.

William
Makepeace
Thackeray,
The
Newcomes

COVENTRY PATMORE'S most famous poem, *Angel in the House* (1854–63), now stands as a byword for an oppressive code imposed on women. The Victorian angel in the house, whether embodied in Honoria Vaughan, Florence Dombey, or Ethel Newcome, has come to represent a cluster of repressions that crippled women, men, and children. Thus we are most familiar with middle-class Victorian homes that were hierarchical, starkly polarized along gender lines, and hand in glove with the ideology of capitalist competition—the "glove," of course, being the cultivation (and isolation) of feminine virtues within the home that made possible, and bearable, the male's ventures into a world of commerce and the cash nexus.[1] The Victorian middle-class home was all these things, but it was something more as well. To focus on its limitations is fair but not complete.[2] Looking at Victorian literature in the context of serialization helps us recover the constructive elements of Victorian attitudes toward home, especially since the virtues that sustain a home and the traits required of serial readers so often coincided.

One of these is a capacity for endurance, perseverence, and patience. Only among those willing to endure unpleasant times, hardship, or conflict through commitment to long-lasting relationships can homes prevail. Those who give up at the first sign of thwarted desire or fulfillment—or merely boredom—can provide no lasting shelter for kin or companions. Homes marred by abuse or tyranny, of course, turn even persistence into a flaw, if not a vice. But any long-lasting human relationship, whether between friends, lovers, or family members, depends for its success on affectionate patience.

The Victorian age most frequently allotted women the task of embodying domestic endurance and patience in its stories, hence the array of long-suffering female heroines represented in this chapter by Jane Graham, Florence Dombey, and Ethel Newcome.[3] Patience and endurance, of course, apply to serial literature as well as to homes: original audiences of the works under discussion had to exercise patience and persistence as readers, withstanding the obstacles of frustrating delays or boredom for nineteen months to nine years. And just as Victorian spouses and parents were called upon to remain loyal to their families, preserving secure homes amidst temporary absences or temptations, so the serial publishing format encouraged a kind of loyalty from its readers that could also transcend the absence of a story's characters in the intervals between parts. Readers who persisted, becoming "loyal fans," lived on intimate terms with characters of the imagination, taking them inside homes and even minds, sharing their acquaintance with others outside the pages, and so extending a kind of intimacy also associated with home.

The congruence between domestic ideology and elements of serial reading could, however, take a less benign turn. In reviewing the first installment of *Angel in the House,* the May 1855 *Eclectic Review* articulated the sense of home as refuge from the commercial world and then connected home and poetry: "[Home] is a place of refuge from the storm and strife that is for ever going on in this competitive world. What should we do were it not for this happy haven [in] which . . . the grim brow grows smooth in the placid smile of love, poetry comes into the face that is furrowed with the hieroglyphs of business, and the shut-up heart opens in the warmth of affection, and expands until it can embrace humanity in the arms of its love" (551). This commentary suggests the marginality of home, poetry, and women to the world of men and business. At regular intervals, in time off from work, men resorted to the enfolding boundaries of home for moral uplift, emotional nurturance, and delight before they returned to the "real world"—the same terms on which they resorted to literature, a point made even clearer with parts publication, which did not demand long investments of time all at once.[4]

Generally, however, the alignment of domestic and serial sensibilities involved affirmation rather than evasion. To cite another instance, life within the Victorian home was seen as a continuing sequence of nonreversible stages, whether applied to courtship leading to marriage, marriage itself, or child rearing. One literary convention derived from this domestic ideology and often used in the serial form is the courtship plot. Robert Kiely discerns a pattern in courtship plots consisting of "encounter, attraction, break, and resolution in either final reunion or separation" (quoted in Boone, *Tradition* 71). Kiely's pattern is evident in Patmore's poem: the 1854 volume, subtitled *The Betrothal,* culminated in Honoria Churchill's acceptance of Felix Vaughan's marriage proposal; the poem then broke off until 1856, when *The Espousals* appeared, to be followed by *Faithful for Ever* in 1860 and *The Victories of Love* (first serialized in three parts in *Macmillan's Magazine* in 1861, then reissued in volume form in 1863).

If these stages of domestic life and their representation in plots occurred in strict sequence, however, they did not culminate in static, fixed endings but remained embedded in process. The entire plot suggested by Patmore's titles (victories of love are not won until long after marriage) thus complicates arguments that "the impetus toward closed endings . . . in . . . variations on the marriage theme reflects the wish to believe in a stable organization underlying social reality and cultural convention; by rounding off the work's vision into a complete and contained whole, the writer attempts to leave the reader in an unquestioning state of repose and acceptance" (Boone, "Wedlock" 69; see also *Tradition* 78). Patmore's 1854 poem ended but did not close with betrothal; the poem again ended but did not close with espousals. In fact Victorians' complete ideology of home, in and out of literature, suggested a larger, gradually occurring and non-reversible sequence that embraced not only engagement and marriage but also the begetting and raising of children, the emergence into late maturity and grandparenthood, and then death that itself led to ongoing spiritual life in which, many Victorians fervently hoped, personal relationships persisted. This larger domestic sequence chimed with the aesthetics of serialization, which presented stories unfolding in strict sequence and stages with pauses and breaks along the way until a distant (but rarely final) closure was achieved.

The same sequence of stages informs stories of Victorian childhood, whether in the bildungsroman or as part of larger stories of life and home.[5] In the twentieth century the sequential (or consequential) plot has lost favor and is often seen as a naive or even domineering imposition on reality (though many insist on developmental sequences for biological organisms, as in Piaget's sequential, nonreversible model of childhood development). Victorian stories of children, then, embody an emphatic sequence affirming that growth and development must occur in stages embedded in linear time. Once again, this view of childhood development was reinforced by serialization, which also depended on elapsed time and a sequence of stages for its story to grow and achieve maturity. Hence, in this chapter, we want to explore not only how domestic virtues within Victorian ideology are particularly apparent in the recovered record of Victorian serial readers but also how serial reading could extend, augment, and influence the perception of domestic themes. Within the serial experience, author, characters, and reader alike contributed their part toward creating a home.

Patmore's depiction of women has become infamous, especially the 1886 version of *Angel in the House* adopted for the standard edition of Patmore's verse.[6] The poem's original, serial version, while offensive to twentieth-century sensibilities, is a less egregious, more interesting poem than the 1886 text. The prologue to the 1886 *Angel in the House* presents an entirely passive and "well-pleased Wife" (*Poems* 63) who receives her husband's poem. In the 1854 prologue to *The Betrothal,* she is an active collaborator on the text: "Then, arguing high artistic laws, / Long did they o'er the plan confer. / 'Twas fix'd, with much on both sides said." In receiving the poem she has an equally active role, for she is not the "well-pleased Wife" but a "kind critic" (*Betrothal* 7).[7] The spouses' interaction rather than fixed, static roles in these lines can remind us of a point about the larger poem itself. Original Victorian audiences did not encounter a tightly bound, static text but one in process, and their reception of it affected their notion of the entire poem.[8] As a reviewer for the *Illustrated London News* remarked on 13 June 1863, by which time the entire poem had been issued,

(651)   *Horace, an invaluable authority, mentions nine years as the proper*
          time for an author to keep his MS. by him before sending it forth to try its

fortune with the public. He does not say whether, on the principle of reci-
procity, the public is bound to suspend its judgment an equal space of time.
By the end of such a period (rather more than twice the lifetime of the
second French Republic) the book and the judgment must both be toler-
ably mature; and, indeed, the fact of any book surviving to be talked of
nine years after publication, may safely be accepted as a symptom of re-
markable goodness or badness, of a superiority to commonplace, at all
events. Exactly this magic period happens to have elapsed since the first
instalment of "The Angel in the House" was given to the world. Warmly
praised, vigorously attacked, the work has, at all events, given ample
proof of vitality. It has lived, it has thriven, it has added to its growth, it
has shed superfluous limbs, it has developed itself from the original germ
into the two handsome volumes before us. Good, bad, or indifferent, as it
may be pronounced, it is, at all events, a fact, something of which the stu-
dent of our modern literature must take cognisance, whether he will or no.

The reviewer's language of development, growth, and vitality can alert us
to similar concerns in the poem itself. Its most important theme is that true
marital love involves gradual development (rather than static possession)
dependent on the passage of time for full realization (see also Ball 4–5,
Burdett 46–47). It was a theme made more compelling by the poem's serial
publishing format, as we shall see in both the details of the first edition and
the reception of its installments.

Three marriages occur in the several parts of *Angel in the House:* one
between Felix Vaughan and Honoria Churchill following an idealized
courtship; one between the disappointed suitor for Honoria's hand, Frederick Graham, and the unidealized Jane (whose maiden name we never
know); and one between John Graham, son of Frederick and Jane, and
Emily Vaughan, daughter of Felix and Honoria—the last clearly a synthe-
sis of the first two and the beginning of a new generation. The clergy are
inseparable from marriage as Patmore conceives it, and so Dean Churchill,
Honoria's father and Frederick's uncle, pronounces on all three unions. In
every case his point is the same: marriage is a starting point, never a
conclusion. To his new son-in-law, Felix, he remarks after the wedding
ceremony,

(*Espousals*
156–57)

>   "She's your's; but I love more than yet
>   "You can: such fondness only wakes
>   "When time has rais'd the heart above
>   "The prejudice of youth, which makes
>   "Beauty conditional to love."

Writing to his nephew after learning the surprising news of his marriage, the dean counsels against placing too much trust in "the fragile youth / Of wedlock" (*Faithful* 140) and emphasizes instead the process of a marriage embedded in daily life—"Love's simple gamut day by day" (*Faithful* 143). The dean articulates the poem's philosophy of marriage as a whole in his final wedding sermon, which first appeared in the December 1861 *Macmillan's Magazine:*

Lovers, once married, deem their bond
Then perfect, scanning nought beyond
For love to do but to sustain
The spousal hour's completed gain.
(114)   But time and a right life alone
Fulfil what is that hour foreshown.
The Bridegroom and the Bride withal
Are but unwrought material
Of marriage.

Patmore challenged and revised the tradition of love poetry that preceded him (Burdett vii–ix) because his poem argued that true love is old love, that love, like people, grows up by growing old. He departed from earlier catastrophic views of love as passion leading to the great singular moment of joining—whether in or out of marriage—and instead espoused a uniformitarian viewpoint whereby love gradually evolves into higher, mature forms by almost imperceptible degrees:

No magic of her voice or smile
Raised in a trice a fairy isle,
But fondness for her underwent
(*Faithful*   An unregarded increment,
216–17)   Like that which lifts, through centuries,
The coral reef within the seas,
Till, lo! the land where was the wave.

This evolutionary view was evident in the titles of the four installments themselves: victories of love are not achieved until after betrothal, marriage, and long-enduring faith in marriage.

The plotting of the installments also furthered the theme of time-dependent growth in love. *The Betrothal*'s last idyl, for example, was entitled, not "The Victory" or "The Coronal," but "The Abdication." Felix is uncertain how to relate the fair beloved he has hitherto worshipped to the earthly woman who accepts him and warmly expresses her love in turn:

> But this of making me her lord
> Appear'd such passionate excess,
>   I almost wish'd her state restored,
> I almost wish'd she loved me less.

(*Betrothal*
182)

Acceptance—in traditional love or courtship poetry the moment of fulfill-ment and completion—is here a moment of extraordinary ambivalence and even defeat. Patmore not only frustrated reader expectations and so revised the tradition of love poetry; he also resisted closure and suggested that the story must continue if their love was to reach a more distant fulfillment.

The poem's original publication format was a formal analogue of Patmore's marriage theme.[9] The prologue to *The Betrothal* described the transition of the husband's poem from the planning to the initial writing and reading stages. The epilogue showed his second book in the very process of being written: the husband read the opening verses of the next book he had begun when his wife objected to certain details; he promised to remove the offending lines, and the poem broke off shortly after. Thus, readers were invited to imagine, once they put the first installment down, the poem continuing to be written, revised, and expanded, just as they were invited to imagine the further developing relationship of the husband and wife in the frame and of the engaged Felix and Honoria in the idyls. Love, marriage, and the poem grew simultaneously.

This was a point caught and expressed by the reviews of the 1854 volume. Aside from the famous parody of the poem published by Henry Fothergill Chorley in the 20 January 1855 *Athenaeum*,[10] most reviews were favorable, praising the poem's realism[11] and the poet's conception of woman-as-angel. The writer for the May 1855 *Eclectic Review*, however, also noted the connection between serial reading and the poem's matter, seeing that first readers, like the newly betrothed, were "engaged" with the poem but did not yet entirely know to what they had committed themselves: "This first part of the 'Angel in the House' only takes us through the phase of courtship, to leave us, like true lovers, eager for what is to come" (549). The reviewer concluded by encouraging readers to woo the poem as Felix does Honoria: "The 'Angel in the House' is somewhat shy, and must be approached with gentleness. . . . only win her regards by kindred sympathy, and then sit down for a long, quiet, loving talk, and she will become eloquent. . . . Her words are healthful as the embrace of mountain air and the draught from mountain springs; and many things that she utters will long remain in memory with an abiding beauty" (556).

The 1856 *Espousals* did not open immediately on the young affianced lovers. Instead the prologue showed this couple on the far side of betrothals and espousals. Even in mature domestic love, surrounded by children, they are far from achieving closure in their relationship:

> Ten years to-day has she been his;
> He but begins to understand,
> He says, the dignity and bliss
> She gave him when she gave her hand.

(*Espousals* 4)

The framing prologues and epilogues of the poem's first two installments, then, both depicted mature love and showed it in the process of continued development, as evidenced by the reference to three successive wedding anniversaries (Ball 210). In the 1856 epilogue, in fact, the husband virtually renounced the courtship story he had related in *The Betrothal* and *The Espousals*:

> A fresh-lit fire
> Sends forth to heaven great shows of fume,
> And watchers far away admire;
>   But, when the flames their power assume,
>   The more they burn the less they show;
>   The clouds no longer smirch the sky;
> And then the flames intensest glow
>   When far-off watchers think they die.
> The fumes of early love my verse
>   Hath figured, but to paint the flame
> Might merit the Promethean curse,
>   And is a task unknown to fame.

(*Espousals* 180–81)

The wife exclaims in response, " 'Do, Dear, go on!' " (*Espousals* 181), and readers once again had the opportunity to imagine the poem, like true marital love, continuing.[12] Indeed, with the publication of the second installment the serial format began to function as an analogue to marriage more than betrothal: both serial reading and marriage depend on a physical, literal coming together at intervals, but more important is the intangible bond that develops and transcends these merely physical encounters.[13]

Published responses to the poem also came in two installments, once in 1856, when *The Espousals* was published, and again in 1858, when the first two installments were revised and published together under Pat-more's name. The 1 September 1856 *Critic* noted the poem's growth over time and space in the two preceding years—"The first book of this poem . . . has been steadily rising in general appreciation, and has arrived at the honour . . . of being reprinted in America, and commanding a large audience in that country" (422)[14]—and looked forward to future install-ments: "We cannot guess whether the plan of this very remarkable poem comprises one, two, or more future volumes; but we, and doubtless many others, look forward with no common interest to its completion" (423). George Brimley's essay-review in the October 1856 issue of *Fraser's* began by endorsing Patmore's argument that love begins with marriage and chided other poets for celebrating only courtship or adultery. He then paused to consider why the latter two topics had been so much more popular than marital love, and his answer underlined the originality of Patmore's theme, the importance of the serial format's ethos toward open-endedness and development over time, and the reader's role in creating meaning: "[Courtship] seems spontaneously to supply that *beginning, middle,* and *end* which narrative or dramatic poems are truly enough supposed to require." A poem celebrating "the love of husband and wife," conversely, "offers no such obvious and facile series of connected inci-dents, with well-marked divisions, and all tending, by due gradations of interest, to one event; and though in proportion as the interest of poetry is made to turn less on striking outward circumstances, a heavier demand is made upon the imagination of both writer and reader, and a mere passive reception of familiar thoughts and feelings becomes no longer sufficient for the enjoyment of the poem" (477–78).[15]

Though the favorable review by Patmore's friend Aubrey de Vere in the prestigious *Edinburgh Review* of January 1858 helped clinch the critical reputation of Patmore's poem,[16] twentieth-century audiences are likely to find the review by Richard Holt Hutton in the May 1858 *North British Review* more interesting. Hutton was among the first to object to Pat-more's treatment of women. Finding Honoria a "toy" and "prudish" (538), he remarked that in general Patmore took "an exaggerated view of women's natural graces, and a very depreciating view of their capacities for growth. . . . he treats them as if they had no more capacity for moral and intellectual growth than a flower or bird; and, in his very fine 'parallel' between men and women, assigns all the gradual progress to those, and attributes an involuntary blossoming to these" (543).

Brimley and Hutton both chafed at the poem's slowness in coming to depict wedded love rather than courtship, and offered suggestions for the next part. Brimley told Patmore to "begin at the real subject—married love—on a different plan and in a different key" (484). Hutton, similarly, insisted that Patmore "must show us the growth of the affection, after the flutterings of gratified vanity and worshipping admiration have subsided; he must show it us in the keen fire of grief, and strengthened by self-sacrifice; he must show it us modifying the intellect, enlightening the conscience by mutual gleams of light and confirming trust" (542). Their demands for direct pictures of married life, fairer treatment of women, and a new "key" are worth noting because the publication in 1860 of *Faithful for Ever* seemed entirely to oblige them.

Patmore himself thought the last two installments of *Angel in the House* the best (Champneys 1:176), and twentieth-century readers are likely to agree. The story of how Frederick Graham (unable to win Honoria though worshipping her as sincerely as Felix) marries Jane, the daughter of the ship's chaplain, and how their relationship evolves from the strained silences and mutual unhappiness born of initial incompatibilities to deeply based and deeply shared love,[17] is generally seen to complement the first installments by depicting unideal, as opposed to idealized, love.[18] Jane, plain of face and manner, lacks Honoria's grace and glamour, and at most Frederick and Jane share quiet fulfillment, never sublime rapture. But the most profound contribution of the poem's last two parts to the marriage theme is their function as an oblique parable of wedded life after the glamour and passion of courtship have passed, when spouses are challenged to integrate mundane, deidealizing details of life with a love until now grounded in romance. These later stages of the poem, in other words, limn the later stages of marriage that an Honoria and Felix would share as well as a Jane and Fred.

Many elements in the last two parts helped to establish this theme, including formal differences from the poem's first two parts. The *Betrothal* and *Espousals* clearly derived from an elite and aristocratic tradition of poetry with the latinate names of hero and heroine; the language and attitudes of the traditional wooing lover; and their division into prologues, epilogues, "accompaniments," "sentences," and "idyls."[19] In *Faithful for Ever* all this vanished. The poem shifted to the direct and simple epistolary format that more readily suggested the modern, bourgeois forms of the novel and the dramatic monologue.[20] The personal letter, after all, is not public but intimate discourse (unlike cantos or idyls); it is generally homely, and written from within the home. Above all, the epistolary format allows more than one voice to sound (Weinig 76): readers heard all Patmore's correspondents directly, without mediation by a poet figure ensconced in a prologue—just as a romantic lover may imaginatively orchestrate the beloved's being before marriage but is likely to encounter a true other, with a distinctive voice, afterward. Hence, the voice of Felix, which had completely controlled the perspective in the poem's first two parts, was excised from the first edition of *Faithful for Ever,* and Honoria spoke in propria persona instead. The very texture and structure of the later parts (their informality, directness, intimacy, manifold perspectives) thus commented obliquely on the nature of wedded versus affianced life.

So also did the contents of the volume. Readers encountered the unlovely realities of life that can displace romance in marriage when Jane wrote to Mrs. Graham of how Frederick had nursed her through fever, how Frederick's fond demonstrations persisted despite her getting "nervous, cross, and uglier still," and how, "for all indignities / Of life in health and in disease, / His friendliness got more and more" (*Faithful* 168–69). Honoria herself descended to earth and wrote to her father that she and Felix actually "fell out" over how much money she had spent on clothes the season before.

More important, Honoria and Jane gradually emerged as doubles, just as Felix and Frederick mirrored each other in their idealistic love for Honoria. When Jane and Frederick visit the Vaughans at their country home, Honoria actually grows jealous, as Felix had earlier been jealous of Frederick, because Jane's unaffected directness and humanity elicit responses from Felix formerly reserved for Honoria:

> "She the first
> Has made me jealous. . . .
> I must not have her stopping here
> More than a fortnight once a year."

(*Faithful* 196)

Eventually (in the final installment) Jane's and Honoria's identities merge in a dream Jane has, just as their blood mingles in the wedding of their two children. Honoria and Jane became doubles because they represented two different phases of married life, the romanticized female icon prior to marriage and the earthy, embodied woman encountered after; and Patmore suggested that in the best of circumstances the two aspects could meet and merge.[21]

Given Victorians' commitment to gradually evolving affections rather than more intense but evanescent passions, and the completeness with which Patmore's third installment met the requests of Brimley and Hutton, one would expect *Faithful for Ever* to have met with an especially warm reception.[22] Instead the volume was roundly attacked for its extreme prosaicness. Almost all reviewers found Frederick's "descent" from love of Honoria to marriage with Jane repellent, and Jane herself repugnant. Those who conceded anything to Jane did so only on the assumption that living with the superior Frederick leavened her manners' coarseness and improved her mind;[23] no one remarked that Jane had improved Fred. If Richard Garnett, writing in the December 1860 *Macmillan's Magazine,* observed that Frederick and Felix were doubles ("Graham is Vaughan's moral and spiritual fac-simile . . . whose preferences and antipathies necessarily correspond to those of his counterpart" [126]), he saw no "fac-simile" of Honoria in Jane, and in fact objected, like so many other reviewers, to the startling shift in perspective on Honoria: "we could well have dispensed with numerous trivial details relative to her husband and children, which vexatiously conflict with the unity of impression already disturbed by the change of *venue* in Book II" (129).[24]

Clearly, Patmore's changes of style and mode went too far for his audience. Perhaps the mostly male reviewing audience preferred a female icon more pliable to male desire than the resistant materials of a woman speaking in her own voice. Some reviewers were also rigid about what constituted poetry as opposed to prose and complained that Patmore had confused the two. Another factor that cannot be ignored was the effect of serialization, which at this stage became as much a problem as a virtue.[25] Readers had, for six years prior to the issuing of *Faithful for Ever,* known only of the love associated with Honoria and Felix, or Frederick's disappointed love for Honoria. Those readers attracted to the initial installments, who had cared enough for what they found to have read and reread the poem over the years, were exactly those who would have found it difficult to respond to Jane or her marriage to Frederick.[26] It was rather like asking Felix, after six years of marriage, to abandon Honoria and elope with Jane.

Still, if serialization helped make Jane's advent seem a kind of breach of loyalty to many, some readers were more receptive to the new installment. The 19 December 1860 *Guardian,* while deploring Frederick's descending scale of taste, Jane's dullness, and the leavening of "poetry" with "prose," nonetheless concluded its review with a statement that offhandedly emphasized the new installment's theme: "We cannot recommend *Faithful for Ever* to readers who can endure in poetry only the high romantic strain. We must own that it is often flat and prosaic; and sometimes descends to the very verge of bathos. Yet it depicts cleverly the working of more than one mind; and its analysis is skilful, if the analysing process is unattractive. There is a tender heart within it; and if we let it keep company with us for a few winter's evenings, we shall find a quiet sympathy growing up between it and us, as between Jane and Fred" (1117). Time, this reviewer suggested, could enhance art as well as marriage.

Patmore's poem never received quite the critical attention after 1860 that it did before, but the last installment, *Victories of Love,* still suggested the relation between theme and serial form. In this narrative Jane sickens and dies, and the poem explored, like Tennyson's *In Memoriam,* how love may last from this life to the next into all eternity. It is as a serial writer that Jane asserts her love for Frederick from beyond the grave, since she writes a daily series of letters on her deathbed for Frederick to read after she is gone.[27] The last installment, serialized in *Macmillan's,* moreover, recapitulated the movement of all of *Angel in the House.* That is, the October installment (like the 1854 and 1856 volumes) ended on a glorious, ideal note with Jane's dream of marital bliss enjoyed in a luminous afterlife, and the 6 October 1861 *Sunday Times* accordingly remarked that Patmore's was a "quiet and beautiful poem," the pages of which "lead us gently on and on to the close" (2). Jane disappeared in the interval between installments; the November number detailed the marriage of Emily Vaughan and John Graham, concluding on a prosaic note (like the 1860 volume) with a letter of worldly advice from Lady Clitheroe (Honoria's sister Mildred) to her newlywed niece. The installment ended when Lady Clitheroe broke off her letter at the sounding of the luncheon bell[28]—at which point the 3 November 1861 *Sunday Times* remarked that the poem "is not so interesting to us this month, and lacks the tenderness which characterised the earlier letters in the poem" (2).[29] Worldliness and spirituality converged in the final December number (as they did in the larger design of all four volumes) in the wedding sermon preached by Dean Churchill, which fused theology and practical advice, praise of the physical bond in marriage and interpretation of it as a type of union with God (see figure 1). Most reviews, however, objected to a long, drawn-out sermon as a poetic conclusion. For the 1863 single-volume edition of the poem, Patmore placed the sermon earlier and ended with Felix's letter to Honoria written on the occasion of their twentieth wedding anniversary.

This letter emphasizes Felix's ever-growing love ("So see I, daily wondering, you, / And worship with a passion new" [*Victories* 93]) and the poem's ongoing development that parallels lack of closure in marriage: "'tis long / Ago I closed the unfinish'd song / Which never could be finish'd" (*Victories* 90), a reference to the epilogue of the 1856 *Espousals.*[30] Patmore then affixed a personal endnote to the 1863 volume that made the

cried to see her old love so degraded. There was no time for crying, or for saying more than a few sharp words, for they were coming towards her.

"What nonsense is this, Charles?" she said, "What is this masquerade? Are you come to double my shame? Go home and take that dress off and burn it. Is your pride dead, that you disgrace yourself like this in public? If you are desperate, as you seem, why are you not at the war? They want desperate men there. Oh! if I was a man!"

They parted then; no one but Lord Welter and Hornby knew who Charles was. The former saw that Adelaide had recognised him, and, as they rode simply home together, said,—

"I knew poor Charles was a groom. He saw his sister the other night at our house. I didn't tell you; I hardly know why. I really believe, do you know, that the truth of the matter is, Adelaide, that I did not want to vex you now."

He looked at her as if he thought she would disbelieve him, but she said,—

"Nay, I do believe you, Welter. You are not an ill-natured man, but you are selfish and unprincipled. So am I, perhaps, to a greater extent than you. At what time is that fool of a German coming?"

"At half-past eleven."

"I must go to that woman's party. I must show there, to keep friends with her. She has such a terrible tongue. I will be back by twelve or so."

"I wish you could stay at home."

"I really dare not, my dear Welter. I must go. I will be back in good time."

"Of course you will please yourself about it," said Lord Welter, a thought sulkily. And, when he was by himself, he said,—

"She is going to see Charles Ravenshoe. Well, perhaps she ought. She treated him d—d bad! And so did I."

To be continued.

THE VICTORIES OF LOVE.

BY COVENTRY PATMORE.

IX.—THE WEDDING SERMON.

DEAR children, God is love, and love
Is everything. The truths thereof
Are as the waters of the sea
For clearness and for mystery.
 Of that sweet love which, startling, wakes
Senses and soul, and mostly breaks
The word of promise to the ear,
But keeps it, after many a year,
To the true spirit, how shall I speak?
My memory with age is weak,
And I for hopes do oft suspect
The things I seem to recollect.
Yet who but must remember well
'Twas this made heaven intelligible
As motive, though 'twas small the power
The heart might have, for even an hour,
To hold possession of its height
Of nameless pathos and delight!

Figure 1. Patmore's *Victories of Love,* third installment (December 1861), in *Macmillan's Magazine* (immediately following installment of *Ravenshoe,* by Henry Kingsley). (*Alderman Library, University of Virginia*)

volume readers held in their hands part of the same never-ending process Felix invokes:

> *The plan of the Poem or series of Poems, of which this volume is the conclusion, involved, as it was schemed more than fourteen years ago, a final section on the subject of the hope which remains for individual love in death. . . . but I no longer have, at every step, the needful encouragement of an approval which was all that my heart valued of fame . . . nor have I the aid of a criticism to which, I am bound to confess,—now the critic does not forbid the confession,—that every page is more or less indebted for such truth and grace as it may have.*
>
> *When, however, I commenced this Work, I foresaw that its composition must extend over so long a period that there was much likelihood of my never being able to finish it. I provided, as far as possible, against the evils of that chance, by so planning my Poem that it should not be fragmentary in form, nor wholly incomplete in the treatment of its subject, in the event of its being terminated at any one of its several stages of publication. I trust I have so scattered, through what I have written, the germs which were to have been unfolded in the Concluding Part, that every attentive reader will be able to perceive no uncertain utterance of the main foundations of the hope which is the justification of the entire work.*

(*Victories* 105)

The serial poem and the theme of marriage here converge: both grow in stages; both depend on collaboration; both are in part constituted by their interpenetration with time; both are forever unfinished; and the continuation of both beyond what is visible to the eye can only be hinted at and must be construed by the conjectures of individual interpreters.

The poem's serial format, then, not only reinforced the poem's central theme but also allowed readers direct participation in the experiences of process, growth, hope, and anticipation so essential to Patmore's vision of marriage. To return to the 13 June 1863 *Illustrated London News* with which we began, Patmore's nine-years' poem had indeed become a living thing, one that may have ended but did not (like Patmore's own hopes of love in a heavenly afterlife) close.

This kind of continuing story—in love and literature—figures prominently in other Victorian installment works, such as Dickens's *Dombey and Son*. In a troubled reunion with her mother, Alice Marwood, one of the many doubles for Dickens's "angel in the house," Florence Dombey, insists that a similar movement from the ideal to the actual be recognized, articulating principles of the Victorian worldview evident in Patmore's serial poem: " 'Why, Mother!' said Alice [Marwood], shaking her ragged skirts to detach the old woman from them: 'there are two sides to that. There have been years for me as well as you, and there has been wretchedness for me as well as you'" (345). Here the passage of time ("years") insists on endurance in those who wish family unity; and understanding (seeing "two sides") requires compassion from anyone seeking domestic harmony.[31] Alice has changed in her dozen years as a transported criminal, and she insists on her independence until her mother recognizes these changes that occurred far away over a long stretch of time. Patience, the element identified as a key in building a lasting domestic relationship, has been shown by both women in waiting so long for the daughter's unlikely return. This important quality is also central to other plots of the novel, particularly the story of Florence Dombey, the daughter of "Dom-bey and Son" and a famous representative of long-suffering love in Victorian fiction. The serial publication of Dickens's novel (twenty parts in nineteen months) actively elicited from his audience similar endurance. Thus, as in *Angel in the House,* the dynamics of reading Victorian serial literature coincided with its major themes.

Patience is needed in these two imagined worlds because both Victorian authors accept a similar model of development, one which asserts that life is organized as a continuing sequence of generally irreversible stages. As Steven Marcus and others have noted, Dombey Sr.'s abuse of his son involves attempting to reverse or subvert the phases of a child's natural development.[32] Florence's ability to endure these violations of natural order until domestic harmony is achieved has earned her a distinct place even among the many women in Victorian literature who devote themselves to their families.[33] The number of times she is referred to as an angel underscores Florence's importance in Dickens's scheme of domestic life for *Dombey and Son*. The omniscient narrator, for instance, identifies her as Dombey's "better angel" who has "repaid the agony of slight and coldness, and dislike, with patient unexacting love" (357).

As a believable fictional character, however, Florence has been faulted by critics at least since Kathleen Tillotson's observation that authors are seldom successful in depicting unchanging virtue: "besides the timeless problem of making perfect virtue, and especially the passive virtues, attractive, [Dickens] has his age's problem of vitalizing a heroine in a period of limiting ideas for girlhood" (*Novels* 172).[34] But Dickens, like Patmore, did more than has been recognized to animate his angel in the house, relying especially on her appearance in a serial mode. Florence's commitment to establishing a loving home in *Dombey and Son* parallels Felix and Honoria's courtship, and Frederick and Jane's marriage in *Angel in the House:* she pursues over great reaches of time and space an ideal domestic scene that is, in fact, only briefly enjoyed.

Florence's patience and compassion, often operating over great distances, become models for Dickens's audience outside the fiction. Indeed, the cover of *Dombey and Son*'s monthly part (see figure 2) typifies Dickens's and other mid-Victorian novelists' aims of drawing readers into a long story that required patience and an interest in others. Because such a drawing announced a familiar format, Dickens's audience knew they were being invited to join in a nineteen-month experience and were ready from the start to admire characters who endure many hardships, steadfastly pursue distant dreams, and are finally (but only finally) rewarded. The many characters depicted in *Dombey and Son*'s cover suggest a large cast; the varied scenes are appropriate to a long story; the climbing little figures assert middle-class aspirations. Images of a man hiking, ships at sea, and someone looking through a telescope are consistent with the idea that the resolution of the novel's plot will require travel over great distance, for characters and for readers. (They also suggest Bunsby and Walter's Uncle Sol, as we explain below.) The elaborate structure of cards and ledgers, along with the bowed figure being helped by a young woman, prefigure a possible collapse in the novel's future. The signs on the cover, then, call for patience and compassion from readers, promising also the expected rewards in the end.

True, there are some limitations in Dickens's achievement. To create an ideal domestic environment in *Dombey and Son* the heroine has to move both backward and forward in time: forward to create the family in which she is the wife of Walter Gay; but backward to the recreation of Dombey's family wherein she is the dutiful and beloved daughter. In this latter sense, Florence seems never to grow up, to be moving retroactively back toward her own origin.[35] Dickens's text asserts that this first family was crippled at its inception by Dombey's merchant vision of life. The death of Paul's and Florence's mother suggests that the marriage that began this family was conceived in terms antagonistic to human life and development, as, indeed, British society in a new commercial age might be, according to Dickens.[36] Florence's effort to recover this Ur-family—so intense that in the last number of the novel she asks Dombey's forgiveness for leaving him—forces the heroine into a curiously static role, refusing to advance from her identity as daughter until her father learns to love her. Brutally rejected by Dombey after Paul's death (February 1847), she often seemed to Victorian readers frozen in a memorable pose of abandonment, as the *North British Review* noted in May 1847: "Nowhere has [Dickens] painted

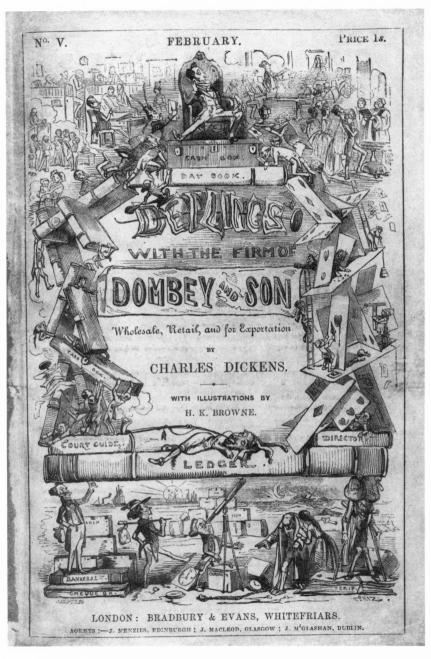

Figure 2. Cover of monthly parts of Dickens's *Dombey and Son* (1846–48) suggesting elements of a long story. (*Alderman Library, University of Virginia*)

with a more vivid pencil, than in drawing the picture, in the 6th Number, of poor forsaken Florence" (116). Yet even in this number, as we shall show presently, Florence is growing and changing on her way to becoming Walter's wife.

In her difficult double role Florence, developing but remaining always the same, can be an unsatisfactory character for whole volume readers, whose perspective on the complete work encourages a final, definitive statement of character. The October 1848 *Blackwood's Magazine* lamented after the novel was concluded that "the extraordinary affection of the daughter [does not] spring from any known principle of humanity" (quoted in Collins, *Dickens* 231). Florence was, however, a favorite for reviewers in the weeklies commenting on the serial version. Philip Collins notes that while Paul's death in the fifth number received great attention, the "pathos of Florence Dombey's situation was also found very moving: Macaulay wept over her as if his heart would break, and so did others" (212). At one moment, then, Florence was expanding her knowledge of the world through reading and imagination ("Florence bloomed . . . like the king's fair daughter in the story" [226]); and at different times she appeared to readers as an unchanging victim of her father ("as if stricken into stone" [182]).

Interest in Florence's developing character begins with sympathy for her plight. Dickens, of course, was a master at eliciting his readers' sympathy for characters in trouble, inspiring "sorrow for the sufferings which have never cost a single tear" (8), as *Lloyd's Weekly London Newspaper* put it in response to *Dombey and Son*'s twelfth number (September 1847).[37] The same paper on 9 April 1848 regretted the end of Dickens's novel because it meant the loss of favorite characters like Florence: "Month after month we have gone onward with the fortunes of the personages who have so strongly enlisted our sympathies" (8). Charles Kent in the 13 April 1848 *Sun* also commended "the eloquent revelations of love which are associated with every fragment in reference to Florence" (quoted in Collins, *Dickens* 229). And the 4 July 1847 *Weekly Dispatch* praised Edith for responding warmly to her new daughter (316).

Some features of the serial version of *Dombey and Son,* therefore, succeeded with its original Victorian audience yet are overlooked by volume readers, who move at a much faster pace through the novel and who are not made to pause at strategic moments in the text.[38] Richard Altick notes of Dickens's installment readers in general: "It was as if they received a monthly budget of news about various sets of characters who, after the first number or two, had become parts of their daily imaginative lives" ("Varieties" 79). Altick also suggests more attention was paid to the individual number than we might at first assume: "In the interval between instalments, many readers must have passed the time by re-reading the latest one. They thereby noticed touches they missed the first headlong time through. And each repeated reading impressed the characters, settings, motifs, and small particulars more deeply in their memories" ("Varieties" 79). The Florence Dombey of the installment novel, then, particularly after the fifth number, in which Paul died and she became a greater center of interest in the narrative,[39] embodied for Victorians an active and evolving spirit of patient understanding, which we hope to recover here.

The principle of change occurring out of sight, at a distance, underscores Florence's development in Dickens's serial text. This principle, evident in Alice's admonition to her mother in the reunion scene, insists that each party in a relationship must recognize change that has occurred in the other over time and in different places. Although the novel does not take the epistolary form of later installments of the *Angel in the House,* the many pairs of characters in *Dombey and Son* (Florence-Dombey, Dombey-Carker, Florence-Edith, etc.) involve a similar dynamics of potential sympathy and understanding. Frequently in Dickens's text these reachings out must overcome a physical separation like that which existed between Jane and Frederick in Patmore's *Victories of Love* (see *Macmillan's Magazine,* October 1861: 439–42).

The enigmatic character of Bunsby may represent this distant vision of sympathy in *Dombey and Son.* J. Hillis Miller has seen Bunsby, whose eye, according to the novel, "continued to be addressed to somewhere about the half-way house between London and Gravesend" (239) rather than his immediate surroundings, as proof there are "apparently unbreakable barriers" (J. Hillis Miller, *Dickens* 149–50) that isolate individuals in Dickens's world. However, Captain Cuttle's philosophical friend, "always on the look-out for something in the extremest distance" (*Dombey* 238), might also suggest a perspective necessary to sustaining relationships in a new age where railroads—"with a shriek, and a roar, and a rattle" (200)—and ocean travel create sudden great separations between individuals.[40] Such a perspective was offered Dickens's audience even in the form of its publication, as we will explain shortly.

In this attention to the faraway, Bunsby is also like Uncle Sol, whose profession involves understanding at great remove from one's subject. Sol's skill, for instance, enables him to remain linked to his missing nephew: "On the table, and about the room, were the charts and maps on which the heavy-hearted Instrument Maker had again and again tracked the missing vessel across the sea, and on which, with a pair of compasses that he still had in his hand, he had been measuring, a minute before [Bunsby and Cuttle arrived], how far she must have driven, to have driven here or there: and trying to demonstrate that a long time must elapse before hope was exhausted" (238). Sol's operation within schemes of great distance ("how far she must have driven") and time ("before hope was exhausted") proves necessary in regaining a family unity. However, his skill is not valued in the commercial society of Dom-bey and Son, and the shop is failing for lack of customers.

The first change of scene in the novel (between chapters three and four in the first installment) required of readers this out-of-fashion perspective that reaches over great distances. The first scenes of the novel had all been within the Dombey house, but the narrative then insisted on making connections:

> *Though the offices of Dombey and Son were within the liberties of the City of London, and within hearing of Bow Bells, when their clashing voices were not drowned by the uproar in the streets, yet were there hints of adventurous and romantic story to be observed in some of the adjacent objects. Gog and Magog held their state within ten minutes' walk; the Royal Exchange was close at hand; the Bank of England, with its vaults of gold and silver "down among the dead men" underground, was their magnificent neighbour. Just round the corner stood the rich East India House, teeming with suggestions of precious stuffs and stones, tigers, elephants, howdahs, hookahs, umbrellas, palm trees, palanquins, and*

(24)

> *gorgeous princes of a brown complexion sitting on carpets with their slippers very much turned up at the toes. Anywhere in the immediate vicinity there might be seen pictures of ships speeding away full sail to all parts of the world; outfitting warehouses ready to pack off anybody anywhere, fully equipped in half an hour; and little timber midshipmen in obsolete naval uniforms, eternally employed outside the shopdoors of nautical instrument-makers in taking observations of the hackney coaches.*
>
> *Sole master and proprietor of one of these effigies—of that which might be called, familiarly, the woodenest—of that which thrust itself out above the pavement, right leg foremost . . . [was] an elderly gentleman in a Welsh wig.*

Of course the sponsor of this midshipman is Uncle Sol, whose business is discounted by the new breed of merchant princes. But Dombey's daughter would not only travel to this new scene but also exercise the same principle of patient vision over time and space, represented in the midshipman's "offensively disproportionate piece of machinery" (24), to recover and create stable homes.

Florence's growing up, then, often occurs in *Dombey and Son* offstage, out of sight, beneath the surface; and special vision, a long-distance perspective, is needed to recognize these changes.[41] She develops not only in her father's large house "on the shady side of a tall, dark, dreadfully genteel street" (16) but also in the house across the street, where Florence watches the "elder child [who] remained with her father when the rest had gone away, and made his tea for him—happy little house-keeper she was then!—and sat conversing with him, sometimes at the window, sometimes in the room, until the candles came" (176). Similarly, at the Skettles's Florence inwardly prepares herself to become someone different, without outwardly changing. She watches "children staying in the house. Children who were as frank and happy with fathers and with mothers as those rosy faces opposite home" (243). And in the reading and study inspired by her efforts to help Paul at Dr. Blimber's, Florence lays the groundwork for a new self awaiting its eventual manifestation in the appropriate setting; she "imagined so often what her life would have been if her father could have loved her" (227) or "she pictured to herself her mother yet alive" (227). In "her books, her music, and her work" she studies so that "the more accomplished she became, the more glad [her father] would be when he came to know and like her" (228).[42] But this more adult Florence cannot appear in the Dombey household until her father recognizes her. Although he has several important opportunities to see her in this light, it is not, of course, until the novel's concluding double number that he sees the Florence who has been growing up before him.

For Victorian readers of the installment text, Florence also often changed offstage; in the months of installment issue the rhythm of her appearances in the fictional world encouraged alterations in the way she was perceived.[43] For instance, Florence did not appear at all in the novel's eleventh number (August 1847), the installment after Dombey's marriage to Edith. At the end of *Dombey and Son*'s tenth part, Florence had hoped, with the second marriage of her father, for a new atmosphere in her home: "The house seems strange and new, and there are loud echoes in it" (320). However, a change for her was no more likely than adherence to the past, which figured prominently in her thoughts: "Florence shuts her book, and gruff Diogenes, who takes that for a signal, puts his paws upon her lap, and rubs his ears against her caressing hands. But Florence cannot see him plainly, in a little time, for there is a mist betwen her eyes and him, and her dead brother and dead mother shine in it like angels. Walter, too, poor wandering ship-wrecked boy, oh, where is he!" (320). In a moment characteristic of this novel, recalling Paul's old-fashioned ways, Florence at the end of number 10 overlooked the immediate surroundings for the distant beings with whom she had shared important relationships. When she reappeared in the novel after a two-month absence, her father and Dickens's serial readers might have been able to sense a newly developed identity.

Interestingly, Lord Francis Jeffrey wrote to Dickens (5 July 1847) that the tenth number, before Florence disappeared for an extra month, was especially moving: "I cannot tell you how much I have been charmed with your last number, and what gentle sobs and delightful tears it has cost me" (quoted in Collins, *Dickens* 217). The *Weekly Dispatch* for 4 July 1847 also noted the tenth installment, "a very excellent Part of Mr. Dickens's popular tale" (316), and quoted a long passage featuring Florence and Edith. Number 11, the one without Florence, was termed, on the other hand, "decidedly the least successful" to that point by Charles Kent in the *Sun*; but, he went on to say, the "indifference of the eleventh number is more than compensated by the extraordinary brilliance of the twelfth. Mr. Dickens begins to develop his plot, and with an art superior to anything of the kind evinced in his preceding fictions" (6 September 1847; quoted in Collins, *Dickens* 227). Similarly, *Lloyd's Weekly London Newspaper* on 19 September 1847 found number 12 especially moving, writing: "The minds of thousands of her Majesty's lieges are already unsettled by the conflict of hopes and fears which have been brought into collision as to the destinies which lie in store for the principal personages in the tale" (8). And the *Illustrated London News* on 11 September 1847 stated that this installment was "admirably sustained, from the first to the last page" (171).

The special attraction of the twelfth number may have been at least in part due to Florence's reappearance in a key scene, linked to that memorable last appearance in number 10. By timing the appearances of Florence in the serial version, that is, Dickens accentuated the stages of a development that had often gone on behind the major scenes of the narrative. Dickens's memoranda to himself for the important twelfth number include these reminders: "Florence's purpose. Remember her old loneliness, and observe her present state of mind" (Horsman 846). Her father, like Dickens's serial reader, has a special chance to recognize Florence's development over time because he has been apart from his daughter during his honeymoon. Number 12 featured in its first few pages the memorable scene in which Dombey, appearing to sleep with a handkerchief draped over his face, observes his daughter. Florence, "his better angel!" (357), tries to focus on some slight domestic work: "There are yielding moments in the lives of the sternest and harshest men, though such men often keep their secret well. The sight of her in her beauty, almost changed into a woman without his knowledge, may have struck out some such moments even in his life of pride. Some passing thought that he had had a happy home within his reach—had had a household spirit bending at his feet—had overlooked it in his stiff-necked sullen arrogance, and wandered away and lost himself, may have engendered them" (357). Although it is qualified by the use of "may," this passage suggests that Florence is not only the unchanging domestic spirit of Dombey's home but also a daughter, "almost changed into a woman without his knowledge," capable of becoming an angel in another house. In the next moment, Dombey combines this close perspective with the distant one that includes the lost Paul: "As he looked, she became blended with the child he had loved, and he could hardly separate the two. As he looked, he saw her for an instant by a clearer and brighter light, not bending over that child's pillow as his rival—monstrous thought—but as the spirit of his home, and in the action tending himself no less, as he sat once more with his bowed-down head upon his hand at the foot of the little bed" (358). At this instant, just after the midpoint of the novel, reconciliation is possible; but Edith's sudden arrival—and the love she spontaneously shows for Florence—breaks the spell, and Dombey's pride regains its hold on him.[44]

Thus, Dickens's installment readers should have recognized how difficult it is to restore a divided family and achieve the ideal Victorian home as they watched Florence's struggles. The key moment of opportunity with her father in number 12 came a full year after the novel's beginning, twelve months after Victorians started to follow the fortunes of this one household. As Dombey's momentary understanding closed down in anger and jealousy—"a darkness gathered on his face, exceeding any that the night could cast, and rested there" (358)—readers could anticipate more suffering for Florence in this broken home.[45] Florence also reminded readers in the next scene with Edith that "Poor Walter is drowned" (359). Her learning about the loss of the *Son and Heir,* on which Walter had sailed, was, once again, an event that occurred offstage, for Captain Cuttle commissioned Susan Nipper, through Toots, to "break it gentle to the young lady" (333) in number 11. Thus, Florence's dealing with yet another death—"I have had a great sorrow since that day of [Edith's marriage]" (359)—added to her character. The new family she and Walter might have begun together seemed as impossible now as a new happy family with herself, Edith, and Dombey, "no home then, for anyone" (362). Thus, serial readers to this point in the novel, rather than being sentimentally idealistic about the hearth, had been made increasingly aware of the difficulties involved in trying to create domestic stability.

Florence's development as a character, often offstage between installments or outside the present focus of the narrative, might be likened to the old Madeira treasured by Sol Gills.[46] A bottle first opened in the initial number introduced "the wonderful Madeira" to the novel; but its aging would go on throughout the nineteen months of reading until its perfection in the final installment. Uncle Sol explains how it has already developed offstage, while other events took the limelight: " 'Think of this wine, for instance,' said old Sol, 'which has been to the East Indies and back, I'm not able to say how often, and has been once around the world. Think of the pitch–dark nights, the roaring winds, and rolling seas . . . that this wine has passed through. Think what a straining and creaking of timbers and masts: what a whistling and howling of the gale through ropes and rigging . . . has gone on, over the old cask that held this wine' " (29). The wine continues to develop offstage, recalled occasionally by the narrator. When Walter sets sail on the *Son and Heir,* for instance, we are told that the "last bottle of the old Madeira, which had had its cruising days, and known its dangers of the deep, lay silently beneath its dust and cobwebs, in the meanwhile, undisturbed" (no. 6: 192). When Walter and Florence are married, "the last bottle of the old Madeira still remains among its dust and cobwebs, undisturbed" (no. 18: 576). And in the final double number a "bottle that has been long excluded from the light of day, and is hoary with dust and cobwebs, has been brought into the sunshine; and the golden wine within it sheds a lustre on the table" (620). One family restored and another begun, the fulfillment promised by and in the novel is represented through the timely perfection of the old wine. Similarly, Florence, come to the perfection Dickens intended for her (if not one modern readers can accept fully), as both beloved daughter and fulfilled wife and mother, appears in the center of the text at last.

Before this final fulfillment, however, one additional stage is added to Florence's development; and, again, her appearance in the serial format highlighted this change and provided a model of patience and compassion for Victorian readers. Florence eventually gave up on her father, or at least on her own capacity to earn his love; but that abandonment of her dream of a restored home came slowly, over a long period of time, a process lengthened and deepened by the installment form of her story. And thus, when her father was brought by events to a new vision, her reunion, at least in Dickens's eyes, was made sweeter by the wait.

In number 14 (November 1847) Florence, observing her father's behavior toward Edith, reevaluated her own mother's fate: "She saw her father cold and obdurate to Edith, as to her; hard, inflexible, unyielding. Could it be, she asked herself with starting tears, that her own dear mother had been made unhappy by such treatment, and had pined away and died?" (429). In her further reflections at this time, she acknowledges how long she has patiently waited for acceptance: "It was a long, long time, she thought, since she used to make her nightly pilgrimages to his door! It was a long, long time, she tried to think, since she had entered his room at midnight, and he had led her back to the stair-foot!" (431) For Dickens's original serial readers, it had been eight months since that scene of rejection for Florence (March 1847). If she began to change her feelings for her father at this point in her life, it would hardly have seemed too quick to that Victorian audience.

In the next installment (December 1847), six months after Dombey's fall from his horse and when the new "home" created by Edith and her father was "nearly two years old" (466), Florence's feelings had changed even more. Her new state, however, was again arrived at slowly, in the discrete stages characteristic of Victorian thought: "Florence loved him still, but, by degrees, had come to love him rather as some dear one who had been, or who might have been, than as the hard reality before her eyes. Something of the softened sadness with which she loved the memory of little Paul, or of her mother, seemed to enter now into her thoughts of him, and to make them, as it were, a dear remembrance" (460). This change came to her in much the same way her growth toward being Walter's wife occurred for Victorian installment readers: "The change, if it may be called one, had stolen on her like the change from childhood to womanhood, and had come with it. Florence was almost seventeen, when, in her lonely musings, she was conscious of these thoughts" (461). When Dombey struck her later in the same installment, after Edith has run away, then, Florence did not have to change much more to recognize that "she had no father upon earth, and [she] ran out, orphaned, from his house" (472).

The final transition from abandoned daughter to new wife occurs quickly in the volume text, but not in the serial version. At the end of number 15, Florence was falling asleep at the Wooden Midshipman, watched by Captain Cuttle: "A louder sob or moan than usual, brought him sometimes to her door; but by degrees she slept more peacefully, and the Captain's watch was undisturbed" (480). Number 16 opened, "It was long before Florence awoke" (481), and readers were told that she is never unconscious "of what had happened in the home that existed no more" (481). For Dickens's serial readers, however, a full month interposed between her falling asleep and this waking, time for the shift from the role of daughter to that of young woman to be more easily accepted.[47] Though Florence cannot in this one night forget the terrible scene at home, Victorian readers would necessarily have let it slip from the forefront of their consciousnesses during the thirty-day interval between parts' publication. Thus, the audience's return to the text after their own absence from the fiction would have stressed the distance Florence had traveled in leaving her only home; the father who drove her from his house was farther back in this audience's past.

The distance Florence travels, not just one night of sleep but a month of Victorian life, was further emphasized in Dickens's text depicting her waking. Returning to consciousness was described in terms of covering great reaches of space and time, enacting that distant perspective frequently endorsed by the novel.

(481) *The sun was getting low in the west, and, glancing out of a red mist, pierced with its rays opposite loop-holes and pieces of fret-work in the spires of city churches, as if with golden arrows that struck through and through them—and far away athwart the river and its flat banks, it was gleaming like a path of fire—and out at sea it was irradiating sails of ships—and, looked towards, from quiet churchyards, upon hill-tops in the country, it was steeping distant prospects in a flush and glow that seemed to mingle earth and sky together in one glorious suffusion—when Florence, opening her heavy eyes, lay at first, looking without interest or recognition at the unfamiliar walls around her, and listening in the same regardless manner to the noises in the street.*

She would have to focus on her immediate situation quickly, but Florence's coming to consciousness, as represented in the structure of this long sentence, paralleled the serial audience's beginning the new installment: Florence finally made the journey from her father's home to her own identity in a larger world; Dickens's readers moved from their own sphere of activity in Victorian England in January 1848 to Sol Gill's shop, recalling from the past Florence's crisis in order to connect it to the present scene. The readers' activity, through its parallel structure, enacted the time Florence had had to complete the break with her father and to see herself as the potential angel in another house, this time as wife and mother. Both in their reading of this complex sentence and in their connecting the end of installment 15 with the beginning of number 16, Victorian readers had to reach out over significant distances.

It is true, of course, that Dickens's presentation of Florence's new maturity was not completely successful with his installment audience. The 9 January 1848 *News of the World,* for instance, expressed disbelief at Florence's sudden new ability as a domestic force (6), particularly when she, surely still exhausted from the previous day's events, "looking into the little cupboard, took out the case-bottle and mixed a perfect glass of grog for [Captain Cuttle], unasked, and set it at his elbow" (484). Still, Walter's reaction helped guide readers to Dickens's intended response: the returned sailor finds her "changed to me. I left you such a child, and find you—oh! something so different—" (492). And since Florence and her story dominated this sixteenth number (her father's condition being presented in the brief last chapter), readers were given sufficient material to get used to her new role.

Victorian serial readers also had time to become accustomed to the Florence who figures as Walter's wife-to-be because number 17 (February 1848) focused on Dombey's pursuit of Edith and Carker, culminating in Edith's dramatic undoing of Carker in Dijon. Florence did not appear in the installment, and when she reappeared in number 18 (March 1848), it was no longer as Dombey's daughter. She tells Susan, "I am going to be [Walter's] wife, to give him up my whole heart, and to live with him and die with him" (559). Their wedding was described in the part's last chapter: "through the light, and through the shade, they go on lovingly together, lost to everything around; thinking of no other riches, and no prouder home, than they have now in one another" (572). Dombey Sr., who appropriately did not appear in this installment, was not a factor in this Florence's life or a part of this new home.

The reversal of the last double number, of course, Florence's returning to her father as the child still seeking a parent's love, did confuse Dickens's audience, both volume and serial readers (see, for instance, *News of the World,* 9 April 1848: 6). However, given Dickens's special desire to see the commercial Dombey humanized, to see the failed parent restored, Florence's character had to revert to the role of daughter seeking a father's love at the same time she figured as perfect wife and mother. Significantly, recognition for Dombey and daughter comes when they are separated by the greatest physical distance. In a scene that includes some ironic echoes of the one between Alice Marwood and her mother, Florence explains to her father: "When [my child] was born, and when I knew how much I loved it, I knew what I had done in leaving you. . . . My little child was born at sea, Papa. I prayed to God (and so did Walter for me) to spare me, that I might come home. The moment I could land, I came back to you. Never let us be parted any more, Papa" (599–600). Home is created by this angel through remarkable (for some, unbelievable) patience and compassion sustained over time and space.

The more important point for the Victorian audience here, however, was that neither home, the one restored or the one created, had come easily or quickly in this literary experience. Victorians may have idolized the hearth, but their best literary portrayals emphasized how tenuous it was and how much time was involved in attaining it. The many months of patient waiting for domestic serenity (nineteen in fact) by Dickens's serial readers far outnumbered the one in which harmony existed for the novel's characters and audience. In this sense, the qualities emphasized by Florence's role in the fiction were realized by Victorian readers. Their separation from the world of the novel was in one sense even greater than England's from China, and yet they sympathetically crossed over into the lives of Dombey and Florence each month for nearly two years to wait patiently for fulfillment.

That such experiences created a "family" of author, characters, and readers in Victorian society is an accepted notion; but the time involved for such relationships to develop and mature in nineteenth-century literature is less often acknowledged. Dickens himself was aware that home is a difficult and often distant prospect, as shown in the preface to *Dombey and Son,* written, of course, at the end of the story:

(included at the end of the final double number)

> I cannot forego my usual opportunity of saying farewell to my readers in this greeting-place, though I have only to acknowledge the unbounded warmth and earnestness of their sympathy in every stage of the journey we have just concluded.
>
> If any of them have felt a sorrow in one of the principal incidents on which this fiction turns [Paul's death], I hope it may be a sorrow of that sort which endears the sharers in it, one to another.

The "greeting-place" of literary experience, distant for both author and reader, is a kind of home, but one that does not exclude loss and suffering. The end of such events, endearing individuals to each other, is worthwhile, but comes only after significant commitments of time, a journey of many stages.[48]

While it is true that whole-volume readers must travel this same distance to Dickens's "greeting-place," the repeated, forced interruptions of the installment experience underscored this separation more forcefully:

serial readers had to put down Dickens's text regularly and for specific lengths of time; on each occasion that they took up another part between October 1846 and April 1848, they were reminded of their separation from the fictional universe. Although the happy ending certainly had a resonance over time for Victorian readers after the novel concluded, modern evaluations of the entire text have given too much weight to this small part of the total event.[49] The difficulty of achieving a rewarding domestic life, the challenge to patience and compassion, was embodied in Victorian readers' nineteen-month search for such resolution in the novel *Dombey and Son.*

As Charles Dickens elicited his audience's patience and sympathy through his story of the long-suffering angelic Florence, and as Coventry Patmore encouraged in his readers a respect for marriage as the product of slow development in the medium of everyday life, William Makepeace Thackeray in *The Newcomes* (October 1853–August 1855) insisted through the twenty-four month publication of his serial novel that understanding the family as a fundamental civilizing element in society must go beyond conventional wisdom. His narrator, alter-ego Arthur Pendennis, observes in the novel's fifteenth part that "a novelist must go on with his heroine, as a man with his wife, for better or worse, and to the end" (2:66).[50] Linking the art of marriage to literary achievement, Thackeray himself "goes on" past the crisis of lost love with his heroine and ultimate "angel in the house," Ethel Newcome, farther than his audience wanted, but for "better" rather than "worse," as the "end" he felt compelled to reach involved necessary challenges to his readers' worldview. Only after this process of disenchantment could a model family relationship be realized by author and audience.

The subtitle of Thackeray's novel, *Memoirs of a Most Respectable Family,* announced on the cover of the monthly part that this work, like *Dombey and Son* and *Angel in the House,* had a domestic subject.[51] The novel is an almost inclusive survey of variations in Victorian family relationships, from the warmth of Aunt Martha Honeyman's cottage at Brighton to the open warfare of Barnes Newcome's household, with a number of other domestic establishments—from Pendennis's and Warrington's bachelor rooms to Mrs. Ridley's multifamily dwelling, Walpole Street, Mayfair—providing alternatives to the conventional home.[52] At issue throughout is the larger question of family duties and affection, what George Warrington calls at one point "Kinsmanship" (2:271) and Edward Burne-Jones in 1856 identified as "the very heart and core of social disease, unhappy wedded life."[53] When, during the campaign for Parliament late in the novel, the crowd calls out, "Where [are] Barnes Newcomes's chil-

dren?" (2:286)—drawing attention to the suffering of both Barnes's legitimate and his illegitimate families—Thackeray links the state of the individual family to the health of the nation: failure in the microcosm of the
home leads to the failure of society.[54] As Robert Colby in *Thackeray's
Canvass of Humanity* has shown, the monthly parts of *The Newcomes* placed
themselves within a national consideration of domestic themes: " 'Home
influence' makes itself felt in many other books advertised in the monthly
parts of *The Newcomes,* in a pictorial ambience of clothing, furnishings,
aromatic teas, home remedies, and patent medicines" (360).[55]

When the troubled unions (Newcome-Hobson, Florac–de Blois, duc
and duchesse d'Ivry, Barnes-Clara and Barnes–Mrs. Delacy, Clive-Rosey)
outnumber the happy ones (the Ridleys, the Pendennises) in Thackeray's
text, the author's theme emerges: in nineteenth-century England "homely
tyranny" (2:370)—as Mrs. Mackenzie's reign in Clive's household is
characterized—is more common than the "happy home" (1:227) once
imagined by the Colonel for Ethel and Clive. And as Léonore, the Colonel's only love, asserts near the end of her life, this state of affairs bodes ill
for the future: "Do you know that the children of those who do not love in
marriage seem to bear an hereditary coldness?" (2:90). Only after a prolonged and thorough disenchantment with inadequate definitions of home
can Thackeray suggest a course of action for the novel's hero and heroine,
as well as for his readers.

This overt theme of failed social relationships is most effective when
the narrator demonstrates that the readers' world is the same as the one
described in the fiction: "I have said this book is all about the world, and a
respectable family dwelling in it. It is not a sermon, except where it cannot
help itself, and the speaker pursuing the destiny of his narrative finds such
a homily before him. O friend, in your life and mine, don't we light upon
such sermons daily—don't we see at home as well as amongst our neigh-
bours that battle betwixt Evil and Good? Here on one side is Self and
Ambition and Advancement and Right and Love on the other. Which shall
we let to triumph for ourselves—which for our children?" (1:377).[56] The
"destiny of his narrative" here is not simply the end of Ethel and Clive's
story, but the readers' own lives, where imagined problems become real,
sentimental tears represent genuine sorrow, children's fate is the actual
future.[57]

Like Patmore with the successive volumes of his work and Dickens in
his traditional nineteen-month installment format, Thackeray cast his
story in a long medium: twenty-four parts in twenty-three months. Thus,
any resolution of domestic problems lay in the distance for Victorian

readers who began the story in October 1853, as was suggested in the *Weekly Dispatch*'s 9 October 1853 comment: "The first number of a new work (edited by a late remarkable hero, Arthur Pendennis, Esq.) will be gladly accepted by all, without a single question as to the merits, interest, and moral of a story that, as yet, lies in the future" (646). Much later in the novel's publication, the 18 August 1855 *Spectator* also noted the length of this particular novel's journey: "more than once we think the land of promise will never be reached: but far off from that mountain-top we spy the shining of its streams of milk and honey, and we see in spirit the wilderness cleared, the Jordan passed, and our wayworn and sorely-tried ones at rest beneath their vine" (859).

Such distance from aspiration to realization necessary for characters in fiction and readers of fiction is underscored by the Colonel's life in India, the miles separating him from those he loves. Of Thomas Newcome's youthful effort to establish his career in the Empire, Pendennis writes that a price had to be paid at home and abroad: "Scarce a soldier goes to yonder shores but leaves a home and grief in it behind him. The lords of the subject province find wives there: but their children cannot live on the soil. The parents bring their children to the shore, and part from them. The family must be broken up" (1:52). Though he marries in India, most of the Colonel's "thirty-four years' absence from home" (1:55) is without a family near him.

When Clive later watches his father depart again for India, this second time to earn the money to support Clive's comfortable life-style, the theme of family division is further emphasized. Pendennis and his friends are present at the parting: "We saw Clive and his father talking together by the wheel. Then they went below; and a passenger, her husband, asked me to give my arm to an almost fainting lady, and to lead her off the ship. Bayham followed us, carrying the two children in his arms, as the husband turned away, and walked aft" (1:255–56). Although his initial concern is for Clive and the Colonel, Pendennis recognizes the analogous plight of these strangers. The incident received further emphasis in the last lines of this number (May 1854): "I scarce perceived at the ship's side, beckoning an adieu, our dear old friend, when the lady, whose husband had bidden me to lead her away from the ship, fainted in my arms. Poor soul! Her, too, has fate stricken. Ah, pangs of hearts torn asunder, passionate regrets, cruel cruel partings! Shall you not end one day, ere many years; when the tears shall be wiped from all eyes, and there shall be neither sorrow nor pain?" (1:256). The eighth installment ended with these words. One of the two full-page illustrations for the number was entitled "Farewell" and

showed, from the point of view of a departing traveler, the crowd waving
on shore, including the one lady fainting beside Pendennis (see figure 3).
Thus, the breakup of families received additional emphasis in the monthly
format: not only would the illustration have stressed the loss involved, but
the fact that the number concluded with this memorable scene would have
helped etch it more deeply on the audience's memory.

This long novel, then, like *Dombey and Son,* posits from its earliest
numbers a world of great time and space across which relationships must
somehow reach if a final and probably temporary happiness for the
characters is to be found. As in the *Angel in the House,* the numerous letters
of *The Newcomes* stress the theme of separation among loved ones, highlighting the situations where face-to-face encounters are impossible.[58] On
the long journey toward a distant future union (or reunion) for characters
and audience, Thackeray took extra time to establish the background
against which his characters could develop and find their places in his
audience's affection. As Gordon Ray has written, the installment form was
appropriate for the slow pace and the wealth of detail necessary to create
this spacious fictional world: "Certainly of all Thackeray's novels [*The
Newcomes*] is the one which benefited most from the circumstances of
serial issue" (248).[59]

Still, after three or four numbers some reviewers began to complain
that there was no plot in Thackeray's newest work. For instance, while the
1 October 1853 *Weekly News and Chronicle* was happy to see the first
number from a familiar and well-liked author ("in all essential particulars,
a continuation of 'Pendennis'" [634]), the same paper lamented a lack of
incident in number two: "but perhaps something is about to occur which
will surprise matters out of their seeming" (5 November 1853: 714). After
three numbers *Bell's Weekly Messenger* also complained on 3 December
1853: "The author of this serial has not proceeded at present very far with
any plot, but seems to have intended nothing more than to devote its pages
to that cynicism, with which all his books are more or less tinged" (6). The
5 February 1854 *Weekly Dispatch* was more tolerant of Thackeray's style in
number 5: "Few incidents as yet occur in the story of 'Newcomes,' to
excite the zest of the reader who likes his viands well-seasoned; but the
author revels in descriptions, and his details of the Colonel's dinner-party
are not among the least graphic and amusing of his efforts" (86). Gordon
Ray also notes, however, that Thackeray had a plan for the full reach of the
novel: "When Bradbury and Evans complained after publishing four
monthly parts, 'the public has found that the story does not move,'
Thackeray remained undisturbed" (237). That Thackeray could build his

"Farewell."

Figure 3. "Farewell," Thackeray's *The Newcomes* (eighth installment, May 1854), emphasizing separation of families. (*Alderman Library, University of Virginia*)

audience over time was demonstrated in the weekly reviews of the next six monthly parts.

Bell's Weekly Messenger was perhaps the least enthusiastic about Thackeray and the early numbers of *The Newcomes*. Reviewing the sixth part on 4 March 1854 this paper had "not been able to trace any plot at all" (6) and was still put off by what it termed the author's "cynicism." And number 7 was considered "very heavy and prolix" (8 April 1854: 6). However, with the issue of the eighth number, *Bell's* began to be won over by Thackeray's art, calling it on 6 May 1854 "the best number . . . of his new tale" and admitting that it included a "sublime passage" that ended the number. That passage is the one depicting the Colonel's departure for India and Pendennis's support of the fainting wife.

The conversion of *Bell's Weekly Messenger* from antagonist to proponent of *The Newcomes* was confirmed in the next few months. On 3 June 1854 the paper observed that Thackeray was more "successful in this [ninth part] than in many previous numbers of his new monthly work" (6). Number 10 was found "even a better one than the last, which was of a much higher order than any of its predecessors" (8 July 1854: 6). And by the appearance of number 11 *Bell's* was among the most enthusiastic readers of Thackeray: "The plot of this tale thickens, and abounds with sparkling writing of a very exciting character" (5 August 1854: 6). This pattern of response was characteristic of other weeklies, as Thackeray slowly but steadily gathered an audience for his extended story of the Newcome family, creating his own family of readers and characters journeying together toward a distant union.[60]

At the heart of Thackeray's appeal in *The Newcomes,* once the story was set more clearly in motion from January to June 1854, were two major elements: the character of Colonel Newcome and the romance of Ethel and Clive.[61] These elements united in the novel's long search for the Victorian ideal, a happy home in which the affections are completely fulfilled. And as this novel's "angel in the house," Ethel embodied key traits like patience shared by Florence Dombey and Honoria Vaughan and Jane Graham. However, her realization of these qualities came only after preliminary failures and an extended process of maturing. Again, Thackeray's twenty-four month format allowed time to introduce Ethel's world in detail to Victorian readers; to involve the audience's sympathy in her situation; and to carry that Victorian public beyond the conventional expectation of a happy ending to new definitions of domestic stability.

Ethel Newcome has become famous to Thackeray readers as the Diana-like figure who appears at a family dinner with a green ticket pinned on her frock suggesting her status as object for sale (no. 9, June 1854); as the witty young lady who dances beyond the end of the ball and rejects Lord Kew (number 11, August 1854); and as the confident mature woman who relentlessly pursues with her grandmother Lord Farintosh and a grand match (no. 17, February 1855).[62] However, Ethel Newcome first appeared in the novel as a potential "angel in the house." A young woman in number 7, for instance, Ethel showed the skills of a domestic manager: she "busied herself delightedly in preparing the apartments which [Clive and his father] were to inhabit during their stay [in Newcome]—speculated upon it in a hundred pleasant ways, putting off her visit to this pleasant neighbour, or that pretty scene in the vicinage, until her uncle should come and they could be enabled to enjoy the excursion together" (1:194). Her family's plans for her marriage, however, push Ethel toward a more public role than that of the traditional wife and mother. To frame her later role as "angel," Thackeray first allows her to try out other possibilities. As Juliet McMaster informs us, "Besides being both vivid and likable, [Ethel] has a dynamism which most of Thackeray's major females lack: she learns about herself, and changes as a result of her knowledge" (*Thackeray* 163).[63]

Ethel's character during her years of courtship was at the center of interest in *The Newcomes* from March 1854 to April 1855, as the 12 November 1854 *Weekly Dispatch's* comment about number 14 suggests: "Miss Ethel, the haughty and the beautiful, still continues to torture and persecute that poor young man—Clive Newcome" (726). Thackeray, however, was preparing this heroine for a fate that his audience, anticipating a match with Clive, did not foresee. The 14 January 1855 *Weekly Dispatch* noted in number 16 "something ominous" (6) for Clive and Ethel, as Laura Pendennis arranges a meeting between the cousins that ends with Ethel in tears and Clive shaking his head and riding away "gloomily" (2:120): the review concluded that between "Ethel and Clive the same distance continues to exist, whatever the undercurrent of magnetism which, sympathetically, at least, draws the young people together" (6). *Bell's Weekly Messenger* similarly worried on 7 October 1854 about the traditional happy ending, wondering at number 14 "how the end will be brought about—the union of the hero and heroine in the bonds of matrimony" (6).

That reader-desired resolution, marriage between Ethel and Clive, seemed nearest in the novel's fifteenth part, particularly its last chapter, "Two or Three Acts of a Little Comedy." Here at the Hôtel de Florac Clive declares his love, and Ethel cites her feelings of duty toward her family; but their obvious feelings for each other encouraged readers' hopes. The 2 December 1854 *Weekly News and Chronicle* noted the "smart dialogue between the rich and beautiful heiress and poor young Clive" (762). *Bell's Weekly Messenger* on 2 December 1854 found number 15 especially effective: "This tale is by many degrees the best that Mr. Thackeray has yet written" (6). And the 10 December 1854 *Weekly Dispatch* termed the concluding moment "a scene full of emotion and feeling, full of deepest tenderness and pathos" (790). Of course, Thackeray chose to keep the central romance in limbo for many months, often frustrating these same readers. *Bell's Weekly Messenger* exploded at number 16 on 8 January 1855:

"By far the worst number . . . dull, insipid, and improbable, leaving his characters in the same plight in which they have remained for the last three months. What he is going to do with his hero and heroine, we are at an utter loss to conceive. He has got them into an awkward 'fix,' and it will take more ingenuity we imagine than he is possessed of cleverly to extricate them" (6).

Ethel's real destination within the novel's plot is as domestic, not romantic, heroine.[64] Thackeray moves his story toward that conclusion by having his narrator Pendennis insist throughout that he cannot manipulate the "facts" of the Newcome family history: he "must go on with his heroine, as a man with his wife, for better or worse, and to the end" (2:66). The voice telling this story is, of course, Arthur Pendennis's, not Thackeray's; thus, in his role as a character the narrator is bound by the limits of the fictional world. Pen explains late in the novel that he merely narrates what has happened, generally without art or disguise: "I disdain, for the most part, the tricks and surprises of the novelist's art" (2:293). This emphasis on the narrative's inalterable events is repeated throughout *The Newcomes,* as in this much earlier passage: "Not always doth the writer know whither the divine Muse leadeth him. But of this be sure—she is as inexorable as Truth. We must tell our tale as she imparts it to us, and go on or turn aside at her bidding" (1:100).

In addition to asserting his history's determined nature, Pendennis also tells his readers that in this case he must go on "to the end" beyond the conventional romantic story, which concludes with marriage. At one point, Mrs. Mackenzie informs the narrator of this mission: "You gentlemen who write books, Mr. Pendennis, and stop at the third volume, know very well that the real story often begins afterwards. My third volume ended when I was sixteen, and was married to my poor husband" (1:219). Since *The Newcomes* ran to four-volume length with twenty-four monthly parts, its form suggests it is following the advice of Clive's mother-in-law. Pendennis makes the same point much later in a rhetorical question: "Now, how will you have the story? Worthy mammas of families— . . . Is life all over when Jenny and Jessamy are married; and are there no subsequent trials, griefs, wars, bitter heart-pangs, dreadful temptations, defeats, remorses, sufferings to bear, and dangers to overcome?" (2:165).

As with *Angel in the House,* then, the real subject of *The Newcomes* is domestic life beyond courtship, where daily mundane cares weigh down the dreams of romantic youth.[65] Although this might be a subject Arthur Pendennis wishes to avoid, Thackeray's plan for *The Newcomes* required him to explore it. While the narrator is still a bachelor, he assumes like many Victorians that the tedium of ordinary life is a fate borne more easily by women than by men:

(2:18)

> *I protest the great ills of life are nothing—the loss of your fortune is a mere flea-bite; the loss of your wife—how many men have supported it and married comfortably afterwards? It is not what you lose, but what you have daily to bear, that is hard. I can fancy nothing more cruel, after a long easy life of bachelorhood, than to have to sit day after day with a dull handsome woman opposite; to have to answer her speeches about the weather, housekeeping, and what not; to smile appropriately when she is disposed to be lively (that laughing at the jokes is the hardest part), and to model your conversation so as to suit her intelligence, knowing that a word used out of its downright signification will not be understood by your fair breakfast-maker.*

While a more intelligent partner in life's journey might alleviate this boredom (as Ethel's history is meant to reveal), the pressure of "what you have daily to bear" is the great subject of this work, one which, according to the novel, dominated English national life in his time: "If you were acquainted with the history of every family in your street, don't you know that in two or three of the houses there such tragedies have been playing? . . . The fate under which man or woman falls, blows of brutal tyranny, heartless desertion, weight of domestic care too heavy to bear—are not blows such as these constantly striking people down?" (1:354).

Ethel is moved toward this national fate of domestic suffering by two forces: compassion for others and disenchantment with her own prospects in society. Sir Brian's stroke and recovery begin Ethel's role as angel in the house: "During all this period of their father's misfortune no sister of charity could have been more tender, active, cheerful, and watchful than Miss Ethel" (1:367). Torn between family pressures to marry well and her own feelings for Clive, she retreats to this domestic duty. She tells Lady Kew, "leave me to take care of my poor father. Here I know I am doing right. Here, at least, there is no sorrow, and doubt, and shame, for me, as my friends have tried to make me endure" (1:379).

Thackeray's habit of anticipating a character's future also warned the reader that Ethel moves through phases toward a final maturity. In the first extended description of her in the novel, Pendennis spoke "of a countenance somewhat grave and haughty, but on occasion brightening with humour or beaming with kindliness and affection. Too quick to detect affectation or insincerity in others, too impatient of dulness or pomposity, she is more sarcastic now than she became when after years of suffering had softened her nature" (1:232). Victorian readers naturally responded strongly to events that hinted at a final happy marriage with Clive rather than to foreshadowings of domestic difficulty for Ethel. They did not want these two to suffer in unhappy homes any more than did the narrator, Pendennis, who assents to his wife's assertion: "Well, my dear; and why should not the poor boy be made happy? . . . It is evident to me that Ethel is fond of him. I would rather see her married to a good young man whom she loves, than the mistress of a thousand palaces and coronets" (2:219).

The dangers of arranged marriages were especially emphasized in number 18 (March 1855), when Clara fled Barnes's household and Ethel could see what might be in store for her in Lady Kew's plan. The 8 April 1855 *Weekly Dispatch* was particularly moved by the narrator's summary of Clara's fate, quoting at length the passage in number 19 that describes her "new home" with Jack Belsize (2:224): "[This number] is emphatically 'good,' and the following is the forcible summing up of a life rendered hopelessly dark by the brutal treatment of him [Barnes] whom it most concerns" (6). That Ethel should reject Lord Farintosh in the same installment seemed to set up the happy resolution desired by most readers.

Of course, on the concluding page of number 19 Laura Pendennis, Ethel, and Thackeray's readers learned in a letter from the Colonel to Mrs. Mason that he has "a very pretty little daughter-in-law . . . Miss Rosa Mackenzie" (2:224). *Bell's Weekly Messenger* stated the audience's disappointment most strongly in a 5 May 1855 review of number 20: "Mr. Thackeray has made a great mistake in this number, by marrying his hero to the lady, for whom he was evidently not at first intended, and in changing the nature of the Newcomes, father and son, from their original cheerful and kind-hearted temperament. . . . It is a violation of all propriety and expectation that Clive Newcome should have wedded anyone but his cousin Ethel" (6).

Although the 5 May 1855 *Weekly Chronicle* was similarly disappointed that the novel's characters were "uncomfortable and unhappy" (282), the paper also noted that Ethel had "changed into a quiet, rural Lady Bountiful" (282). As was the case when her father needed her, Ethel responds to the suffering of others in her family: "The deserted little girl, Barnes's eldest child, ran, with tears and cries of joy, to her Aunt Ethel, whom she had always loved better than her mother; and clung to her and embraced her; and, in her artless little words, told her that mamma had gone away, and that Ethel should be her mamma now" (2:205). Ethel must also provide the center for Victorian domestic life: "Miss Newcome had to take the command of the whole of this demented household, hysterical mamma and sister, mutineering servants, and shrieking abandoned nursery, and bring young people and old to peace and quiet" (2:205). While modern readers certainly lament the limited options available to Ethel, they would still agree with Victorian readers and Thackeray's text: "She is a very different person from the giddy and worldly girl who compelled our admiration of late in the days of her triumphant youthful beauty, of her wayward generous humour, of her frivolities and her flirtations" (2:256).[66]

Two other characters, Arthur and Laura Pendennis, provide additional depth to the heroine's characterization in *The Newcomes*. Laura arrived late in this novel, first appearing in number 16 (January 1855). Similarly, her husband, after appearing as a character as well as narrator in the opening numbers of the novel, generally disappeared into the distant omniscient point of view until about number 17, when he began to intervene more directly in the affairs of the Newcome family. These characters affected Victorian readers primarily during the last six months of the reading experience, a time when audience familiarity with and commitment to Thackeray's story were already well established. Such newcomers to the front stage of this narrative, both familiar characters from their own novel (*The History of Pendennis,* November 1848–December 1850), were secondary to Clive and Ethel's relationship.[67] Arthur and Laura's domesticity reeks of complacency and sentimentality, particularly next to Ethel's difficult plight; but it is the rare product, the narrative reminds readers, of good fortune: "To us Heaven had awarded health, happiness, competence, loving children, united hearts, and modest prosperity. To yonder good man [the Colonel], whose long life shone with benefactions, and whose career was but kindness and honour, fate decreed poverty, disappointment, separation, a lonely old age. We bowed our heads, humiliated at the contrast of his lot and ours; and prayed Heaven to enable us to bear our present good fortune meekly, and our evil days, if they should come, with such a resignation as this good Christian showed" (2:331). Laura's and Pen's happiness is the product of good fortune delivered in another novel to which *The Newcomes* is, in a sense, a sequel. Thus, as Patmore deepened his treatment of domestic love by continuing his poem beyond the idealistic romance of Felix and Honoria, Thackeray here added to his audience's understanding of love and marriage by considering a couple less smiled upon by fortune.

Of the systems of belief offered, however, Laura Pendennis's seemed to answer Ethel's situation most fully.[68] Again, more modern alternatives are certainly desirable; but Thackeray explored in this novel what his own society contained. If an arranged marriage in high society was now unacceptable, and marriage based on love no longer available, Ethel had to take the only remaining option. And, as with Florence Dombey and Jane, patience was the best quality to carry her through this difficult time, the best quality, Thackeray argued, for all those in conditions for which there is no visible remedy: "Death, never dying out; hunger always crying; and children born to it day after day,—our young London lady, flying from the splendours and follies in which her life had been passed, found herself in the presence of these; threading darkling alleys which swarmed with wretched life; sitting by naked beds, whither by God's blessing she was sometimes enabled to carry a little comfort and consolation; or whence she came heart-stricken by the overpowering misery, or touched by the patient resignation of the new friends to whom fate had directed her" (2:227).[69] Whitwell Elwin epitomized this important value of *The Newcomes* in the September 1855 *Quarterly Review:* "Duration is of more importance than intensity" (362).

When Ethel thus finds herself a husbandless mother attempting to help the suffering around her, Thackeray is rounding off a process begun in the novel's first number, the domestication of society.[70] That is, the feelings that make the home sacred for Victorians are to be extended throughout the nation, and, indeed, the Empire. The Colonel set the pattern for this domestication in that male world, "The Cave of Harmony."[71] The Colonel's rejection of baseness in the name of family in that scene is consistent with Ethel's character at the end of the novel: "You must go home to Rosa," Ethel tells Clive after his father's death. "She will be sure to ask for her husband, and forgiveness is best, dear Clive" (2:369).[72] Although both characters are excluding for the moment what they wish did not exist, Ethel and the Colonel stand for a fundamental Victorian assertion of domestic virtues as the best weapon against corruption in their time.

In insisting on this fate for Ethel, Thackeray forced his readers to feel the cost such a social system exacts. In its 6 May 1855 observation about number 20 the *Weekly Dispatch* found of all the characters Ethel "alone seems most at her ease," though this writer is very much aware of unhappiness dominating the fictional landscape: "Ominous clouds and sinister forebodings seem to hover about the chapters of the present number, while the personages of the story are oppressed with a sense of advancing misery, which weighs with more or less effect upon all" (6). Similarly, *Bell's Weekly Messenger* predicted on 9 June 1855, after reading number 21, "we much fear the close will only add to the disappointment, which the last three or four numbers have engendered" (6). When we recall that Thackeray coaxed many of these readers from disinterest in the early numbers to enthusiastic involvement through number 19, we begin to see how masterful his direction of the Victorian installment audience was. He made them care about characters who were admittedly not perfect; and when their world did not allow them happiness in the end, these readers felt the need for change.

Some of the audience's anxiety about the cast of *The Newcomes* was resolved in the final double number, where all the important personages came together at a variety of homes for a final though limited resolution. The 12 August 1855 *Weekly Dispatch* noted "a mingled feeling of awakened tenderness, respect and reverence" (6) in the final pages. This paper was strongly moved, as most were, by the Colonel's death: "But what fine human feelings are thus awakened, what pity almost divine, what sympathies almost celestial, what impulses in the superlative of heroism, what religion of 'nature' is evolved in our inmost being while we follow the grand old Belisarius to his temporary lodging and his final home!" (6). *Bell's Weekly Messenger* on 4 August 1855 also accepted Thackeray's ending, even after its own previously expressed worries: " 'The Newcomes' is at last concluded, and just as it ought to be. Mr Thackeray has evidently taken the greatest pains with the ending, and by so doing he has brought it to a happy termination, though many of his deeply-interested readers doubted whether he would do so" (6).

The gathering around the hearth at the conclusion of the novel, however, involved more than a select few of the novel's characters who are to be at least momentarily protected from the dangers of the outside world; into this circle are drawn also the narrator Arthur Pendennis, the author Thackeray, and finally the readers of the fiction themselves. Among the "Old Friends Come Together" (the title of the second chapter in the final double number, August 1855) is the text's narrator, Arthur Pendennis. Through much of this history, of course, Clive's friend had been simply a confidant and a record keeper. At the end of number 18, however, he became a more direct agent in the family's affairs (though still a minor character in the novel's plot) when he attempted to remove Lord Highgate from Newcome.[73] Clara's tragedy increased the connection between the Pendennises and the Newcomes, as Laura became Ethel's chief counselor in number 19. And in number 22, after the crash of the Bundelcund Bank and the Colonel's bankruptcy, Pendennis visited Clive in Boulogne to offer him money and more: "Whatever he wanted was his as much as mine" (2:315).

This movement from observer to agent, from distance to involvement, has seemed to modern readers simply a failure to control point of view.[74] Yet it also represents a central value of the form in which Pendennis works as narrator, the long history: he cannot in the end stay removed from the fate of individuals he has known for so long and whose situation he understands so fully.[75] He does not remain detached in the idyllic domestic retreat of Fairoaks, but travels to Newcome and London in the effort to aid friends in trouble. His movement, in fact, is analogous to those installment reviewers in the weeklies who disliked the early numbers of *The Newcomes,* but eventually, learning more about the fiction's characters, came to care very much for the ongoing story. That is, Pendennis finds he "must go on with his heroine" and her circle because he feels for them, "as a man with his wife"; and this affection carries "to the end" (2:66) even though it causes him pain.

The same pressure to enter more fully into the world of his acquaintances, which ultimately inspires Arthur to write the history of the family, also animates Thackeray himself, the author of the novel. In that famous epilogue to Pendennis's narrative, Thackeray appears in his own person for the first time since the overture:[76] "As I write the last line with a rather sad heart, Pendennis and Laura and Ethel and Clive, fade away into fableland" (2:373). Thackeray has been drawn out from behind the cover of his alter ego–narrator Arthur Pendennis, addressing directly his Victorian installment readers. Walking "with my children in some pleasant fields near to Berne in Switzerland," Thackeray appears as the head of a family, the father of real as well as fictional children. His distance from England and the fact that no wife or mother appears here place him, not in the domestic isolation from the world where many argue Victorian novels conclude, but on a journey away from home, although perhaps moving, like so many of his characters, toward such a safe haven.

This Thackeray appearing at the end of the novel is the parent of the Newcomes's story, "which for three-and-twenty months the reader has been pleased to follow" (2:373). And in predicting a novel about J. J. Ridley, Thackeray posits another fictional family of his creation, whose history "may be told some of these fine summer months, or Christmas evenings, when the kind reader has leisure to hear" (2:374). Just as Pendennis found himself more and more deeply involved in the lives of the Newcomes, even when he had his own concerns as suitor, husband, father, writer, and member of Parliament, so Thackeray, Victorian citizen, had grown increasingly attached to his created characters over time: "I hardly know whether they are not true: whether they do not live near us somewhere. They were alive, and I heard their voices, but five minutes since was touched by their grief. And have we parted with them here on a sudden, and without so much as a shake of the hand?" (2:377). Thackeray too, that is, developed over time strongly felt relationships with his characters, "as a man with his wife," which blended sadness with aspiration in readers' last vision of them.[77]

As with Dickens at the end of *Dombey and Son* and Patmore in *Angel in the House,* however, Thackeray shared a closeness with his readers, a family relationship of artist and audience whose home was in the literary experience.[78] Referring to a "Fable-land" much like Dickens's imagined "greeting-place," Thackeray addressed his audience: "Friendly reader! may you and the author meet there on some future day! He hopes so; as he yet keeps a lingering hold of your hand, and bids you farewell with a kind heart" (2:375). Like his memorable character Colonel Newcome with a song in the "Cave of Harmony," Thackeray attempted through this story of the Newcome family to domesticate a Victorian audience, creating a family by the hearth stretching across all England.

Since more such stories were predicted and desired, the novel itself concluded in a brief moment of longed-for happiness before difficulties were once more encountered, underscoring the truth that domestic stability is less realized than pursued in Victorian literature. While Thackeray's final authorial statement, like Dickens's April 1848 preface and Patmore's 1863 endnote, may not conform to rules in the art of fiction or to dictates about closure in literature, they all demonstrate an allegiance to the values of serial literature: domestic virtue comes out of the literature, from the homes of Ethel and Clive, Florence and Walter, Honoria and Felix, on long and difficult journeys through authors to readers, whose homes are suggested in "fine summer months, or Christmas evenings," when Victorian families in life, fictional families in literature, and extended families in authors and readers are assembled, they sincerely believed, for the welfare of all.

III

Living in History

The passenger booked by this history, was on the coach-step, getting in.

Charles Dickens, *A Tale of Two Cities*

She turned her back on Florence, not meaning to look at it till the monks were quite out of sight; and raising the edge of her cowl again when she had seated herself, she discerned Maso and the mules at a distance where it was not hopeless for her to overtake them, as the old man would probably linger in expectation of her.

Meanwhile she might pause a little. She was free and alone.

George Eliot, *Romola*

if it might but last!
Always, my life-long, thus to journey still!
It is the interruption that I dread.

Robert Browning, *The Ring and the Book*

VICTORIANS EAGERLY QUESTIONED what living in history meant to themselves, their predecessors, and their projected successors. Whether they subscribed to Macaulay's Whig view of history or merely acknowledged the uniform action of time and change, they generally saw their own age as the end result of continuous growth and development over time.[1] Yet this process had also produced a culture that, insofar as it was truly new, truly "modern," represented an abrupt break with preceding eras. This dual awareness of links to, yet separation from, their forebears, as well as the general "discovery of time" and history detailed by Toulmin and Goodfield or Jerome Buckley, led Victorians to consider from multiple vantage points their relation to the past, the status of the present, and their possible directions into the future.[2] As Carlyle remarked in his 1830 essay "On

History," "Let us search more and more into the Past; let all men explore it, as the true fountain of knowledge; by whose light alone, consciously or unconsciously employed, the Present and the Future can be interpreted or guessed at" (89).

A related issue for Victorian thinkers was the shape history took. If Macaulay's *History of England* encouraged readers to see history as a straight line of progress leading to the mid-nineteenth century, others posited a far more complicated view of history. As Richard Altick notes, some evidence pointed Victorians to the conclusion that "for every mile of progress there might well be a neutralizing mile of retrograde action" (*Victorian* 111). If at times it made most sense to figure history as a straight line, many Victorians also felt impelled (Carlyle among them) to see history as a series of cycles, each cycle becoming an embodied whole.[3]

Victorian explorations of history, then, were a dominant element in the age's treatises and literature.[4] And these explorations took on additional resonance when they were embodied in serial publication (as was Macaulay's *History of England,* issued in separate volumes from 1849 to 1861). For a serial work is itself embedded in the linear unfolding of time, yet—especially in the case of novels and poetry—also aspires to a wholeness of shape and meaning. We wish to show how installment literature and an awareness of history are related phenomena in the nineteenth century by focusing on three serial works: Charles Dickens's *A Tale of Two Cities,* in both weekly and monthly installments (30 April to 26 November 1859); George Eliot's *Romola,* in the monthly *Cornhill* (July 1862–August 1863); and Robert Browning's *The Ring and the Book,* in four separate volumes issued at monthly intervals (November 1868–February 1869).

Peter Brooks has stated the general case about the meaning of reading over time, as in serial publication: "the time it takes, to get from beginning to end—particularly in those instances of narrative that most define our sense of the mode, nineteenth-century novels—is very much part of our sense of the narrative, what it has accomplished, what it means. . . . if we think of the effects of serialization (which, monthly, weekly, or even daily, was the medium of publication for many of the great nineteenth-century novels) we can perhaps grasp more nearly how time in the representing is felt to be a necessary analogue of time represented" (20–21).[5] Focusing more specifically on historical literature published in installments, we can state that to understand history in the Victorian era meant to find oneself on a line running from the past through the present to the future; this sense of the linearity of time and its forward-moving nature was embodied in the serial form, in which readers repeatedly found themselves in the middle of a story whose past was earlier installments and whose future was "to be continued."[6]

At key points in each work of literature, however, characters paused amidst the hustle and hurry of life to assess where they stood and to understand the shape of history, which was usually but not always progressive. In "the space between numbers," or the gaps between published parts,[7] serial readers also paused along the line of narrative and attempted to define the shape of the whole work of art, an embodiment of the author's understanding of historical events. Being within each number was for installment readers living in history, a fictionalized past in which one was not completely sure where all events lead; being between numbers or at the end of the entire text was inhabiting one of those moments at which one glimpses or creates larger patterns, fixing oneself more securely within a scheme of history. A unique feature of the serial historical novel or poem is often the rhythm of these two states of consciousness, awareness of the ebb and flow of change.

For Victorians no single event figured more prominently as "historical" than the French Revolution. A. Dwight Culler cites Goethe's statement that "Anyone who has lived through the Revolution feels impelled toward history. He sees the past in the present, and contemplates it with fresh eyes which bring even the most distant objects into the picture." Culler concludes that such a person moreover "wishes to see whether he can project the line of development into the future and see what lies ahead" (5–6). Thus, Charles Dickens's most overtly historical novel, *A Tale of Two Cities,* is about the single event that itself most shaped Victorian concepts of history.

Philip Collins has stated that this particular Dickens novel "has been little discussed by the critics. At the time [of first publication], it was reviewed coolly and without much acumen" (*Dickens* 421). But he is talking primarily about the more learned reviewers of literary journals rather than the average readers in Dickens's popular audience. Michael Wolff reminds us that "there is no question but that *A Tale of Two Cities* was a popular success despite the critics" (274). The *Examiner* (5 November 1859) noted the success of the periodical in which Dickens's story appeared, a popularity probably "due to the fact that the new story by Mr. Dickens, the 'Tale of Two Cities,' which runs through [*All the Year Round*'s] numbers, has earned wide applause as one of the best things that he has written" (709). Such enthusiastic response to this serial is more visible in the popular weekly press than in the more prestigious monthlies and quarterlies.[8]

Readers of Dickens's serial generally responded more to characters than to the depiction of significant historical events, as *Bell's Weekly Messenger* noted on 17 December 1859: Dickens's success in *Tale* "has been far less in detailing the most striking events of French history, than in pourtraying [*sic*] the conduct and suffering of individuals" (6).[9] John Forster in the 10 December 1859 *Examiner* claimed similarly that the domestic subject underlying the historical framework was compelling: "in his broadest colouring of revolutionary scenes, while he gives life to large truths in the story of a nation, he is working out closely and thoroughly the skilfully designed tale of a household" (788). The obvious romantic heroine, Lucie Manette, naturally captured the hearts of these readers interested in individual lives, but she has also been recognized as Dickens's spirit of history in *Tale,* "the golden thread that united [her father] to a Past beyond his misery, and to a Present beyond his misery" (11 June 1859: 145).[10] Lucie's identity as "baby, girl, and woman, all in one" (9 July 1859: 243) underscores, as Alexander Welsh has written in *The City of Dickens* (210), her angelic nature that stands outside of time and yet unifies it. However, in a novel where names are linked in interesting pairs, another *L* character also plays an important role in representing history: Jarvis Lorry, the man of business and friend of the family with seemingly little personal identity. At times caught up in the rush of history, Lorry also sometimes stands back from events to measure their meaning and direction. Thus, as the representation of an individual living in the ceaseless movement of time, Jarvis Lorry figures as an important focal point for Victorian readers' interest in the dynamics of history.

Indeed, the novel began with Lorry stepping into history. After the splendid opening chapter setting the scene in prerevolutionary France and eighteenth-century England ("It was the best of times, it was the worst of times"), readers saw Lorry on the road from London to Dover: "The passenger booked by this history, was on the coach-step, getting in" (30 April 1859: 3; see figure 4).[11] Getting into the coach, Lorry is committing himself to the journey, to the confusion of events in time as opposed to the more static, protected world of Tellson's Bank. Accepting Jerry's words, "Recalled to Life," in the subsequent scene further confirms Lorry's position in relation to actions and consequences. By suggesting that journeys set events in motion and that putting ideas into words gives shape to past, present, and future, this passage introduces the reader to two central metaphors for history in the novel, travel and narrative. As Lorry affirms his involvement with events (he is "booked" on this mission), he also inaugurates a story, "this history," which is to be our "book," *A Tale of*

Figure 4. Lorry stepping into history in Dickens's *Tale of Two Cities* (first installment, 30 April 1859). (*Alderman Library, University of Virginia*)

Two Cities. The *Weekly Dispatch's* later review of the novel (11 December 1859) linked Lorry's role as agent of history to the author's role in originating literature, saying of Dickens: "He possesses in an eminent degree the power of calling back to life, by a few minute touches, the actual past" (6).

In addition to starting up this story or history, Lorry's appearance in the narrative stresses for Victorian readers two central responses to history, feeling caught up in the rush of passing events and seeing oneself essentially motionless within the greater sweeps of time. His position in this early scene, one foot in the coach and one on the ground, might represent these two states, as he is suspended in the movement from one to the other. The alternation between travel and rest, between movement and cessation evident in the Dover road scene is central both to Dickens's understanding of history and to Victorian reading of serials. Progress and pause, that is, make up an essential rhythm of nineteenth-century life. Both history's rapid pace and the opportunities for achieving timeless perspectives are aspects of the novel extended and strengthened by Dickens's serial form.

Lorry's being caught up in the swirl of events is evident in his first trip to Paris to rescue Manette from prison and on his last retreat with the entire family toward England. In the later scene, the identification of readers with characters as citizens of a changing world is accomplished through the use of first-person narrative: "Houses in twos and threes pass by us, solitary farms, ruinous buildings, dye-works, tanneries, and the like, open country, avenues of leafless trees. The hard uneven pavement is under us, the soft deep mud is on either side. Sometimes, we strike into the skirting mud, to avoid the stones that clatter us and shake us; sometimes we stick in ruts and sloughs there. The agony of our impatience is then so great, that in our wild alarm and hurry we are for getting out and running—hiding—doing anything but stopping" (12 November 1859: 49). The echoes of the novel's opening journey—the mud, getting in and out of the vehicle, a fractured landscape—are part of a dominant mood in much of the novel, an aspect of Dickens's style in this particular work. The breathless rush of words often matches the characters' feelings of being swept along by wild, uncontrollable events. Readers of the novel in its weekly parts in *All the Year Round* often found that individual, short installments raced past in a blur that seemed appropriate to the tumultuous events being represented.[12]

As J. Don Vann shows us (71–72), eighteen of the thirty-one weekly installments of *Tale of Two Cities* were made up of a single chapter; twelve consisted of two, closely related, often paired chapters (such as "Monseigneur in Town" and "Monseigneur in the Country" or "One Night" and "Nine Days"); and only one, the first, included three chapters.[13] The careful composition of each unit led to broad appreciation of the novel's tight structure. On 25 August 1859 Dickens himself wrote of the special character of this novel, which featured less description than was typical for him: "I set myself the little task of making a *picturesque* story, rising in every chapter with characters true to nature, but whom the story itself should express, more than they should express themselves, by dialogue" (cited in Collins, *Dickens* 423). After reading six weekly parts, *Lloyd's Weekly London Newspaper* on 5 June 1859 noted the work's careful construction: "We have now read enough of the story to discover that there is a well—an artistically—laid plot in it" (8). *Bell's Weekly Messenger* on 17 December 1859 similarly praised the author's craft: "Mr. Charles Dickens has certainly not written a more clever, or connected story, nor one which exhibits larger specimens of his talent and skill" (6).

Although installments in the weekly format were quite short (four and one-half double-columned pages of *All the Year Round*), each contained a memorable subject presented in remarkable detail. As *Lloyd's*

Weekly London Newspaper for 1 May 1859 suggested, readers took up Dickens's tale at the appearance of the first installment in *All the Year Round:* "The literary event of the week is the appearance of the first number of Mr. Charles Dickens's new periodical—the chief contribution to No. 1 being the opening of a new story by the editor. . . . We shall afford our readers a peep at Mr. Dickens's 'Night Shadows,' requiring from our readers in return that they will read the 'Tale of Two Cities' from the beginning" (8). While many readers must have purchased the monthly numbers Dickens also offered (containing the same material as the weekly magazine parts in his traditional thirty-two page format), commentary in the popular press seemed to respond to the novel's being read in weekly installments. The *Critic,* for instance, noted on 17 December 1859 that this story had "for thirty weeks kept the readers of *All the Year Round* in anxious expectation" (602); and the 11 December 1859 *Weekly Dispatch* reported that, as "it appeared piecemeal in the columns of *All the Year Round,* it was read by many thousands" (6). The *Critic's* reviewers acknowledged that the "monthly green parts" now "are gathered together, the preface and title-page are set before, and the binder has made the scattered leaves a book"; but they derived their final review from "our recollection of the weekly instalments from which, like so many more, we pieced out the story from week to week" (602).

The final outcome of events was always clear for readers in the middle of any installment, weekly or monthly. For instance, we read in the first pages of *Tale:* "It is likely enough that, rooted in the woods of France and Norway, there were growing trees, when that sufferer [one accused by the French government of treason] was put to death, already marked by the Woodman, Fate, to come down and be sawn into boards, to make a certain movable framework with a sack and a knife in it, terrible in history" (30 April 1859: 1). Yet how individuals might escape immediate danger within one part or the next was generally not known: "What do you expect, Mr. Darnay?" Carton asks at the trial in London; and Charles can only answer "The worst" (4 June 1859: 125), giving no clues to Dickens's readers about the outcome of this particular sequence of events.

The careful planning for tight, short parts led to a drive and density in Dickens's style that has been remarked from the novel's first publication to the present. The *Illustrated London News* on 12 November 1859 credited some of the narrative's power to the novel's appearance in weekly parts, saying that *All the Year Round's* "popularity is attributed to the very obvious circumstance of the issue of Mr. Dickens' 'Tale of Two Cities.' . . . which probably carries most of its readers along with it. In the form in which it has been produced, whether artfully or not we cannot say, it has the effect of keeping up the desire to ascertain what it is all about through every successive number" (458). John Forster in the *Examiner* for 10 December 1859 similarly noted the "energy," "single purpose," and "force" (788) of Dickens's novel. And *Bell's Weekly Messenger* in 17 December 1859 remarked on "the evident closeness of the story" and the "unalterable purpose from the very first" (6). In this century John Gross among others cites the novel's "rapid tempo which never lets up from the opening sentence" ("A Tale" 195).[14]

Of course, some Victorian critics took an opposite view of Dickens's achievement. Sir James Fitzjames Stephen cleverly damned Dickens's text and the medium in which it appeared for the *Saturday Review* on 17 December 1859: "in order to extend the circulation of the new periodical he published in it the story which now lies before us. It has the merit of being much shorter than its predecessors, and the consequence is, that the satisfaction which both the author and the readers must feel at its conclusion was deferred for a considerably less period than usual" (741). Nevertheless, the serial readers' response to the rapid weekly issue of Dickens's novel in *All the Year Round,* both favorable and unfavorable, seemed to place them in a position similar to that of the characters in the novel, swept along by the explosive events of revolution and change. Within each individual installment, readers encountered a moment from the past presented in a style that is powerful and forward-moving; they found themselves living in history, being carried along by the rapid pace of events toward uncertain destinations. The novel's serial form thus heightened a major theme, the nature of history.

The merging of characters and readers in the experience of history is developed further through the figure of Jarvis Lorry traveling throughout England and France. Of all the characters in the novel dislocated by events, he might seem the most secure, the least affected. Some critics have, in fact, dismissed Lorry as someone bound to the traditions and forms of the past.[15] Though committed to an older way of life, Lorry still accepts changes brought about by history and ultimately moves toward the England of Dickens's own day, toward the lives of Dickens's actual readers. Admittedly, Lorry's employer, Tellson's Bank, "an old-fashioned place . . . very small, very dark, very ugly, very incommodious" (28 May 1859: 97), is a representative of the established social order in England, ominously analogous to the doomed, corrupt aristocracy of France. Yet throughout the novel Lorry, like the later Victorian citizens who read his story, is caught up in events, moving down the road of history.

In his inaugural relationship to Manette, for instance, Lorry's job is to bring Lucie's father into the present, releasing him from entombment in the past.[16] As the narrative emphasizes many times in the opening pages, Lorry is "on his way to dig some one out of a grave" (30 April 1859: 5), to free someone from an old dispensation. The operation is less physical (opening the doors of prison) than mental (opening the consciousness to the passage of time); thus, Lorry's travels on the road to Paris are paired with inner activities: "When it was dark, and he sat before the coffee-room fire, awaiting his dinner as he had awaited his breakfast, his mind was busily digging, digging, digging, in the live red coals" (7 May 1859: 26). His mental digging matches the reader's metaphorical traveling back into the past, a search for historical understanding from Dickens's text.[17] Lorry's place in the novel is, then, not simply that of a fossil from England's unchanging, deadening institutions; rather he, like Dickens's middle-class audience, represents someone with a firm commitment to conservative values seeing himself propelled along the path to a new future.[18]

The object of Lorry's search at the novel's opening is, of course, a man with no past, someone taken out of history. As he awakens Manette, Lorry represents a spirit of change, of movement into the future. Furthermore, Lorry has already given Lucie her past: the man from Tellson's narrated for Lucie "the story of one of our customers" (7 May 1859: 27), her father. Lorry assures Lucie that she will find her identity in time; she will know "the history of [her] father" (28). Thus, Lorry is the agent of historical consciousness, though he himself does not suffer the personal shock of change as much as the other characters.

This sense of the force of change is, as indicated earlier, often conveyed through travel. In opposition to images of change and travel, however, the novel also contains instances of rest or stasis, in which events are slowed and the shape of history is glimpsed.[19] Just as Jarvis Lorry represents at some points the individual caught up in action, he is also seen at other moments to stand in the ebb rather than within the flow of time. These pauses outside of time are matched in the serial novel's form by key uneventful installments and by gaps between installments.

In his good fortune at remaining personally untouched by some of the tumultuous events of his time, Jarvis Lorry thus models for Victorian installment readers a second important response to history, finding a fixed point of reference from which to determine one's own place in it. These moments are often signaled in the text by a pause from travel. After a "long journey" (10 September 1859: 457) across France in 1792, for instance, Lorry sits "by a newly-lighted wood fire (the blighted and unfruitful year was prematurely cold), and on his honest and courageous face there was a deeper shade than the pendent lamp could throw, or any object in the room distortedly reflect—a shade of horror" (24 September 1859: 505). His study of France at this point in the revolution has opened his eyes to the process and results of the most recent events in history.

Just as Lorry surveys his place in time on such breaks from travel, the serial reader is also given resting places along the linear journey of reading *A Tale of Two Cities*. For instance, the first individual installment almost totally dedicated to rest within the flux of events is the eighth installment, 18 June 1859. Here the quiet retreat of Doctor Manette's Soho residence, "a very harbour from the raging streets" (169), is described under the ironic chapter title "Hundreds of People." No major characters travel great distances in this part, and very few people—none but friends—invade this house. In his review of the novel for the 10 December 1859 *Examiner* John Forster gave detailed attention to this part as representative of Dickens's achievement: "We may recall as one example of the manner of the book, the art with which the echoes of the future are suggested by the echoes in Doctor Manette's quiet street corner, near Soho square" (788). For Dickens's first readers, then, this uneventful installment provided an opportunity for reflection on the story thus far, on what has happened and how it is "to be continued."

One of the particular moments within this 18 June 1859 part at which readers might have reviewed and assessed what happened comes at an exchange between Lorry and Miss Pross. Lorry's role in initiating events is recalled when Miss Pross tells the man from Tellson's that too many people are calling on Lucie at their quiet home in Soho:

> *"All sorts of people who are not in the least degree worthy of the pet, are always turning up," said Miss Pross. "When you began it—"*
> *"I began it, Miss Pross?"*
> (170)
> *"Didn't you? Who brought her father to life?"*
> *"Oh! If that was beginning it—" said Mr. Lorry.*
> *"It wasn't ending it, I suppose? I say, when you began it."*

Lorry brought to life the events of the novel, much as Lucie restored her father to consciousness of his past, by embarking on his memorable journey.

Installment readers were not only reminded of what had happened at this point in the reading experience; they also were encouraged in the eighth part to look ahead to how the story might be continued. In this chapter readers were told how even the protected corner of Dr. Manette's residence is not guaranteed exemption from history: "It was such a curious corner in its acoustical properties, such a peculiar Ear of a place, that as Mr Lorry stood at the open window, looking for the father and daughter whose steps he heard, he fancied they would never approach. Not only would the echoes die away, as though the steps had gone; but, echoes of other steps that never came would be heard in their stead, and would die away for good when they seemed close at hand" (171). Thus Lorry, pausing from the ordinary rush of events, anticipates imagined and real future actions; similarly, Dickens's original readers had opportunities to anticipate what might happen in future installments of *A Tale of Two Cities*.

Later in the same installment, those gathered in the house for tea are also told that the future is likely to contain mystery: "the wonderful corner for echoes resounded with the echoes of footsteps coming and going, yet not a footstep was there" (173). Lucie's apprehension provides readers with a foreshadowing of how these private lives might be touched by public events: "I have sometimes sat alone here of an evening, listening, until I have made the echoes out to be the echoes of all the footsteps that are coming by-and-by into our lives" (173). The ominous note of Lucie's thoughts is picked up by the narrator, who concludes the installment by directing us toward that busy outside world: "see the great crowd of people with its rush and roar, bearing down upon [those gathered in Manette's house], too" (173). Again, serial readers of *All the Year Round* could expect this small band of citizens to come into contact with the larger world in subsequent installments. This particular expectation would be heightened by the novel's installment structure, as this narrative look into the future comes as the last sentence of the 18 June 1859 part, assuming an important place in the reader's consciousness for the ensuing week between installments.

This particularly quiet and reflective number, the eighth, then, came approximately one quarter of the way through the novel of thirty-one parts. Another installment with less dramatic events, which inspired in readers an assessment of past and future events in the fiction, was the sixteenth, coming at about the midpoint of the text (13 August 1859). This part includes the marriage of Lucie and Darnay (the chapter called "One Night") and the time of the honeymoon, when Dr. Manette suffers a relapse to his prison days (the chapter entitled "Nine Days"). On the night before the wedding, Lucie and her father recall the past and project the future: her father recollects the distant "period of his suffering" and assures her that his "future is far brighter, Lucie, seen though your marriage, than it could have been—nay, than it ever was—without it" (361). Their thoughts might have inspired similar summations from readers.

In "Nine Days," the other half of this installment, Jarvis Lorry also figures as an inspiration for readers to gather together the pieces of narrative into comprehensible patterns. At one point he considers the shape of his own life, exclaiming to Miss Pross: "To think that there might have been a Mrs. Lorry, any time these fifty years almost!" (363). When Dr. Manette reverts to his ahistorical character, making shoes, Lorry leaves the protected world of Tellson's once again to bring his friend back to the present: "He therefore made arrangements to absent himself from Tellson's for the first time in his life" (364). Since Manette believes himself a prisoner, Lorry's strategy is to insist on his own place in the present: Lorry "remained, therefore, in his seat near the window, reading and writing, and expressing in as many pleasant and natural ways as he could think of, that it was a free place" (364). Thus, again Lorry acts as the agent of historical consciousness, insisting on the existence of a past from which we have advanced to the present. Readers, recalling the earlier events of the narrative that account for this crisis, similarly find themselves along a line of time moving forward toward the conclusion of the novel. That Lorry is, in fact, reading here reinforces the parallel between character and readers.

For much of the second half of the novel, in which event follows event with increasing speed, the primary pause for Victorian readers was not any individual part but the gap between installments, the week in which the story was halted. There Victorian serial readers had the opportunity to fix their understanding of the story thus far, discussing with others the more memorable scenes and perhaps making predictions about the future. Such a situation occurred after the end of installment 22 (24 September 1859). The Defarges have made a visit to Lucie and her daughter in their Paris apartment. Although Lorry tried to dismiss Lucie's worries about what "that dreadful woman" intended toward her imprisoned husband and his family, he is apprehensive about the future: "the shadow of the manner of these Defarges was dark upon himself, for all that, and in his secret mind it troubled him greatly" (509). Serial readers were encouraged by this passage, which ended the number, to review past events in the novel and to foresee the future—that is, to find the shape of history.[20]

Such pauses in literary experience are interestingly represented in the novel by the breaks of Dr. Manette's own historical narrative, the account of his arrest and imprisonment rediscovered by Defarge: "Where I make the broken marks that follow here, I leave off for the time, and put my paper in its hiding-place. ★ ★ ★ ★ ★ " (1).[21] This "history" makes up almost all of the novel's twenty-seventh part (29 October 1859), as only a brief account of the jury's deliberation and judgment concludes the chapter. The shape of this particular narrative underscores two features of serial literature in general: first, gaps in narrative create meaning; and second, the experience of literature is often more powerful and meaningful than any specific conclusion drawn from it as lesson or moral.

The breaks in Dr. Manette's narrative are often as suggestive as those in the whole novel. For instance, the revelation that there is a second patient in the nobleman's house ends one section of the prisoner's record: "Is it a pressing case?" asks Manette; and then we read: "You had better see," [the elder brother] carelessly answered; and took up a light. ★ ★ ★ ★ ★ " (2). Such pauses encourage an organization and shaping of message for author and reader: "I am so fearful," Manette writes at one point, "of being detected, and consigned to an underground cell and total darkness, that I must abridge this narrative. There is no confusion or failure in my memory; it can recal [sic], and could detail, every word that was ever spoken between me and those brothers" (4). Manette's "abridgement" occurs around the breaks in his text. In those spaces, clearly, Manette makes decisions about what goes in his narrative and in what order. Thus, these spaces are structurally important and contribute to the narrative's final effect.

The lesson of Manette's narrative seems initially to be unequivocal and powerful: "them and their descendants, to the last of their race, I Alexandre Manette, unhappy prisoner, do this last night of the year 1767, in my unbearable agony, denounce to the times when all these things shall be answered for. I denounce them to Heaven and to earth" (6). Manette's conclusion about the meaning of his experience is immediately taken up by the later audience hearing the tale: "The narrative called up the most revengeful passions of the time, and there was not a head in the nation but must have dropped before it" (6). Yet Dr. Manette, years after the event, wishes to retract this absolute condemnation. The substance of the narrative is never denied or altered, but one conclusion toward which it leads is rejected by its author and by the novel's narrator, who expands the context for this document's meaning: "Little need, in presence of that tribunal and that auditory, to show how the Defarges had not made the paper public, with the other captured Bastille memorials borne in procession, and had kept it, biding their time" (6). Dickens's representation of narration and its meaning suggests that, whereas the experience of reading (in this case, hearing) is undeniably valuable, conclusions about the meaning of such literary experience are sometimes problematic. How it feels to be living in history as one reads Dickens's novel may be more important to its author than a moral about history arrived at after the book has been read.[22]

As Manette's record with its parts and its gaps suggests, essential to the nature of historical experience in Dickens's view is the rhythm of activity and cessation, movement and rest. While there are few pauses or rests in the second half of Dickens's narrative, other than the breaks between parts, there is one brief moment early in the twenty-fifth part that does provide a momentary glimpse of the full sweep of history as Dickens understands it. In this part, chapter 8 of book 3, "A Hand of Cards" (15 October 1859), Sydney Carton lays the groundwork for his daring plan. Bringing Miss Pross and the spy Barsad to Mr. Lorry, he finds a man he has come to respect reflecting on the course of events:[23] "Mr. Lorry had just finished his dinner, and was sitting before a cheery little log or two of fire—perhaps looking into their blaze for the picture of that younger elderly gentleman from Tellson's, who had looked into the red coals at the Royal George at Dover, now a good many years ago" (579). As this passage recalls the opening of the novel, the first journey, it encourages the reader to evaluate the meaning of the past and to measure the length of time that separates beginning from end.

Dickens's final view of history was not, of course, a radical one, nor one that departed in significant ways from accepted Victorian notions. He stated this position directly at the beginning of the last installment on 26 November 1859:

> *And yet there is not in France, with its rich variety of soil and climate, a blade, a leaf, a root, a sprig, a peppercorn, which will grow to maturity under conditions more certain than those that have produced this horror [the violence of the French Revolution]. Crush humanity out of shape once more, under similar hammers, and it will twist itself into the same tortured forms. Sow the same seed of rapacious licence and oppression over again, and it will surely yield the same fruit according to its kind.*
>
> *Six tumbrils roll along the streets. Change these back again to what they were, thou powerful enchanter, Time, and they shall be seen to be the carriages of absolute monarchs, the equipages of feudal nobles, . . . No; the great magician [Time] who majestically works out the appointed order of the Creator, never reverses his transformations.*

(93)

In the view of Dickens and his age, there is a fixed, linear order to time and progress. Even cataclysmic changes ("this horror") are part of a steady forward movement (the "fruit" of earlier "seed," a process that clears the way for new growth), though they may not seem so at the moments they occur. God's shape for history has an "appointed order" and contains no "reversals," as the narrator later confirms, using the novel's travel metaphor to describe the last moments of Carton and the girl he supports: "These two children of the Universal Mother, else so wide apart and differing, have come together on the dark highway, to repair home together, and to rest in her bosom" (26 November 1859: 94). That such a view of history was widely accepted by Dickens's readers is evident in the *Weekly Dispatch*'s 11 December 1859 review of the novel: "The outburst of popular wrath which swept away the monarchy of France and laid so many proud heads in the dust, was no sudden impulse; it was the result of years of silent, sullen brooding over real miseries and countless wrongs" (6).[24]

This lesson confirmed at the novel's end, however, as we have argued, may not be more crucial to Dickens's effort than the experience of living in history generated by the long middle of his text. The long middle, for instance, would have intensified the warning to his contemporaries, since it embodied the realization that we are always in the midst of history, as serial readers are in the midst of narrative, and cannot always see where they are going. By insisting that his readers live in history for the duration of the novel's publication (seven months), Dickens deepened the audience's understanding of the causes and development of revolution.

That the mimetic art of Dickens should take a form (serial) analogous to its subject (history) is evident in a letter the author addressed to his friend Wilkie Collins (6 October 1859): "I think the business of art is to lay all that ground carefully, not with the care that conceals itself—to show, by a backward light, what everything has been working to—but only to *suggest,* until the fulfilment comes. These are the ways of Providence, of which ways all art is but a little imitation" (quoted in Collins, *Dickens* 423). As Providence directs history to a final, appropriate conclusion, according to Dickens, so he places his readers along a line from beginning to end of this serial novel, suggesting how events will end, but also letting his audience live in a moment of the past depicted in each installment.

Reinforcing the belief of Dickens and his audience that history is a journey in stages from past through present toward the future, then, *A Tale of Two Cities* takes a serial form, an irreversible, forward moving story in a linear shape.[25] Along the path of thirty-nine weeks traveled by Victorian serial readers in 1859 are alternating accounts of swiftly moving events and of momentary cessations in time's continuing changes (with

many pauses simply the gaps between installments). Victorian serial readers repeatedly found themselves, like Lorry with one foot on the road and
the other in the Dover mail, shifting from points of timeless perspective
into the rush of time. Dickens's insights into the French Revolution as
historical event perhaps are not, as many have argued, particularly brilliant; yet his novel deserves some praise it has not received for its presentation of the past through the installment format, alternating the rush of
events with the pauses for reflection that inspire a sense of living in
history. [26]

While characters like Mr. Lorry in *A Tale of Two Cities* often felt
themselves pushed forward by the swift flow of events, and only occasionally lifted out of the movement of time to places where they could glimpse
the shape of past, present, and future, the personages of George Eliot's
Romola were more aware of being at pivotal moments in history, standing
at the end of one sequence of related events and attempting to prepare
themselves for the next. Living in history, they knew in varying degrees
that where they were headed was a consequence of the actions they were
taking in the present. But for them the grand sweep of human events was
less obvious than it appeared in Dickens's world, and their sense of the
future insisted on by the line running from the past through the present
was clouded by confusions about the motives of others and the complexity
of their own personalities. Thus, if Jarvis Lorry travels frequently in
Dickens's novel, Romola often pauses in Eliot's world; one is caught up in
the flow of time, while the other stands at the end of a phase in life. Readers
of the novel *Romola* in its serialized version (*Cornhill,* July 1862–August
1863) often felt themselves to be in a position similar to Romola's, understanding with unusual clarity what had happened in the fiction to that
point, yet less able than expected to predict how the story was "to be
continued." The installment form once again was an important extension
of the artist's vision and a significant manifestation of the age's beliefs.

This "historical novel" has been analyzed more as a study of timeless
moral dilemmas than as an examination of the past's relationship to the
present. [27] The *Athenaeum,* for instance, in its review of the completed
work, was quick to focus on questions of conduct, finding the clearest
effect on the audience to be "a desire to cease from a life of self-pleasing,
and to embody in action that sense of obligation, of obedience to duty,
which is, indeed, the crowning distinction that has been bestowed on
man, the high gift in which all others culminate" (quoted in Carroll 197).
Modern critics similarly tend to pay most attention to ethical issues in the
novel. [28]

True, in Eliot moral issues are almost always set within temporal contexts. That is, both individual and collective responsibility require an awareness of the past's relation to the present, according to the novel: "Our lives make a moral tradition for our individual selves, as the life of mankind at large makes a moral tradition for the race" (February 1863: 158). Furthermore, the novel's lessons about history involve more than an intellectual ability to chart the past or predict the future. Tito, for example, is shrewd at predicting events, but he does not admit to their human contexts: he often experiences "the mild self-gratulation of a man who has won a game that has employed hypothetic skill, not a game that has stirred the muscles and heated the blood" (July 1863: 22). Not only does Eliot insist that we see ourselves within an ethical tradition, but her characters must do more than let that moral heritage guide them into the future; they must create the next phase in that pathway by making choices of conduct. Savonarola offers a philosophy of divine guidance to Romola: "I am but as the branch of the forest when the wind of heaven penetrates it" (November 1862: 593); but she must find and define her own history as part of a larger humanity. In such a scheme, the consequences of our actions are not always obvious, as the narrator insists: "our deeds are like children that are born to us; they live and act apart from our own will" (October 1862: 440). Understanding history for Eliot, then, involves not just seeing events in sequence but placing such patterns within larger schemes of value: "the fortunes of Tito and Romola were dependent on certain grand political and social conditions which made an epoch in the history of Italy" (November 1862: 577). Living in history for Eliot involved, as it did for Dickens, finding oneself on a line running from the past through the present to the future; however, in Eliot's world time's linearity and its forward-moving nature are more difficult to see and to act on.

Some early readers, like the *Home and Foreign Review* (October 1863), did insist on the importance of specific historical context in determining moral questions: "In *Romola* the population of Florence is not only made the setting and background of the tale, but it takes a prominent part in the conduct of the story" (quoted in Carroll 230). Of course, many readers had such difficulty assimilating the densely presented historical material that interpretation was unlikely. The *Weekly Dispatch,* reviewing the first installment on 20 July 1862, expressed a common preference for subject matter: "The author of 'Adam Bede' has left the story of the 'ignorant present time,' and English life, scenery and character for Italy in the fifteenth century. Lifted from the fixed and firm-set earth of solid reality away back into the 'dim religious light' of the past, we think he or she is borne away from the strength that has sustained the peculiar genius that has attracted us. . . . as author and readers know little or nothing of the real inner life of Italy so very long ago, we think we should have preferred to hear something of what we really *do* know" (6). A year and one week later, 26 July 1863, the *Weekly Dispatch* correctly noted that most Victorians read through the historical material to the human story of the major characters, as they had with *A Tale of Two Cities:* "Addressed to a Tuscan instead of an English audience, the work might excite interest if not enthusiasm, for neither labour nor research has evidently been spared in its composition, and its merit in an antiquarian sense is unquestionable. But details of which we are unable to test the accuracy are merely tedious, and the central figures, Romola and Tito, are those which the reader will chiefly regard with interest" (6). Even the more sophisticated *Guardian,* 6 August 1862, was somewhat puzzled about how it should react to this novel's setting in its second part: Eliot "treats of Italy when the 'revival of learning,' as it was called, was rooting up all the old traditions in literature, art, and religion. It has a strange, unreal, and somewhat tame effect, coming after a tale [Thackeray's *The Adventures of Philip?*] conversant entirely with the every-day realities of the nineteenth century" (763).

In general, then, contemporary Victorian understanding is represented by the *Westminster Review's* assertion (October 1863) that "the external machinery of the tale is but the means by which [the "deep moral maxim"] shall be set in an adequate light" (quoted in Carroll 214). The 16 September 1863 *Guardian* stated of the novel that the "historical details which determine its outward form are well chosen and carefully drawn; but they are, after all, only the frame of the picture, or the setting of the gem" (875). We wish here to examine more carefully elements within "the frame of the picture" (both the parts structure of the novel and its historical setting) to determine how they affect the "gem" itself. In particular, we wish to study turning points of the plot, which often occur at pauses in the text inspired by its installment form. Such pivotal moments constitute a significant element in Eliot's concept of historical process.

Among recent studies of *Romola* taking up the question of history is Mary Wilson Carpenter's *George Eliot and the Landscape of Time: Narrative Form and Protestant Apocalyptic History*. She presents a convincing explanation of Romola's and Tito's lives as reflections of biblical interpretations of history: "Just as Western civilization may be construed as moving through periods dominated by Greek civilization, the Roman Empire, Christianity, and a visionary post-Christian period, so the major spiritual influences of Romola's life are Tito's love, the Stoic philosophy of her father and godfather, and Savonarola's Christian 'reformation,' after which she passes into an independent but community-oriented stage of post-Christian and postpatriarchal values" (80). Carpenter's analysis makes a convincing case about Eliot's intentions, but her scheme is based on viewing the novel as a single whole text divided into individual chapters.[29] Seeing Romola's life broken into a variety of phases (two, three, four, or seven), each presented in a group of related chapters, Carpenter does not consider Eliot's original audience and its serial experience; their story was enacted in fourteen discrete units, one each month for over a year. This fourteen-part structure underscores more basic elements of Eliot's vision than apocalyptic sequences. Here the author emphasizes that living in history means assessing one's past at the pivotal present in order to shape a correct future.[30]

In her study of Eliot's novel and its sources, Felicia Bonaparte (165) explains that *Romola* begins at a pivotal moment in history, as the Proem takes readers from their Victorian setting back to the year 1492: "our imagination pauses on a certain historical spot" (July 1862: 2). That year, of course, marked the division of European history into two phases, one that looked eastward and another aware of the New World to the west: "Columbus was still waiting and arguing for the three poor vessels with which he was to set sail from the port of Palos" (2). Further, Lorenzo de' Medici's death at the novel's opening ends an era in Florence's history, placing its citizens at a moment of transition between old and new (a position, of course, similar to the one Victorians felt they occupied between the medieval and the modern[31]). The Florentine citizen of that time, evoked by Eliot's muse in the Proem, would not have been able to foresee the path the city would pursue into the distant nineteenth century, for, according to the narrator, "the changes are great" (7) after such a turning point in history. The Florentine's questions would be focused too narrowly on the nature of events immediately after this pivotal moment: "How has it all turned out? Which party is likely to be banished and have its houses sacked just now? Is there any successor of the incomparable Lorenzo?" (6). Most characters of the novel share the limited vision of this spirit, never achieving a full perspective on history's larger patterns. Only select characters, like the heroine—and readers who arrive at the end of the novel—are permitted to see the shape of the centuries to come.

Although the distant future is hard for fifteenth-century citizens to foresee, Eliot's narrator reminds characters and readers that certain rhythms of human life endure: "These things have not changed. The sunlight and shadows bring their old beauty and waken the old heart-strains at morning, noon, and even-tide; the little children are still the symbol of the eternal marriage between love and duty; and men still yearn for the reign of peace and righteousness—still own *that* life to be the highest which is a conscious voluntary sacrifice" (7). To identify Eliot's idea of historical progression, then, we must distinguish between what she sees as recurring, eternal questions of human conduct and those issues that change as conditions alter in time. In contemplating Eliot's completed text, Victorian and modern readers stand poised at a transitional moment in history, 1492, seeing the ancient world behind and a more modern age ahead. This broad pattern of centuries-long change, most visible at the beginning (Proem) and end (Epilogue) of the novel, is the constant background for specific actions within the text. Reading *Romola* in installments, the original Victorian audience found themselves frequently at pivotal moments in the lives of individual characters, the pauses beween morning and noon, noon and eventide. Such moments along the linear experience of reading were basic structural features of *Romola;* generally unexplored by modern scholars, they provide important clues to Eliot's vision of history. At these points characters and readers were poised between stages in one human story, aware of the broad unchanging shape of existence but more concerned with how the issues of today would shape tomorrow.

As in *A Tale of Two Cities,* characters in Romola sometimes find themselves so hurried by everyday events that larger perspectives are lost. Tito perhaps best represents the individual controlled by outside forces, even though for much of the novel his political talent encourages him and others to think he is making his own destiny. A "shipwrecked stranger" (July 1862: 8) from the beginning, however, Tito is charting a course more in reaction to his world than as an expression of his own intentions. At one seemingly successful moment in his career, for instance, he is carried "above the shoulders of the people, on a bench apparently snatched up in the street . . . in smiling amusement at the compulsion he was under" (December 1862: 736). Tito is unaware here that he is controlled by events, just as he will be in his final drifting down the "dark river" toward Baldassarre: "The current was having its way with him: he hardly knew where he was: exhaustion was bringing on the dreamy state that precedes unconsciousness" (July 1863: 32).

Tito is not alone in such moments of confusion caused by swiftly moving events, often represented by hurried or aimless travel. His unofficial wife, Tessa, explains to Tito later that she had been carried along by crowds at the Peasants' Fair: "Somebody took my bag with the bread and chestnuts in it, and the people pushed me back, and I was so frightened coming in the crowd, and I couldn't get anywhere near the Holy Madonna, to give the cocoons to the *Padre,* but I must—oh, I must" (September 1862: 314). Even stronger characters, who understand far more deeply the nature of individuals and crowds, are sometimes swept away: late in the novel (and his life) Savonarola "felt himself dragged and pushed along in the midst of that hooting multitude" (July 1863: 27). The heroic Bernardo is forced by events along an unhappy course: he is one of "the five condemned men [who] were being led barefoot and in irons through the midst of the council" (June 1863: 698). And Romola herself at times finds her movement though Florence's streets directed by others, as when her husband encounters Dolfo Spini and she learns about their plot against Savonarola: "she was aware now of footsteps and voices, and her habitual sense of personal dignity made her at once yield to Tito's movement towards leading her from the loggia" (March 1863: 308). As in *A Tale of Two Cities,* then, characters in this historical novel sometimes find themselves propelled toward an uncertain future by individuals or events beyond their control.

Similarly, some individual installments of the *Cornhill Romola* stressed for readers the rapid pace of events within which it was difficult to gain a sense of direction, since these numbers provided few pauses for readers to assess the meaning of the narrative. In such parts, characters travel frequently, as did Jarvis Lorry in Dickens's story, insisting on the movement of time and events. For example, the ninth installment, March 1863, reveals the escalating turmoil in Florence as different forces maneuver for control. In this number Victorian readers saw Romola moving through the streets of Florence "tending the sick and relieving the hungry" (283) as both plague and shortages of food afflict the city (chapter 42); Tito arrives with a message for the rulers of Florence (chapter 43)—"pressing at full gallop along by the Arno; the sides of his bay horse, just streaked with foam, looked all white from swiftness" (290); Baldassarre wanders "up the narrowest streets" (294) plotting revenge against Tito (chapter 44); Tito moves "in a sauntering fashion" (297) toward Nello's barbershop where the latest political gossip is being aired (chapter 45); and Dolfo Spini encounters Tito walking with Romola "By a Street Lamp" (chapter 46), revealing the most recent intrigues that endanger Savonarola. With this much activity in one number, readers did feel themselves and the characters being pulled along in the current of history. R. H. Hutton, for instance, admitted in the 18 July 1863 *Spectator* that in the second half of the novel "the reader is drawn into that rushing tide of Savonarola's revolution" (2267).[32]

In general, however, Victorians were not swept along by reading this

novel as often as they had been in Dickens's depiction of the more tumultuous French Revolution. Hutton observed in the same issue of the
Spectator that Eliot "has Sir Walter Scott's art for revivifying the past,—but
not Scott's dynamical force in making you plunge into it with as headlong
an interest as into the present" (2265). Instead, each long installment
covered a basic phase in the action, bringing up to date most major
elements of the plot so that a more or less static state of affairs was finally
realized. The 16 September 1863 *Guardian,* for instance, in its review of the
completed novel said, "the lights and shadows of the whole picture are
very clear, and the story goes its way with a directness which is very little
interrupted by the play of the minor characters or the necessary details of
actual history" (875). At the end of a typical installment, serial readers
knew where characters stood in relation to each other and against the
backdrop of larger forces; but what that combination of individuals,
confronted with new circumstances in the next number, might do was not
always apparent.

    This aspect of the installment structure, the tendency of each part to
advance all matters of the plot through a complete phase of action, is
consistent with another narrative feature, the fact that time generally does
not pass in *Romola* during the gap between numbers. In many serials by
Dickens and others, days, weeks, or months frequently pass in the world
of the novel after one installment ends and before the next begins. The
beginning of each part in *Romola,* however, generally takes up the action
exactly where the last left off. For instance, at the conclusion of the first
installment (July 1862) Romola stands by her father awaiting the entry of
Tito: "She was standing by him at her full height, in quiet majestic self-
possession, when the visitors entered. . . . [She was] in a state of girlish
simplicity and ignorance concerning the world outside her father's books"
(43). The next part (August 1862) begins, "When Maso opened the door
again, and ushered in the two visitors" (145). Similarly, the ninth number
(March 1863) ends with Tito escorting Romola back to their house after
the embarrassing meeting with Dolfo Spini: " 'Pray go to rest with an easy
heart,' [Tito] added, opening the door for her" (309). The next installment
(April 1863) again picks up at the same moment in time: "It was very
seldom that he walked with Romola in the evening, yet he had happened
to be walking with her precisely on this evening when her presence was
supremely inconvenient" (417). The installment breaks, then, generally
do not coincide with gaps in the narrative.

    There are two important exceptions to this structural principle in
Romola: between October 1862 (installment 4) and November 1862 (in-

stallment 5) eighteen months passed in the world of the novel, during which Tito and Romola married and began their life together. A second major gap occurred between installments 8 and 9. Eliot's text in the February 1863 issue of *Cornhill* concluded with "the most memorable Christmas Eve in her life to Romola, this of 1494" (171) because she has decided to return to Florence at Savonarola's direction. The March 1863 installment then began, "It was the thirtieth of October, 1496" (281), when there is famine in Florence and dangers from outside her borders. These two major instances of time's passing between numbers occurred at the divisions between books 1 and 2 and between books 2 and 3.[33]

Although gaps in the narrative do not often coincide with the space between numbers, there are many references to elapsed time within individual installments, often at the beginnings of chapters. For instance, midway in the September 1862 installment Tito and Romola declared their love, and chapter 12 concluded with her father's saying he would speak to Bernardo "about the measures needful to be observed" (301). The next chapter began, "It was the lazy afternoon time on the seventh of September, more than two months after the day on which Romola and Tito had confessed their love to each other" (302). In the June 1863 installment time also passed between chapters 57 and 58. The first chapter of that part ended with Tito galloping "toward Siena" (685); the next chapter began, "Tito soon returned from Siena" (686). A greater gap occurred between chapters in the July 1863 issue of *Cornhill:* chapter 62 portrays "the last morning of the Carnival" (1), and chapter 63 begins "A month after that Carnival" (5).

Thus, the installment structure of *Romola* encouraged Victorian readers to expect that the author would narrate all significant actions within individual parts, skipping over less significant times, not between but within numbers. The fourteen serial parts are discrete units of plot, each advancing the story through a significant phase. In general, serial readers found themselves completing an installment of the novel at the same time as the characters completed a sequence of related actions in the plot. Furthermore, because the story's chronological time usually passed within installments rather than between them, the end of each installment was often a pivotal moment in the plot, a turning point in the causal sequence of events that presented Eliot's moral vision. Characters had arrived at the end of one major phase of their lives (described in that number) and were about to begin a new one (the subject of the next installment). As readers reviewed everything that had happened up to that point in Eliot's serial *Romola,* then, they recognized that they would soon begin a new phase in the story. Thus, subscribers to *Cornhill* felt like characters living in history, pausing at pivotal moments in their ongoing story.

Romola's seventh number (January 1863), for instance, seems particularly to have made a lasting impression on Victorian readers because of its pivotal place in the plot of the entire novel. This installment describes the heroine's decision to leave her husband and her home, "violently rending her life in two" (23), for a new existence and identity in Venice. The number ends with Romola outside Florence, pausing on her way to a world apart from Tito, exactly at the midpoint of Eliot's fourteen-part text:

(342)
> *She turned her back on Florence, not meaning to look at it till the monks were quite out of sight; and raising the edge of her cowl again when she had seated herself, she discerned Maso and the mules at a distance where it was not hopeless for her to overtake them, as the old man would probably linger in expectation of her.*
>
> *Meanwhile she might pause a little. She was free and alone.*

The scene is further emphasized in the *Cornhill* text by the illustration (see figure 5), which closes the number, "Escaped."

Modern readers have frequently thought of Romola as moving from subservience in her marriage with Tito directly to control by another domineering male in the form of Savonarola, since she hears the "arresting voice" (163) of the Frate only moments after this stop for rest. Yet, because this scene occurs at the end of the installment, Victorian serial readers would have had a full month to envision Romola as free from all men and to project a future path of independence for her. In fact, it would not be until the very end of the next monthly number, after a lengthy account of Baldassarre's adventures and the extended debate with Savonarola, that Romola would choose to return to Florence.

Although Romola thinks she is "free and alone" in this central scene, she is, of course, poised between twin restrictions on her future: ahead of her on the road away from Florence, Maso represents her past and her father's values of independence and scholarship, which she cannot easily abandon; behind her on the way back to the city is Savonarola, whose ties to Florence and her brother Dino will soon compel her to return. Thus, her future is guided by her past, though she does not yet recognize fully the path she will take. Savonarola's appeal to community and to a selfless identification with suffering will direct her back to Tito and Florence. As is often the case in Eliot, Romola will not be forced into this action but must make the choice about her own future, one that calls on her fullest sense of

W.J.LINTON sc.

Figure 5. Romola pausing outside Florence in *Cornhill Magazine* (close
of seventh installment, Eliot's *Romola,* January 1863). (*Alderman
Library, University of Virginia*)

commitment to self and others.[34] Central to her decision is the recognition, just taking its clearest shape with the words "free and alone," that she stands at a pivotal position in her life.

This key moment in the novel made a significant impression on Victorian serial readers of the *Cornhill* in part because it came at the end of an installment; subscribers naturally tended to carry away from their reading in January 1863 this final image of Romola, on "a great flat stone against a cypress that rose from a projecting green bank" (30),[35] poised between great stages in her life. Further, as already noted, readers did not know which way Romola would go in the next installment and had to wait a full month to learn her future. She appeared headed to Venice, but readers were also aware that the sight of "two monks, who were approaching within a few yards of her" had made "her heart beat disagreeably" (30). Her nervousness was probably caused, as the narrator suggested, by "uneasiness in her religious disguise" (30), but her earlier responses to Dino's prophecy, to Savonarola's preaching, and to the crucifix she had just taken out of the tabernacle hint that there may be a more direct connection between these figures and herself, a connection that could make itself clear in the next installment and change her course in life. Thus, Eliot's original readers too were at a pause in the narrative's progress, pondering the direction of the story in January 1863 just as Romola contemplated her next steps in life.

Eliot made further use of the installment structure to emphasize the importance of turning points in one's moral history by describing Baldassarre's recovery of memory at the beginning of the next installment (February 1863), before resuming Romola's story. After a month of suspense for her serial readers, that is, Eliot continued Romola's story by studying an analogous situation involving another important character. The incident that opens the next installment, Baldassarre's recalling Greek language and literature, provides an interesting further commentary on Romola's situation, as well as extending Eliot's examination of the meaning of history, for he too stands at a turning point in life.

Through earlier installments, Tito's stepfather had resembled *A Tale of Two Cities'* Dr. Manette, a man separated from history. After his trials as a prisoner, Baldassarre "had the vague aching of an unremembered past within him—when he seemed to sit in dark loneliness, visited by whispers which died out mockingly as he strained his ear after them, and by forms that seemed to approach him and float away as he thrust out his hand to grasp them" (740). Suddenly, Baldassarre's memory returns. He finds himself along a line from the past through the present and can for once project a future consistent with that direction: "he sat surrounded, not by the habitual dimness and vanishing shadows, but by the clear images of the past: he was living again in an unbroken course through that life which seemed a long preparation for the taste of bitterness" (February 1863: 147). Along this "course" Baldassarre stands at a pivotal moment, committing all the resources of his education and experience to future revenge upon Tito, the man who had wronged him in the past.

Such knowledge of history is linked to the mastery of language, since Baldassarre's memory is sparked here by moonlight shining on the pages of a book: "at this moment [the black marks] were once more the magic signs that conjure up a world" (148).[36] Finding himself in time, then, he also finds the world as well: "That sense of mental empire which belongs to us all in moments of exceptional clearness was intensified for him by the long days and nights in which memory had been little more than the consciousness of something gone. That city, which had been a weary labyrinth, was material that he could subdue to his purposes now" (148). Of course, Baldassarre fails at the subsequent confrontation with Tito in the Rucellai gardens, sadly losing the moment and his last clear consciousness of the world he inhabits.

The pivotal instant of understanding the past's relation to the present, an analogue to Romola's acceptance of Savonarola's call to return to Florence, seemed to make a significant impression on Victorian readers. In its review of the entire text, the 18 July 1863 *Spectator* recalled Baldassarre's recovery of memory as a key point in the novel and praised the way it showed "that sense of large *human* power which the mastery over a great ancient language, itself the key to a magnificent literature, gave, and which made scholarship then a *passion,* while with us it has almost relapsed into an antiquarian dryasdust pursuit" (quoted in Carroll 201). This linking of historical study (sometimes an "antiquarian dryasdust pursuit") with the reading of "magnificent literature" nicely suggests that Eliot's aim did have the desired effect in at least this one case: reading *Romola,* with all its potentially dulling historical detail, this element of the Victorian audience brought to life with a certain passion one moment from within the past and was thus living in history.

Just as Baldassarre's history for the rest of the novel seemed fixed by key turning points like the one that began the eighth part, much of Romola's subsequent life derived from events at the pivotal moment when she rested outside Florence at the conclusion to part 7. The novel resumed Romola's story in the middle of installment 8; free from "the accustomed walls and streets," Romola "felt alone in the presence of the earth and sky,

with no human presence interposing and making a law for her" (163).
While critics have stressed Romola's second flight from Florence, her
dreamlike floating away to a distant plague-stricken village, this earlier
moment in the novel also embodied fundamental elements of Eliot's
vision of history.[37]

Savonarola's message in this scene is to obey not only conscience
(morality) but also the obligations Romola's own past actions have created
for the present (history). Stressing Romola's "debts" (164) to Florence and
"pledges" (165) to her husband, he links ethical demands to responsibilities
carried forward in time: "But can man or woman choose duties? No more
than they can choose their birthplace or their father and mother" (164).
Morality ("duties") is inextricably bound up with origins ("birthplace" and
parents). The Frate's exhortations not only derive from a sense of the past
but also insist on a related future. Pointing to other Florentine women,
each of whom "waits and endures because the promised work is great"
(166), he asks Romola to justify a future unconnected to her past, particularly the past represented by the crucifix she carries with her. Her
response is appropriately represented in a travel metaphor: "What a length
of road she had travelled through since she first took that crucifix from the
Frate's hands! Had life as many secrets before her still as it had for her then,
in her young blindness?" (166). Savonarola's rhetoric relies on a fundamental concept of life as a clear line running from past through the present into
the future; he returns to the example of one who "beholds the history of the
world as the history of a great redemption in which he is himself a fellow-
worker, in his own place among his own people!" (167). Thus, in the end,
Romola returns reluctantly to the journey she had been on: she "shrank as
one who sees the path she must take, but sees, too, that the hot lava lies
there" (168).

Serial readers of *Romola* in the *Cornhill* too had to accept the path the
novel was taking after the eighth installment in February 1863. Romola
would not leave her husband or Florence, and Eliot's story would unwind
within limits set by those decisions. Some readers did not find the central
character appealing here.[38] R. H. Hutton, for instance, termed Romola in
the 18 July 1863 *Spectator* the "least perfect figure in the book, though a fine
one" (quoted in Carroll 203–4). He agreed with the October 1863 *Westminster Review* and others that Romola seemed closer to "a modern English-
woman" than any medieval Italian (quoted in Carroll 217). Her modern
dilemma, being trapped in an unhappy marriage, particularly after the
pivotal eighth installment where she accepts Savonarola's call, was a major
factor in Victorian uneasiness with her story. Eliot herself knew that her

heroine's fate touched on tender nerves in her readers; she wrote to R. H. Hutton after the novel was completed (8 August 1863): "I am sorry [Romola] has attracted you so little; for the great problem of her life . . . is one that readers need helping to understand" (quoted in Carroll 207).[39]

The crucial exchange between Romola and Savonarola made a lasting impression on Victorian readers of the novel, both as it unsettled them and as its power impressed them. The 11 July 1863 *Athenaeum* said, "The scene beween Romola and Savonarola, when she is flying from her husband, is noble, and puts an end to all inclination to criticize or complain" (46). R. H. Hutton admired Savonarola's part in the scene and Eliot's mastery of her medium: "Nothing can be finer and more impressive—nothing more difficult to make fine and impressive—than Savonarola's exhortation to Romola to return to the home from which she was flying" (quoted in Carroll 204). The 16 September 1863 *Guardian* felt that Savonarola rose "to sublimity" (876) in his persuasion, and that journal concluded even more forcefully: "The preceding incidents, the gradual accumulation of difficulties, the growing deterioration of Tito's character, and the exquisite anguish inflicted by it on Romola, have all contributed to produce a state of exultation in which the reader is ready to accept, not only as true and right, but as natural and fitting, the lofty sentiments which pour from Savonarola's lips" (876). Some Victorian readers, then, in "a state of exultation" generated by Eliot's serial text, shared the commitments to duty and to history manifest in Savonarola's speech to Romola and in her response.

The Victorian readership also shared a sense of the importance of such pivotal moments in individual and collective history emphasized by the installment structure of Eliot's novel. Though not all turning points in *Romola*'s plot came at the conclusions of monthly numbers, a great many did. Tito stands on the threshold of Bardo's house at the end of the first installment, July 1862, about to change Romola's life forever. Word arrives from Baldassarre that he is alive but a slave for whom ransom is required at the end of the second number, August 1862, inaugurating a new phase in Tito's life. Tessa believes she has just been married to Tito at the end of the September issue, and October's text ends with Romola's day of betrothal. Tito puts on his metal armor as the November part concludes, while Romola finds her father's library has been sold on the last pages of the December installment. Romola's resting outside Florence, as already described, finishes the January 1863 part, and she resumes her old life at the end of the February issue. Romola then learns of Tito's plotting against Savonarola as the March *Cornhill* text concludes. Both the April and the May parts end on notes of continuation more than at turning points, as

Romola comforts a harrassed Brigida in the tenth part and in the eleventh learns that Tito has eluded danger, while others in Florence are threatened by the latest political developments. Romola drifts away from Florence at the end of the June issue, however, a major turning point in her life; and the deaths of Tito and Baldassare conclude the July installment. Clearly, then, the parts structure of Eliot's novel insists that we know the turning points in our lives because they structure experience into patterns of morality and history.

Indeed, Romola's second decision to return to Florence, after having drifted away to the stricken village, represents a final understanding of her place in history. In the concluding installment (August 1863) the narrator describes Romola's coming to accept the shape of her own life: "In those silent wintry hours when Romola lay resting from her weariness, her mind, travelling back over the past, and gazing across the undefined distance of the future, saw all objects from a new position" (136).[40] At this last major turning point in the novel, Romola reexamines the line of events that runs from the beginning of her life through the present and on into the future: "And then the past arose with a fresh appeal to her. Her work in this green valley was done, and the emotions that were disengaged from the people immediately around her rushed back into the old deep channels of use and affection" (137). This experience inspires Romola to a firmer understanding of history and morality, allowing her in later life to focus more on the eternal, unchanging rhythms of human life. She looks beyond her present surroundings, which she knows will alter in time, to more fulfilling patterns: "Her hands were crossed on her lap and her eyes were fixed absently on the distant mountains: she was evidently unconscious of anything around her. . . . there was a placidity in Romola's face which had never belonged to it in youth" (151). She is now most likely to see the importance of the pivotal year, 1492, in Florentine history, an understanding the reader of the completed historical novel *Romola* also finds with the end of the fiction.

As Eliot's Victorian readers of the serial text of *Romola* in the *Cornhill* arrived at this conclusion, then, they were presented with the author's summary vision of history. The heroine's story showed that the patterns of the past insist on a certain future and that the consequences of one's actions should be measured at pivotal moments in life. Readers had engaged a text structured around important turning points, generally at the ends of installments, at which they, like the characters living in history, assessed the past (what they had read so far) and attempted to foresee the future (the story to be continued). The experience of being in individual moments of

Romola's story, seated with her on the road outside the city of Florence, inspired an understanding of historical process, learning to see how one phase of life or sequence of events comes to an end when another is ready to begin. This conception of history fit perfectly with that suggested by the novel as a whole, since the complete text presented the collective turning point in Western history, 1492. Living in history, then, for both Eliot and Dickens meant finding oneself along a line running from the past through the present and into the future.

Henry James thought that Robert Browning's skill in adapting historical detail in *The Ring and the Book* exceeded even that of Eliot's in *Romola* (79), and Browning's emphasis on "repristination" of course echoes Dickens's "Recalled to Life!" theme (Gent 15). But if Dickens's *Tale of Two Cities* embodies the sense of being swept up in the rush of history and Eliot's *Romola* explores the turning points of individual and public history, Browning's *The Ring and the Book* focuses on how we know and interpret history. His emphasis on interpreting (rather than experiencing) history is immediately evident in his poem's structure. In contrast to Dickens and Eliot, Browning rejects a linear, consequential plot and instead tells his Roman murder story multiple times from multiple points of view, highlighting the theme familiar to Victorian and twentieth-century readers alike: the relativity of truth and the fallibility of interpretation. The circular structure that results from Browning's abandonment of linear plot, furthermore, suggests simultaneity, either because Browning's ten speakers indicate the complex cross sections of events occurring at once rather than in sequence, or because the mythic overtones of Caponsacchi's conversion, Pompilia's martyrdom and death, and the Pope's judgment invoke the eternal and eternally recurring. The poem's circular structure also suggests, then, the cycles of history. In these respects Browning's treatment of history again seems to differ from the patterns we have traced in Dickens and Eliot.

But a rarely considered factor in the poem's approach to history is its own publishing history, that is, Browning's deliberate decision to issue the poem in four monthly parts (each consisting of three books) rather than all at once. William Allingham records Browning's discussion of publication format with him. Browning scholars frequently note this conversation, but generally ignore the fact that Allingham's own *Lawrence Bloomfield in Ireland* was serialized in twelve monthly parts in *Fraser's Magazine* from November 1862 to November 1863, an occurrence that gives particular point to Browning's remarks: " 'And now! can you advise me? I'm puzzled about how to publish it. I want people not to turn to the end, but to read

through in proper order. Magazine, you'll say: but no, I don't like the
notion of being sandwiched between Politics and Deer-Stalking, say. I
think of bringing it out in four monthly volumes, giving people time to
read and digest it, part by part, but not to forget what has gone before' "
(181). If serialization was on one hand a device to prevent readers from
skipping over certain monologues (which readers have been doing ever
since the whole poem appeared), serialization was on the other hand an
implicit validation of linear time and sequence ("time . . . part by part").
Serialization thus balanced and qualified the poem's impetus toward circularity and simultaneous perception. If Browning's poem, like Dickens's
and Eliot's novels, at once pondered the relation of the nineteenth-century
present to the past and especially considered the shape, whether linear or
cyclic, into which history might be absorbed, the poem's serialization
ensured that neither the linear nor the cyclic dimension of history would
be ignored; instead, the problematic relation of these two perspectives
would be maintained and emphasized.

Browning scholarship of our century has stressed the circularity and
simultaneity of *The Ring and the Book*. The 1968 Altick and Loucks study,
for example, maintains "the necessity of reading the poem simultaneously
on . . . numerous levels" and argues that the "ideal method of reading *The
Ring and the Book* would require the suspension of time or the adoption of
an extra dimension" (35). Mary Ellis Gibson's 1987 *History and the Prism of
Art,* which places Browning's treatment of history in the context of
Hayden White's theoretical work on historical narrative, also asserts that
Browning "rejects linear progression and creates instead circularity and
repetition or patterns requiring us to consider at once all parts of a work
and to place them in historical, social, or moral contexts" (113).[41] But for
Browning's original readers, such simultaneity was impossible. Three
months after starting the first installment, readers could not yet glimpse all
four parts simultaneously; serial publication forced these readers to absorb
the work, in Browning's words, "part by part." Since twentieth-century
criticism has given so little attention to linear sequence in the poem,
especially as influenced by serialization, we will reassess the poem's structure and meaning in this context.[42]

The Ring and the Book approaches linear shape in several ways. Twentieth-century commentators tend to note only in passing that the poem
takes the form of a trial (see, e.g., Chell 96, Crowell 233), but the most
common motif in Victorian reviews published while (or just after) Browning's installments were appearing was the poem's relation to the courtroom.[43] John Addington Symonds, writing in the January 1869 *Macmillan's*

Magazine, observed that Browning's poem made "the modern public judge and jury of a crime" (258), a point echoed in the January 1869 *Tinsley's Magazine,* which remarked that "If your wife has run away from you (which is not improbable in these days), you will . . . see in Count Guido's crime a natural act of punishment; if you are a lady, and consider that your husband does not pay you sufficient attention (which is at least possible in these days), you will claim Pompilia's conduct quite justifiable" (670). The March 1869 *British Quarterly Review,* whose notice followed closely upon the poem's final installment, asserted that "The effect produced upon the mind [by a story "told over and over again, from various points of view"] resembles that which results from reading through a long trial in the newspapers—evidence *in extenso,* speeches of all the counsel, the judge's summing up, and the subsequent comments of a dozen different journals" (456). This review's emphasis on a linear, periodic sequence dependent on the passage of time was anticipated by the 26 December 1868 *Saturday Review,* whose review of the poem's first installment clarifies why original audiences seized on the trial analogue: "there is no more consecutiveness in the narrative than in the story elicited from different witnesses in a court of justice. Many parts are repeated over and over again; the murder, the central point of the whole, is related at length three several times. Still, in spite of this prolongation and intricacy, the result is attained that the reader does in the end understand the plot; the sense of conflicting evidence, and of the different movements of the popular mind, is vividly given; and when we have come to the close of the volume, we are anxious to know how the real fact will develop itself out of the maze of conjecture and inconsistency" (833).[44]

These reviews draw out features common to a trial and a serial publication: judge and jury are not given "the facts," the witnesses' stories, all at once. Testimony is scheduled (like the release of serial parts), and auditors must wait to hear certain versions until witnesses are called. Moreover, judge and jury (or vicarious jurors who follow newspaper accounts) live with a trial, enfolding it into the daily rhythm of life, just as serial readers live with an ongoing story for a season. Yet courtroom activities are based on the faith (similar to that of Browning's first readers awaiting the whole poem) that at the end of the trial truth will emerge, judgment will be rendered, and all participants will be able to view the entire case from a point beyond it. In this respect the poet's attention to judicial sequence in each volume could have had intensified meaning for the audience following the serial poem in the same linear sequence demanded by a trial. The poet refers to the sequencing of court documents in the first book (1.1.160–77, 198–200); Tertium Quid asserts in the second installment that Guido's impending trial is the "last link of a chain / Whereof the first was forged three years ago. . . . / Can't we look through the crimson and trace lines?" (2.4.22–23, 40). The lawyers compose their court pleadings in the third installment; and the Pope asserts in the final installment that "All till the very end is trial in life" (4.10.1303).[45]

Indeed, the Pope articulates a method for extracting truth that applies equally to a trial or to a serial poem: "Truth, nowhere, lies yet everywhere in these— / Not absolutely in a portion, yet / Evolvable from the whole" (4.10.228–30). And Tertium Quid's reference to a Punch and Judy show is an apt analogue for being in the middle of a trial or a serial work—or, for that matter, of history:

> You've seen the puppets, of Place Navona, play,—
> Punch and his mate,—how threats pass, blows are dealt,
> And a crisis comes: the crowd or clap or hiss
> Accordingly as disposed for man or wife—
> When down the actors duck awhile perdue,
> Donning what novel rag-and-feather trim
> Best suits the next adventure, new effect:
> And,—by the time the mob is on the move,
> With something like a judgment *pro* and *con,*—
> There's a whistle, up again the actors pop
> In t'other tatter with fresh-tinseled staves.

(2.4.1282–92)

As with a trial or a serial, or merely the act of living in history, participants go along, start to form judgments, especially during a recess (or pause) in events (or installments); just when they arrive at interpretations, new testimony, text, or events resume with a change of scene or venue requiring renewed interpretation. The pause after the poem's first installment, in fact, would have removed readers from the midst of a trial, forcibly enjoined upon them a recess in time and truth, and left them in the middle (and muddle) of judgment after the conflicting testimony of Half-Rome and Other Half-Rome.[46] This contrast between linear progress and pause reminds us that, in the poem, four levels of such linearity and pausing are dealt with at once: the trial versus judgment, reading the poem versus interpreting (or judging) it,[47] journeying versus pausing (especially for Caponsacchi, Pompilia, Guido), and living in history versus understanding it.

Those who read the poem over four months not only manifested the rhythm of journey and pause,[48] history and its interpretation, so central to the poem, but also perceived a different shape to the poem from those who approach the completed work. Altick and Loucks discern three triads (Half-Rome, Other-Half Rome, Tertium Quid; Guido, Caponsacchi, Pompilia; Arcangeli, Bottini, the Pope) each culminating in a high point, plus Guido's second monologue—all surrounded by the "ring" of the poet's commentaries in books 1 and 12. Following Browning's grouping of speakers into observers, principals, and legal agents (1.1.838–1329), Altick and Loucks also map a progressive focus in these triads, the first providing an "exposition of the externalities" of the story, the second the character of the participants, and the third the "poem's great issues, such as truth, deceit, language, and religion" (39–40).

But again, this pattern was unlikely for Browning's first readers, whose conception of triads was affected by the material publishing format of four volumes spaced a month apart. Not only could serial readers not hold the whole poem in their minds, they could not hold the whole poem in their hands. And when they did handle one of the four volumes, they encountered these groupings: the poet's introduction, Half-Rome, Other Half-Rome; Tertium Quid, Guido, Caponsacchi (see figure 6); Pompilia, Arcangeli, Bottini; and the Pope, Guido, and the poet's conclusion. That the publishing format—determined by linearity rather than simultaneity—shaped the way first readers saw the work is made clear in the 12 December 1868 *Spectator:* "As Mr. Browning issues his new poem in instalments, we may well suppose that he wishes it to be read, and studied, and conceived in instalments; indeed, that, with the help his prologue gives us, each of the subsequent parts . . . will form a whole in itself, organically complete, though suited, like each of the parts of the old Greek trilogies, to constitute, in conjunction with the other poetic facets or developments of the same story, a still more impressive and various whole" (1464).[49]

The most frequently cited lines in reviews of the first installment were the "lyric love" passage that concludes book 1, which Victorian readers recognized as an expression of Browning's love for Elizabeth Barrett Browning. Sexual love thus might have served as a unifying theme of the first volume. The volume's three monologues ring three changes on the theme of sexual love, from passionate married love in the first, to adultery in the second, to romantic but Platonic love in the volume's concluding monologue. As the 26 December 1868 *Athenaeum* observed, "nothing could well be finer than the graduation between the sharp, personally

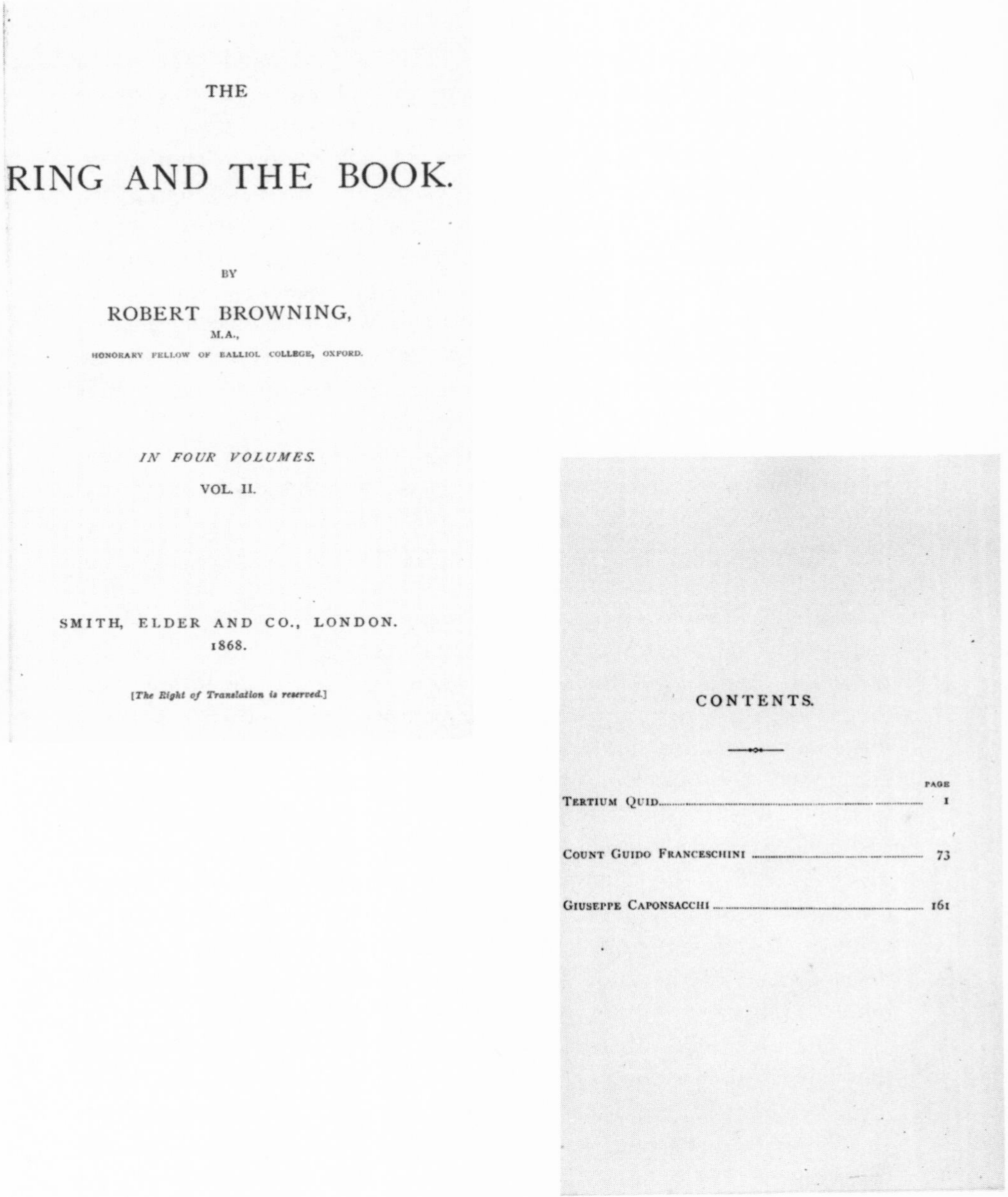

THE

RING AND THE BOOK.

BY

ROBERT BROWNING,
M.A.,
HONORARY FELLOW OF BALLIOL COLLEGE, OXFORD.

IN FOUR VOLUMES.
VOL. II.

SMITH, ELDER AND CO., LONDON.
1868.

[*The Right of Translation is reserved.*]

CONTENTS.

Figure 6. Title page (*a*) and table of contents (*b*) of Browning's *Ring and the Book* (second installment, December 1868), showing serial triads of monologues. (*Armstrong Browning Library, Baylor University, Waco, Texas*)

anxious, suspicious manner of the first Roman speaker, who is a *married man,* and the bright, disinterested emotion, excited mainly by the personal beauty of Pompilia, of the second speaker, who is a *bachelor*" (875).[50]

The issue of social status attracted attention in the second installment, since Tertium Quid, Guido, and Caponsacchi are all linked by their aristocratic lineage.[51] Tertium Quid, as the 30 January 1869 *Spectator* noted, favors Guido's side (139),[52] and the 20 January 1869 *Guardian* remarked that "Franceschini goes back to his ancestry and informs his Judges that he represents one of the first of the old families in Arezzo; Caponsacchi, troubled as he is at learning that Pompilia is dying, does not omit to claim descent from Capo in Sacco" (74). These reviews illuminate the significance of an earlier comment in the 5 December 1868 *London Review,* which, responding to the first installment, asserted that Half-Rome is tinged with "Cockneyism":

(620)
> The reader may ask how the vulgarest of Roman citizens could possibly be guilty of Cockneyism; but does not Mr. Browning, perhaps using the handiest form of indicating the social grade and training of one of his Roman citizens, make the man say—
> "Beside I'm useful at explaining things—
> As how the dagger laid there at the feet," &c.?

Hence, the second triad was set apart from the first not only by a month's interval in publishing but also by differences in class.

Pompilia, of course, most often attracted attention in the third installment. The reference to her as "true woman and true mother" (322) by the 27 March 1869 *Illustrated London News* reminds us that the role of parents figures prominently in the third volume. Arcangeli's doting on his son parodies Pompilia's passionate devotion to her own. And Bottini picks up the domestic theme in his hypothetical portrait of the Holy Family on its journey to Egypt (3.9.17–83).

The final installment gives repeated consideration to endings, whether of the lives of the Pope and Guido, the century, or the poem itself. This installment explores whether things ever can end or whether there is an essential ongoingness to existence, questions equally appropriate to a Christian pope, a man facing execution, and a poem that, in its first appearance, was grounded in a rhythm of pauses followed by the resumption of text.[53] The Pope may announce at the outset that "The case is over, judgment at an end, / And all things done now and irrevocable" (4.10.207–8), but he also avows that "The divine instance of self-sacrifice / . . . never ends and aye begins for man" (4.10.1656–57). Guido's monologue is grounded in ongoing time and process, since we are to imagine some twelve hours passing as he talks and talks; but in his case each moment's gradual progression leads to an abrupt and final end for him.[54]

If the Pope and Guido (for different reasons) resist endings, so does the final book, which begins, "Here were the end, had anything an end" (4.12.1). Indeed, the 24 March 1869 *Guardian* complained that Browning's "poem becomes more fragmentary as it proceeds, and terminates, like an ill-written letter, in a series of abrupt and almost unconnected postscripts" (343). But this arrangement was in many ways fitting. The serialization of the poem had demonstrated three times that a poem could come to an end point and yet not end. Moreover, if, by the twelfth book, Pompilia and Guido are dead and the Pope's judgment delivered, the "postscripts" reveal that the case did not have a clear terminal point; Bottini later brought suit, and one hundred fifty years later the Old Yellow Book fell into the hands of a poet who renewed the story for his own and future audiences. The poem's refusal to end also accords with an important truth about the experience of living in history: to *be* history, data, details, events must be shaped into a phase, a cycle complete unto itself. Yet the details from one cycle of events bleed over, as it were, into the next, serving as a motivating force for the next linear sequence.[55] The resistance to endings therefore suggests the linear progression that forever surges forward to complicate and undermine the perspectives constructed during pauses in experience.

Serialization affected not only the shape of the poem's triads and their suggested themes but also the entire experience of reading and judging the poem. As John Morley stated in the March 1869 *Fortnightly Review* at the end of the poem's run, "When the second volume, containing *Giuseppe Caponsacchi,* appeared, men no longer found it sordid or ugly; the third, with *Pompilia,* convinced them that the subject was not, after all, so incurably unlovely; and the fourth, with *the Pope,* and the passage from the Friar's sermon, may well persuade those who needed persuasion, that moral fruitfulness depends on the master, his eye and hand . . . more than on the this and that of the transaction which has taken possession of his imagination" (331).[56] Morley's comment underscores the importance of provisional judgment inherent in serial reading, a feature that complemented thematic materials in *The Ring and the Book.* As noted earlier, the pause after the first installment helped reinforce and extend the quandary of judgment, as indicated by the reviewer's sense in *Tinsley's Magazine* that grounds could exist for sympathizing most with Guido or with Pompilia. Just as, in the poem itself, Other Half-Rome remarks that Pompilia conflated time and truth during her pause from journeying at Castelnuovo

("She makes confusion . . . mix[ing] both times, morn and eve, in one"
[1.3.1189, 1193]), so readers' pauses complicated time and truth. Should
readers pay most attention to the poet's preview in book 1 or to the line-
by-line accounts of all three books? Readers were asked to judge not only
the poem's events, furthermore, but the poem itself, and the January 1869
Westminster Review grumbled at being denied the whole-poem perspective
that could prop up a more certain pronouncement on Browning's performance: "It is unfortunate that 'The Ring and the Book' is published in
instalments. Author and critic both stand at a disadvantage. What the
effect may be when seen as an organic whole we cannot say" (141). Besides
inducing uncertainty of judgment, the pause after the first installment also
helped align volume 1's characters and Browning's audience. Just as
Browning presented public gossip about a newsworthy story in "Half-
Rome" and "Other Half-Rome," so the interval between the first two
volumes enabled Browning's British public to "gossip" about his poem,
whether by reading reviews or discussing the poem with friends.[57] Finally,
the pause in publication shored up the importance of the second and third
monologues. If in the long run (or the end of the run), "Half-Rome" and
"Other Half-Rome" seemed of subordinate interest, they were vitally
important for readers in the midst of the poem, since they were (along
with the poet's prologue) all readers had.

The pauses after the second and third installments, equally relevant to
audience interpretation (discussed below), were also spots along the way
for judging the poem. What emerges from the reviews, once again, is a
record of tentative judgment that, like the Italian history Browning documents, changed with time. The reviewer in the 27 December 1868 *Sunday
Times,* for example, identified the organizing principle of the work as
"that of representing a number of different people, more or less interested
by personal motive" (7). The reviewer in the 26 December 1868 *Saturday
Review* objected to a story of "vice pure, unadulterated, and unrelieved,"
and remarked that "If there is anything morally better to come in the
succeeding volumes, there is small sign of it in the present; unless it be in
the character of the Pope" (833). These reviewers had not yet encountered
the monologues of Caponsacchi, who scorns self-interest in his testimony,
or of Pompilia, who came to represent purity and virtue to so many. The
30 January 1869 *Spectator,* more aware of the pitfalls of judgment, proposed after the poem's second installment that the dilemma in judging
innocence or guilt was only apparent, and that Browning endorsed Pompilia's innocence. In that case the reviewer questioned the need of so many
speakers, but meanwhile refused to make a final judgment: "the truth

appears to be, not *between* the various representations of it, but almost wholly in one of them. Surely Mr. Browning could have given us in this case the pure gold of 'the ring,' almost without the alloy, if he had given Count Guido's, and Canon Caponsacchi's, and Pompilia's versions of the matter only, with the old Pope's final judgment upon it? It may be, however, that this criticism is premature, and will be rebutted by the third or fourth volume" (141). If in the end many (the *Spectator* included) decided that several monologues should be removed, they at least read the whole poem part by part and treated their judgment as both tentative and potentially fallible, thus helping further exemplify the poem's lesson that "our human speech is naught, / Our human testimony false, our fame / And human estimation words and wind" (4.12.834–36).

Another pattern of progression and pause is the journey, a synechdoche in *A Tale of Two Cities* and *Romola* for the entire process of living in and understanding history. One such journey in *The Ring and the Book* again involves the reader. To a greater extent in serial than in whole-volume reading, the poem became a journey to and away from Pompilia, who indeed lay at the center—the heart—of the poem (see also McElderry, "Narrative" 194; Harrold 34–35). It is not merely that the first two installments anticipated her deathbed testimony through several references but also that serial readers had to wait two months to read her monologue, enduring enforced pauses that heightened their desire to journey toward her.

In book 2 Half-Rome and one of the spectators of the Comparini corpses at San Lorenzo insist Pompilia must die that night (1.2.134–35, 1444–50); in addition Half-Rome twice states that Pompilia has made a confession, and he expresses his eagerness to hear her story. Other Half-Rome opens his monologue by announcing that "Another day . . . finds [Pompilia] living yet" (1.3.1), proving incidentally that linearity—Pompilia's life span—can outlast and flout Half-Rome's fiats and judgments. Indeed, Mary Rose Sullivan argues that a "sense of [Pompilia's] continuing presence" permeates Other Half-Rome's monologue, especially since he has just come from observing her on her deathbed (44). Other Half-Rome also narrates the climactic moment when Pompilia and Caponsacchi at last meet, but if this meeting endorses catastrophic moments of passion or conversion, readers' own delay in encountering Pompilia paralleled Caponsacchi's earlier experience of hearing much of her from others' accounts before meeting her directly—a reminder that if catastrophism is essential to their story, gradualism and slow progress are still the norm.

Thus, even if Victorian readers easily understood how central Pompilia's story is to the poem ("the story of Pompilia stands out clear and naked as a Greek statue, against a lurid background of tragic pain and wrong," asserted the 5 December 1868 *London Review* [620]) or wished to rush to her story, they were forced to pause and wait instead. As the 20 January 1869 *Guardian* confided, "we are decidedly anxious to hear, some time early in February, the story of a brief and unhappy life, as it drops in low tones from the lips of the dying Pompilia" (74).

The *Guardian's* review was published after the second installment appeared, and the second volume certainly intensified both the progression toward Pompilia and the enforced pause before she was reached. The volume opened with the announcement yet again that Pompilia lived on ("she's not dead yet" [2.4.2]). This opening to the second installment could have assumed greater power for serial readers because Pompilia's ability to endure and survive a pause (literally, a month-long pause) could have recalled her surviving the disastrous pause from journeying at Castelnuovo and hinted that her life might persist even when she was (through death) permanently out of sight. With Guido's monologue, second in the installment, the pace of the poem lurched forward and brought readers closer to Pompilia, since they now encountered her husband. Guido, however, while glancing at the confession of his wife yet to be heard (2.5.1687–89), prefers to speak of her as already dead (2.5.936). It was in Caponsacchi's passionate monologue, then, that the rush toward Pompilia quickened and intensified, as the Canon's own heart yearns toward her. For the first time Victorians heard, not her voice directly, but quotations of her voice, since a significant portion of Caponsacchi's monologue consists of quotes from Pompilia; she resides at the heart of the poem, at Caponsacchi's heart, and at the heart of his own voice and testimony: "Pompilia spoke, and I at once received, / Accepted my own fact, my miracle / Self-authorised and self-explained" (2.6.918–20). Caponsacchi's monologue, infused by passion, rushes forward to give a sense of the rushing journey that forms the central event of his life. But for Victorian readers this forward rush culminated in a great pause: volume 2 broke off (see figure 6b), and readers had to wait a full month before reading Pompilia's monologue. In whole-volume editions of the poem, Pompilia's monologue immediately follows Caponsacchi's, so that the two texts lie next to each other and, as it were, hug each other. But in the serial format they were sundered in both space and time, just as Caponsacchi is exiled from Pompilia first after their flight toward Rome, and forever after Guido murders her. The effect of serialization, then, was to make Caponsacchis of readers who yearned toward and wished to rush to Pompilia but were prevented from doing so by publishing format.[58]

Readers at last encountered the voice of Pompilia in February 1869 and then journeyed from her climactic testimony on to the end of the poem. Most Victorian readers, like those in the twentieth century, were impatient at the lawyers' monologues that followed, yet within the linear perspective of serialization their inclusion was appropriate. To travel two months through six books to reach her voice, only to have her utterance overlain by accounts that distorted her life and absorbed it into a legal system, was to recapitulate the action of history. As the Old Yellow Book attests, Pompilia after her death became merely a piece of evidence in the trial and suits that followed; indeed, as Browning indicated, a trace of her history remained only because of lawyers' business (4.12.225). The final pause before the fourth installment gave readers time on their journey away from Pompilia to question whether Pompilia's or others' voices would triumph.

From the low point at the end of Bottini's monologue ("Still, it pays" [3.9.1577]) to "the opening of the fourth volume," commented the 24 March 1869 *Guardian,* "we rise again to a much higher level" when the Pope speaks (344; cf. DeVane 325). The impact of encountering the Pope after the lawyers was also recorded by Julia Wedgwood, who wrote to Browning on 14 February 1869 to say, "I felt for a while after reading it as if something in me were released. . . . I can feel, as I listen to Innocent, that this poor little planet is a good inn for our souls to rest in, before they start on the long journey" (Browning and Wedgwood 167). The Pope, of course, reasserts the virtue and innocence of Pompilia, just as, by quite contrary means, Guido does (4.11.2302–5, 2425).[59] If, at the very end of the poem, the journey from Pompilia turns into a mere sequence of documents that give no direct glimpse of the woman at the center of the story, that is precisely what happened, according to Browning, in the course of history itself.[60]

Seen within the context of linearity emphasized by serial publication, the characters of the poem, and the main events of their story, also reveal an intensified reliance on linear forces. Pompilia is frequently approached as a timeless, mythic presence on the brink of eternity who pauses before death to try to understand her strange life; Caponsacchi is seen as a quester who moves along a path of action (see, e.g., Culler 193). Yet it is Pompilia, not Caponsacchi (though he relays her words), who exclaims that she wants " 'Always, my life-long, thus to journey still! / It is the interruption

that I dread' " (2.6.1312–13). Like Lorry in Dickens's *Tale,* Pompilia opts
to enter a coach for a journey that determines the outcome of her later life,
and the journey, insofar as it constructs a line from the past through the
present and into the future, becomes a key to Browning's treatment of
history as well. A prime motive in the events of the murder story is
lineage—family history—a genetic line traversing time. Guido must perpetuate his lineage, and so marries Pompilia; because Pompilia's lineage is
distorted and "debased," she can be used as a pawn by the Comparinis and
Guido; the conception and birth of Gaetano incite Pompilia to flight and
Guido to murder. Pompilia, Caponsacchi, and the Pope affirm history and
linear progression, while Guido, the Comparini's, and minor characters
like Bottini deny or distort history.[61]

Like Dr. Manette in *A Tale of Two Cities* and Baldassarre in *Romola,*
Pompilia is a victim whose past is denied by her victimizers. Even the
forgiving Pompilia sees a strict causal line running from Violante's lies
about Pompilia's parentage through the arranged marriage, which in turn
led to all else:

(3.7.314–
15, 320–
21).

> this falsehood hatched,
> She could not let it go nor keep it fast. . . .
> This it was set her on to make amends,
> This brought about the marriage.

Guido's tyranny and bestiality in marriage further stripped her of any
personal history:

(2.6.776–
81)

> He laid a hand on me that burned all peace,
> All joy, all hope, and last all fear away,
> Dipping the bough of life, so pleasant once,
> In fire which shrivelled leaf and bud alike,
> Burning not only present life but past,
> Which you might think was safe beyond his reach.

He had this power over her because Violante and Pietro first obliterated
the traces of Pompilia's biological parentage, then denied their own par-
enting:

(2.6.782–
87)

> He reached it, though, since that beloved pair,
> My father once, my mother all those years,
> That loved me so, now say I dreamed a dream
> And bid me wake, henceforth no child of theirs,
> Never in all the time their child at all.
> Do you understand? I cannot: yet so it is.

Because she has suffered so much from these denials of her personal history, Pompilia at times (like Dr. Manette after learning Charles Darnay's identity) purposely "forgets" elements of the past and herself denies the line of history threading through her life. Hence she claims that Gaetano has no father (cf. Altick and Loucks 87) and cannot will herself to remember occasions in her marriage that were too dreadful.

To balance her obliterated past, however, one purpose of her monologue is to recover and embrace history and the flow of time.[62] Her opening words show her desperately clinging to the flow of weeks and years she can claim: "I am just seventeen years and five months old, / And, if I lived one day more, three full weeks"; "I [have] been a mother of a son / Exactly two weeks" (3.7.1–2, 13–14). She reconstructs the history of her mother's life (3.7.863–77), then forges a line leading back to her mother so that she can address her mother directly:

(3.7.878–   If she sold . . . what they call, sold . . . me her child—
88)[63]   I shall believe she hoped in her poor heart
             That I at least might try be good and pure,
             Begin to live untempted, not go doomed
             And done with ere once found in fault, as she.
             Oh and, my mother, it all came to this?
             Why should I trust those that speak ill of you,
             When I mistrust who speaks even well of them?
             Why, since all bound to do me good, did harm,
             May not you, seeming as you harmed me most,
             Have meant to do most good?

As a victim whose past life is denied by others, Pompilia emerges as a character committed to history, at least to a meaningful personal history that constructs patterns among her own past, present, and future. Equally important of course is the pause prior to death that affords her the simultaneous, even timeless, perspective on her past; but as she approaches this timelessness of eternity she nonetheless also affirms linear progression.

The process of time is a key to Pompilia's character in another way. As Other Half-Rome observes, "Thus saintship is effected probably; / No sparing saints the process!" (1.3.111–12). To view Pompilia in timeless, mythic terms may slight the process of her martyrdom and so repeat Pietro and Violante's mistake of obliterating actions embedded in time. Even a speaker so unsympathetic to Pompilia as Tertium Quid reminds us of the process of Pompilia's martyrdom, which he describes precisely in linear terms: "Circumvallated month by month, and week / By week, and day by day, and hour by hour, / Close, closer and yet closer still with pain" (2.4.791–93)—a vantage point confirmed by Pompilia herself, who states that her life "by step and step . . . / got to grow so terrible and strange" (3.7.117–18). It is Caponsacchi's distinction to see something like her sainthood while she is still alive, entrenched in linear progression, instead of on her deathbed and approaching eternity, and so he alone can help her.

What commits Pompilia to ongoing history and to her journey with Caponsacchi, of course, is the conception of a child who gives her a future to care about, who carries her biological line and her love into the future. Because the pursuing Guido would blot out this future as he has blotted out her past, any pause in the onward progression of her life or her journey is a threat.[64] After his momentous first encounter with Pompilia, nonetheless, Caponsacchi mistakenly pauses for two days (Irvine and Honan 428, Hassett 64), denying life and his involvement in history. He determines to journey with her only when he recalls Pompilia's ongoing process of martyrdom. In this respect, Caponsacchi's moment of conversion is not enough; the journey is as necessary as that instant in which he sees a new direction and meaning for his life.[65] Hence, he removes Pompilia from the circle in which Guido has penned her (3.7.1546–54) and leads her into time, history, and ongoing life. Though Caponsacchi is the first to propose a pause (2.6.1281), which Pompilia resists ("'Oh, no stay! . . . / On to Rome, on, on'" [2.6.1288–89]), Pompilia credits Caponsacchi with enabling her to continue her journey on the first day by narrating a tale "Which lifted me and let my soul go on!" (3.7.1542). Both the literal journey and the unfolding of a story are here seen as linear progressions that impart life and hope.

If Pompilia on her deathbed thinks back to the journey as "one milky way" (3.7.1566), a phrase suffused with romantic, maternal, spatial, and temporal overtones, she thinks of the dreadful pause at Castelnuovo as one that destroyed time's flow:[66] evening and morning became "two red plates / That crushed together, crushed the time between, / And are since then a solid fire to me" (3.7.1582–84). If the entire journey is viewed from the vantage point of this dreadful pause, it seems a futile, tragic failure. Yet viewed from within time it assumes a different aspect. Caponsacchi, for one, hardly denies its validity, but Pompilia above all insists that the journey guaranteed a further progression through time, first by saving the life of her child (3.7.1656–58), and second by enabling her on her deathbed to begin constructing her personal history and glimpsing a future life:

Weeks and months of quietude,
I could lie in such peace and learn so much—
Begin the task, I see how needful now,
Of understanding somewhat of my past,—
Know life a little, I should leave so soon.
Therefore, because this man restored my soul,
All has been right; I have gained my gain, enjoyed
As well as suffered,—nay, got foretaste too
Of better life beginning where this ends—
All through the breathing-while allowed me thus.

(3.7.1662–71)

Even on her deathbed, as a result, Pompilia directs herself toward the future, considering, for example, the sort of memories of his mother Gaetano will have (3.7.65–107).[67] For Pompilia, then, the journey not only took her into history and the future but also granted her an emotional triumph, and at the moment of her death—"now, when I am most upon the move" (3.7.1775)—she announces that she is journeying still: "And I rise." If the timeless and the mythic are important (and amply studied) elements of the poem, so is the temporal progression that receives articulation in Pompilia's last words, a temporal progression underscored when viewed within the context of the poem's serial issue.

At the end of the poem's own journey to its Victorian audience in March 1869, John Morley remarked in the *Fortnightly Review* that "Mr. Browning's close would be no unfit epilogue to a scientific essay on history, or a treatise on the errors of the human understanding and the inaccuracy of human opinion and judgment" (338). Morley most likely referred to book 12's multiple documents and their conflicting testimony, but Browning's famous opening image of the firerocket can also suggest a "scientific" view of history:

Thus, lit and launched, up and up roared and soared
A rocket, till the key o' the vault was reached,
And wide heaven held, a breathless minute-space,
In brilliant usurpature.

(4.12.2–5)

If directed toward Guido's hold on Rome's attention until (after the execution) he gradually faded from memory, the passage also forms an apt metaphor of the complex relation of living in and understanding history. In the pause of the rocket's upward journey (the "breathless minute-space") comes the great moment of brilliant illumination, but that explosion of light cannot occur without the rocket's "roaring" and "soaring" journey "up and up." Similarly, the illuminations of history's significance come when we step outside or pause amidst the press of history; but without history's sequence that gets us from the past into the future, there is no looking back for further understanding. Yet one must journey and then pause, pause and then journey, never pause and journey at once. At best these two acts of journeying through time, then pausing to understand the shape of the journey, complement and complete each other, as in Lorry's moments of fireside meditation and Romola's inner debates about her duties and obligations. But as separate entities (the line of forward progression versus the circle of simultaneous perception), journeying and pausing can also jar against one another, a point conveyed in Browning's poem by the fact that pauses can be constructive (e.g., Pompilia's pause before death to comprehend her life) or destructive (the pause at Castelnuovo),[68] just as Pompilia's journey to Rome saves her while Guido's journey to Rome destroys her.

Browning's suggestion that journeying and pausing can produce very different outcomes or perspectives also applies to conducting a trial and judging innocence, reading and interpreting a poem, or living in and understanding history. The poet himself distinguishes journeys and pauses in book 1. First he journeys, or walks, as he reads the Old Yellow Book; but he has his moment of understanding after the walking ceases:

<blockquote>
Still read I on, from written title-page
To written index, on, through street and street,
At the Strozzi, at the Pillar, at the Bridge;
Till, by the time I stood at home again
In Casa Guidi by Felice Church,
Under the doorway where the black begins
With the first stone-slab of the staircase cold,
I had mastered the contents, knew the whole truth
Gathered together, bound up in this book,
Print three-fifths, written supplement the rest.
</blockquote>

(1.1.110–19)

His second time through the Old Yellow Book, he pauses and remains stationary to read, then turns away and walks:

<blockquote>
. . . from the reading, and that slab I leant
My elbow on, the while I read and read,
I turned, to free myself and find the world,
And stepped out on the narrow terrace, built
Over the street and opposite the church,
And paced its lozenge-brickwork sprinkled cool.
</blockquote>

(1.1.476–81)

As he paces, he takes an imaginative journey to Arezzo and reenacts the murder story, until

(1.1.520–
23)

> The life in me abolished the death of things,
> Deep calling unto deep: as then and there
> Acted itself over again once more
> The tragic piece.

In the first instance he journeys through the text, then has a simultaneous vision of its complete shape and truth "gathered" and "bound" within a book. In the second he devours the text in a single act, then imaginatively relives the process of the story. The Pope, too, alternates between simultaneous and sequential judgment in his monologue, now relying on instant, intuitive judgment, now carefully tracking a sequential argument (cf. Mary Rose Sullivan 124)—an alternation he ultimately relates to humankind's differences from Christ:

(4.10.375–
78)

> He, the Truth, is, too,
> The Word. We men, in our degree, may know
> There, simply, instantaneously, as here
> After long time and amid many lies.

The Pope's observation that on earth we know what we know only after "long time" suggests a rationale for both the poem's length and its serialization. W. David Shaw particularly illuminates the function of the poem's enormous length: "Most paraphrases of *The Ring and the Book* distance us from what actually happens to us as we read. They translate the discomforts and anxieties into safer, less demanding fictions. To return to the text is to stretch oneself out on the rack of a tough, obscure poem. By combining the tortures of the Roman murder trial with a real trial of the reader's own endurance Browning uses the physical extent of his poem, its great duration, to disclose the inconclusiveness and agony of history" (54). Shaw stresses the "agony" of historical interpretation, since interpretation can proliferate endlessly only to result in "amorphousness" (54). For us the poem's "great duration" implies the discontinuity between the linear process of reading the poem and the interpretations we construct during pauses, and between living in and understanding history.[69] As we go through life, we experience a vast succession of meaningful moments and details, and the details on which we focus shift from moment to moment. To get some kind of perspective on our lives, we must relinquish our hold on the millions of details and construct larger patterns of the whole, but this is not the same as actually living in time. In *The Ring and the Book,* similarly, each image, each metaphor, is important as we read through successive lines, but there is so much imagery in a given monologue (not to mention the shifts in imagery as we move from monologue to monologue) that we cannot hold it all in our minds at the same time.[70] We can either grasp the large outlines of the poem all at once—Pompilia's innocence and passion, the Pope's wisdom, the instability of language and truth—or we can experience the flow of the poem in its sinuous unfolding of some twenty thousand lines.[71] The poem affirms both kinds of experience: after all, Browning's decision to serialize was partly prompted by his insistence that readers follow every line of the poem, yet he also took care to short-circuit a strictly linear approach by telling the outcome of the trial in the opening book. But readers cannot affirm both kinds of knowing or experience at once.

Serial publication would have intensified this separation between journeying through the text over time and constructing its significance during pauses. If readers had difficulty holding a single monologue in their minds as they were reading (or just after), the attempt to remember individual lines would have been even more difficult when three months intervened between reading the first and last lines of this massive work. Serialization, in other words, factored literal time into the reading and interpreting process; Browning himself took care to mention that he lived with the Old Yellow Book for four years (4.12.227), a duration to which serial readers' four months of company with the poem formed an apt analogue. This factoring in of time was complemented by the work's sheer bulk and publication format, which factored in space. Together, this largesse of time and space made memory and fidelity to details almost impossible for a text that nonetheless insisted on striving for accuracy and wholeness of interpretation and memory (cf. Menaghan 264).

In this respect the poem's title gains an additional facet of meaning. The title, of course, is usually connected to Browning's metaphor of the alloy of poetic imagination and its mysterious relation to the truth of a book. Victorian audiences also recognized the title as a reference to his wife based on the poem's closing lines: "that inscription on the Casa Guidi at Florence, which suggested to Mr. Browning half of the title of his poem, may fittingly terminate this review. It may at once make us proud of her in whose honour it is written, and grateful to those who wrote it," remarked J. R. Mozley in the April 1869 *Macmillan's Magazine* (552). From the perspective of serialization, the title can suggest the circular, simultaneous truths grasped when reading stops and interpretation begins ("The Ring"), yet also the linear sequence through time demanded of readers moving line by line through the poem ("The Book").[72] Browning's readers, like Jarvis Lorry, became "booked" on a historical journey as they read; his readers also paused at critical moments as did Romola on her journeys. But *The Ring and the Book* suggested that the views obtained while journeying could vary significantly from those obtained in pauses, and thus challenged and complicated notions of history.

Publication format, in fact, extended Browning's theme because the poem's structure looked different from within versus after its issuance in parts. Especially in the first three months of publication, readers tended to view each part as a connected installment, with triads of monologues dictated by each volume's boundaries. Once publication ended, however, and readers began to focus on the poem as a whole, most subordinated material conditions (the book's layout) to intellectual conceptions (the poem grasped as a whole), leaping across the physical boundaries of each volume's covers to perceive the triadic structure still emphasized today.

If the serialization of *The Ring and the Book* posed some of the same interpretive challenges for its readers that Browning applied to history, serialization of this poem, and of *A Tale of Two Cities* and *Romola*, also affirmed the value of tracing stories, and histories, along a linear path. The three works we have examined together illustrate the complexity and range of Victorian patterns of history, and of the Victorian serial. Dickens's *Tale* stresses being caught up in history's movement, Eliot's *Romola* the pauses that serve as pivotal points in life and perception, and Browning's *Ring and the Book* the difficulties of interpreting from within a process or during a pause. Yet even if they demonstrate the complications of living in and understanding history, all three works affirm in their very publication format the process of moving along a line from the past through the present and into the future.

IV

Building the Empire

> *"There is nothing to be done," said the Duke almost angrily.*
> *"Then you should make something to be done," said the Duchess, mimicking him.*
>
> Trollope, *The Prime Minister*

> *"Watch what thou seest, and lightly bring me word."*
>
> Tennyson, "The Coming of Arthur"

> *"Then tell me what better I can do," said Gwendolen, insistently.*
>
> George Eliot, *Daniel Deronda*

IN THEIR MAJOR LITERARY WORKS Victorian authors shared a principle of influence with the representatives of the British Empire outside literature. Building railroads, bridges, roads, irrigation systems, telegraph and postal services (while also, of course, annexing formerly independent states for the Crown), Andrew Broun Ramsay brought the British system to India in the middle of the nineteenth century. Though their materials and economic networks were quite different, Victorian writers can also be viewed as establishing an expanding network of communication and innovation. Even before the nineteenth century began, at least one periodical editor saw the link between the two forms of enterprise, as Jon Klancher makes clear in discussing the *Bee:*

> *As another expanding order that drew social groups within its grasp, colonialism offered an almost inevitable metaphor for the universalizing of public discourse in the periodicals. The journal, one might say, built the greater reading public by colonizing social groups previously excluded from it:*
>
> (Klancher 25)[1]
>
>> *Nor does the editor [John Anderson of the Bee] confine his views to Britain alone. The world at large he considers as the proper theatre for*

literary improvements, and the whole human race, as constituting but one great society, whose general advancement in knowledge must tend to augment the prosperity of all its parts. . . . British traders are now to be found in all nations on the globe; and the English language begins to be studied as highly useful in every country. By means of the universal intercourse which that trade occasions, and the general utility of this language, he hopes to be able to establish a mutual exchange of knowledge, and to effect a friendly literary intercourse among all nations. . . . till it shall comprehend every individual of the human race.

Similarly, constructing significant works of prose and poetry for the edification of the world, Victorian writers were pleased at their own originality in conceiving ideas, at their industry in developing the fullest expression of those visions, and at the justification for such enterprises visible in the acceptance of their efforts by reading publics at home and abroad.

Often such works focused on characters who themselves built or contributed to the building of empires, such as Plantagenet Palliser in Trollope's *The Prime Minister,* Daniel Deronda in Eliot's novel of the same name, and King Arthur in Tennyson's *Idylls of the King.* Like so many other major works of the age, these three titles appeared serially: *The Prime Minister* and *Daniel Deronda* in eight half-volumes published at monthly intervals (November 1875–June 1876 and February–September 1876, respectively); *Idylls of the King* in separate volumes (1859, 1869, 1872) and in other forms (1842, 1862, 1871, 1873, 1885). The temporal and spatial growth of a serial, which starts with a single, limited part, then grows through the issue of additional installments, and finally comes to a conclusion with the appearance of the whole work, parallels the Victorian principles of empire.

For an empire to be established and to spread in a nineteenth-century literary work, a leader must gain the trust of a growing community through action and words; similarly, successful serial literature is written by an author whose voice and vision compel an audience to increased commitment over space and time. In this chapter we wish to link Victorian belief in empire and the serial form by exploring three models of leadership in serial works appearing as the empire reached its zenith. As Richard Altick points out, "When Disraeli bestowed upon the Queen the additional title of Empress of India in 1876, her country was approaching the height of its influence and achievement as an imperial power" (*Victorian* 15).

The impulse to empire is an undisguised element of Trollope's writing, as for him British politics, celebrated in his six-novel Palliser series (1864–80), is clearly the most advanced form of social organization in the world. And Plantagenet Palliser in *The Prime Minister* embodies the devotion to principle central to Trollope's ideal of one who governs well. Yet in the shape of his serial fiction Trollope presents an even more subtle endorsement of empire, for from no other Victorian writer flowed more deftly and consistently the stuff of fiction to a ready audience. In this apparent ease of production, installment after installment, novel following novel, Trollope demonstrated a harmony with nineteenth-century British society, creating more and more features of an imagined world as he (in the postal service) and his fellow citizens (in other walks of life) constructed the many parts to a genuine empire.

Some two decades ago Ruth apRoberts identified a feature of Trollope's work that much criticism since has pursued: "There is something of a mystery in the case of Anthony Trollope. His novels constitute a phenomenon of acknowledged success and importance, but still go largely unexplained" (11). In discussing nineteenth-century heroes, Peter Brooks may have touched on one of the forces in Trollope that is so appealing, if not addictive: "The ambitious heroes of the nineteenth-century novel—those of Balzac, for instance—may regularly be conceived as 'desiring machines' whose presence in the text creates and sustains narrative movement through the forward march of desire, projecting the self onto the world through scenarios of desire imagined and then acted upon" (39–40). Trollope the author, however mechanical his record of production, is a similar "desiring machine" in the unstoppable creation of fiction. A deceptively easy style disguises the incredible energy that went into his novels (and into his work for the postal service as well).[2] Such drive and achievement impressed the Victorian audience; and such drive is also essential to empire.

The central character in Trollope's novel about empire, *The Prime Minister,* is driven, not at first to be the head of the government, but rather simply to serve his country as a member of Parliament. Coral Lansbury insightfully comments, however, that to "*be elected* to the House of Commons in Trollope's day was to feel oneself seated on the throne of the world. Beyond England were the colonies and an empire that other countries could only envy or imitate" (212). When he does accept the queen's call to form a cabinet, he arrives at the very center of power in the known world. To evaluate Palliser's success as prime minister, leader of the empire, we must first establish the political and historical context within which his term occurs and then measure his achievements against the possibilities that context allows. When Plantagenet Palliser's success is appreciated, we can then understand more fully why Victorian readers admired Trollope's work.

Palliser's appearance as prime minister is framed by the depiction of another character who represents the principle of empire gone bad.[3] Lopez, the interloper who threatens the central characters, boasts a foreign origin (he might have "fallen out of the moon" [1:60]) and appears in middle-class Victorian society more as an invader than through any invitation (he asks a favor of Sextus Parker "not at all on his knees, but, as one might say, at the muzzle of a pistol" [1:14]). Despite such external disadvantages, however, the man who does not know or will not say "who were his grandfathers and who were his grandmothers" (1:1) marries into a prominent British family and very nearly gains a seat in Parliament: "he was imperious, and he had learned to carry his empire in his eye" (1:8). The power to project an idea, to gain support for a particular cause, and to reorganize society along new lines does belong to some individuals outside the traditional ruling families of England, as the 8 July 1876 *Illustrated London News* recognized when it referred to Lopez as "one of those adventurers who spring up like mushrooms" (34). The 22 July 1876 *Examiner* admitted that many found it "difficult to know whether one ought to sympathize with [Lopez] or not" (826). As many critics have written since, confusion about Lopez derives from the fact that he represents more fundamental elements of Victorian society than many of Trollope's readers would admit, and his destruction at Tenway Junction creates as much doubt about equality in a modern capitalist country as it reflects his own emotional bankruptcy.[4] In evaluating Plantagenet Palliser as prime minister, then, we can view his actions against the sinister background of Lopez's career.

Palliser is a coalition leader, one whose ministry bridges periods in which majorities devise and institute specific policies and actions. As Ruth apRoberts reminds us, the coalition "in actuality occurred rather often in Trollope's time" (140). Interestingly, Duke Plantagenet Palliser's novel in the Palliser series, *The Prime Minister* (1875–76), also bridges two different eras, an earlier time presented in *Phineas Redux* (1873–74) and the later era chronicled by *The Duke's Children* (1879–80). Thus, again there is a correspondence in this serial novel's form and its content. Victorian readers placed this novel within a sequence of related stories, as was evident in the 25 December 1875 *Bell's Weekly Messenger* review of the first installment: "In this, the first [part], we have already renewed once again our acquaintance with several old friends, with whom we have passed many a pleasant bygone hour in other productions of this always interesting author" (6). The 22 July 1876 *Examiner* similarly suggested how this novel's identity was determined in part by its context of past and future stories: "old characters with which we have already some acquaintance are more interesting than new. It is like meeting old friends whom we have not met for some years, and who have made for themselves in the interval a story worth telling. Then not only do we hear the tale of their new enterprises and adventures, but we hear also the story of new people with whom they have been brought in contact" (826). Such linking of a present story with a known past (and an implied future) is a necessary strategy in assessing the Duke of Omnium's three-year term as a coalition prime minister within Trollope's fictional political history.

As Robert Polhemus (*Changing* 198) argued some years ago (and as Geoffrey Harvey more recently has repeated [150]), "coalition" might be termed the novel's central theme, figuring in social, emotional, moral, and financial areas as well as in the political world. What *coalition* means in the political realm is that the country's many interests are essentially balanced, with no great issues of dissatisfaction demanding immediate action.[5] Geoffrey Harvey has argued that Palliser is thus "in charge of the best Government, theoretically, that can be devised, a non-partisan Coalition serving the national interest" (144). Palliser's challenge is to sustain a basic equilibrium for as long as no single issue—suffrage reform, Home Rule, imperial crisis—demands action. In the same way that he came to be prime minister in the first place—gradually but steadily—Palliser himself comes to realize his special task: "The policy confided to him and expected at his hands was that of keeping together a Coalition Ministry" (2:285).

The young Plantagenet Palliser first appeared in Trollope's world with *The Small House at Allington* (1862–64). Twenty fictional years later (after four more long novels from Trollope's pen adding to the chronicle of Palliser's life), the now Duke of Omnium had risen to the highest echelons of power in his country. When Palliser first speaks to Glencora about the possibility of office, he doubts "whether I have any gift for governing men"; his wife replies, "It will come" (1:86), and the novel proves her correct, at least in part. Although it takes some time for him to realize it, his skill is an extension of his basic character, particularly his willingness to accept the differences of others so long as high ethical principles are not violated.[6] Palliser's career as prime minister, a continuation of the life narrated in Trollope's previous fiction, is presented in stages, the novel's eight monthly parts, whose neat sequential structure appealed to Victorian readers: Palliser is led reluctantly to his new role (part 1, November 1875);

holds office but is unsure of his responsibilities (part 2, December 1875); struggles to establish his leadership indirectly rather than through action (part 3, January 1876); is recognized as a successful Prime Minister (part 4, February 1876); encounters the first signs of the difficulties that will end his ministry (part 5, March 1876); resists the pressure to alter his policies in order to remain in office (part 6, April 1876); loses control of the support that made the coalition possible (part 7, May 1876); and retires gracefully at the recognized end of his term (part 8, June 1876).

The central character's "gift for governing men," which already exists at the beginning of the novel, his tolerance of other viewpoints, is an appropriate quality for the leader of a coalition government. The success of his approach is measured by the additional individuals it brings into the government as time passes and by the repeated sessions in which a majority is not threatened. At the beginning of his term, many politicians "expected that the seeds of weakness, of which they had perceived the scattering, would grow at once into an enormous crop of blunders, difficulties, and complications" (2:188). However, after several months "there grew up an idea that the Coalition was really the proper thing" (2:188) for the country at that time. And by part 4 "the Government was carried on and the country was prosperous. A few useful measures had been passed by unambitious men, and the Duke of St. Bungay declared that he had never known a Session of Parliament more thoroughly satisfactory to the ministers" (5:5).

Some of Trollope's readers also did not think of Plantagenet as a potentially successful prime minister when the novel began; the 25 December 1875 *Bell's Weekly Messenger* suggested as much by the tone of surprise in its review of part 1: "The Prime Minister proves to be none other than Planty Pal" (6). The 22 July 1876 *Spectator,* reviewing the novel at its completion, also thought it unlikely that the familiar figure from earlier works could have developed into a leader of the government: "Mr. Palliser has become Duke of Omnium and Prime Minister, and is in the process changed for the worse to a degree which could never have occurred [in real life]" (922).[7] However, other readers found the evolution of Palliser's character perfectly reasonable and commended Trollope's control of his art. The 18 August 1876 *Times* stated: "perhaps, Mr. Trollope has never given more convincing proof of his easy command of materials that are apparently anything but plastic than in developing the Duke of Omnium into the Prime Minister. Plantagenet Palliser, when we first met him, was as little interesting and almost as disagreeable as a man could be, who had the manners and feelings of a gentleman" (4). While the *Spectator* (cited above) found Palliser "vulgar" (922), the *Times* concluded: "we were scarcely prepared to find that Mr. Trollope should actually make us know him and like him better in that exalted post [as prime minister] than we had ever done before" (4). Thus, Trollope's method in presenting his central character was well received by significant portions of his reading public; and basic to both praise and criticism of the duke is a belief that character in fiction and personality in life should develop consistently in stages over time.

Palliser begins his term as prime minister with a restraint that has long been a key feature of his identity. Because he does not initiate new policy at the beginning of his ministry, Palliser directs the nation in the first four parts of the novel (November 1875–February 1876) more by opposing unwise practices than by acting himself. Palliser knows in part 1 that "there was wanting to him a certain noble capacity for commanding support and homage from other men" (1:104); yet he is able to ensure that others follow the national interest rather than personal desire. Sir Orlando Drought, for instance, draws out Palliser's methods of leadership when he insists in part 2 that the government pursue expansive action, such as building more ships. When Sir Orlando tries to bring up his recommendation for "increased armaments" (2:337) at Gatherum, the duke is inspired to make a clear statement of policy, which was given added resonance for Victorian serial readers because it came at the end of this part: "Things to be done offer themselves, I suppose, because they are in themselves desirable; not because it is desirable to have something to do" (2:336). Nonetheless, Sir Orlando presses in part 4 for a policy of "building four bigger ships of war than had ever been built before" (4:191) under the slogan "The Salvation of the Empire" (4:192). Since the duke is convinced "that the Empire [is] safe" (4:192), he, of course, refuses to urge that the ships be constructed. Rather than taking action against Sir Orlando, however, he simply lets that member make the decision to retire.

Although Palliser took no direct action against Sir Orlando, he established the policy of his cabinet by opposing actions he felt unnecessary or antagonistic to the continued growth of the empire. In fact, Sir Orlando's entire frame of reference involved an inappropriate definition of a leader for the time of Palliser's coalition. Looking for the prime minister at Gatherum (part 2), he imagined their interaction in these erroneous terms: "Emperor meets Emperor, and King meets King, and as they wander among rural glades in fraternal intimacy, wars are arranged, and swelling territories are enjoyed in anticipation" (2:333). England's territories are "swelling," but through Palliser's different policy (explained below in connection with John Grey). As the 18 August 1876 *Times* put it, "If [Palliser] could not mould men easily and pleasantly to his purpose, at least he had some art of commanding them and making them follow his lead at a respectful distance" (quoted in Smalley 424).

Palliser, then, leads by establishing the outer limits of policy. Balancing the many demands of the coalition's different parties, he puts his faith in the British system itself, already in place and functioning. The duke pursues a similar course in his marriage, which, as many critics have noted, provides a microcosm of the state and illuminates Trollope's theme of governance.[8] This analogous relationship of government to marriage was suggested by the cover for individual parts, which featured the political title and a romantic illustration (see figure 7). Allowing Glencora her idea of "conquering people . . . by feeding them" (2:292) at grand parties in parts 1–4, Palliser takes action only by stopping her at the boundary of proper policy. Interestingly, *Bell's Weekly Messenger* anticipated danger from Glencora's ambition in its 22 January 1876 review of part 2. Noting "the political vortex through which [Glencora] tries to steer the Prime-Ministerial boat" (6), this review worried: "We are led to fear, however, that Lady Glencora is going beyond even this [exercise of traditional feminine power]; but we hope, that as on former occasions, her good sense prevailed, so in the present it will get the better of her daring originality" (6).

When in the next part one of Glencora's guests, Major Pountney, breaches political decorum in the duke's view, Palliser orders him, in writing, off the grounds of Gatherum. Even though "gradually there had crept upon him a fear that his wife was making a mistake" (2:283) in giving such parties, Palliser continues a marital policy of forbearance; he tells her, "I love you the better for [trying to help], day by day" (2:300). Though she will resent his later criticism, Glencora is "so surprised" that "her eyes were filled with tears" (2:300) at this recognition of her efforts. Indeed, Palliser appears by part 4 as a more romantic figure than ever before in his relation to Cora: "His manner to her lately had been more than urbane, more than affectionate;—it had almost been that of a lover" (4:190). At the same time that Palliser is learning that he is an effective prime minister, then, he is also developing as a husband—in Victorian terms, as the leader in a marriage.[9]

Many Victorians, of course, were less tolerant of Glencora's political schemes than was her husband. The 8 July 1876 *Illustrated London News*, for instance, referred to "the vain manoeuvers of the Duchess to be a Prime Ministress of Society" (34). And the 22 July 1876 *Examiner* admitted that

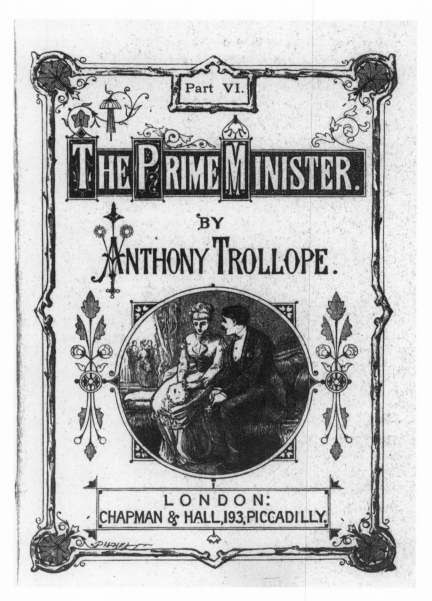

Figure 7. Cover of monthly half-volumes of Trollope's *Prime Minister* (1875–76), linking government and marriage. (*Alderman Library, University of Virginia*)

"she proves a certain impediment to [the duke's] high-minded ideas of his office" (826). The 22 July 1876 *Spectator* found Glencora's character to be "utterly unrecognisable" in her new role of "parvenue" (923). In fact, this journal made the bold claim, actually expressed fairly frequently by serial readers, that fictional characters belong, not to authors, but to audiences! The *Spectator* accused Trollope of having "chosen also to smirch old characters, people who have become a possession of the reading world, and whom he had no right to degrade in its estimation" (922). The power-seeking Glencora of *The Prime Minister,* then, was "not the woman whom so many of Mr. Trollope's readers have admired" (923); yet she retained her husband's affection.

As Coral Lansbury points out, the duchess, like Sir Orlando, possesses at the beginning of the novel an "idea of a prime minister [that] is a century and more out of date" (219). Her unrealistic concept is visible in a crucial scene almost exactly at the midpoint of the story.[10] As part 5 opens, Palliser is beginning to be bothered by Quintus Slide's criticism that there is a "lethargy on the country" (5:9); Glencora tries to urge action on her husband. However, as the Duke of St. Bungay reminded Palliser, there had been "ever-recurring majorities" (5:9) to support the cabinet's policies in the last session, and nothing more momentous than naming a replacement for Sir Orlando Drought is called for at this time. Unwilling to "keep Parliament sitting in order that more ribbons might be sold," the duke "almost angrily" but quite correctly tells the duchess, "There is nothing to be done" (5:11).[11] Her response, "mimicking him," reveals how little she understands the situation: "Then you should make something to be done" (5:11).

Although she never fully accepts the duke's style of government, Glencora does come to suspect that her own approach contained weaknesses; by part 4 she realizes that the "world was not taken captive as she had intended. . . . she had almost thought that she could rule England by giving dinner and supper parties, by ices and champagne" (4:281). She argues in part 6 that she, rather than Plantagenet, "should have been made" prime minister, because, whereas her husband is "a god," she is "not a goddess" and would "have done all the dirty work" (6:273–75). But by part 8 the "system on which the Duchess had commenced her career as wife of the Prime Minister had now been completely abandoned" (8:270). Her policies failed in their imperial goal: "There never had come the happy moment in which she had felt herself to be dominant over other women" (2:343). Nor were her ambitions for her husband fully realized, as she tells her friend Mrs. Finn: "He never understood that to be Prime Minister in

England is as much as to be an Emperor in France, and much more than being President in America" (8:342).

Once again, the wisdom of Palliser's philosophy is underscored by the opposite system characterizing the Lopez marriage. Emily Wharton, a subject of the relatively benevolent "tyranny" (2:209) of her father in parts 1 and 2, comes to see her marriage to Lopez in part 3 as the complete loss of her independent identity: "She must learn to look at the world with his eyes" (2:73). Lopez takes over Emily's life, in fact, as if he were colonizing her: "there came upon her gradually a feeling that by her marriage she had divided herself from her own people" (3:162). This tragedy for Emily was hardly a surprise to most Victorian readers, whose view of the world contained fixed stereotypes, as the October 1876 *New Quarterly Magazine's* comment suggested: "so far as the moral of her fate can be discerned, it is to serve as a warning to romantic young ladies not to be led away by the fascinations of Jewish stockbrokers who bear a foreign name" (256).

The effect of Lopez's imperial policy in marriage is further underscored by a parallel between serial form and actual experience. In part 4 (February 1876), readers learned that Emily might be pregnant: "And then she thought of other coming joys and coming troubles,—of how in future years she might have to teach a girl falsely to believe that her father was a good man, and to train a boy to honest purposes whatever parental lessons might come from the other side" (4:326). This hint that Lopez's empire might be expanded was confirmed in part 5 (March 1876), as the husband encourages a new relationship with the Parkers. When Emily says "I'll help her spoil the children" (5:81), Lopez responds: " 'You can get a lesson there, you know,' he said, looking into her face. The little joke was one which a young wife might take with pleasure from her husband, but her life had already been too much embittered for any such delight. Yes; the time was coming when that trouble also would be added to her. She dreaded she knew not what, and had often told herself that it would be better that she should be childless" (5:81–82). Where the prospect of a child ought to be drawing the couple together here, it becomes instead one more weapon, a joke, Lopez uses to control Emily.

In the long months of pregnancy parents-to-be like the Lopezes can measure and appreciate the prospects of a larger family. This period of expectation has its parallel for readers in the extended time of serial publication: Trollope's Victorian audience had many weeks in February and March 1876 to contemplate what the new member of the family would mean to Emily. Modern single-volume readers, on the other hand, move more quickly to the discovery in part 5 that "the poor child did not live a couple of days" (5:152). For Trollope's contemporaries anticipation of the next installment paralleled the waiting of Emily, who later would look "at all the preparations she had made,—the happy work of her fingers when her thoughts of their future use were her sweetest consolation,—and weep till she would herself feel that there never could be an end to her tears" (5:153). Victorians who anticipated the consolation of a child for Emily would have looked back at their serial reading experience with similar disappointment that a happy resolution to this part of the plot had been denied them.

Because Lopez's philosophy is corrupt, however, his debts (marked by an "inky devil" [3:75]) increase and the number of people who care for him decreases during the course of the novel's publication. (As in *Daniel Deronda,* in fact, the twin financial principles of interest and debt underscore this society's deep faith in development over time.) The patience of Arthur Fletcher, consistent with Palliser's insistence on taking action only when it is needed, provides the correct framework for Emily to recover from the loss of her child and the collapse of her marriage. Whereas Lopez had failed to initiate his wife "by degrees" (5:63) into the realities of his character, Arthur is markedly deliberate in letting Emily come to see his superior qualities: "There must be time" (7:70) for her recovery, he says repeatedly to family and friends. As an effective member for Silverbridge, Fletcher also demonstrates the qualities of leadership appropriate to Parliament as well as the Victorian home. Talking to Emily's father, for instance, he explains long-term investment and return in government policy: "We are going to lend money to the parish on the security of the rates for draining bits of common land. Then we shall sell the land and endow the unions so as to lessen the poor rates, and increase the cereal products of the country" (4:270).

In its presentation of Fletcher's perseverance and restraint, the serial structure of the novel again coincides with its theme. Lopez dies at the conclusion of part 6 (April 1876), but Arthur and Emily are not united until part 8 (June 1876). In fact, part 7 (May 1876) closes with Arthur not yet having pressed his suit: "loving her as I do,—by heaven! I cannot hurry her. . . . I shall do it [propose] in time, I suppose;—but I must wait till the time comes" (7:168). Some Victorian readers resented this postponement. The 8 July 1876 *Illustrated London News,* for instance, commented: "The suicide which closes the career of Ferdinand Lopez occurs at the end of the sixth part of 'The Prime Minister,' and there the novel might have been opportunely wound up with the promise of future happiness to Emily Lopez and Arthur Fletcher, as some recompense for their long-suffering"

(34). But, as Mary Hamer has shown, Trollope always planned the structure of his novels carefully (46), and the delayed resolution of the romantic theme, even Emily's excessively coy and protracted rejection of Arthur, is meant to underscore a proper sense of time and process.

As Lopez's failure to govern well is revealed in his marriage, so his political role, the opposite of Palliser's, proves empty. Impatient to leap over the necessary stages of development to power within the empire, in the end he does not even take office. In contrast, two characters familiar to Trollope's readers provide examples of slowly developing, positive service in the empire: Phineas Finn (protagonist in two Palliser novels, 1867–69 and 1873–74) and John Grey (a central character in *Can You Forgive Her?* [1864–65]). Phineas serves the ministry effectively in his native Ireland (1:123–26); takes Sir Orlando's place as first lord of the admiralty (5:10); speaks for the prime minister in Parliament (chapter 57); and provides the sounding board for Palliser's political philosophy (chapter 68). John Grey gives up the important seat in Silverbridge to serve the ministry in Persia (3:5), a country that is, according to Jennifer Uglow, believed to be "threatening the stability of Afghanistan and Herat, leaving the 'gate of India' open to possible Russian invasion" (2:414). Quietly and undramatically, then, Palliser governs through competent associates like Grey and Finn, sustaining and strengthening the British Empire. Grey and Finn move gradually toward greater power in England just as they develop slowly over the many years of their appearances in the Palliser novels. Lopez, unmentioned before *The Prime Minister,* is a man with no history in his world or in the Victorian audience's experience; hence, his aspirations run counter to fundamental principles of his society.

Grey, Finn, and Fletcher all represent individuals brought into the government by Palliser, the coalition leader whose ministry serves the country well at a particular moment in history. In the second half of the novel, parts 5–8 (March–June 1876), however, the national mood begins to change, calling for a change in leadership. Palliser's three-year term as prime minister comes to a natural end. As late as part 6, the "country was thriving under the Coalition" (6:265). The spirit of continuing reform, however, calling for altered behavior from government officials as well as for new bills in Parliament, inspires a new mood, one distorted and magnified, of course, by Quintus Slide. Trollope makes it clear that Palliser has done well with important matters while the people's worst instincts are exploited to effect change: "Had the welfare of the Indian Empire occupied the House [rather than Finn's "explanation" of the duke's role in the Silverbridge election], the House would have been empty. But the hope that a certain woman's name would have to be mentioned, crammed it from the floor to the ceiling" (6:290).

Even as late as in part 7 Mrs. Finn can size up the state of affairs in England by saying "The world is going on very smoothly" (7:38). And Mr. Monk tells the duke, "the country is very prosperous. I don't know that I ever remember trade to have been more evenly satisfactory" (7:93). We are reminded, however, that Palliser had been able to govern because "neither of the two old and well-recognized leaders of parties could command a sufficient following for the carrying on of the government" (7:49); and the Duke of St. Bungay recognizes a new situation emerging. Either a Liberal or a Conservative majority should now rule because the coalition "had done its work" (7:51).[12] Palliser angers his more conservative supporters by appointing Lord Earlybird a Knight of the Garter (part 7) and the more liberal members by trying to pass a county suffrage bill that does not go as far as many desired (part 8). As his majority dwindles, Palliser must confront the nature of his service as prime minister, pointing out to his old friend the Duke of St. Bungay,

(8:202–3)
> "[The county suffrage bill] is the first large measure that we have tried to carry."
> "We did not come in to carry large measures, my friend. Look back and see how many large measures Pitt carried,—but he took the country safely through its most dangerous crisis."
> "What have we done?"
> "Carried on the Queen's Government prosperously for three years. Is that nothing for a minister to do?"

Admitting to Finn later that "We shan't make this step [county suffrage bill] towards the millenium just at present," Palliser hears his friend insist: "But we shall have made a step towards the step" (8:215). Since such actions ("to march on to some nearer approach to equality" [7:128]) formed the essence of the duke's own political philosophy as he presented it to Finn on that memorable walk at Matching (chapter 68), Palliser does come to accept his own accomplishments as fulfilling.[13]

In a meeting with Mr. Monk on the last pages of the novel, the duke hears once again how his policy was appropriate and fruitful because it allowed the natural strengths of the country to operate and because it was an expression of his own best qualities: "The Government was carried on, and was on the whole respected. History will give you credit for patriotism, patience, and courage" (8:344). And when Palliser questions whether or not that was "a great part to play," Monk answers: "Great enough to satisfy the heart of a man who has fortified himself against the evil side of ambition. After all, what is it that the Prime Minister of such a country as this should chiefly regard? Is it not the prosperity of the country? It is not often that we want great measures, or new arrangements that shall be vital to the country" (8:344–45).[14] Palliser's faith in the essential rightness of the British system made him the right leader of a coalition for a specific time in the nation's history.

In fact, Palliser's commitment to decimal coinage, a cause he continues to urge at the end of the novel in his conversation with Monk, is a key instance of his vision and method. Such a change would not alter the underlying forces that account for the country's prosperity, but it would make their integration easier and the nation's exchange with other states more efficient. Some modern critics have dismissed the duke's obsession, saying, for instance, that Palliser "retains some illusions he can always go back to jamming five farthings into a penny" after his term as prime minister (Kincaid, *Trollope* 223). Decimal-based coinage is more rational and efficient than the old system in a society that uses a base-ten number system (the metric system) for its arithmetic. Hence, that central Trollopian concern, national prosperity, might have been increased had others seen the wisdom of the duke's ideas; yet the action taken would not have been as concrete and visible as, say, four new ships of war.[15]

Palliser's obsession with a base-ten system might be seen as analogous to Trollope's interest in structuring his fiction into even units, stages of the narrative's development. As Mary Hamer has explained, he planned each work according to numbers of pages, chapters, books, and serial installments, consistently completing the writing according to an exacting prearranged scheme. In fact, each of *The Prime Minister*'s eight parts is divided neatly into ten chapters (decimals) and provides a way to see Trollope's art of fiction as similar to Palliser's style of government. The spread of both Trollope's fictional world and his actual audience over time links his creative impulse to the forces at the very heart of empire.

This ease of composition has troubled some readers from Victorian times to the present. A consistent complaint about Trollope is that later novels repeat earlier ones, as the January 1876 *New Quarterly Magazine* suggested when it called the first part of *The Prime Minister* "almost indistinguishable from its predecessors" (491). Other Victorian reviewers argued that the author's powers fell off later in his career, a point made by *Bell's Weekly Messenger* in reviewing part 5 and 6 on 6 May 1876: "we find ourselves sighing, and looking, but sighing in vain, for something like novelty—the striking and utilizing of some new line of thought that will give us glimpses of cleverness, which were so abundantly prominent in those earlier efforts, by which he made his reputation, and persevered in keeping up the standard he had well and worthily won" (6). Yet Trollope never lost his readers, and reservations about his work often neglect the imaginative achievement of the whole—forty-six novels, many of three-volume length. His ability to generate new characters and plots that appealed to audiences was admitted by the *Examiner* in its review of *The Prime Minister* on 22 July 1876: "Mr. Trollope has long settled down into his peculiar method, and there is no reason why he should not go on producing this kind of manufacture by the volume, with the regularity of a calculating machine, as long as the machinery lasts. He is likely to tire of it as soon as his readers. For, whatever may be said about the Philistinic realism of Mr. Trollope's work, it cannot be denied that it interests. It is not fascinating, but it interests" (825). And, of course, it has interested new generations after this original Victorian readership, as Trollope's voice and vision have earned him a larger audience in our time.[16]

Trollope's fiction "interests," as the *Examiner* suggests, through its realism. That is, his audience viewed his always expanding and moving world in almost the same way they looked at reality. The October 1876 *New Quarterly Magazine* explained: "Reading Mr. Trollope's novels is very like looking out of the window. It is an occupation that can be taken up at any time, and is never enslaving" (251). Although some reviewers offered this observation as a complaint, it remains testimony to his powers of observation, narration, and creation. The 22 July 1876 *Examiner,* for example, admitted that "Mr. Trollope has his own political history, his own public incidents and personages, more or less adumbrations of contemporary realities, and he narrates the events of that history, and admits us freely to the company of the persons who are supposed to make it" (825). Trollope seems able to create a world that expands and develops as rapidly and consistently as his audience's own world.

Trollope's narration was criticized for its prosiness, its matter-of-fact style. The October 1876 *New Quarterly Magazine* likened his fiction to simple journalism: "if the Duke of Omnium were a living person, and his ministry a reality, the comments of the daily papers upon its fortunes would be almost identical with the political portion of 'The Prime Minister'" (255). This review concluded that Trollope, thus, had "a shallow and imperfect vision of the world" (253–54), which accounted for his popularity with "superficial" readers (254). The 22 July 1876 *Spectator* arrived at a similar judgment: "[*The Prime Minister*] contains some pleasant chapters, full of characters whom we have all met, of incidents so natural as almost to seem undeserving of acute and humorous observations" (922). And the 14 October 1876 *Saturday Review* said of the novel's political plot: "It might serve for a somewhat tame account of events that actually happened, but it can scarcely claim to possess any sort of imaginative value" (482). However much some individuals might dislike this realism, it inspired increased commitment from a widening audience in the last century, through many serial stories appearing over many years. Trollope's style reveals, then, a nearly absolute faith both in the world he inhabits and in conventional modes (such as journalism) of representing that world in language.

Another element of Trollope's fiction, its multiplot construction, also had an appeal to nineteenth-century readers. Garrett explains how each novel is made up of individual characters, each with his or her own unique perspective: Trollope's "narrator represents only the corrective of pluralism, setting one limited perspective against another, attempting to represent each side of a situation fairly" (190). Trollope's plot construction insists on a certain tolerance, then, a recognition that others see things from their own situations. D. A. Miller agrees: "Instead of loving this character and hating that one, Trollope is at once charmed and irritated by them all, thus cultivating a pluralistic appreciation of the value—as well as the limitations—that each in one context or another proves to have" (26). Thus, Trollope as author and narrator exhibits the key quality of Palliser, his central character, tolerance. The blandness and tolerance found in Trollope's fiction are in the end appropriately matched by the undramatic, undistinguished method of Palliser's governing.[17] Both are based on faith in the system of English life in the nineteenth century. As the coalition formed around the duke and made him a successful prime minister, so the world around Trollope gave him a subject for fiction and a language to develop it, which, as his audience expanded and deepened through the stages of his career, led him to a major position among Victorian men of letters. The larger reality of British life carried along both politician and writer to empire.

Tennyson was an integral part of the British Empire from 1850, when he became poet laureate; and before the last of *Idylls of the King* appeared he had been made a peer of the realm. Trollope represented the civil service of empire and, in art, a genre similarly unpretentious. Tennyson represented, ultimately, the offices and aristocracy of empire, and he wrote in a genre approaching the epic.[18] King Arthur, not surprisingly, embodies a far more active leadership role than does Planty Pall. And yet the two characters, one so mundanely "real," the other wrought from mythic materials, similarly reject rule by conquest and pursue the ideal of leadership through shared beliefs.

More than any other poem we discuss in this book, *Idylls of the King* has received attention as a serial work, starting with Kathleen Tillotson's influential essay "Tennyson's Serial Poem," published in 1965. Yet as a serial poem *Idylls of the King* represents a special case: of the serial works we discuss, only Tennyson's Arthuriad was published out of the sequence of the completed work. The *Idylls'* serialization did not (as with *The Ring and the Book*) counterbalance cyclic movement by emphasizing linear progression. The *Idylls'* publication order instead counterbalanced the linear progression toward the kingdom's downfall in the finished poem with an emphasis on cyclic recurrence.

As with Arthur's origins, so those of the poem featuring this king are vague and debatable. The first installment, entitled *Idylls of the King,* appeared in 1859 and was seen by many as a self-contained unit. Many others, however, saw that installment as a sequel to "Morte d'Arthur" and "The Epic," which (along with "Sir Galahad," the revised "Lady of Shalott," and "Sir Launcelot and Queen Guinevere") had appeared in 1842. Several reviewers of the 1859 volume even suggested that the *Idylls* be reprinted with the "Morte" as the fifth poem. For these Victorian readers, the poem began with Arthur's death in 1842, followed by his resurgence in 1859. Yet another ten years later, the resurgence of Arthur was unmistakable. The glimpse of Arthur fading into the mists in "Guinevere" was succeeded in 1869 by the advent of the king in "The Coming of Arthur." With this poem, as well as "The Holy Grail," "Pelleas and Ettarre," and the reworked "Morte" (now "The Passing of Arthur"), most reviewers thought the poem complete. But "The Last Tournament" appeared in the December 1871 *Contemporary Review,* and the volume containing "Gareth and Lynette" and the reprinted "Last Tournament" appeared in 1872. Yet once more the death—or rather the passing (less terminal, more open to ongoing process)—of Arthur was followed by his return.

The result of all this was not only to heighten Victorians' perception of cycles in the poem but to allow participation in them, since each of the 1859, 1869, and 1872 installments reopened on the early days of the realm after a previous poem had depicted Arthur's downfall or death. For Victorian audiences of 1872, that is, Tennyson's Arthur had returned three times. Theirs was a more hopeful poem than the one known to readers of the completed work, who start at the founding of the table and chart a narrative of irreversible decline. And since idylls about the early days of the realm so often followed rather than preceded tales about the realm's last days, any incident might refer forward and backward in time at once. For the poem's first readers the description of Arthur's gate on which "New things and old co-twisted, as if Time / Were nothing, so inveterately" ("Gareth and Lynette" 1872: 16), must have read as a direct gloss on the poem they had been reading for a generation. No one should have been surprised when the *Idylls* failed to end even in 1872, or when the final installment, which appeared thirteen years later, narrated events not at the end or beginning of the realm but events in the middle: "Balin and Balan" was the last idyll to appear, but Tennyson's footnote to the poem in the 1885 *Tiresias and Other Poems* identified this work as an "introduction" to "Merlin and Vivien" (1885: 117).[19]

Audiences' reception of the *Idylls* took place in the context of a larger Arthurian revival.[20] As Mark Girouard has shown, the nineteenth-century cult of chivalry was closely connected to concepts of empire. At first an assertion of monarchy in reaction to the French Revolution, the renewal of chivalry gradually became linked by the 1840s with English history and nationhood, as seen in the design of the houses of Parliament (see also Mancoff 65–135). By the 1850s, Girouard argues, the cult of chivalry bifurcated into romantic chivalry among the Pre-Raphaelites and kindred figures, and moral chivalry as represented by Tennyson and, later, those who emphasized muscular Christianity, games, the boy scouts, and a code of gentlemanly behavior increasingly associated with imperialism as the century neared its end.[21] Victorian readers of Arthurian poems, then, had an implicit framework of nationhood and empire not always immediately apparent today, a framework that gives added importance to Victorian approaches to leadership and the fate of nations in such works. That Tennyson's poem celebrated the governance of an ideal monarch and was written by the official court poet further promoted links between the *Idylls* and notions of empire.[22]

Today the poem is generally approached as a skeptical treatment of empire and civilization: Tennyson is praised for demonstrating the futility or destructiveness of ideals (e.g., Ryals, Rosenberg), the pessimism of waning nineteenth-century society in a realm that seems to deliquesce almost as soon as it is founded (Buckley), or the stark reality that civilizations can fall or lapse for no good reason at all, simply because they exist and are doomed one day to die (Kincaid, *Tennyson*). To late twentieth-century readers, the *Idylls* most often embody the poetics of entropy. Insofar as there is a poet figure in the *Idylls,* that personage is of course Merlin, whose foreglimpse of doom immobilizes him and whose fall by means of crude seduction leaves him forever in a self-enclosed world, a hermeneutic circle impenetrable to future audiences. In this respect the poem is often praised as a reflexive poem about narrativity itself (Reed), or as a text so full of various threads it is easily unraveled.

When *Idylls of the King* is restored to its serial context, its themes of empire appear quite different. Its publication sequence validated the ability of an Arthur to return and hence suggested (along with the poem's contents) the potential within Arthur's realm for renewal, growth, and expansion from a clear center. That center was identified with Arthur the leader, who conveyed to most Victorian readers exemplary rather than futile traits. In the many reviews written in response to each installment there emerges an Arthur who suggested growth as much as failure, triumph as well as doom. And the counterpart of the poet for Tennyson's serial readers was less Merlin than Arthur himself: both the king and the laureate gradually built their kingdom of Camelot and extended their range of followers (if also losing many to rivals toward the end). Their form of empire building depended above all on an ability to induce others to share a vision, and these visions were alike subject to forces of decline and renewal.

Since "Morte d'Arthur," which began Tennyson's serial poem, was written soon after the death of Arthur Hallam, criticism of that poem has naturally focused on the coalescing of the legendary and mortal Arthurs, and on the similar plights of Alfred Tennyson and Bedivere, both bereft of a former focal point for their lives. "The Epic," in which the "Morte" was encased in 1842, is sometimes noted for its function in distancing the "Morte" from its intensely private poet, or, more constructively, for helping establish the "modern" points of relevance in the Arthurian poem, especially the decay of faith and tradition. Another connection exists between frame and inset, however, for Everard Hall and King Arthur share a similar dilemma, the need to induce others to share a vision based in the past—a vision deriving from archaic materials and traditions for the poet, from the eclipsed glories of his early reign for Arthur.

Arthur is the center around whom all his men have fallen: "King Arthur's table, man by man, / Had fall'n in Lyonness about their Lord, / King Arthur" (1842: 4), as he was once the focal point of Camelot in its glorious days. But he is wounded and weak, left with one knight, dependent on this knight and the knight's compliance to carry out his last plan. And here Arthur twice fails; Bedivere, on quite plausible grounds, twice refuses to cast Excalibur in the lake, choosing instead to follow his own counsel. Bedivere fails to obey because Arthur fails to lead. For Arthur this

leadership is intimately bound up with Excalibur, the badge of his kingship, and he relates to Bedivere the vision of its conferral:

>   thou rememberest how
>   In those old days, one summer noon, an arm
> (1842: 5)   Rose up from out the bosom of the lake,
>   Clothed in white samite, mystic, wonderful,
>   Holding the sword—and how I row'd across
>   And took it, and have worn it, like a king.

In telling Bedivere to fling the sword, "Watch what thou seest, and lightly
bring me word" (1842: 5), Arthur insists not merely on an extension by
Bedivere of his own experience but also on a recreation of his own vision
in language: he wishes Bedivere to bring back, not a sword, but a word.
Arthur's faith in his vision remains staunch, and he insists after Bedivere's
first—and false—report from the lake that "surer sign had follow'd, either
hand, / Or voice, or else a motion of the mere" (1842: 7) if Bedivere had
done what he was told. Bedivere's slow striding (1842: 7, 9) rather than
light return back to the king after his first two visits to the lake shows his
resistance to Arthur's inner world, especially when Arthur is, as Bedivere
reasons, "sick, and knows not what he does" (1842: 8)—a charge potentially lodged against all leadership. At the poem's low point, Arthur
resorts to compulsion—a sign of failed leadership—instead of compliance, threatening to slay Bedivere if he fails one more time to obey.
Bedivere responds to this show of force, especially since he has no competing ideal or idea to follow, and his compliance validates and extends
Arthur's underlying vision. First, the unnamed narrator relives (by re-
iterating) Arthur's inner vision (1842: 10), then Bedivere himself does so:
" 'when I look'd again, behold an arm, / Clothed in white samite, mystic,
wonderful, / That caught him by the hilt' " (1842: 11). Bedivere thus
comes to see and articulate the same mystic arm that Arthur first described, and Arthur, even as he is dying and his realm dispersed, manifests
leadership by extending his vision to others.

In "The Epic," Everard Hall, too, appears against the backdrop of a
dying tradition, the poetic tradition of epic and legendary materials that
seem out of place in the new order:

>   nature brings not back the Mastodon,
> (1842: 3)   Nor we those times; and why should any man
>   Remodel models rather than the life?
>   And these twelve books of mine (to speak the truth)

Were faint Homeric echoes, nothing worth,
Mere chaff and draff, much better burnt.

Hall, too, speaks amidst dispersal, the burning of his own work, from
which Francis Allen (like an unfaithful Bedivere) has rescued a fragment
that Hall then reads. Hall loses at least one follower among his audience—
the parson falls asleep—but he is so successful with the narrator of "The
Epic" that the latter sails with Arthur in dreams and witnesses his return in
the current age as a leader beloved of the people (1842: 17–18). With at least
one auditor, then, Everard Hall has succeeded, like Arthur with Bedivere,
in gaining adherence to his inner vision and so expanding it outward to
others; despite the larger loss of the epic, there is a triumph within the
smaller world of the frame poem.

It was left to Tennyson's Victorian readers of 1842 to validate or
rebuff his own hint of an Arthurian epic to come. While many responded
warmly to the poem, John Sterling's censure of the subject as remote and
lacking human interest effectively stopped the growth of the poem (Tillotson, "Tennyson" 88–89), and Tennyson "built" no more for another
seventeen years. The "Morte," however, had established a model of
leadership and planted the expectation of an epic to come in many minds.
The sequel clearly had to move backward in time, not forward. The end of
the realm had already been shown, yet only teasing hints were given of the
golden earlier days when knights walked "about the gardens and the halls /
Of Camelot" delighting their "souls with talk of knightly deeds" (1842: 5),
or when Arthur himself "shot thro' the lists" (1842: 14) in tourney.

In this respect Tennyson's adopting the epic convention of beginning
each idyll in medias res recapitulated the entire genesis of the *Idylls,* with
the end, or "Morte," coming first in 1842, and the preceding tales of
"Enid," "Vivien," "Elaine," and "Guinevere" appearing in 1859. By 1859
significant changes had occurred in both Tennyson's career and the British
nation. In 1842 Victoria had been on the throne five years, and she and
Albert were both only twenty-three. Tennyson was just emerging from
his ten years' silence and the sometimes hostile reviews of 1832, and his
followers tended to think of themselves as a coterie. Seventeen years later,
Victoria and Albert were forty, the throne and succession secure. Tennyson himself had become poet laureate of their court and a familiar presence
within the nation. He was no longer the favorite only of the cognoscenti
but a poet whose work received increasing recognition and whose audience and popularity were expanding. Both the expansionism of the
British throne and of Tennyson's reputation and powers were to play a role
in the reception of the 1859 volume.

There are, for example, unmistakable reflections of imperialism in some reviews: the 16 July 1859 *Athenaeum* praised Tennyson's depiction of a "true ideal" of chivalry, which it identified with "national honour and patriotism" (73); the September 1859 *Eclectic Review* deemed the *Idylls* a superior "offspring of Christianity and civilization" (289); Gladstone (writing anonymously) similarly pronounced in the October 1859 *Quarterly Review* that Tennyson's subject was "national: it is Christian . . . [and] though highly national, it is universal" (468); the April 1860 *Dublin University Magazine* (498–99) and September 1860 *Blackwood's* (337) both compared modern British soldiers in India or the Crimea to Arthurian knights. Yet if the *Idylls* are approached in light of what they have to say of leadership, they reflect far less saber rattling and far more extension of the treatment of Arthur's role in 1842.

Contemporary reviews suggest that the *Idylls* attained their popularity because they focused on love and because Tennyson's readers were so struck by the vividness of his characterization. Reviewers were also struck by the central role of Arthur himself. In addition to the numerous reviews that commented on the idealism embodied in Arthur and the vows he asks his knights to take, the 16 July 1859 *Examiner* remarked that in each idyll "the King incidentally appears, as an image of pure manhood" (452); in the August 1859 *North British Review* Coventry Patmore asserted that "The several pieces are connected . . . by the reappearance of the same characters, especially King Arthur himself, who constitutes the ideal standard of purity and honour and prowess, around which all else is grouped" (151). The 10 September 1859 *Times* applauded the obliqueness with which Arthur's character was revealed, remarking that although Arthur is never at the forefront of any idyll, his design for the realm pervades them all (5). The September 1859 *Eclectic Review* observed, similarly, that all the events of the poems hinge on the way different characters react to Arthur or are influenced by him, concluding that "There can be no more artistic mode of showing us the real form of a character than by exhibiting it as reflected through different media" (290). Gladstone, in the *Quarterly Review,* contended that Tennyson departed from Malory in making Arthur, rather than Lancelot, the focal figure (476–77); and *Sharpe's London Magazine* noted that while Arthur was not prominent in the first three idylls, he was always present as the standard of action: "In Arthur (in the glimpses we see of him), the supreme hero, to whose delineation all else is subservient, we have the ideal of the perfect man—no goddess-born partaker in superhuman divinity, but strictly human" (September 1859: 330).[23] The centrality of Arthur as unifying device, character, leader, and model differs from most twentieth-century assessments and suggests the usefulness of examining his role as leader in the 1859 installment.

The opening lines of "Enid" firmly establish Arthur at the center by making Geraint's identity dependent on the king's existence: "The brave Geraint [was] a knight of Arthur's court, / A tributary prince of Devon, one / Of that great Order of the Table Round" (1859: 1). As the tale moves back in time to relate the meeting and marrying of Geraint and Enid, Arthur's presence at the center of his people inaugurates the flashback:

(1859: 8)
> For Arthur on the Whitsuntide before
> Held court at old Caerleon upon Usk.
> There on a day, he sitting high in hall,
> Before him came a forester of Dean.

But as in "Morte d'Arthur," Arthur can extend his vision only to the degree that others acknowledge him as a center. In each of the four idylls, someone abandons the court (Geraint, Merlin, Lancelot, Guinevere), and most of the action takes place at the margins of Arthur's realm. The issue then becomes the degree to which the margin is an extension of the center or a free-floating domain without subordination or relation.

Geraint's first fault in fleeing Arthur's presence is that, doubting Enid's love, he is "Forgetful of his promise to the King" (1859: 3). He eventually renews his faith in Enid and the power of their love and, the domestic issue resolved, can actively exercise fealty to the king once more. At this point Arthur appropriately enters the scene, since the renewal of Geraint and Edyrn (formerly the renegade Sparrow Hawk) suggests the replication of Arthur's own renewal (evidenced in the movement from his death in 1842 to his resurgence in 1859). In these circumstances Arthur is equally viable at the center and the margin of his realm. He is shown, significantly, moving outward and extending the physical domain of his kingdom even as he has extended his ideals and experiences to his knights:

> But while Geraint lay healing of his hurt,
> The blameless King went forth and cast his eyes
> On whom his father Uther left in charge
> Long since, to guard the justice of the King:
>
>   · · · · ·
(1859: 95)
> He rooted out the slothful officer
> Or guilty, which for bribe had wink'd at wrong,
> And in their chairs set up a stronger race
> With hearts and hands, and sent a thousand men
> To till the wastes, and moving everywhere

Cleared the dark places and let in the law,
And broke the bandit holds and cleansed the land.

At the end of the poem Geraint again leaves court and goes to Devon, but he now goes, significantly, as an emissary or extension of Arthur ("there he kept the justice of the King" [1859: 96]) rather than fleeing from the court. And as Arthur appeared at the head of the idyll, so he figures in the end and literally has the last word, for we are told that Geraint "fell / Against the heathen of the Northern Sea / In battle, fighting for the blameless King" (1859: 97).

Of the next poem in the 1859 volume Gladstone asserted, "The achievement of Vivien bears directly on the state of Arthur by withdrawing his chief councillor—the brain, as Lancelot was the right arm, of his court" (479–80). Merlin, too, flees the court rather than extending Arthur's realm, yet unlike Geraint he acts, not on the basis of vague rumors, but of oppressive visions he endures from within court:

"O did you never lie upon the shore,
And watch the curl'd white of the coming wave
Glass'd in the slippery sand before it breaks?
Ev'n such a wave, but not so pleasurable,
(1859: 108)   Dark in the glass of some presageful mood,
Had I for three days seen, ready to fall.
And then I rose and fled from Arthur's court
To break the mood."

Vivien, who has caused Merlin's departure, deliberately praises and repeats the song Lancelot has sung in court and hence invokes the adulterous love that, in Tennyson's version of the legend, is so destructive:

"Unfaith in aught is want of faith in all.

"It is the little rift within the lute,
That by and by will make the music mute,
(1859: 113–   And ever widening slowly silence all.
14)
"The little rift within the lover's lute,
Or little pitted speck in garner'd fruit,
That rotting inward slowly moulders all."

The song also introduces a rival principle of expansion, a widening breach of loyalty that is to be accompanied by inward collapse.

The widening rift is evident in the next idyll, "Elaine," since it depicts the first direct disobedience of the king's vows: Lancelot and Guinevere are clearly lovers, and if Gawaine begins a quest at the king's command, he resents the order and leaves Elaine to carry out the mission. Arthur still retains a measure of his efficacy, however. If Guinevere repudiates Arthur as her lover and husband, she is, ironically, the first among the 1859 characters to articulate the principle of his rule, which suggests that she is sufficiently attuned to his vision to understand it correctly. She sees that his kingship depends on sharing his vision with others when she calls Arthur "Rapt in this fancy of his Table Round, / And swearing men to vows impossible, / To make them like himself" (1859: 154); she perceives as well that Arthur's proof of kingship is its reflection in the acts of others: "No keener hunter after glory breathes. / He loves it in his knights more than himself: / They prove to him his work" (1859: 155). Lancelot not only sees but also shares Arthur's vision; he cannot, however, make his acts consistent with what he sees, though he acknowledges Arthur as the center of the kingdom: "there lives / No greater leader" (1859: 162–64). Lancelot articulates the expansion of Arthur's realm when he relates the twelve wars Arthur waged against the pagans at Duglas, Bassa, Gurnion, Badon, and elsewhere. But the expansion he lauds is an expansion of the past, not the present, as in "Enid." Arthur can still hold the center, as seen in his presence on the throne at the Diamond Jousts (1859: 169–70), but the margins of his realm are increasingly fractious and dissonant with the center.

In "Guinevere" the center collapses: Guinevere flees the court, and when Arthur also abandons the center to wage war, first on Lancelot, then on Modred, the fragmented margins of the realm are all that are left. The one image of expansion is that of Guinevere's shadow on the land (1859: 229), which wreaks destruction as it extends outward—the end result of the "widening rift" begun earlier. The Round Table is now dispersed, and instead of expanding, the realm is subject to invasion and colonization: " 'For now the Heathen of the Northern Sea, / Lured by the crimes and frailties of the court, / Begin to slay the folk, and spoil the land' " (1859: 232). Yet as the realm disperses and shrinks, the articulation of Arthur's ideals actually grows, for Arthur for the first time identifies the vows previously alluded to but never explained.[24] As he states these vows, he speaks, appropriately, with a "Ghost's" voice (1859: 247), not simply because he is near death or articulates spiritual ideals but because these ideals are no longer embodied and hence exist only as ghostly rather than as living forms.

Arthur is at this point a shadow of himself as king, too, and this may explain why, ironically, Arthur is progressively evident in the 1859 installment as his influence wanes. Only present at rare intervals in the first two poems, he receives far greater attention in "Elaine" and utters his first— and only—extended monologue in "Guinevere." This feature of the 1859 *Idylls* is perhaps a structural device indicating Arthur's declining efficacy as a leader; as Guinevere points out in "Elaine," Arthur's proof of leadership is the reflection of his ideas and ideals in others. When a Geraint or Edyrn can extend the principles of Arthur's life, or when Merlin never doubts Arthur's leadership even if the mage succumbs to seduction, Arthur is little in evidence. When his vision is increasingly confined to himself, he becomes more visible since less able to extend his principle of rule outward through others who can represent him.

Certainly when Arthur speaks to Guinevere he identifies an expand- ing vision and realm as the key principles of his kingship. Looking back upon his early reign, he takes special pride in having been the "first of all the kings who drew / The knighthood-errant of this realm and all / The realms together under me, their Head" (1859: 249). And he reveals that each knight's vows began with the promise to share Arthur's vision: "I made them lay their hands in mine and swear / To reverence the King, as if he were / Their conscience, and their conscience as their King" (1859: 249). He has failed as a leader, however, in the domestic sphere, for he could not induce Guinevere to share his vision as well: "And all this throve until I wedded thee! / Believing, 'lo mine helpmate, one to feel / My purpose and rejoicing in my joy' " (1859: 250).[25] But as in "Morte d'Arthur," Arthur in his last extremity and defeat validates his leadership by inducing one who formerly resisted his vision to share it at last. Guinevere, after Arthur has left, also brings him back a word, his own words, just as Bedivere in 1842 finally duplicated Arthur's vision of the silk-clad arm brandishing Ex- calibur. Thus Guinevere exclaims, "Let no one dream but that he loves me still" (1859: 260), an echo of Arthur's own claim (1859: 254). As Gladstone remarked in the October 1859 *Quarterly Review,* "in the last speech of Guinevere, she echoes back, with other ideas and expressions, the senti- ment of Arthur's affection, which becomes in her mouth sublime" (478). Guinevere also acknowledges Arthur, belatedly, as a center ("My own true lord!" [1859: 257]) and as the realm's greatest leader: "now I see thee what thou art, / Thou art the highest and most human too, / Not Lancelot, nor another" (1859: 258). In this respect Arthur's story is, like the 1842 "Morte," one of triumph in the midst of defeat.

Though not as striking as it was to be in 1869, reaction to the immensely popular 1859 *Idylls* lauded Tennyson in terms that linked him to the king he celebrated. For both poet and king, expanding their realms of influence was essential, and Tennyson was praised for extending his skills, his audience, and in the future, it was hoped, the *Idylls* themselves. Essential to these responses was the sense of Tennyson's Arthurian poems as a serial work that grew over time. The September 1859 *Sharpe's London Magazine* made the most explicit link between conquering king and poet when it began its review observing that "It is understood, whether rightly or wrongly, that Mr. Tennyson has set to himself the task of writing the epic of the 'Table Round.' Undeterred by failures or successes of predecessors . . . this poet—so rumour says, and the tenor of the present volume would indicate—steadily advances into that mythic region, gaining upon and overtaking, one by one, the giant-phantoms which people it; and, by magic of human insight, transforming them into living men" (329–30). And both the September 1859 *Eclectic Review* and Gladstone in the October 1859 *Quarterly Review* saw the *Idylls* as a pinnacle for which Tennyson's earlier work had been preparation, the first noting "this latest work [as] the product of maturer years and wider sympathy" (294), and Gladstone assserting that "for this higher effort [Tennyson] has been gradually accumulating and preparing his resources" (465; see also 480).

Other reviews noted Tennyson's growing fame and increasing audience. The 31 July 1859 *Weekly Dispatch,* in fact, connected Tennyson's fame with a slow process of growth that would continue even after his death: "During the past twenty years the fame of Alfred Tennyson has grown and widened with an unfaltering steadiness which gives a sure promise of the 'All hail hereafter!' " (6). The August 1859 *Tait's Edinburgh Magazine* was among the minority of journals far less sure of the poem's merit than the *Weekly Dispatch,* but even its review began and ended by acknowledging Tennyson's popularity and foreseeing a growing audience for the *Idylls: "The Idylls of the King* is already the most popular volume of modern poetry, and it has not been more than three weeks among the booksellers"; "although it can hardly enhance the fame of its author, yet it will enlarge the circle of his readers" (464, 470). And insofar as Tennyson's poem helped further popularize and inform the public about Arthurian legend, it also became identified with Arthur himself. As the September 1860 *Blackwood's Edinburgh Magazine* noted, "The British king is more ubiquitous in his resuscitation than even in the days of his mortality" (311), and the journal called the revival of interest in the legend "one of the most remarkable resurrections in the history of fiction" (313).

Review after review, moreover, treated the 1859 poems as an installment promising future expansion into a finished poem. The 23 July 1859 *Spectator*'s anticipation is especially interesting in its equation of the method of the poem and of the Round Table itself: "when he has completed his work, the whole cycle of the Arthurian legends will come from his hands an image of the Round Table itself, no member of it made subordinate to another, but all equally free to assert their individual claims to honour for intrinsic worth" (764; cf. Pattison 149). Thus, Victorian response to the 1859 *Idylls* not only viewed Arthur in more positive and central terms than do late twentieth-century audiences but also often praised the poet laureate for the same principles of expansion and growth lauded in the mythic king.

Arthur himself pointed to a sequel—his rendezvous with Guinevere in heaven—near the close of the 1859 volume, and while that scenario must have seemed distantly echoed in the 1862 Dedication of the *Idylls* to Albert, who had died in 1861 and left a queen longing to be "at his side again," the actual sequel published in 1869 brought Arthur back to earth at the outset of his reign. The 22 December 1869 *Guardian* and 25 December 1869 *Illustrated London News* reflected a sense of renewal, of slow (serial) development, and of Tennyson's success since 1842 in extending his vision of Arthur to the British public; both reviewers noted the Christmastide appearance of the 1869 volume and imagined themselves amidst the crowd that had awaited the return of Arthur as a "modern gentleman" in the 1842 "Epic":

> *A large fraction of a long life has passed since Mr. Tennyson first gave the world that jewel of poetry, the "Morte d'Arthur," having previously set it in a frame of gold, and inscribed on the outer rim of the setting—*

(*Guardian* 1439)
> At this a hundred bells began to peal,
> That with the sound I woke, and heard indeed
> The clear church-bells ring in the Christmas-morn.

> *Christmas is just with us again; the new year is soon coming; and Mr. Tennyson has given us another volume of verse, in time to blend with the sweet music of the bells.*

(*Illustrated London News* 654)
> *We feel ourselves, as in the dream of one who then heard it ["our companion this quarter of a century past"] read aloud, waiting in a crowd of others—here in England, in the reign of Victoria—for the arrival of a bark that, blowing forward, bore King Arthur to our shore, not like a mailed knight of the Middle Ages, but rather*
> Like a modern gentleman
> Of stateliest port. . . .

Crowds now awaited the sixty-year-old laureate's poem, too. In "Our
London Letter," the 18 December 1869 *Leeds Mercury* reported that "Mr.
Tennyson's new poem seems to be everywhere. The rush for it at Mudie's
was almost unprecedented. . . . The orders for new copies are still pouring
in upon the publishers, and it is expected that forty thousand copies will
have been printed before the end of the year" (5). While the *Quarterly
Review* and *Academy* sounded the disparagement of overrefined verse that
was to become a hallmark of critical reaction to Tennyson among the
intelligentsia in coming decades, the great majority of reviews were as
enthusiastic as the patrons at Mudie's. And this glowing response, once
again, was to become a factor in the way the first audience understood the
1869 *Idylls.*

    "The Coming of Arthur" extended the realm of Arthur backward in
time and showed its genesis, one developed partly in terms of expansion
versus contraction and dispersal. The time prior to Arthur's coming was
characterized by warring factions and invasion:

> For many a petty king ere Arthur came
> Ruled in this isle, and ever waging war
> Each upon other, wasted all the land;
> And still from time to time the heathen host
(1870: 3–4)
> Swarm'd overseas, and harried what was left.
> And so there grew great tracts of wilderness,
> Wherein the beast was ever more and more,
> But man was less and less, till Arthur came.

Arthur's success is evident when he

>   drave
(1870: 6–7)
> The heathen, and he slew the beast, and fell'd
> The forest, and let in the sun, and made
> Broad pathways for the hunter and the knight.

—when, that is, he literally enlarged the kingdom.

    Arthur's other great act was to take what had formerly been separate
and haphazard and transform these into a larger whole:

> first Aurelius lived and fought and died,
> And after him King Uther fought and died,
(1870: 4)
> But either fail'd to make the kingdom one.
> And after these King Arthur for a space,
> And thro' the puissance of his Table Round,

> Drew all their petty princedoms under him,
> Their king and head, and made a realm, and reign'd.

This action could have had particular significance for the poem's first readers because Arthur effected among his dominions what the 1869 installment was perceived to have wrought upon the 1859 poems, transforming what had been loosely related individual poems into a larger, well-regulated, and masterful whole. This achievement was emphasized by the list facing the title page of *The Holy Grail and Other Poems,* which reassembled the 1859 and 1869 volumes in a new order (see figure 8) and ended with an assertion of overarching design: "This last, the earliest written of the poems, is here connected with the rest in accordance with an early project of the author's." The keynotes of both the poem and the poet were therefore expansion and order, a celebration of the governance of empire and of art. The laureate's "governance" was due to his introduction, noted by many in Tennyson's day and our own, of metaphysical and spiritual themes into the *Idylls,* the stronger identification of Arthur as a type of Christ or as the conscience or soul (with Guinevere representing the flesh), and the clear indication of cycles in lives and empires.

These elements are clear enough no matter in what time frame or order the *Idylls* are read, but the difference for serial readers was that the clinching of the carefully patterned design in the *Idylls* would have been evident in "The Coming of Arthur" rather than in later idylls. That is, because readers were already familiar, through the 1842 "Morte" and the 1859 idylls, with events at the end of Arthur's realm, the echoes of other parts came in the "first" instead of in later idylls. For twentieth-century readers of the completed poem, for example, the reference to Bedivere as "the first of all his knights" (1870: 11) is echoed and completed in "The Passing of Arthur," with the reference to Bedivere as "First made and latest left of all the knights" (1870: 131; see also 147). But for serial readers long familiar with the "Morte" and its reference to Bedivere as "the last of all his knights" (1842: 4), the echo and completion occurred in "The Coming of Arthur": the end point of a symbolic pattern came in the beginning. Thus, as Victorians first read of Arthur's founding and expansion of his realm, they were also witnessing the establishing and extension of Tennyson's aesthetic design (see also Staines 86). For them, design and order would be most apparent at the beginning of the realm, after which things then ran their course. As the 25 December 1869 *Spectator* observed, " 'The Coming of Arthur,' and the new opening of 'The Morte d'Arthur,' contain in some sense the key to the whole" (1531).

THESE four 'Idylls of the King' are printed in their present form for the convenience of those who possess the former volume.

The whole series should be read, and is to-day published, in the following order :—

THE COMING OF ARTHUR.

𝔗𝔥𝔢 ℜ𝔬𝔲𝔫𝔡 𝔗𝔞𝔟𝔩𝔢.

GERAINT AND ENID.
MERLIN AND VIVIEN.
LANCELOT AND ELAINE.
THE HOLY GRAIL.
PELLEAS AND ETTARRE.
GUINEVERE.

THE PASSING OF ARTHUR.*

* This last, the earliest written of the poems, is here connected with the rest in accordance with an early project of the author's.

Figure 8. Frontispiece of Tennyson's *Holy Grail and Other Poems* (1869) announcing Tennyson's design for integrating new idylls into older order. (*Department of Special Collections, Kenneth Spencer Research Library, University of Kansas*)

This analogue between king and serial poet underlies the numerous reviews hailing the growth of the poem and its design, which was often compared to the growth of a building, especially a Gothic cathedral. The 22 December 1869 *Guardian* was the first to connect the growth of the poem, the growth of its artistic design, and the growth of Arthur himself (though of course the last suffered an eventual decline): "Mr. Tennyson is to be heartily congratulated on having given so large a measure of unity to the intermittent work of many years. In the Arthurian poems, as they are now arranged, there is a genuine growth and development. The child passes into the man; the weird legend gains a meaning which did not at first belong to it; the knights that gather about the round table are scattered here and there by the force of an idea more definitely sacred than that which first formed their circle; the amour of Lancelot is a condition of the repentance of Guinevere; the last battle and the life of the King die away into a profound but hopeful mystery. To deal thus with the story of Arthur is not to remodel models, but to study from the inner life of thought and of man" (1439). The 25 December 1869 *Spectator* argued that, "To the present writer, at least, the Arthurian idylls have risen from a very exquisite series of cabinet pictures, into a great tragic epic, from this re-reading of the series in order" (1531); "The *morcellement* of the Arthurian poem, due to its slow and gradual growth, may have popularized, but has certainly hitherto disguised its unity and greatness, even from students of Tennyson" (1533). James T. Knowles, whose 1 January 1870 essay in the *Spectator* presented a full reading of the newly wrought poem's "parabolic drift," also compared its growth to that of Canterbury Cathedral and said that even as the poem had grown, so had its meaning: "Bit by bit the poem and its sacred purport have grown continually more and more connected and impressive" (16–17). The 8 January 1870 *Graphic,* similarly, thought that "these new Idylls are the completion of an edifice which, grand as it appeared to be in detachments, is now grander than ever," and termed "The Holy Grail" a poem "of the highest value, as crowning with a tall severe spire, that points heavenward, a structure which, nearer the level of the eye, is rich with all that is most beautiful in human story" (130). The 26 February 1870 *Chambers's Journal* also connected the poem's growth in extent and meaning: "with each successive portion brought before the world, new light has been continually thrown upon the meaning of the story" (138). And Dean Alford, writing in the January 1870 *Contemporary Review,* argued that the poem's mediate status between parts and a unified whole was one of its triumphs: "We seem to require, in these introspective days, a whole, composed of parts which can justify their own separate existence: and, casting off the artificial requirements of the epic, we ask no more than that those parts should be connected by a great central interest, and, by their common assumptions and allusions, should recognise and presuppose one another" (105).

While the 1869 poems modify some of the motifs of the 1859 poems, Arthur's central role and his extension of vision to others remain in place. Tennyson separated "The Coming of Arthur" and "The Passing of Arthur" from the "Round Table" section, suggesting that if Arthur is alone in his advent and death, he is submerged and sublimated in his Round Table while it is in effect, so that no inner idylls bear his name.[26] "The Coming of Arthur" in fact enlarges Arthur's point in "Guinevere" that the key to his kingship is the knights' sharing his vision. Bellicent tells Leodogran that Arthur's knights are "Few, but all brave, all of one mind with him" (1870: 16), and reports that at his coronation "I beheld / From eye to eye thro' all their Order flash / A momentary likeness of the King" (1870: 16–17). The

concluding lines of the idyll (see also Homans 697, Solimine 110–12) state
the significance of this sharing:

> And Arthur and his knighthood for a space
> Were all one will, and thro' that strength the King
> (1870: 29)   Drew in the petty princedoms under him
>
> . . . . .
>
> and made a realm and reign'd.

In the second of the 1869 idylls, "The Holy Grail," Ambrosius reveals
that Arthur still has power to impress his inner likeness upon his knights, if
less consistently than in the past:

> I knew [Percivale]
> For one of those who eat in Arthur's hall;
> (1870: 34)   For good ye are and bad, and like to coins,
> Some true, some light, but every one of you
> Stamp'd with the image of the King.

Early in the reign, when Arthur's power to extend his vision to others was
at its height, the grail did *not* come (1870: 38–39). Only when Arthur's
efficacy is compromised can the grail exert influence. Galahad and Percivale's sister, a nun, emerge as a kind of rival king and queen who
establish a rival vision mutually exclusive with Arthur's own (Homans
700, Gray 29), and which has the power to draw many knights away from
Arthur and undermine his realm. Thus, when the nun tells Galahad of the
grail, she declares that "thou shalt see what I have seen" (1870: 43), and the
result is that "he believed in her belief" (1870: 43). Galahad calls Arthur
"Sir," not "King Arthur" (1870: 51), because he *is* a rival. As rival leader,
Galahad also conquers pagans, and on the eve of his departure he is
likewise concerned to extend his vision to a single follower. Meeting
Percivale at a hermitage, Galahad declares, " 'hence I go; and one will
crown me king / Far in the spiritual city; and come thou, too, / For thou
shalt see the vision when I go' " (1870: 62); and Percival "grew / One with
him, to believe as he believed" (1870: 62). The effect of this rival vision is
evident in the contrasts between the realm at the start and at the close of the
grail episode. Early in the idyll Arthur's winged statue atop the highest
spire of Camelot announces his centrality to his people ("the people . . . /
Behold it, crying, 'We have still a king' " [1870: 48]). Later, Arthur's
knights have dispersed, only a tenth returning; one of the wings on
Arthur's statue has been "Half-wrench'd" (1870: 77) by the same storm
that served as dramatic backdrop for Galahad's glorious exit; and Arthur,

if enunciating his doctrine of centrality at the idyll's end (1870: 87–88), cannot win so much as understanding from the Percivale who has grown to share Galahad's vision: " 'So spake the king: I knew not all he meant' " (1870: 88).

"Pelleas and Ettarre," next in the 1869 volume, presents a knight who begins fully sharing Arthur's vision: "him his new-made knight / Worshipt, whose lightest whisper moved him more / Than all the ranged reasons of the world" (1870: 100; see also Fulweiler 156). But Pelleas's utter disillusionment by Ettarre, Gawaine, and others leads him at the end to reject all that Arthur stands for:

the king

(1870: 119)
Hath made us fools and liars. O noble vows!
O great and sane and simple race of brutes
That own no lust because they have no law!

As the 25 December 1869 *Spectator* remarked, "the gentle and wise king does not appear to bring back to the spirit of faith the maddened soul of the poor young knight" (1533). Pelleas comes from the margins of Arthur's realm, from the waste isles (1870: 96), and his story indicates Arthur's inability to extend outward his hold at the center in this late stage of the realm.

By "The Passing of Arthur," the last of the 1869 idylls, Arthur seems to himself to be "but King among the dead" (1870: 138). It is clear from earlier idylls why "The king who fights his people fights himself" (1870: 134), since " 'My house are rather they who sware my vows, / Yea, even while they brake them, own'd me king' " (1870: 139). But of course, as in the 1842 "Morte" from which the "Passing" was refashioned, Arthur achieves a victory amidst death and defeat in battle. The 1869 victory, however, expanded in scope. Here Arthur not only reasserts his kingship and extends his vision to Bedivere but is also accorded a triumphal entry into Avillion:

Then from the dawn it seem'd there came, but faint
As from beyond the limit of the world,

(1870: 157)
Like the last echo born of a great cry,
Sounds, as if some fair city were one voice
Around a king returning from his wars.

He is no mere "modern gentleman," as in the 1842 "Epic," but a victorious monarch; his rank and power, as well as his terms of victory, have increased. And of course the disappearance of the funeral barge amidst the resplendent dawn of the new year intensifies the promise of renewal and return.

As much as these new lines, however, the poem's publication process had already made cogent Bedivere's hope that " 'He passes to be king among the dead, / And after healing of his grievous wound / He comes again' " (1870: 156–57); Arthur had twice "died" (in 1842 and 1859) and had twice returned (in 1859 and 1869) to Victorian audiences in the triumphal work of the poet laureate. In this context the resounding optimism expressed in the 25 December 1869 *Saturday Review* is also made more cogent to late twentieth-century audiences: "In the 'Passing' of Arthur, who does not die, but goes to 'heal him of his grievous wound,' and who will come again, there lies the visioned assurance that the 'defeat of worth' which seems to meet us at every turn in the history of the world and of Christianity, and in the events of to-day, is no real defeat after all, nor the vanishing of old things a real and permanent disjunction; there is the guarantee of restitution and rediscovery in future of all that in the past was worthiest and best" (828).

One other effect of the 1869 idylls on the whole Arthuriad should be noted. The new order (see figure 8) increased the duration of the realm both because its beginnings were extended back into the past[27] (since events prior to Arthur's advent are alluded to), and because its demise was greatly retarded. The Round Table section began with the same first three idylls that opened the 1859 *Idylls*: "Enid," "Vivien," "Elaine," though the titles in 1869 were expanded to mention male characters as well. But now "Lancelot and Elaine" did not lead directly to "Guinevere"; into the gap between Lancelot's remorse and Guinevere's repentance were inserted the stories of the Holy Grail and of Pelleas and Ettarre, providing a new "late summer" before the fall. This sense of extended duration was evident in the April 1870 *St. James's Magazine,* which, after discussing "The Coming of Arthur," commented before turning to "The Holy Grail," "Long years of the knightly story passed away, already related in the tales of Enid's patience, Merlin's retributive fate, the funeral barge of the 'lily maid of Astolat' " (789). Yet if the two new inner idylls expanded the duration of the realm, they also expanded the "widening rift" caused by Lancelot and Guinevere's illicit love, the rotting process evident in the decimation of knighthood's ranks during the grail quest and Pelleas's process of disillusionment. Just as serial publication out of the sequence of the completed poem meant that virtually every detail in "The Coming of Arthur," "Geraint and Enid," or "The Holy Grail" could point backward and forward in time at once, so serial publication brought, simultaneously, a sense of increased plenitude and of increased deliquescence to the realm in the new idylls inserted into "The Round Table."

The immense popular and critical success of the 1869 idylls compli-cated the reception of the three remaining installments of the poem. The single biggest problem was that so many readers (as indicated in the reviews) considered the *Idylls* complete in 1869 and celebrated the strong aesthetic design they discerned. Any further augmentation of the poem meant that Tennyson risked competing with his own earlier achievement and disrupting what had quickly assumed a sense of settled order to his audience.

Tennyson's decision to publish "The Last Tournament" in the De-cember 1871 issue of *Contemporary Review* must have puzzled many. True, a note appended to the poem explained that "This poem forms one of the 'Idylls of the King.' Its place is between 'Pelleas' and 'Guinevere' " (1871: 1). And as in earlier installments, details in "The Last Tournament" pointed backwards and forwards. When Guinevere, watching Arthur leave court with his young knights, unconsciously sighs and recalls Mer-lin's rhyme—" 'Where is he who knows? / From the great deep to the great deep he goes' " (1871: 5)—readers could recall not only "The Com-ing of Arthur" or the young knights left after the grail quest but also, in "Guinevere," Arthur's leaving the court to see the queen at Almesbury and her own eventual recognition of him as true king. At least one review, moreover, noted that the story of Tristram and Iseult had been prepared for by the allusion to these lovers in the 1859 "Guinevere" (*Saturday Review* 9 December 1871: 754). Thus, as in 1869, individual lines could resonate backwards and forwards in the "finished" sequence of the *Idylls* and in the audience's reading history.

But "The Last Tournament" was the first poem since the "Morte" to be published by itself, and it must have seemed a kind of dark inversion of that poem. "The Last Tournament" was published, like the 1869 idylls, in the Christmas season, just as "The Epic," in 1842, depicted the "Morte" as being read during Christmastide. Both the 1842 and 1871 poems, more-over, deal with endings—of tournaments and of whole kingdoms. But if the "Morte" presents a story of triumph in failure, "The Last Tourna-ment" is about failure in triumph. Arthur succeeds in establishing safe passage in the north, hence in extending his realm once more, but his kingship fails utterly when his knights ignore orders—and their leader's vision—and massacre the Red Knight's followers. Because the poem appeared by itself, there was no counterweight to this idyll's grim pessimism. It is a dark poem published in a dark time of the year, with little hint of the "new sun" hailed at the end of the 1869 volume.

Tennyson's choice to publish "The Last Tournament" as a satellite cut adrift from the larger whole was at least appropriate to the poem's theme, the disappearance of Arthur from the center of the Round Table (Staines 99). Arthur himself is aware that fewer and fewer share his vision when even Lancelot resists his decisions: " 'The foot . . . loiters, bidden go,—the glance / . . . only seems half-loyal to command,— / A manner somewhat fall'n from reverence' " (1871: 4). Arthur's words may still compel Lancelot, but they do so as a haunting nightmare (1871: 5), not as a shared dream of order. In these circumstances it is not surprising that the Red Knight, a far more savage rival to the king than Galahad, has set up an opposing center in the north and has invaded Arthur's very court in the form of a mutilated peasant sent as emissary. As a result Arthur for the first time leaves the center while others stay, an oblique commentary on his dilemma of leadership, which is the problem of not being able to "take" others "with" him. He can no longer inspire Lancelot, Tristram, least of all the young knights, with his vision, but only the fool who remains in Camelot as the lone surviving type of the king. In his absence the rules of the tourney fall apart and Mark commits a vile murder. Arthur still has the ability, as in "Geraint and Enid," to venture out to the margins of his realm and to return, but now when Arthur returns to the center, the court has, except for one fool (Wilkenfeld 292–93), abandoned him:

> The great Queen's bower was dark
>
> . . . . .
>
(1871: 22)   and the voice about his feet
> Sent up an answer, sobbing, "I am thy fool,
> And I shall never make thee smile again."

Reviewers of the 1871 poem tended to ignore Arthur, however, and focus on Tristram and Iseult as a lesser Lancelot and Guinevere who prefigured the end to come. Several reviewers even expressed weariness with the continuing expansion of the poem. "Very few, we imagine, of Mr. Tennyson's sincere friends desire to see any more Arthurian idylls from his hand," announced the 9 December 1871 *Illustrated London News* (558). Such reviewers made it clear that one reason they disliked receiving "The Last Tournament" was that it disrupted their old sense of the Arthuriad without providing a coherent new view of the whole. As the 9 December 1871 *Saturday Review* noted, "It is perhaps unlucky for the first generation of readers that the order of publication has not coincided with the natural sequence of the poetic narrative. . . . A poem, although it may be produced in instalments, ought to be regarded as a whole" (754). And the *Illustrated London News* asserted that "The Last Tournament" "should never have appeared dissociated from the rest. Its significance depends entirely upon its position as a constituent of an organic whole. Isolated from its context, its suggestiveness is destroyed" (558). Most interesting is the response of the 13 December 1871 *Guardian*. It expressed concerns similar to the above reviews when it complained that "we see him marring the effect of his previous labours." It also derided the unrelieved pessimism of "The Last Tournament": "it is the province of poetry to nurse, rather than to destroy, wholesome and innocent illusion" (1484). But as so often happened in the course of the *Idylls'* publication, this review also connected the state of Arthur's realm with Tennyson's poetic "empire":

(1484)

Beginning the cycle of his Arthurian poems with some misgiving and hesitation, he gained fresh confidence, if not greater skill, as he proceeded. . . . Of late he has not been like a knight riding at dawn or dusk along doubtful ways, keeping his visor down and his lance in readiness, and singing in a cheerful but carefully sustained tone a goodly strain that might scare the fiends and encourage such of his friends as happened to hear him. His course has been an easy one, in the full light of day, through fields and groves; he has overcome his enemies, and the crowds that have met him from time to time have somewhat teased him with their noisy demonstrations of applause. He has consequently been a little off his guard, and has failed to bear himself in his old knightly fashion. Our metaphor will be no riddle to readers who turn from the poem which, for old association's sake, we will still call the Morte d'Arthur *to that* Last Tournament. *. . . in* The Last Tournament *we see too clearly that the manner and matter of the writer are alike of a lower order. Having already used the best parts of the tale of Arthur, he now falls back on some of the worst.*

The review concluded, "To use words which he employs more than once in his latest idyll, the glory of the Round Table is no more" (1484).[28]

After the images of sodden leaves, trampled faces, cloven skulls, bedraggled clothing, and mud-laden cups in "The Last Tournament," "Gareth and Lynette" (first published in 1872 along with the reprinted "Last Tournament") was an astonishing sequel, one of the most dramatic of Arthur's returns after the unrelieved darkness of the 1871 poem. And since "Gareth and Lynette" appeared with "The Last Tournament," the whole became a true installment, another cycle of return and fall, with the first poem (as in the 1869 installment) underscoring the theme of resurgence because it was a sequel and yet at the head of the new volume.

"Gareth and Lynette" also continued the theme of expansion even as it expanded Tennyson's *Idylls*. In the first half of the idyll, Gareth stays put within the domestic sphere, first at home, then in the kitchen. In the second half he moves out into new and unknown territories, achieving victory in the name of the king who remains at the realm's center (in pointed contrast to the king who left the center in 1871). Arthur's empire is expanding, too; he has cleared a safe passageway into the wild and pledges to make the kingdom equally safe at the margins and the center: " 'so my knighthood keep the vows they swore, / The wastest moorland of our realm shall be / Safe, damsel, as the centre of this hall' " (1872: 38). Insofar as Tennyson's poem expanded successfully from its previous state, it shared the traits of a secure empire that, complete already, can accept and integrate new satellites. Richard Holt Hutton supported this view in the December 1872 *Macmillan's Magazine:* " 'The Last Tournament,' and 'Gareth and Lynette,' which furnished respectively almost the last and first links in the chain, except the 'Passing' and 'Coming' of Arthur themselves, seem to me to have wrought up the poet's conceptions into a far completer expression, and to have put the final touches to a very great, though not quite perfect whole" (157–58).

The 1872 idyll also shed new light on the ruler at the center of the realm. Since this is set early in the kingdom, when Arthur successfully extends his vision to others, the king is seen relatively little. Still, when Gareth first approaches Camelot, he sees the outward signs of Arthur first ("all about a healthful people stept / As in the presence of a gracious king" [1872: 21]), and subsequently the king at the very center:

Then into hall Gareth ascending heard
A voice, the voice of Arthur, and beheld
Far over heads in that long-vaulted hall
The splendour of the presence of the King
Throned, and delivering doom.

(1872: 21–22)

As these lines indicate, this idyll presented a new element in Arthur's governance. Just as, for the first time, the idyll presented a full-blown and successful quest, so for the first time it showed Arthur actively administering his realm and handing down justice. As the 26 October 1872 *Spectator* observed, this was "the first idyll in which King Arthur's work is seen" (1363). Thirty years after his first introduction to the Victorian audience,

Arthur began to assume the mundane, day-to-day duties of a king. The idyll perhaps suggested that such actions had, all along, been going on out of sight, rather like the smooth running of government overseen by Plantagenet Palliser.

Serial publication, after "The Last Tournament," also gave added force to the rebirth imagery (phoenix, butterfly, rainbow, springtime, blooming boy emerging from Death) that pervades "Gareth and Lynette" and to a marked shift in tone hard to have imagined in December 1871. Even Arthur's subjects share in this renewal: Merlin, his prophetic and bardic powers at their height, greets Gareth outside the city gates; Tristam is as yet loyal to his vows (1872: 26); and Lancelot is still truly "the King's friend" (1872: 87). But the renewal above all suggests Arthur's renewal, both past and future. Insofar as Gareth is a type of Arthur (a point noted by the 26 October 1872 *Spectator* [1365]), his defeat of the knights calling themselves Morning, Noon, Night, and Death overcomes the linear sequence of time. This victory represents a principle embodied not only in Arthur's wondrous city gate (1872: 16) and in Arthur himself but also in the poem in which the theme first appeared. To the degree that Tennyson convinced readers that his powers and poem could spring back into life fully renewed with each additional idyll, the principle was also embodied in the laureate. Like the gates that seem to move before viewers' eyes and to intertwine new and old things until time becomes nothing, so the *Idylls* twisted and intertwined old and new poems and kept moving into new shapes of significance.

In contrast to the overwhelming critical applause in 1869, however, critical response in 1872 was mixed. If many were convinced by the renewal embodied in "Gareth and Lynette," many rejected it, though published responses may not have accurately gauged popular response (as they apparently did not with "The Last Tournament"). As the 3 November 1872 *Sunday Times,* itself a popular newspaper, contended,

(7)

> *Judging by the notices which have already appeared of Mr. Tennyson's new contribution to the Arthurian Legends, disappointment seems to be a feeling generally entertained. That this is so is a little strange. It is true that the journals of higher authority, so far as they have spoken, have bestowed serious criticism and praise upon the work, and that those journals which have derided or scoffed at it have belonged to the daily press, little given to concern itself with literary questions. It is hard, however, to think that any newspaper above the level of the professedly libellous, should reward with a sneer such services as the laureate has*

rendered to literature. . . . Whatever may be said by a few impetuous and unappreciative critics, the world is not tired of Arthurian Legends, and the later poems of Mr. Tennyson are not subjects for contempt.

As suggested by the *Sunday Times,* it appears that those who repudiated Tennyson's vision expressed weariness and boredom with Arthurian legend in general and the *Idylls* in particular. In addition, they often asserted the decline of Tennyson's poetic powers or sided with Swinburne's critique in *Under the Microscope.*[29]

When reviewers were receptive to Tennyson's Arthurian vision, they viewed the *Idylls* as the pinnacle of Tennyson's career, often associating the continuous growth of Camelot ("the city . . . built / To music" [1872: 19]) with art or empire, and the laureate with his king. The 26 October 1872 *Spectator* concluded its notice by asserting that "Gareth and Lynette" had not "been surpassed in beauty by any other" in Tennyson's "slowly completed epic" (1365); and it began by saying that "To his great Arthurian building Mr. Tennyson has added the porch last" (1363). The 2 November 1872 *Saturday Review* (though expressing some reservations about the new additions to the series) asserted, "The three paradoxes which puzzled Gareth are to the readers of the *Idyls* [sic] both intelligible and true. The whole world of Camelot and Arthur has up to this time been in building still, because it is built to a fine and creative music" (569). The 3 November 1872 *Sunday Times* argued that "The two poems included in his latest volume are entitled to stand beside what has gone before, and will form two fitting columns in the temple of the completed poem" (7). Richard Holt Hutton remarked in the December 1872 *Macmillan's Magazine* that Tennyson "himself has told us very finely in his newest poem, when describing the building of Arthur's great capital,—which, like Ilium, was rumoured to have been built to a divine music,—how the highest works of the human spirit are created" (143).[30]

The 30 October 1872 review in the *Guardian,* however, reflects more than any other the identifications (if not entirely reverent) that could be made between Arthur's efforts and Tennyson's own:

(1369)   *Mr. Tennyson, we are given to understand, has now completed his cycle of Arthurian legends. As Excaliber long since sank in the mere, so the peculiar pen that has told of the weapon and its wearer, whether made of steel like that which formed the trusty blade of the sword, or of gold . . . or of a goose-quill as noble in virtue of the service it has done as quill plucked from any full-breasted swan that has fluted its wild carol before dying, is, we must suppose, to be withdrawn by a magic hand from curious eyes, and sleep within the verge of a consecrated inkstand. A special interest therefore attaches to* Gareth and Lynette, *in one sense the last idyll, in another sense the second of the series.*

The association between Arthur and Tennyson was all the more striking because this praise for the poem was a resurgence of critical esteem after the journal's negative reaction to "The Last Tournament."

As Tennyson's poem expanded from its first center, the "Morte d'Arthur," Arthur remained the political and ideological center of the kingdom and of the poem's aesthetic design. But Tennyson's poetic sway over the British public was, like Arthur's reign, subject to decline as well as increase. If many continued to see in each installment of the *Idylls* an augmentation of the laureate's achievements or of the aesthetic power and design of the poem, others were listening to rival voices by the 1870s, and Tennyson's unquestioned command over his audience began to wane.

"To the Queen," first appearing in the six-volume Library Edition of 1873, has some truly imperialistic lines—the English are called "mightiest of all peoples under heaven" (1873: 6:298) and the colonies hailed for providing "boundless homes / For ever-broadening England" (1873: 6: 298). But the poem also addresses issues of governance and leadership less tainted by self-congratulation. Though "To the Queen" is usually cited for its gloss of the central theme of the *Idylls* ("Sense at war with Soul" [1873: 6:299]), it also places the *Idylls* firmly in the context of empire. It begins with yet another renewal and recovery, here of the Prince of Wales from serious illness, and so establishes, like the winged statue of Arthur in "The Holy Grail," that the people "have still a King." The prince's recovery not only assures England of a future through succession but also redresses the past loss of Albert to disease that would have been an implicit framework for Tennyson's readers and was the explicit frame (in the Dedication) of the *Idylls* themselves. Rather like the volume just published in 1872, "To the Queen" moves from renewal at the opening (as in "Gareth and Lynette") to a host of social ills and threats of dissolution at the close (as in "The Last Tournament"). The lines on the *Idylls'* shadowing of "Sense at war with Soul" lie in between the expression of hope and of doubt for the British realm, suggesting that the Arthuriad has a bearing on these issues of empire and leadership. The very end of "To the Queen" then modulated into a muted expression of hope for "our slowly-grown / And crown'd Republic" (1873: 6:300), a suitable close for an Arthuriad that had itself "slowly-grown."

Tennyson himself became a peer of the realm in 1883 and took a seat in the House of Lords in 1884. In 1885 this lord and laureate published the last of the *Idylls,* "Balin and Balan," which appeared in *Tiresias and Other Poems.* By now the poet who had published "Morte d'Arthur" at the age of thirty-three was seventy-six, yet the final idyll from a poet himself near the end of life was not about endings. In its content and its place in the *Idylls'* sequence "Balin and Balan" inhabits the realm of the middle. Though the last idyll published, "Balin and Balan" is termed "an introduction to Merlin and Vivien" in a footnote to the text (1885: 117). It is neither a beginning nor an end—just as each preceding installment might have seemed an ending to its first audience but was transformed into a middle by a succeeding part.

"Balin and Balan" commands interest today as a psychological drama, but insofar as the idyll is about leadership, it is about one who can see, validate, and share a leader's vision only so long as the follower is in the leader's immediate presence. Such a subject can thrive *at* the center but is doomed if he or she goes outward to the marge, a theme Conrad was to pursue with such power at the end of the century (see chapter six). At the idyll's outset, readers would have once again encountered embodiments of renewal: to Arthur "The light-wing'd spirit of his youth return'd" (1885: 118), and he set off in disguise to joust with Balin and Balan without anyone's knowing of his exploit (a benign version of the wood demon who rides invisibly later in the poem). That Arthur can so ride and return means he can as yet mediate between the center and the margin of his realm. As subject, moreover, Balin twice renews his ability to share the king's vision, when "he felt his being move / In music with his Order, and the King" (1885: 129).

But these instances of a secure center or of renewal are fragile. Lancelot may still try to assert the ideal of purity, represented by the lily he praises, but his sensual response to Guinevere is stronger. Dependent on external props of order, Balin cannot withstand the threats to order posed by Lancelot and Guinevere, and after witnessing their encounter in the flower walk Balin flees the court (like many in the 1859 idylls). First he flees to the court of a rival king, Pellam, whose court mirrors the same unnatural suppressions Balin has hitherto imposed on himself. When Balin's violence erupts, he flees again, and further from court he encounters the demon of the wood and Vivien, an indication that conditions at the margin of Arthur's realm are becoming more problematical. If the beginning of the idyll reflects a state of promise, the close suggests the potential for demise. Balan still has hope of future life and future encounters ("'Goodnight, true brother here! goodmorrow there!" [1885: 154]), as did Arthur in leaving Guinevere in 1859. But the two brothers die a needless and sordid death, and now Vivien is at large in the kingdom.

Balin's ultimate difficulty is his potential for disruption, his inability to be integrated into the Order. The last idyll could be said to have had the same problem. At worst, "Balin and Balan" was seen as having no relation to the *Idylls* at all. Tennyson had given a casual, even offhand introduction of "Balin and Balan" to the public, placing it after "The Spinster's Sweet-Arts" (a comic monologue in Lincolnshire dialect) and before the prologue to the "Charge of the Heavy Brigade" (addressed to General Hamley) in his new volume. T. H. S. Escott, in what must have been a hasty perusal of the volume, failed even to identify the poem with the *Idylls* when he reviewed for the 1 February 1886 *Fortnightly*: "Balin and Balan not only bears a structural resemblance to, but in more than one passage contains a distinct reminiscence of *Idyls* [sic] *of the King*" (271). The 12 December 1885 *Illustrated London News* at least gave "Balin and Balan" a place in the Arthuriad, but it rejected the relevance of the larger enterprise: "'Balin and Balan' . . . might have its place in that series, but the garb and cant of a fabulous chivalry, after all, cannot be made to fit the morality of the present age. English society in the nineteenth century will not sit and learn lessons at the fantastic Round Table, though a sincere teacher of Christian righteousness be poetical usher to the Royal presence" (600).

Only the 26 December 1885 *Athenaeum* and the April 1886 *Edinburgh Review* remained steadfast in loyalty and appreciation; both also insisted on the thorough integration of "Balin and Balan" into the larger *Idylls*. "Fused in the alembic of poetic genius," the *Edinburgh Review* argued, "the incoherent details that cluster round the Hero King assume a common meaning," and "The new book helps materially to fill up the outline of the Arthurian tragedy, and contributes directly to the final catastrophe" (495, 496). For this reviewer, the legends themselves remained relevant, the poem served as an expression of empire, and Tennyson's powers renewed themselves: "the 'Idylls of the King' are less remote from common interests, less local, and less partial than they at first sight appear. They are national and Christian poems. To the oppressed and dreamy Celt, Arthur was a secondary Saviour, and his mission, at once a retrospect and a future, appeals directly to religious sentiment. . . . Lord Tennyson does not, like the late Lord Lytton in 'King Arthur,' recall his characters to poetic life by a copious use of the supernatural, nor does he veil his figures in the dim transparency of the Spenserian allegory, but teaches living lessons by the universality of the humanity he portrays" (488).

Ultimately the Victorian reception of *Idylls of the King* defies any neat pattern; its issue lasted so long, and its emerging order was so quirky, that the poem remains a singular case among serial works. Still, it is possible to say that for those in sympathy with the poem, its growth over the years reinforced faith in an expanding realm based on a shared vision of value and aspiration. For these readers Arthur remained a compelling presence whose leadership drew its power from his residing at the center of an expanding kingdom that could draw independent satellites into a unified realm, and above all from Arthur's ability to inspire followers by extending his vision to them. Tennyson likewise retained his hold upon his audience by loyal readers' conviction that each new idyll extended the scope, power, and aesthetic structure of his Arthuriad through a vision of a king who at once served as a warning of dissolving empires and a hope of survival and renewal.

For all who read the poem, advocates or not, however, the work was bound up with Tennyson's own life story—and hence with the empire, its monarchs, its laureate, and one of its lords—in a way that was not true for any other serial work, not even Byron's *Don Juan*. This was partly because of Tennyson's prominence, partly because of readers' own experiences. A youth of twenty who read the "Morte d'Arthur" eagerly in 1842 would have been sixty-three when the *Idylls* assumed the form we know now. The poem was not just an artwork but an inextricable part of readers' own lives. As the 30 October 1872 *Guardian* remarked of what it thought a complete poem (thirteen years before its close), "A whole generation, perhaps, must wait before seeing, in its mellow perfection, the general effect of a poem that has been growing in a great mind for some forty years. We can no more really read it, as a whole, for the first time by a sudden effort than we can revive our first impressions of London by taking a cab, or a succession of cabs, and driving through street after street" (1370). Later generations have indeed seen the poem as a whole, but have not seen the warmth and hope embodied in Arthur that those who lived with his presence so many years did. For original audiences reading the parts in their published order rather than in the poem's finished form allowed Arthur to return again.

Tennyson's *Idylls of the King* as a serial poem explored with Victorians the possibility of reestablishing an empire once (or more) fallen in the past. Trollope's *The Prime Minister,* a serial novel, had approached the same subject more optimistically, picturing a system established and expanding in the fictional world even as the readers' own British way of life made new conquests in other lands. George Eliot's novel of empire, *Daniel Deronda,* published almost simultaneously (February to September 1876) with Trollope's (November 1875 to June 1876), accepted the same principle of a vision's spreading throughout a nation or people; but she retreated even further than Tennyson from endorsing the ideal of British imperialism celebrated in Trollope's fiction. Eliot's last completed novel is about the possibility of regaining a national unity and then offering its special virtues to others ("separateness with communication"). The leader of this potential empire, however, unlike Plantagenet Palliser or King Arthur, is seen only at the beginning of his career, never as a functioning head of a prosperous state.[31] With a mere handful of followers Daniel Deronda proposes to rebuild society in a future far beyond the end of the novel. For this story Eliot assumed an audience that, like Gwendolen Harleth desperately asking the hero for direction in her life, might just be beginning to realize it lacks a vision sufficient for the times. And, as Deronda directs Gwendolen, so Eliot leads her readers toward a new consciousness.[32]

Eliot paralleled Trollope and Tennyson by insisting that many years are necessary to produce someone who can influence the shape of society,[33] though she narrated only the initial stages of her central character's development in the eight months of the novel's publication. The author of the Palliser series took the large form of multiple novels and more than a decade to bring his hero to the office of prime minister; and Tennyson, of course, was forty years filling out the career of Arthur in Camelot. Still, a central feature of all three works is the slow emergence of a leader in society, matched by a literary audience's gradual recognition of his important characteristics.[34] The 13 February 1876 *Weekly Dispatch* commented on the value of the serial format in this regard at the publication of the first book. Pointing out that for volume readers "the first impulse" would probably be "to rush to the end to see what becomes of Gwendolen Harleth," this review insisted that serial readers better study "the gradual development of character" (6). Henry James, reviewing book 1 in the 24 February 1876 *Nation,* was also sensitive to the potential of an expansive installment format: "we must express our pleasure in the prospect of the intellectual luxury of taking up, month after month, the little clear-paged volumes of Daniel Deronda. . . . For almost a year to come the lives of appreciative readers will have a sort of literal extension into another multitudinous world" (362–63).

Just as the *Idylls* contained the antagonist to the just leader in Modred, and whereas *The Prime Minister* included a foil to the benevolent duke in Lopez, so *Deronda* presents a history of misuse of power in the character of Henleigh Mallinger Grandcourt.[35] Much discussed by critics from Eliot's time to our own, Grandcourt cast "an imperious spell" (April: 154) in his world through "long, narrow, impenetrable eyes" (April: 180). And since Gwendolen Harleth based her life on "winning empire" (February: 110), her relationship to Grandcourt becomes a battle described repeatedly in terms of "mastery" (May: 222), "power" (July: 285), and "will" (August: 122). Although Gwendolen predicted Grandcourt would become her "slave" (February: 167) and thus allow her to regain "a sort of empire over her own life" (April: 163) after the family's loss of fortune, she soon had trouble even "governing herself" (May: 231), whereas "Grandcourt within his own sphere of interest showed some of the qualities which have entered into triumphal diplomacy of the widest continental sort" (July: 337). In the end he leads her "captive" (August: 106) with a spirit of "domination" (August: 121).

On the other hand, the true leader Daniel Deronda, like Arthur in his many appearances in separate idylls over the decades, is meant to grow gradually in the audience's understanding as the representation of Europe's genuine hope for the future. Like Palliser's, Deronda's leadership begins with a tolerance of many viewpoints, which ultimately suggests some form of coalition, where many sides turn their unique gifts toward a collective government. We can trace this hero's development toward a future leadership through the eight books and months of Eliot's fiction: in book 1 (February 1876) Deronda appears briefly as an English gentleman at a cosmopolitan European gambling spot; his youth and education as the apparent illegitimate son of Sir Hugo Mallinger are narrated in book 2 (March 1876), to the point where he rescues a suicidal young Jewish woman from the Thames; in book 3 (April 1876), affected by Mirah's story, Deronda reviews his own life and values; still in the service of Sir Hugo, he moves closer to an understanding of Judaism in book 4 (May 1876); Deronda accepts new responsibilities in book 5 (June 1876), directing Gwendolen in her troubles and responding to the longings of the Jewish philosopher Mordecai; book 6 (July 1876) has Deronda more closely tied to Mordecai, now recognized as Mirah's brother and as a man with a profound mission; learning his parentage in book 7 (August 1876), Deronda contemplates a new destiny, which is an outgrowth of his individual character and his historical circumstances; and in book 8 (September 1876) the hero embraces his role as a leader for the future. This eight-month movement toward the stature of potential leader represents a gradual development in stages familiar to Victorian audiences; both the form of his development and the ideas that he articulates embody Eliot's vision of empire.

We can also see in the same months of 1876 the author's growing influence over her audience. Her choosing twin strands of narrative and different fictional landscapes was an analogue to Deronda's tolerance for other experiences, different stories.[36] The slow pace of the story's unfolding fit expectations in many cases, as the 4 March 1876 *Examiner* revealed in a review of book 2, stating that an advantage of serialization is "the ample time thus afforded for the study and free social discussion of the characters, for speculation as to their unrevealed past and their unreached future" (265). As Eliot moves her English story and its characters more and more into the world of Judaism, however, even to the point where the Christian hero appears ready to abandon his heritage, her empire of readers diminished with the appearance of the final two books of *Daniel Deronda*. However, since that setback, George Eliot's last novel has gained rather than lost support in the literary canon of England. As with Trollope in *The Prime Minister,* we can best understand Eliot's use of a serial structure after we have examined her character Deronda as a representation of leadership in Victorian terms.

One important element of Eliot's thought frames Deronda's developing ability as leader throughout the entire novel: the belief that ideas shape action in the world, and perhaps even shape the world itself.[37] Eliot's epigraph, "Let thy chief terror be of thine own soul" (printed facing the title page of each monthly installment), announced that her subject was the emotional and spiritual life. Further, the novel begins, not with a description of physical reality in time and place, but with a representation of thoughts in the mind of the central character, asserting from the outset that this is a novel about ideas: "Was she beautiful or not beautiful? . . . She who raised these questions in Daniel Deronda's mind was occupied in gambling" (February: 3–4).[38] What he thinks seems to alter Gwendolen's behavior and her world, undermining her superficial idea of an imperial destiny represented in the coins she holds: "Deronda's gaze seemed to have acted as an evil eye. . . . she had been winning ever since she took to roulette with a few napoleons at command" (February: 9). The power Deronda later assumes in her thoughts as a guide and counselor derives from a set of ideas rather than his physical being. Deronda himself says "generally in all deep affections the objects are a mixture—half persons and half ideas" (June: 31). Thus, Deronda's career is largely a product of his ideas.

The ideas of Deronda's class in England, particularly those about empire, are often shown as superficial in the novel; and a central feature of the hero's development is to move beyond them to a more accurate and enduring vision.[39] Gwendolen Harleth, for instance, "had no notion how her maternal grandfather got the fortune inherited by his two daughters; but he had been a West Indian—which seemed to exclude further question" (February: 34). Warham Gascoigne has a vague notion that "the welfare of our Indian Empire [was] somehow connected with a quotable knowledge of Browne's Pastorals" (February: 96–97). Eliot dismisses talk about "the rinderpest and Jamaica" (May: 232) among the British middle and upper classes as "polite pea-shooting" (May: 233), no one having a genuine knowledge of other nationalities or political events outside England. Serious threats to the empire, like the rise of Germany under Bismarck, do lie behind the action of the novel, as Barbara Hardy reminds us ("Notes" 887–88),[40] making British confidence in their system less substantial than in the past. Eliot's carefully ironic description of Grandcourt and Gwendolen in Genoa reveals the gap between a Victorian ideal of empire and the current reality: "This handsome, fair-skinned English couple manifesting the usual eccentricity of their nation, both of them proud, pale, and calm, without a smile on their faces, moving like creatures who were fulfilling a supernatural destiny—:it was a thing to go out and see, a thing to paint" (August: 123).

Such grand, satisfying figures as Grandcourt and Gwendolen, rather than the title character and future leader Deronda, won the interest of Victorian readers at the time of the novel's serial publication. It took, in fact, some months for the weaknesses in these characters to be fully realized by Eliot's readers and for interest to settle on the more important figures of Deronda, Mirah, and Mordecai. Deronda, for instance, is little discussed in reviews of book 1 (February 1876), in part, of course, because he appears so little. The 29 January 1876 *Spectator* noted in a section entitled "Topics of the Day" that "no young lady with a flesh and blood existence is likely to be half as much discussed in English drawing rooms for the next eight months as [Gwendolen Harleth] is" (138). This heroine, continued the review, will perhaps "eclipse Daniel Deronda himself in the interest she excites" (138). The 20 February 1876 *Sunday Times* stated simply, "As yet, the hero is scarcely seen" (7). The 13 February 1876 *News of the World* also admitted that Deronda "is only shown to us for a moment" (6). Perhaps most intriguing are the *Guardian*'s speculations about the novel on 2 February 1876: "Why call the book *Daniel Deronda*? . . . That [gambling incident] is all we hear about him for the present: if we want to know anything more, we are reduced to guessing at the meaning of the odd-looking name. *Deronda* is an obvious anagram of *adorned*. Will that suggest to any ingenious reader a clue to the story in which he is to figure? Is he merely to be an Admirable Crichton? Or is the 'n' redundant, or intentionally misleading, and must we suppose that he is to be *adored* by the wilful Gwendolen?" (154).[41] That this prediction was fairly accurate, and that the journal was willing to reveal the degree of its speculation about the novel's future, underscores how thoroughly Victorian society engaged its serial texts from the first month of publication to the last.

Not only Gwendolen, but even less important characters in book 1 attracted Eliot's readers more than the apparent hero. The same review in the *Guardian,* for instance, found Mr. Gascoigne to be "excellently drawn" (153), demonstrating "sound practical sense and clear judgment" (154); the magazine then quoted several passages about him, perhaps because he was a familiar character of Victorian fiction and also because he probably represented someone who would enjoy Eliot's fiction.[42] The 13 February 1876 *News of the World* also revealed this general interest in the Gascoignes, "of stronger character than [Gwen's] mother" (6). This weekly seemed to express a romantic expectation of the audience when it argued that Gwen "rejects the suit of 'Rex' with a violence that seems to show that he has made some impression on her" (6). This desire for a happy romantic resolution was inspired in part by Eliot's own careful prose: she encouraged "that futile sort of wishing . . . —if only these two beautiful young creatures could have pledged themselves to each other then and there, and never through life have swerved from that pledge!" (99).

The hope running throughout the novel's publication that Rex and Gwen would finally come together, coupled with the appeal of the Gascoigne family for the Victorian audience, suggests that Eliot knew well what needed to be included in her first volume of a new novel to secure her readership.[43] Rex, in fact, represents a standard version of future bureaucrat in the empire, as his sister's excited description to Gwen suggests: "He is so clever, and such a dear old thing, and he will act Napoleon looking over the sea. He looks just like Napoleon. Rex can do anything" (February: 93). Of course, like others in his set, Rex has little real understanding of the larger world. When he is rejected by Gwen, he tells his father, "I will go to Canada, or somewhere of that sort"; but the narrator notes that "Rex had not studied the character of our colonial possessions"

(February: 150). With such familiar figures satisfying readers, Eliot's popularity did not suffer in these first numbers.[44] The 20 February 1876 *Sunday Times,* for instance, after acknowledging that the first book had been criticized for its sensationalism (even using the term *outcry*), stated: "There is nothing, however, in the portion yet written to denote any falling-off in strength of style, in descriptive power, in perception, or in characterization, from the masterpieces which have taken up permanent rank in our literature" (7). Similarly, the 5 February 1876 *Bell's Weekly Messenger* stated that "each and all will be eager to receive what is to follow" (6). The popularity of *Deronda,* in fact, as reflected in serial reviews, remained high until the final two books in August and September 1876.

Some reviews in the weeklies of *Deronda's* book 2 were almost glowing, particularly in discussing the central character. The 15 March 1876 *Guardian,* for instance, stated emphatically, "The redeeming feature of the book is, however, to be found in Deronda. It is a great satisfaction to discover that we are to be allowed one character at least whom it is possible to like and admire. Deronda is a youth, splendid in body and mind, full of amiable impulse and utterly self-forgetting" (357). Similar enthusiasm was shown by the 19 March 1876 *Sunday Times:* "The character of the hero is admirably painted" (7); and the 4 March 1876 *Examiner* added: "Deronda himself, a chivalrous high-souled dreamy youth, educated as an English gentleman but devoid of the practical energy of the race, is a fine character, and sure to prove interesting" (265).[45] Although it is hard to determine exactly what in Deronda's character appealed most to these Eliot readers, he is linked in the text of book 2 to several important leaders. He tells his tutor before he goes to Cambridge, "I don't want to be a Porson or a Leibnitz, . . . I would rather be a greater leader, like Pericles or Washington" (March: 314–15). Sir Hugo later teases Deronda by asking him if he plans to challenge Grandcourt for Gwendolen: "The best horse will win in spite of pedigree, my boy. You remember Napoleon's *mot—Je suit un ancêtre*" (March: 296). With his uncertainty about his parentage, however, Deronda does not wish at this point to be a public figure, to be a singer and "take the house by storm" (March: 306), for instance, as his guardian suggests at another moment.

Deronda may be compared to such figures as Napoleon and Washington, but he is also distinguished from another imperial figure; he is said to be "unlike the great Clive," who established the British Empire in India (March: 324). Deronda is characterized by "a subdued fervour of sympathy, an activity of imagination on behalf of others" (March: 323) that inspires a respect and restraint also characteristic of Trollope's Palliser. Deronda tells Sir Hugo that he wants "to get rid of a merely English attitude in studies" (March: 334), a comment that distinguishes him from characters like the Gascoignes and that also put off some readers (see George Saintsbury in the 9 September 1876 *Academy* [253–54]). Eliot goes on to insist that it was "a mistake, however, to suppose that Deronda had not his share of ambition" (March: 324).[46] She is taking pains to define for her audience new qualities of leadership: "Certainly Deronda's ambition even in his spring-time, lay exceptionally aloof from conspicuous, vulgar triumph, and from other ugly forms of boyish energy; perhaps because he was early impassioned by ideas, and burned his fire on those heights" (March: 325). Interestingly, Deronda early rejected an army career, but also "set himself against authorship—a vocation which is understood to turn foolish thinking into funds" (March: 337). Throughout the first half of *Daniel Deronda,* in fact, the hero is one whose capacity to lead awaits the appropriate situation for action.

The appeal of this rather unconventional hero, then, when added to the more evident interest in Gwendolen's developing story, allowed Eliot's popularity to continue with book 2 through March 1876.[47] Reviewing books 1 and 2 in April 1876, the *New Quarterly Magazine* termed the work so far the "first and second acts of a great tragedy" (270) that "promises to equal or surpass any of her previous works" (273). This review found that the novel to this point demonstrated the author's social responsibility to enlarge her audience, to build an empire of readers: an artist's "first duty . . . is to be widely popular. To be influential she must appeal, not alone to persons of strong thought and fine taste, but to those also who are little endowed with thinking power and not at all with taste. . . . George Eliot knows her public, and what captivates it" (275). One character who did not excite much interest in reviews of book 2 is Mirah. The 19 March 1876 *Sunday Times* did admit that "the rescue of the Jewess, with all its attendant circumstances, is thoroughly moving" (7) but did not attach much importance to Mirah herself. The 15 March 1876 *Guardian* also mentioned only briefly the hero's attentions to "an attractive young Jewess from Prague" (357).[48] Not surprisingly, then, the English elements of Eliot's story generated its first appeal for readers.

The novel's readership remained faithful through the next several books, watching with interest the ongoing stories of the central characters. *Bell's Weekly Messenger* termed *Deronda* on 3 April 1876 "by far the most clever specimen of the author's powers, that she has ever given to the world" (6). The 1 April 1876 *Examiner* agreed, calling book 3 the best of

Deronda so far, "perhaps superior in interest and in workmanship, to anything that the authoress has ever written" (381). Such reviews generally gave most space to the courtship of Grandcourt and Gwendolen. The 23 April 1876 *Sunday Times* assumed closer links would soon be formed between the figures they thought of as heroine and hero: "As yet, the relations of Gwendolen Harleth to Daniel Deronda are scarcely hinted" (7). Mirah's story was referred to frequently, but sometimes condescendingly, as in the same *Sunday Times* review: "Skillful treatment was required to bring the Jewess to the point of attempted suicide, and preserve our faith in her purity" (7). Deronda's capacity for leadership continued to evolve slowly in book 3, marked more by a set of ideas than as a specific course of action: "Something in his own experience caused Mirah's search after her mother to lay hold with peculiar force on his imagination" (April: 4); his interest in Judaism is thus inspired.

In book 4, "Gwendolen Gets Her Choice" (May 1876), Deronda and Mirah naturally form secondary lines to the main plot, which sustained the readers' interest. The 6 May 1876 *Bell's Weekly Messenger* said: "This fourth part of George Eliot's newest and most absorbing creation is the best of all that have preceded it" (6). And the 14 May 1876 *Sunday Times* agreed, calling book 4 "the most interesting installment of the novel yet given" (7). Some reviewers were puzzled that the novel seemed now to be going in a direction they had not anticipated. The 14 May 1876 *Sunday Times* explained: "We are far, however, from guessing what are to be the relations between Daniel Deronda, who is obviously the author's favorite, and Gwendolen. That something is to come of their intercourse may fairly be inferred, since George Eliot is not the writer to bring two characters into so close accord for the mere purpose of separating them again" (7). Here Eliot's plan (a connection between British and Jewish cultures) began to stretch her audience's conventional expectations (marriage of traditional romantic hero and heroine).

The Jewish parts of book 4 were noted, even praised in many reviews; but they were consistently seen as unconnected to what was considered the main, that is the English, story. *Bell's Weekly Messenger* on 6 May 1876 commented on Mirah and the Cohens after discussing what this reviewer considered an unattractive marriage between Grandcourt and Gwendolen: "The remaining features of the Book are transferred exclusively to the search after the relatives of the Jewish girl by Deronda, and are so charming and winning in their characteristics that they tend most considerably to remove very much of that disagreeable feeling, which the former portion can but produce" (6). The 14 May 1876 *Sunday Times* suggested that this part of the novel was interesting, but surely unrelated in the end to Deronda and the other major characters: "He makes some curious acquaintances, and witnesses some of those ceremonies of Jewish domestic worship which seldom fail to prove impressive when first seen, and of which a minutely faithful account is given. There are few who have beheld the interior of Jewish households in which the observances of the Hebrew religion are maintained, without feeling a sense of that impressiveness which the words of the novel so well convey" (7). In other words, this reader does not object to the subject of Jews in Victorian fiction; but such people are seen more as "curiosities" than as vital parts of British national life.

In book 4 Deronda's potential for leadership began to be more clearly established for Victorian serial readers. Helping Sir Hugo research "an after-dinner speech on a burning topic" (May: 330), Deronda demonstrates rhetorical and intellectual skills that suggest a political future. Mallinger says, "If you would seize an occasion of this sort to make an impression, you might be in Parliament in no time" (May: 331); and then he uses exactly the logic Trollope had in describing Palliser's call to high government office: "The business of the country must be done—her Majesty's Government carried on, as the Old Duke said" (May: 331). Deronda, however, has not been inspired to action by his British education (which he terms "borrowed opinions" [May: 331]), and he awaits some stimulus to direct his energy and desire: "what he most longed for was either some external event, or some inward light, that would urge him into a definite line of action, and compress his wandering energy" (May: 295). His restraint resembles Palliser's in *The Prime Minister* as he tells Sir Hugo, "if I were to set up for a public man I might mistake my own success for public expediency" (May: 332).

Both novel and hero maintained a solid popularity with reviewers of book 5, "Mordecai" (June 1876).[49] The 18 June 1876 *Sunday Times* stated that *Deronda* "remains the most masterly product of its author's pen" (7); and the 21 June 1876 *Guardian* added: "The interest of *Daniel Deronda* has grown considerably in the last two books" (825). As with the early parts the main interest was Gwendolen's story, within which readers continued to place Deronda. The *Sunday Times* credited Eliot with describing "the conditions that gradually bring the heroine and Daniel Deronda into closer contact" (7). Other journals noted a change in the hero's role; the 3 June 1876 *Examiner,* for example, stated that Deronda is "more prominent in this than in any of the preceding books" (632). The hero's new stature might be traced to the key scene in which Deronda accepts the role of leader for one individual, Gwendolen Grandcourt.[50]

Throughout the first half of the novel, Deronda had influenced Gwendolen primarily as an idea: "whatever I do before him," she tells Sir Hugo, "I am afraid he will cast an evil eye upon it" (June: 15). However, Deronda has kept his distance from Gwendolen, and, though more aware of her troubles as Grandcourt's wife, he thinks to himself, "I can't do anything to help her" (June: 23). But as the narrator reminds us, "Those who trust us educate us"; and Gwendolen's need will bring Deronda to action, to a more committed self: "in that ideal consecration of Gwendolen's, some education was being prepared for Deronda" (June: 57). With a following of exactly one, then, Deronda begins his career of leader at almost the exact same point—early in book 5—that Palliser explained to Glencora, "there is nothing to be done," and thus articulated his policy of leadership.

At the abbey Gwendolen appeals for Deronda's help: "You must tell me then what to think and what to do; else why did you not let me go on doing as I liked, and not minding?" (June: 85). Inspired by his own situation as well as hers, he responds with "unconscious fervour" (86), finding himself taking action as he directs her. She asks again, "Then tell what better I can do" (86); and in response he articulates a philosophy that will later animate his larger political role as potential Jewish leader: "Look on other lives besides your own. See what their troubles are, and how they are borne. Try to care about something in this vast world besides the gratification of small selfish desires" (86).[51] As Gwendolen takes his words to heart—words she will repeat at key moments in her subsequent life— she resembles one of Arthur's knights who has accepted the king's vision of chivalry.

This more involved character—a Deronda who, "offering her his arm," asks an unhappy Gwendolen, "Shall I lead you back?" (June: 87)— thus presented to Victorian serial readers a more decisive, forceful figure as hero in the novel's book 5. Several reviewers were particularly sensitive to Deronda's unusual style of leadership, guiding others discreetly and indirectly, as Palliser had in Trollope's fiction. R. E. Francillon in the October 1876 *Gentleman's Magazine,* for instance, noted that Deronda "justly gives his name to the novel in so far as he, if not the principal actor in any drama, is a moving influence in three dramas which are very subtly and indirectly connected—the stories of Gwendolen, of Mirah, and Mordecai" (quoted in Carroll 391). Similarly, the 16 September 1876 *Saturday*

Review argued: "Deronda does nothing, but he has a curious influence. . . . what is wanting in himself Deronda yet seems to supply to others" (357). Deronda also resembles here Arthur in the 1859 and 1869 *Idylls,* where the king's presence inspires others to just action.

The first step in Gwendolen's moral education inspired by this emerging hero certainly pleased Eliot's readers, familiar with similar situations in *Middlemarch* and earlier novels; and the scenes between heroine and hero contributed to the novel's continuing popularity in June 1876. However, many readers found Deronda's increasing involvement with Jewish characters in book 5 somewhat ominous. The 21 June 1876 *Guardian* commented: "Deronda himself comes more to the front, and he is altogether a very amiable and accomplished and pleasant young man; but he hardly comes up to the force and substance and reality of nature which we have been accustomed to expect in George Eliot's heroes. A new element, however, has been thrown into the story by the Jewish family with whom his search after Mirah's family involves him" (825). The 18 June 1876 *Sunday Times* found the most prominent Jewish character, Mordecai, "mysterious" and stated: "It is quite impossible to surmise what will come of the intimacy between him and the hero" (7).

Even more threatening to middle-class readers was the potential romantic link between Deronda and Mirah. The 3 June 1876 *Examiner* noted: "In the next book we are promised 'Revelations,' which are generally expected to materially alter Deronda's relations with the mysterious Mira [*sic*]" (632–33). The 21 June 1876 *Guardian* expressed greater apprehension and concluded: "it becomes increasingly obvious that Deronda's mysterious birth is in some way bound up with a Jewish origin, and, therefore, bringing him into close kindred with Mirah" (825). The prospect of Deronda's marriage to Mirah, in fact—clearly foreseen in book 7 and achieved in book 8—seems the greatest single blow to the novel's popularity.[52] The 3 June 1876 *Examiner* identified the feature that Eliot no doubt hoped would encourage her audience's acceptance of Deronda as a Jew and as suitor to Mirah. That paper linked novel reading to the hero's central characteristic: "[Receptivity] is the faculty most to be desired by readers of novels that appear in installments. The opposite and more common faculty, that of 'supercilious prejudgment,' cannot be exercised without risk in the case of a half-finished story" (632). Despite Eliot's efforts through the installment format to reduce "supercilious prejudgment," a significant number of readers were unable to accept the conclusion toward which she was moving in books 6 and 7.

The novel moved slowly after book 5 toward establishing Deronda's

Jewish identity and toward his realization of his love for Mirah. Although book 6 (July 1876) was called "Revelations" (see figure 9), the discoveries that would explain fully Deronda's history were delayed until the novel's final two books. Only at the very end of book 6 does the hero learn that his mother is still alive; and her story of his roots will not be told until the next installment. From Mordecai, however, Deronda hears a Jewish political philosophy consistent with Victorian notions of empire.[53] That is, Mordecai believes in a vision's expanding in space and time through many people: "I believe in a growth, a passage, and a new unfolding of life whereof the seed is more perfect, more charged with the elements that are pregnant with diviner form. The life of a people grows, it is knit together and yet expanded, in joy and sorrow, in thought and action; it absorbs the thought of other nations into its own forms, and gives back the thought as new wealth to the world; it is a power and an organ in the great body of nations" (July: 231). Such descriptions of development, of course, could also apply to works of serial literature, which in origin, growth, and completion are analogues in Victorian terms to nations. Another effect, however, of Mordecai's Zionism is to diminish England's distinctive place among nations: "Let the reason of Israel disclose itself in a great outward deed, and let there be another great migration, another choosing of Israel to be a nationality whose members may still stretch to the ends of the earth, even as the sons of England and Germany, whom enterprise carries afar, but who still have a national hearth and a tribunal of national opinion. Will any say 'It cannot be?' " (July: 250). This blurring of England's special place among nations and in history was unlikely to please all of Eliot's readers.

Deronda remains in book 6 sympathetic to, but not completely identified with, Mordecai's philosophy, telling his new friend, "Everything I can in conscience do to make your life effective I will do" (July: 257). Readers, however, could still continue to view the Jewish portions of the novel as secondary to the English narrative centered on Gwendolen. Deronda, in fact, feels himself pulled in two opposite directions: "on the one side the grasp of Mordecai's dying hand on him, with all the ideals and prospects it aroused; on the other this fair creature in silk and gems [Gwendolen], with her hidden wound and her self-dread, making a trustful effort to lean and find herself sustained" (July: 301). Eliot's readers could project at this point a future for Deronda either as Mordecai's disciple working abroad toward the establishment of a Jewish national center or as an emerging political figure making a place for himself in English society and within his country's government. At the "Hand and

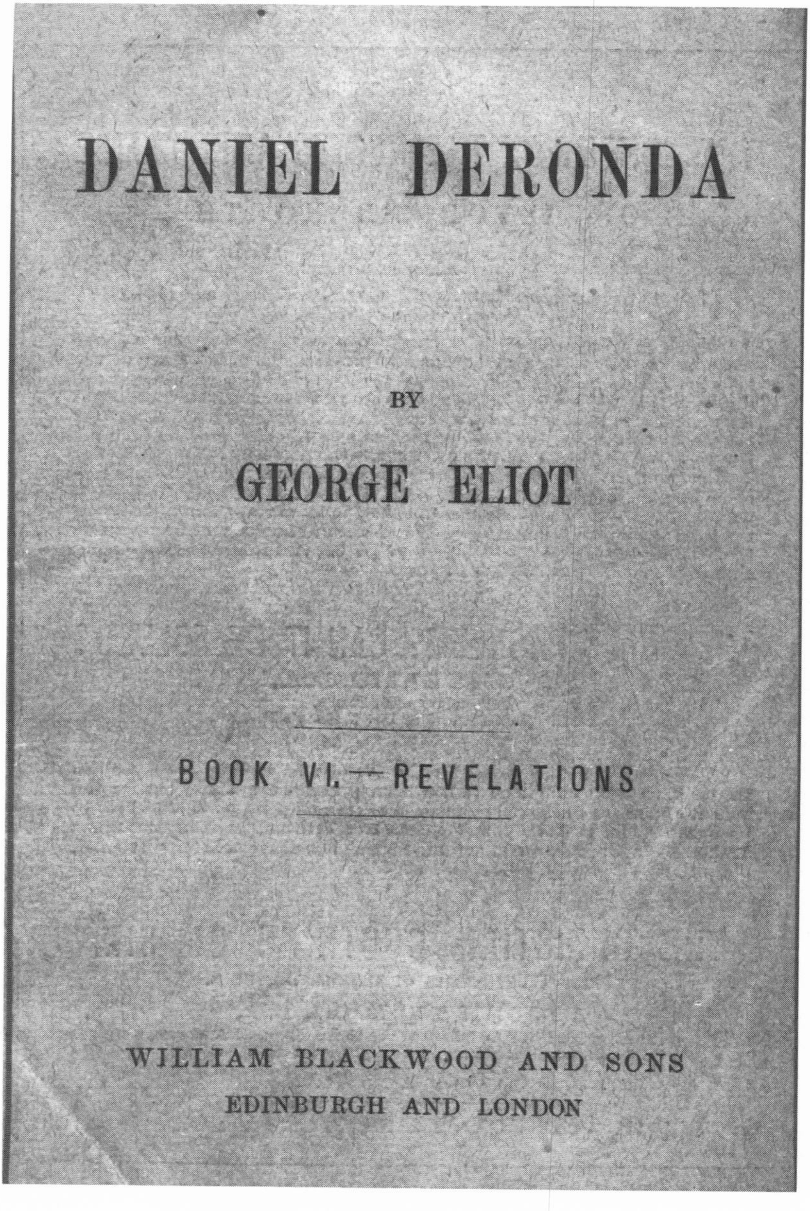

DANIEL DERONDA

BY

GEORGE ELIOT

BOOK VI.—REVELATIONS

WILLIAM BLACKWOOD AND SONS
EDINBURGH AND LONDON

Figure 9. Cover of sixth half-volume (July 1876) of Eliot's *Daniel Deronda*, the last installment to meet widespread popular approval. (*Alderman Library, University of Virginia*)

Banner" Deronda "made a decidedly winning impression on the company" (July: 226) with a "smile breaking over [his] grave face [that] was so
agreeable, that there was a general indistinct murmur, equivalent to a
'Hear, hear' " (224). Although readers could still see Deronda as potential
member of Parliament or even prime minister, Mordecai is imagining him
one of Judea's "heroes" (July: 253) who will "choose our full heritage,
claim the brotherhood of our nation, and carry into it a new brotherhood
with the nations of the Gentiles" (254).

Many reviewers found book 6, even with its hints of several directions for the plot, just as satisfying as they had the first five parts. *Bell's
Weekly Messenger* on 1 July 1876, for instance, insisted the fifth and sixth
parts "go far to prove that our conviction, expressed on the appearance of
the first 'Book'—that it would turn out to be the most perfect in all its
parts that she has ever written—is thoroughly confirmed" (6). The 23 July
1876 *Sunday Times* showed how Victorian readers continued to see the
novel as a romantic story involving Deronda and Gwendolen. This paper
said that Mirah, "interesting as she is, we decline to accept as our heroine,
pinning our faith in preference upon Gwendolen, who, with all her
weaknesses, has been from the first the favorite with most readers" (7).[54]
Since Deronda learned that Mirah was Mordecai's sister in this book, and
thus moved even closer to their world, the *Sunday Times* found expectations frustrated, terming relations between Deronda and Gwendolen
"more and more complicated" (7). Those who actually disliked the novel
at this point seemed to be reacting to the increased importance of the
Jewish characters in the novel. The July 1876 *New Quarterly Magazine,* for
instance, noted "a sensible abatement of the enthusiasm which greeted the
appearance of the first chapters" of a work that will "not turn out to be
among the greater of the author's productions" (514); but their primary
objection to the novel was that "English modern life it certainly is not"
(515).

With the discovery of Daniel's Jewish parentage and his probable
marriage to Mirah, Victorian installment readers were, then, predictably
dissatisfied at *Deronda*'s book 7.[55] A blatant anti-Semitism emerged in
these reviews, not so much because the Jews were favorably portrayed in
the novel but because the English identity could no longer be seen as
distinct from and superior to the Jewish character. The 20 August 1876
Sunday Times commented on the scene with Deronda's mother: "Of
course, Deronda is a Jew. The matter of late has been as little open to doubt
as the nationality of Aaron Solomon, the second-hand clothes dealer, of
Petticoat Lane, who, when asked by a magistrate his religion, answered, "I

am Quaker, don't you shink zo?" (7). *Bell's Weekly Messenger* on 29 July 1876 similarly found Deronda's mother "unnatural" and "repulsive," concluding: "One thing, however, is ascertained—as must have been suspected from the very beginning—that Daniel Deronda is a Jew by birth; yet it is somewhat strange, that he himself, although not without his own suspicion of the fact, had not ascertained his nationality, by means of those positive indications, which can never be mistaken or obliterated" (6).[56] The 13 August 1876 *Weekly Dispatch* was somewhat less harsh: "In Daniel Deronda we have a remarkable sketch of a perfectly good and perfectly priggish young man, in whose gradual conversion from a sort of Christianity to a sort of Judaism, concurrent with the discovery that, though brought up as a Christian, he is a Jew by birth, it is impossible to take much pleasure" (6). The 20 August 1876 *Sunday Times* believed that this book was "in no aspect up to its predecessors" (7); and the 29 July 1876 *Bell's Weekly Messenger* asserted that the hero "by no means shines in so bright a light as he has appeared in the foregoing portions of the story" (6).

Eliot's serial format provided time for change in Deronda's character, allowing, for instance, the month between books 6 (July 1876) and 7 (August 1876) for hints about his future to take effect. His journey to Genoa to meet his mother took this month in the audience's life, during which Mirah's relationship to Mordecai—and Deronda's changing feelings toward both—evolved: "When he set off to Genoa, the interest really uppermost in his mind had hardly so much relation to his mother as to Mordecai and Mirah" (August: 23). The discovery of his parentage inspired a new forcefulness in his character that ought to have been attractive to those Victorian readers who had found him too accepting of others' values: "He was fired with an intolerance that seemed foreign to him" (August: 23). Learning of his grandfather's hope ("Every Jew should rear his family as if he hoped that a Deliverer might spring from it" [August: 88–89]), Deronda acted quickly to identify with the movement for a new Israel, a recovery of an ancient empire.[57] When his mother asked, "What shall you do, then?" Deronda responded: "I consider it my duty—it is the impulse of my feeling—to identify myself, as far as possible, with my hereditary people, and if I can see any work to be done for them that I can give my soul and hand to, I shall choose to do it" (August: 86). Into that new role (not yet articulated in any clear policy like Palliser's campaign for decimal coinage[58]) Deronda takes his special gift; as he tells Sir Hugo before meeting his mother, "What I have been most trying to do for fifteen years is to have some understanding of those who differ from myself" (August: 27).

Eliot's ideal leader, then, after a long season of learning through seven books of the novel, blends tolerance and commitment. He represents the gradual growth and development of a national unity that would then offer (with a new tolerance for other views) its special insights to the rest of the world (separateness with communication).[59] If Victorians disliked Deronda's new identity as a potential Jewish leader, they continued to appreciate his relationship to Gwendolen, the one individual so far who had tried to accept completely his vision for an improved humanity. Before he arrives in Genoa, Gwendolen's "figure entered into the pictures of his present and future" (August: 12); and even after his first interview with his mother, "his mind went towards Gwendolen" (August: 128) because he recognizes that he has accepted a responsibility to act in her behalf. Like Palliser, whose loyalty to an individual (Glencora) overrides political considerations, Deronda feels the necessity of responding to one who has a prior claim on his support. When she comes ashore after the boating accident, Deronda, "in a tone of authority," does act: "If you will get her on to the *Italia* as quickly as possible, I will undertake everything else" (August: 132). His advice to her later about explaining her thoughts during the tragedy recalls Palliser's statement to Glencora at the time of Sir Orlando's call for more ships: "There is no action that ought to be taken in consequence" (August: 156).[60]

After Grandcourt's accident and Gwendolen's widowhood, some reviewers revived their romantic resolution for the novel. Despite Eliot's movement in book 7 toward Deronda's marriage with Mirah, readers hoped that he and Gwendolen would somehow be together.[61] The 20 August 1876 *Sunday Times* said: "With all her faults, Gwendolen is the most sympathetic character in the book. We prefer her far away to Mirah, who apparently is the author's favorite, and who obviously is intended as the consort of his [*sic*] hero" (7). The 13 August 1876 *Weekly Dispatch* was even more interested in Gwendolen and still assumed her ultimate union with the hero: Gwendolen, "we suppose, is in the end to marry Daniel Deronda, if not against his own will, against his better interests" (6). *Bell's Weekly Messenger* on 29 July 1876 foresaw Deronda as instrumental in reconciling Mordecai to his father, but did not predict Daniel's marriage to Mirah. This review identified Eliot's "chief purpose—the fate of the heroine, Gwendolen Grandcourt" (6) and called this "the most important portion" so far.

Book 8 of *Deronda* did leave many Victorian serial readers disappointed in September 1876; but its opening out onto new possibilities was consistent with its own interior logic, with nineteenth-century ideas of empire, and with the dynamics of serial literature.[62] The October 1876 *New Quarterly Magazine* identified the major cause for readers' disappointment, the separation of Deronda from Gwendolen: "In the situation that is presented by his abandonment of Gwendolen and attachment to the insignificant Mirah, the author appears to have intended to reinforce the philosophy [that] the exclusive prejudices of race, if not caste, must be obeyed" (250). The 2 September 1876 *Examiner* sounded a similar note: "We know not which to admire most in 'Daniel Deronda'—the profound moral earnestness which could create two such characters as Gwendolen and Daniel Deronda, or the giggling flippancy which could place at Deronda's wedding feast 'the entire Cohen family, with the one exception of the baby, who carried on her teething intelligently at home'" (993). George Saintsbury, writing in the 9 September 1876 *Academy* also disliked Deronda, finding him "human" only when he "should like to be a Jew, solely because (as that very sensible woman his mother, the Princess, discovers at once) he wishes to marry a fascinating Jewess" (253).[63]

The *Illustrated London News,* however, noted the novel's artistic consistency in its 9 September 1876 review: "The eighth and concluding part of 'Daniel Deronda' (*Blackwood*) is likely to disappoint those readers who look for sudden surprises. The story follows throughout a level and obvious course. . . . It could not have been otherwise without treason to the truth of nature; at the same time, some elements of dramatic effect have certainly been neglected. We are disappointed, for example, at seeing nothing more of Mrs. Glasher" (246).[64] Eliot, as always, prepared carefully for the resolution of the novel, encouraging readers to hope still for a romantic ending.[65] The vision of Deronda's grandfather matches Mordecai's philosophy: "What he used to insist on was that the strength and wealth of mankind depended on the balance of separateness and communication, and he was bitterly against our people losing themselves among the Gentiles" (September: 202). Deronda, in accepting his grandfather's ideas, in fact, adopted a Victorian theory of expansion, as Mordecai's explanation reveals: "See, then—the nation which has been scoffed at for its separateness, has given a binding theory to the human race. . . . and in this way human life is tending toward the image of the Supreme Unity: for as our life becomes more spiritual by capacity of thought, and joy therein, possession tends to become more universal, being independent of gross material contact; so that in a brief day the soul of a man may know in fuller volume the good which has been and is, nay, is to come, than all he could possess in a whole life where he had to follow the creeping paths of the senses" (September: 221–22). Mordecai's hope of regaining a national unity recalls the promise of Arthur's return in the serial *Idylls of the King*.

Even Gwendolen, whose life seems to close with her husband's death, is offered an expanding horizon consistent with these views of new unity. When she asks Deronda once again "what I ought to do" (September: 282), he insists on her own future development: "once beginning to act with that penitential, loving purpose you have in your mind, there will be unexpected satisfactions—there will be newly-opening needs—continually coming to carry you on from day to day. You will find your life growing like a plant" (September: 288). When she expresses further anxieties that her guilty thoughts will wear her down, Deronda explains, "By degrees they will be less insistent" (290), arguing the gradual nature of change and progress that is a key to Victorian thought and literature.[66] Gwendolen's story remained popular with nearly all readers even in this last book. The 9 September 1876 *Illustrated London News* said that "Gwendolen fully and fairly gains our interest and compassion" (246); and the 4 October 1876 *Guardian* claimed that this heroine was "quite equal to anything that has been produced before" (1312).

The novel at its conclusion received mixed reviews, though some critics deemed that a strength for the future. R. E. Francillon in the October 1876 *Gentleman's Magazine* argued: "Not a few critics have already said that *Daniel Deronda* is not likely to extend George Eliot's reputation. . . . But whether *Daniel Deronda* is not likely to *heighten* her reputation is an entirely different question, and will, I firmly believe, meet with a very different answer when certain natural and perhaps inevitable feelings of disappointment have passed away" (quoted in Carroll 382). Eliot's own hold on her audience continued to grow, despite those who resisted her vision in 1876, if the printing of editions and the teaching of her works in the century that followed is any measure.[67] Like Trollope, whose remarkable body of work has inspired addiction in generations of readers, and Tennyson, whose story of Camelot has been read by countless students of his own work as well as Arthurian enthusiasts, Eliot created an empire in the Victorian literary world of the 1870s and beyond. All three writers, themselves leaders in society, embodied in their achievements fundamental principles of Victorian empire: their voices and visions spread slowly but steadily throughout audiences at home and abroad. As underscored by their works' installment format, the Victorian ideal of empire is seen to involve a tolerant furthering of growth more than an imposition of will on helpless victims. The reality, it is true, often departed from this course; but the goal remained. So unforced seems this process that sometimes it appears to occur without direction, through leaders who have the wisdom *not* to act and who therefore may appear undistinctive, even bland. Yet as happens with installment readers whose interest in fictional worlds builds and deepens over time, members of an expanding community reveal a commitment to a new vision of humanity increasing over space and time.

V

Expressing Doubt

"*Good by, Mr. Montague. I think you had better lose no time in going—back to Mrs. Hurtle.*" *All this she said with sundry little impedimentary gurgles in her throat, but without a tear and without any sign of tenderness.*

Anthony Trollope, *The Way We Live Now*

O thou who clingest still to life and love, Though nought of good, no God thou mayst discern.

William Morris, *The Earthly Paradise*

Let us fear—and press forward where few dare to go; Let us falter in hope—and plan deeds for the morrow.

William Morris, *The Pilgrims of Hope*

Thus was the erratic woman stricken; and those who care for more of Diana of The Crossways will find it in the extended chronicle.

George Meredith, *Diana of the Crossways*

IN ALL THEIR ASSERTIONS of progress—personal, national, global—Victorians also maintained an element of doubt, a scepticism that encouraged them to avoid easy assertions that all was right with the world. In the face of scientific discoveries and a weakening religious faith, Victorians injected this element of doubt into all their endeavors, resulting at times, as Walter Houghton has stated, in "prolonged introspection, analysis, and indecision; or the sudden collapse of a philosophy or a religion which had been the motivation of action, with nothing to take its place; or the vision of a mechanistic universe without purpose or meaning" (*Victorian* 73). For the many patient spouses holding together threatened families in long stories, there were also individuals in other or even the same works of literature whose adultery, widowhood, or unhappy marriage insisted that the happy home was not universal in nineteenth-century society.[1] Even though many authors of historical works offered a continuous line of improvement for British society from the past through the present and into the future, these same writers acknowledged that humankind was not always committed to the right path in individual cases. And with the benevolent leadership of Palliser, Arthur, and Deronda also appeared their counterparts, Lopez, Modred, and Grandcourt.

Middle-class experience in the nation at large was also characterized by an interweaving of doubt and progress. As Eric Hobsbawm remarks, "By the 1870s the progress of the bourgeois world had led to a point where more sceptical, even more pessimistic, voices began to be heard. And they were reinforced by the situation in which the world found itself in the 1870s, and which few had foreseen. The economic foundations of advancing civilization were shaken by tremors. After a generation of unparalleled expansion, the world economy was in crisis" (33).[2] Yet even among Socialists, whose major premise was radical doubt about the bourgeois ideal, economic or social collapse was seen as a preliminary step backward on the way to profound and lasting progress.

After moments of lost faith or oppressive doubt, then, many Victorian literary characters of the 1870s and 1880s recovered and went on to later success or achievement in the extended time frame that governed their world.[3] The installment form of some major Victorian works—such as Trollope's *The Way We Live Now* (1874–75), Morris's *Earthly Paradise* (1868–70) and *Pilgrims of Hope* (1885–86), and Meredith's *Diana of the Crossways* (1884)—expressed a society's reservations about accepted beliefs, a caution that authors and readers shared in their approach to the world. Although their vision was ultimately one of progress and optimism, there was sometimes one step back for every two steps forward in the life of the protagonist and in the shape of the work itself. The characteristic alternation between progression and pause in serials' publication intensified hesitation and progression in the stories themselves.

The Way We Live Now (twenty monthly numbers, February 1874 to September 1875) is frequently isolated in Trollope's canon, a novel of satire unrelieved by characters his audience could admire and love. Robert Polhemus links the tone of this novel to larger cultural confusion: "The seventies were comparatively bleak and disillusioning years for Victorian intellectuals. Confidence in the future faded, Victoria's reign was at its nadir, she was in seclusion, 'progress' seemed more and more a naive outworn creed" (*Changing* 186–87). In such a scheme, we might treat the entire novel as one expression of doubt, an opposite to *The Prime Minister,* which follows it in Trollope's career (see chapter four).[4] However, Polhemus perhaps goes too far in concluding that Trollope was a "profound pessimist" (186) at this point in his life and *The Way We Live Now* a manifestation of a totally "dark" view of the world. James Kincaid and Christopher Herbert explore comic patterns that balance or even override cynicism in Trollope's later works.[5] Ruth apRoberts argues that *The Way We Live Now* does not differ "from the rest of his work as much as some critics claim" (167) and concludes that this "'dark' book is nevertheless a melioristic one" (172). Thus, in *The Way We Live Now* doubt is an important, even a dominant theme, just as empire was for *The Prime Minister;* but both novels include both themes in different mixes.

Many critics of *The Way We Live Now* agree that several lines in the novel's construction are at odds; neither wholly comic nor all bleak pessimism, the novel attracts readers with varying interests.[6] The 7 March 1874 *Bell's Weekly Messenger* found Trollope's style mixed in the novel's first installment: "Mr. Anthony Trollope's new novel does not begin pleasantly, for the first part is full of unusual peculiarities, in which a degree of coarseness is too much blended with the talent he unquestionably possesses" (6). Some oppositions within the novel did derive from the many plots characteristic of the long Victorian novel. Susan Peck Mac-Donald notes: "The central thematic conflict occurs between a traditional system of values represented by Roger Carbury and the challenge to those values—the 'way we live now'—posed most dramatically by Augustus Melmotte" (80). A distinctive quality of this Trollope novel is suggested by Kincaid when he states that early critics spoke of "a split between plot and character . . . arguing that in many cases Victorian authors became so fond of their created people [Melmotte, for instance] that the primary demands of plot were more or less forgotten" (*Novels* 20). David Skilton in *Anthony Trollope and His Contemporaries* also notes that the Victorian audience's expectation of any work of fiction was disappointed by Trollope in this case: "It was more or less universally agreed among Trollope's reviewers that there should be a distribution of virtues and vices in any novel—that the evil which must necessarily be shown should at least be counterbalanced by goodness" (65). The 17 July 1875 *Saturday Review* said of *The Way We Live Now:* "If there is a rogue to hate, there should be somebody to love and pity" (88). In *The Way We Live Now,* however, Trollope refused to provide such clearly balanced elements—good and bad characters, a plot featuring the success of virtue and the failure of evil.[7]

Trollope's own analysis of his society must be seen as a first source of mixed reaction to this novel: "I was instigated [to the writing of *The Way We Live Now*] by what I conceived to be the commercial profligacy of the age. Whether the world does or does not become more wicked as years go on, is a question which probably has disturbed the minds of thinkers since the world began to think. That men have become less cruel, less violent, less selfish, less brutal, there can be no doubt;—but have they become less honest? If so, can a world, retrograding from day to day in honesty, be considered to be in a state of progress?" (Trollope, *Autobiography* [1883]; quoted in Smalley 394).

Contrasts between "retrograding" and "progress" characterized the style of this novel, from individual sentences to serial installments.[8] Trollope established the rhythm of doubt or hesitation in one of the earliest memorable sentences of the novel. Speaking of Lady Matilda Carbury in the first installment (February 1874), the narrator states: "The woman was false from head to foot, but there was much of good in her, false though she was" (1:12).[9] Readers are first told to withhold sympathy from this character (one step back), then are encouraged to reverse their feelings and care for Lady Carbury (a step forward), and then once again to resist liking her (another step back). Thus, the structure of this sentence represents a mixture of faith in and doubt about the character of Lady Carbury. The 17 July 1875 *Saturday Review* was sufficiently struck by this sentence to repeat it in its review of the whole novel: "Let us look at the characters thus brought together. Lady Carbury, described as 'false from head to foot, but with much good in her, false though she was,' the good being her blind devotion to her son" (88).

Even the novel's chief romantic plot was developed in emphatic fits and starts. In number 16 (May 1875), for instance, Hetta Carbury finally hears Paul Montague's explanation of his past with Mrs. Hurtle, "from beginning to end" (2:164). Although Paul tries to say his only tie now is to Hetta, she learns from his account that Mrs. Hurtle still thinks herself engaged to him. Telling him several times that he must go "back to Mrs. Hurtle" (2:165), she attempts to end the conversation and their relationship (see figure 10): " 'Good bye, Mr. Montague. I think you had better lose no time in going—back to Mrs. Hurtle.' All this she said with sundry little impedimentary gurgles in her throat, but without a tear and without any sign of tenderness" (2:165). Both the break in her speech (between "going" and "back") and the "sundry little impedimentary gurgles" are signs of her doubt about exactly how to proceed. She feels her faith in his honor and in the purity of her motives weakening in these hesitations, but she cannot give up on them entirely. The phrases "without a tear" and

Figure 10. "You had better go back to Mrs. Hurtle" from Trollope's *Way We Live Now* (sixteenth installment, May 1875), depicting Hetta Carbury's hesitations about Paul Montague. (*Alderman Library, University of Virginia*)

"without any sign of tenderness" conjure up their opposites, letting read-ers know that she feels sorrow for herself and sympathy for Paul. Her shaken belief, however, almost blocking with "impedimentary gurgles" her ability to speak, makes it difficult for her to go forward at this time.

Such descriptions and the actions they report might be assessed as one step forward and two steps back, thus creating a pessimistic decline in the novel as a whole.[10] In more places, however, the narrative moves forward twice for every retrograde action, ultimately following a more optimistic model. For instance, Lord Nidderdale moves forward in such a fashion when he is finally accepted by Marie Melmotte in number 15 (April 1875): "So the interview was over and Nidderdale walked back to the house thinking of his lady love, as far as he was able to bring his mind to any operation of thinking" (2:149). Nidderdale concludes the necessary inter-view (one step forward), even though he does not understand much of what he has done (a step back), and then returns home (a second step forward).

Mr. Broune, feeling "pangs of doubt" (1:196) in the August 1874 number, nevertheless presents his proposal of marriage to Lady Carbury in a similar form: "It is so hard to know the nature of another person. But I think I understand yours;—and if you can confide your happiness with me, I am prepared to entrust mine to your keeping" (1:195). Here an obstacle (the difficulty of reading another's heart) inspires a step back, but the specific case (he does, he thinks, understand her) allows him to contemplate two steps forward (each accepting responsibility for the other's happiness). Later, of course, he will regret having offered, feel relief at being rejected, but also finally offer again and be accepted. His doubt at one point, thus, is described in terms very similar to those used by Houghton (above) to describe the Victorian age: "Who does not know that sudden thoughtfulness at waking, that first matutinal retrospection, and pro-spection, into things as they have been and are to be; and the lowness of heart, the blankness of hope which follows the first remem-brance of some folly lately done, some word ill-spoken, some money misspent,—or perhaps a cigar too much, or a glass of brandy and soda-water which he should have left untasted?" (1:227). Such doubts assailed not only characters but readers in this novel.

Some reviewers echoed Trollope's hesitant forward movement in their own prose. The 26 June 1875 *Spectator,* for instance, wrote about Marie Melmotte in sentences that seemed to move a step back for every one forward: "She is base, though there is some strength in her, and so are all the women, except the dull heroine, Hetta Carbury" (825). Similarly, discussing the male characters, the *Spectator* stated: "There is not a decently honest man in the book who is not a fool, except the squire, Roger Carbury, and he is an overbearing prig" (825). The 24 August 1875 *Times* explicitly noted this structural principle of assertion followed by hesitation, writing that Trollope's "great anxiety seems to deal an exact and even-handed justice to each of his characters. Does he describe a Melmotte, with his odious, purseproud, pompous manners?—then he hastens to add some line or two, giving the man credit for powers of concentration, boldness of conception, and financial pluck" (4).

If individual sentences and paragraphs enacted doubt, holding back for a moment the forward movement of the plot, so too did larger units of the novel. Several early reviewers claimed the novel progressed unevenly. The 28 August 1875 *Examiner* concluded that "Mr. Trollope's narrative is somewhat jerky, in consequence of its numerous transitions from one set of persons and scene to another" (971). The *Examiner* also noted the "frequent and confusing retrogressions to which [Trollope] has recourse in order to keep the several movements equally advanced" (971). As Mary Hamer has shown, however, Trollope was by this time in his career a master of the multiplot novel, linking different narrative strands and moving smoothly among them.[11] The Victorian sense of "retrogression," then, may have had more to do with the fact that no element of the plot moved forward consistently (that is, in patterns familiar to Trollope's audience) from beginning to end of the novel. The drag on the novel's development of traditional plots was given additional emphasis in the original parts structure of the novel; for one installment frequently took away what another had given. While the overall scheme still showed a progress typical of most Victorian literature,[12] the regressions suggested Trollope's own doubts.

One of these doubts was whether individual liberty was truly possible in the Victorian age. Marie Melmotte, for instance, is a character who over the course of the novel's publication developed from reliance on others to a new independence; yet her strength was devoted to alliances first with Felix Carbury, seen by all except his doting mother as without redeeming social value, and later to Hamilton Fisker, a brash and unpredictable American. Thus, Marie moved forward only to regress, particularly in the first ten installments of the novel, concluding this stage of her development at the sad scene in which she is called back to her father at the Liverpool train station.[13] The passage of nine months in the life of Trollope's audience (February–November 1874) provided a framework to underscore Marie's development and growth; but her limited progress in establishing her own private and social identity during that time under-scored crucial doubts about freedom in Victorian society.

Marie Melmotte appeared in number 1 (Febuary 1874) simply as "the great heiress" (1:15) Lady Carbury hopes her son will marry. In a charac-teristic construction, the narrative took away virtues almost as fast as it attributed them to this potential heroine: "She was not beautiful, she was not clever, and she was not a saint. But then neither was she plain, nor stupid, nor, especially, a sinner" (1:22). Particularly in the phrase "nor, especially, a sinner," Trollope advanced Marie as a potentially interesting character in the same breath that he held back his endorsement. Her development was suggested in the same installment, after her father rejected Lord Nidderdale for her; from this point on, readers learned, Marie "began to have an opinion" (1:22) about her own future. However, she would advance her own independence by seeking a doomed alliance with Sir Felix Carbury.

Marie's story did not take any significant steps forward in the novel's second number (March 1874), and in number 3 (April 1874) the narrative stepped back in time to recall Marie's childhood in New York, her life with an unsuccessful father in Germany, a sudden prosperity coming with a new stepmother in France, and her presentation to English society. In-spired by his mother, Felix Carbury did offer himself to Marie. When he asked her if he could speak to her father, the narrator reported: "It was thus that the greatest heiress of the day, the greatest heiress of any day if people spoke truly, gave herself away to a man without a penny" (1:73). The qualifying phrase, "if people spoke truly," typically held back the novel's presentation of Marie's story, though there appeared to be some progress toward a romantic resolution in the overall structure of this part.

Number 4 (May 1874), however, tended to take away Marie's move-ment toward a new freedom from her father as it dropped back to repeat the most important fact of Marie's present story: "She had once told [Felix] that he might go to her father" (1:108). A similar lack of progress was exhibited in the romance itself: "Since that [*sic*] she had seen him, indeed, but he had not said a word to press his suit, nor, as far as she knew, had he said a word to Mr. Melmotte" (1:108). When she was walking with Felix at Carbury Manor, the narrative once more retraced its steps: "Sir Felix Carbury, she knew, had made her an offer. She knew also, or thought that she knew, that she loved the man" (1:110). This sentence took one step back ("or thought that she knew") for two steps forward (she has an offer; she loves the man). While the engagement was reaffirmed in this walk, the couple did not go far beyond the "first step" (1:117) in their romance:

Marie talked to her stepmother, but Felix avoided confrontation with Mr. Melmotte. Her story, then, regressed before it made its small progress forward in number 4.

The fifth number of *The Way We Live Now* (June 1874) did feature Sir Felix's interview with Melmotte, but the latter's request for a financial statement delayed the romance's progress. The more substantial development occurred in Marie's own character. Felix saw how she was now maneuvering for him; thus, it "certainly did seem to Sir Felix that the very nature of the girl was altered" (1:146). Having found that "her courage grew within her" (1:157), Marie doubted Felix's love, if not yet love itself: "Sir Felix was her idol, and she abandoned herself to its worship. But she desired that the idol should be of flesh and blood, and not of wood" (1:157). Signing a letter to her "own, own, own darling Felix" as his "own, own, affectionate ladylove, Marie" (1:158), her prose expressed her own doubt through the repeated emphasis on commitment. Thus, this installment left most of the issues in Marie's situation hanging.

Number 6 (July 1874) included the dramatic confrontation between Marie and her father, he threatening violence and she saying she is willing to be "cut into bits" (1:183) for Felix. However, once again the novel's sentences contained elements of doubt. Marie, for instance, said that it "is not more disgraceful to love [Felix] than that other man [Nidderdale]" (1:184), unintentionally but correctly linking Carbury with disgrace. This "very enterprising young lady" (1:184) had matured in the six months of the novel's publication so far, as the narrator's summary insists: "She had had a will of her own when the mother had none. She had not been afraid of her brutal father when he, Sir Felix, had trembled before him" (1:185). Examining these comparisons closely, however—neither her mother nor Felix had provided a model of courage—reveals again Trollope's habit of taking away half of what he has provided.

Marie remained in the background of the novel's number 7 (August 1874) until the conclusion. At the end of the installment the narrative backed up again to remind readers that Marie "had changed her mind" (1:223) about marrying Nidderdale. She informs Nidderdale that "I have seen more of things since" (1:223) their engagement was proposed by their parents, but her confidence in Felix is shaken. Not having seen or heard from her lover for "more than a week" (1:224), Marie appeared still dependent on others in the number's last sentence: "As soon as Lord Nidderdale was gone she wrote again to Sir Felix begging that she might hear from him,—and entrusted her letter to Didon" (1:224). Didon and Lord Nidderdale are so far fairly trustworthy, perhaps willing to let Marie establish her freedom from a tyrannical father; but Felix himself signifies the usual step backward in Trollope's representation of the way things are.

The novel's eighth number (September 1874) presented Felix Carbury's written admission to Melmotte that he would not press his suit for Marie, a clear regression in this romantic plot. Marie herself did not appear again until number 9 (October 1874), when she was "by no means contented with her lover's prowess" (1:257) in pursuing their relationship. Felix would perhaps go forward with their elopement, but characteristically, by retreating from more unpleasant possibilities: "there was the girl at his elbow, and he no more dared to tell her to her face that he meant to give her up, than he dared to tell Melmotte that he intended to stick to his engagement" (1:258). Thus Marie, "certainly a clever girl" (1:261), continued to progress toward independence, but in pursuit of an unworthy goal.

Marie's attempted elopement, presented in chapter 50, "The Journey to Liverpool," concluded the novel's first volume (ten numbers). After ten installments, nine months in readers' lives, Marie found herself still a prisoner of her father. One of the two illustrations for this number featured Marie stopped by her father's agent.[14] When he says, "You, I think, are Miss Melmotte" (1:315), the agent asserts her identity within the law; no matter how far she has traveled, she comes back to this definition of herself. Of course, this apparent step back is ironically a step forward, freeing her from loyalty to an unworthy object: "We who know how recreant a knight Sir Felix had proved himself, who are aware that had Miss Melmotte succeeded in getting on board the ship she would have passed an hour of miserable suspense, looking everywhere for her lover, and would then at last have been carried to New York without him, may congratulate her on her escape" (1:317).

Although her desire to choose her own lover would, after more setbacks involving Lord Nidderdale, lead her to a problematical fate with Fisker in America, she was more in command of her own fate in the end than when she began. Thus, progress is embodied in the novel's form (the many installments do finally lead somewhere); but there is considerable doubt built into the fiction as well (some parts retard the forward movement). As with many other elements of the novel, her story inspired contradictory reactions among Victorian readers. The 26 June 1875 *Spectator,* for instance, tried but failed to like Marie Melmotte: she has " 'spirit,' " but she "conducts herself . . . like a plucky barmaid, and is at heart utterly sordid" (825). The 17 July 1875 *Saturday Review* found Marie's devotion to Felix unrealistic ("neither the world we live in nor hear about") but consistent with the realm Trollope had created: "it does not seem so very much out of place where it stands" (88). And the 28 August 1875 *Examiner* listed Marie as one of many characters in the novel who are, "in spite of their troubles and struggles, singularly uninteresting" (972).

The pattern of Marie's progress toward maturity and independence, many steps back for just a few more steps forward, is echoed in other elements of the novel's plot. Paul's effort to end his romance with Mrs. Hurtle, first referred to in the initial installment, regressed at almost every meeting in each monthly part, as he most often ended up with her in his arms, their relationship back where it stood when he had proposed to her. Mrs. Hurtle's own history, particularly her emergence as wise counselor to Ruby Ruggles and dispassionate friend to Hetta Carbury, proceeded through stages that represented throwbacks to her wilder American character.[15] Mr. Broune's gradual movement toward the man Lady Carbury can accept as a husband began in the first chapter; but it was concluded in the final installment only after many setbacks in the intervening parts. Ruby's appropriate marriage to John Crumb came also after many months of falling back on the hope that Felix Carbury would rescue her from a common destiny.

A dominant movement of the second ten installments (December 1874–September 1875) was the collapse of Melmotte's financial empire. The 28 August 1875 *Examiner* claimed that "we follow the stages of his certain ruin with considerable excitement" (972). That process too, however, was not presented as a straight line of descent from success to failure, but as a series of single steps forward followed by double steps backward until Melmotte reached ruin and suicide. And again, the serial structure of *The Way We Live Now* reflected a fundamental doubt about Victorian social values, this time that falseness would be revealed and justice served.[16]

As early as the first number (February 1874) Melmotte appeared as a great power in his society, but his authority rested on questionable grounds. He "could make or mar any company" (1:21), yet "he was regarded in Paris as the most gigantic swindler that had ever lived" (1:21). Citizens of Trollope's world and readers of his novel were continually made aware of the double nature of his career: he appeared, at least through the first volume, to be growing ever more powerful and successful; but there was also evidence that he was moving toward an eventual collapse. In number eleven (December 1874), the first part of the second volume, Melmotte was just slightly overreaching himself: "there had grown upon the man during the last few months an arrogance, a self-confidence inspired in him by the worship of other men, which clouded his intellect, and robbed him of much of that power of calculation which undoubtedly he naturally possessed" (2:13). The first rumors that his financial empire might be overextended and that he "must be much pressed for money" (2:20) suggested a sudden collapse was possible—an event, of course, with clear precedent for Trollope's audience in the real world.[17] Still, Melmotte was pursued by the Conservatives to run for Parliament, a sign that his power and his reputation had not completely faded. Thus, the story of his collapse began with another step forward in his continuing rise to eminence, but an equal step back toward the truth about his past dealings.

Number 12 (January 1875) found the word *forgery* (2:45) linked with Melmotte, and suddenly his fall seemed imminent: "what a fiasco would it be, if at this very instant of time the host should be apprehended for common forgery!" (2:52). Yet this too was only one slip backward, resulting in some empty seats at Melmotte's dinner and some nervous moments for the host. Melmotte rebounded in number 13 (February 1875). As the narrator continued to use the word *rumor* rather than *fact,* serial readers saw a resolute financier deciding he could weather the storm: "Perhaps never in his life had he studied his own character and his own conduct more accurately, or made sterner resolves, than he did as he stood there smiling, bowing, and acting without impropriety the part of host to an Emperor" (2:70). Even though he was shortly pictured burning incriminating documents, even in one remarkable instance "chewing the paper into a pulp till he swallowed it" (2:79), Melmotte gave "the only good speech he had ever been known to make" (2:80) in his campaign for Parliament. Furthermore, "something of the old arrogance had come back upon him" (2:87), and he learned the next day that "he had been elected for Westminster" (2:89). Thus, any collapse was delayed at least for this number, even though "he was in danger of almost immediate detection and punishment" (2:89).

Number 14 (March 1875) featured Melmotte on the one hand standing "amidst the ruins" of the party he had thrown for the emperor and on the other sitting "in the British House of Commons" (2:109). He had, again, "in a certain degree recovered his position" (2:115) when he was introduced to the House; but his agent Cohenlupe was at the same time "meditating his own escape from the dangerous shores of England" (2:122). Thus, this installment also balanced a step forward with one back in Melmotte's career.

Melmotte's forgery of Dolly Longestaffe's signature (2:143) was recalled in number 15 (April 1875), revealing that the rumors had been accurate. The holding action Melmotte was capable of waging against loss was in this part indirectly linked to his life in a monthly serial format when Cohenlupe told the financier he must "tide over the evil hour,—or rather over an evil month" (2:147). Indeed, Melmotte's collapse was still several months and numbers away, and the engagement of Marie to Lord Nidderdale seemed to help consolidate his position once more. In one of his characteristic sentences, Trollope summed up the condition of this society, which clearly had its doubts that justice would finally prevail: "The world at large, in spite of the terrible falling-off at the Emperor of China's dinner, in spite of all the rumours, in spite of the ruinous depreciation of the Mexican Railway stock, and of the undoubted fact that Dolly Longestaffe had not received his money, was inclined to think that Melmotte would 'pull through'" (2:154). This sentence took four steps forward in its faith that material success must be deserved (counting the evidence that indicts Melmotte), but fell back one when it asserted that he might still escape accountability. Even though an increasing number of individuals like Squercum believed that Melmotte now was "not a falling, but a fallen star" (2:154), the great financier was able to hold off his creditor Mr. Longestaffe until "Friday at noon" (2:160), two days hence. For Victorian readers, of course, that deadline was one month away and Melmotte's fall still two months in the future.

Melmotte once again felt growing pressure to meet his debts in the sixteenth number (May 1875), finding that "day by day, every resolution that he made was forced to undergo some change" (2:168). Unable, even with violence, to make Marie give up money in her name, he had to forge her signature as well as his clerk's in order to prevent collapse. Mr. Cohenlupe's flight to the Continent occurred in number 17 (June 1875), forcing even Melmotte to suspect that his collapse was imminent: "What would be the end of it? Ruin;—yes" (2:197). This frame of mind inspired a flirtation with suicide: a "razor in his hand," he thought, "How easily might he put an end to it all!" (2:201). But he attempted several more maneuvers before accepting the inevitable: "On that Thursday afternoon it was known everywhere that there was to be a general ruin of all the Melmotte affairs" (2:208). The facts had finally erased society's doubt: "As soon as Cohenlupe had gone, no man doubted" (2:208). Trollope's description of Melmotte's end, however, still questioned society's ability to mete out justice: "Drunk as he had been,—more drunk as he probably became during the night,—still he was able to deliver himself from the indignities and penalties to which the law might have subjected him by a dose of prussic acid" (2:213). This sentence interposed the oblivion of drink and a final deliverance between Melmotte and a rendering of his accounts before society. The parts structure of his story from December 1874 to June 1875 similarly interposed many backward steps in society's continuing effort to bring him to justice.

Uncertainty about Melmotte's character and his fate was consistently revealed in periodical reaction to Trollope's novel. Clearly a fraud, Melmotte nevertheless earned a certain amount of respect from this audience. The 17 July 1875 *Saturday Review,* for instance, linked positive Victorian qualities to the man they viewed as a villain: "Melmotte['s] . . . is a life of fraud demanding such constant vigilance, such habits of self-control, such foresight and preparation, such self-reliance and courage, that it is almost great" (88). Similarly, the 24 August 1875 *Times* recognized Melmotte's ultimate failure but still could admire his "audacity, his courage, his resources, and—his success" (4). The 26 June 1875 *Athenaeum,* although calling Melmotte a "swindler," still referred to him as "the hero of the tale" (851). And the 28 August 1875 *Examiner* stated: "The best, strongest, and most carefully finished character in the book is undoubtedly that of Melmotte" (972). Thus, Melmotte's story resembled various Victorian paradigms, but did not follow as neatly predictable a course as many desired: he was a criminal who would be brought to justice; but he possessed the force that creates empires. Trollope raised doubts about success and status in this world by allowing his villain's strength, remarkably like the strength of eminent Victorians, to delay his fall over many months of the novel's serial publication.

That Trollope accepted for this story the favorite Dickensian format of twenty monthly numbers more than a decade after its greatest popularity draws attention to authorial doubt about the power of literature and the serial form itself. Trollope had already questioned the terms of his own literary reputation, twice in the 1860s publishing novels anonymously to test whether his work's quality or his established name determined reviews and sales (Smalley 18–20). He would have been well aware, too, that the critical reputation of a serial novel's first number helped determine the entire work's success. The opening number of *The Way We Live Now* asked how literary reputations were made. With three carefully crafted letters, Lady Carbury courts favorable reviews for her historical romance from the "Three Editors" of chapter 1's title: Mr. Broune, who was "fond of ladies" (1:2); Mr. Booker, on whom the "stress of circumstances" (1:4) made adherence to professional standards difficult; and Mr. Alf, who very much desired to "come up" (1:6) in the world. Lady Carbury believes, and Trollope suggests he does too, that her literary reputation might be created out of such weaknesses.[18]

It is quite possible that Trollope irritated both professional reviewers and the general audience with this direct assault on the publishing industry in February 1874, delaying widespread recognition of the quality of this novel. His first step forward with *The Way We Live Now* might well have contained its own step backward; by attacking the reviewing process, Trollope risked losing critical notice and thus a large audience for the rest of the novel. The novel's content, then, raised doubts about a fundamental principle of serial form and literary worth, that early response determined the overall success of the work. (In Victorian terms, of course, popular success was a necessary ingredient of true literary quality.[19])

There are few reviews of the novel during its serial run in those weekly papers that customarily followed magazines and works in installments, such as the *Weekly Dispatch*, the *Guardian*, the *Illustrated London News*, and the *News of the World*.[20] The novel might have been neglected simply because it was not liked, but reviewers might also have responded to Trollope's satire by ignoring his novel and denying it publicity. Trollope was certainly aware that even negative reviews sometimes helped sales, for he has Lady Carbury's publisher, Mr. Leadham, tell her in number 3 (April 1874): "Never fight the newspapers, Lady Carbury. . . . Anything is better than indifference, Lady Carbury. A great many people remember simply that the book has been noticed, but carry away nothing as to the purport of the review. It's a very good advertisement" (1:66). Such comments may have inspired reviewers to believe that Trollope himself had decided to "fight the newspapers," and they then used "indifference" as a counterattack.

Since there were so few reviews during its serial run, original reaction to *The Way We Live Now* is harder to determine than response to other Victorian serials. The 24 August 1875 *Times* claimed to have been intensely interested in the novel from its first scenes: "our hearts are with Lady Carbury from the moment we first see her scribbling diplomatic little notes at her desk, until we take leave of her, a more sensible woman by far, kneeling at stout, elderly Mr. Broune's feet, his promised wife" (4). And this paper concluded that this was "one of Mr. Trollope's very best stories" (4). Trollope himself claimed in his *Autobiography*, "Upon the whole, I by no means look upon the book as one of my failures; nor was it taken as a failure by the public or the press" (quoted in Smalley 395).

On the other hand, the rather personal note in the 17 July 1875

Saturday Review might suggest that Trollope's criticism of reviewers had hit home and damaged his own novel's chances: "We must begin by quarrelling with the incivility of Mr. Trollope's title. 'The way *we* live!' We will not retort by requesting the author to speak for himself" (88). It is true that the same review professed to approve of Trollope's satire of the literary marketplace, but it emphasized the authors' more than the reviewers' roles: "One subject on which our author has justly relied for interesting many of his readers, and which to himself may have presented the attraction of a vein less worked than those of more common resort, is that of bookmaking without a vocation, which certainly may be pronounced one feature of the world we live in" (88). The review also suggested a relationship between Trollope as author and Lady Carbury as hack: "Mr Trollope implies for himself a very exact and intimate knowledge of the editorial status and its chances" (88). This was a point made even more strongly by the October 1875 *Westminster Review*: "Of Mr. Trollope's own novel we also feel inclined to wish that it was reviewed by his own Jones, that particular Jones who writes such slashing reviews on novels. . . . Jones might fairly point out how closely Mr. Trollope himself resembles Lady Carbury—how he too has written all sorts of books, a hack translation of Caesar, a scratch volume of hunting sketches, a boys' Christmas book of Australian adventure, all of them with no higher aim than Lady Carbury's" (257). Thus, the limited reputation of this novel during his lifetime may be at least partly the product of Trollope's strategy in depicting literary effort, particularly his assault on the review process in the very first number.

Trollope's doubt about the system of literary production in 1874–75 led him to step back from the business of literary production (attacking the way in which audiences were created) at the same time that he took other steps forward (writing new installments in a long work). Several central figures in that work, Lady Carbury and Melmotte, attracted investors in cheap books and in a virtually fictional railroad much as Trollope worked to get paying believers in his imagined world. Such unsettling commercial mirrors of the author's role slowed recognition of Trollope's achievement. His choice of an outdated format, the twenty separate monthly parts, was itself a retreat to an earlier mode in the history of the novel (see figure 11; the illustrations on the cover of the monthly part recall the covers on Dickens's long stories). As J. Don Vann shows us, the previous seven novels in his career had appeared in periodicals. Trollope's next novel, *The Prime Minister* (1875–76), was in a new form (eight monthly half-volumes) and returned to the subject of his very successful Palliser series. This

Figure 11. Cover of monthly parts of *Way We Live Now* (1874–75), harking back to serial publication formats at mid-century. (*Alderman Library, University of Virginia*)

suggests that Trollope wanted to recapture his audience after the episode of doubt represented by *The Way We Live Now*.

Finally, however, the fact that he was able to complete this major expression of Victorian uncertainty underscores how the dominant pattern of Victorian ideology was still a forward-moving one. Indeed, this novel, consistently praised by modern critics for its tight structure and thematic unity, was made up of twenty installments, each with exactly five chapters, the whole being a neat one hundred chapters (recalling once again Palliser's interest in decimal coinage). Trollope's ability to create, especially with such mathematical precision, confirms how deep was the age's belief in progress even as it expressed doubts about its own future.

William Morris's *The Earthly Paradise*, like Trollope's *The Way We Live Now*, is considered one of its author's best works yet a kind of anomaly. Alfred Austin praised Morris in the November 1869 *Temple Bar* as the poet most likely to contribute to the poetry of the period because he deliberately turned his back on it (46–47, 51). The Apology's declaration that the poet cannot set straight the time and is the "idle singer of an empty day," moreover, seems to contradict Morris's tireless efforts in the Socialist movement in later years. But if atypical in some respects, *The Earthly Paradise*, published in three separate volumes from 1868 to 1870, still illuminates the relationship between literature first issued in parts and Victorian treatments of doubt.

As we have seen in *The Way We Live Now*, its duration (nine months for Marie's attempts to marry Felix) as well as its sheer mass of pages meant that readers remained in the midst of the work far longer than those who read it through as a completed unit. The serial work generally, like Trollope's particular plot in this novel, refuses to move ahead quickly to the end but goes forward (in an installment) only to step back into the work's middle ("to be continued").

The prolonged middle of *The Earthly Paradise* reinforced the poem's central theme, a desire to avoid life's end. This theme was announced in the poem's "Prologue," subtitled "The Wanderers." After the last installment of *The Earthly Paradise* appeared in December 1870, the 28 January 1871 *Spectator* praised the 1868 prologue for providing a key to the whole: "This seems at first sight to be only a pretty fantastic device for establishing an apparent connection amongst a series of tales which might just as well be independent. . . . Yet if the reader will pause to gather up the accumulated impressions left in his mind by the poems in their successive course, he will find that this is not so; there is beneath all the wandering melodies a steady under-current whose minute impulses give at last a certain direction to the whole" (104). Not only did "The Wanderers" provide "a certain direction to the whole," but this frame tale also endorsed the importance of life's middle and provided the narrative device by which the poem's middle could be similarly extended.

The Wanderers' story is preeminently a tale of doubts about the future. Young men of medieval Norway become wanderers when plague rages in their homeland. Having become entranced by the dream of a terrestrial paradise, they flee Norway, and mortality, to search for an earthly paradise and lasting life. Instead, in their four landings on shore, they encounter barbarism, war, death, and cannibalism. Thirty years after leaving Norway, they have no expectations or illusions left: "hope was dead" (1:97). After Nicholas, the Breton squire and chief visionary of the band, dies and supplies dwindle, "we needs must think / That in mid ocean we were doomed to die" (1:99). They are still in the middle of their quest, having neither returned to Norway nor achieved their goal. And they expect to die there, in "mid ocean."

Instead they come to a "nameless city in a distant sea" (1:4) where descendants of Greek sailors have settled and preserved much of their classical culture. The Norsemen arrive "shrivelled, bent, and grey" (1:5), the ironic outcome of a journey meant to move forward to everlasting life. The Greek and Norse elders agree to hold feast days twice a month, sharing a classical tale at the first, a northern one at the second. The body of the poem follows the feast days through an entire year, beginning in March, and presents twenty-four tales within the ongoing frame tale. In that frame tale the Wanderers gradually relinquish their bitterness and accept both death and (in the days left them) life. If the Wanderers' journey in search of an earthly paradise was a form of regression, they eventually progress to a more mature understanding of life and themselves as the poem draws to a close.[21]

The entire poem has an intricate structure: the poet's apology, the Wanderers' prologue, brief lines from the poet to readers, and then a division of the main body of the poem into twelve sections called by the months of the year. Each section begins with a lyric or invocation to the month; there follows a brief narrative of the circumstances under which the Greek and Norse elders meet, a classical tale, the audience's reaction to the tale, a narration of the setting for the second, northern tale, the tale itself, and again the audience's reception of the tale. At the end of the entire cycle comes a brief epilogue and the poet's envoi. This intricacy befits the poem's complex attitudes toward moving forward in time versus transcending it. The Wanderers must move forward from Norway into unknown lands to preserve their lives; yet if they persist in moving forward they simply move closer to death.[22]

A paradise escapes the relentless movement toward death, as seen in "The Story of Cupid and Psyche" (a May tale) and "Ogier the Dane" (an August tale). But paradise, insofar as it implies changelessness, also threatens separation from life's processes, becoming in the end just another form of death. Thus, when the Wanderers are deluded into thinking they are to become gods in a new land, they regret their severance from ongoing life and memory: "Can man be made content? We wished to save / The bygone years; our hope, our painted toy, / We feared to miss, drowned in that sea of joy" (1:85). They are loth to lose life's middle, a state that depends on hope for the future and awareness of the past. Reaching an end, or death, may be a threat, but so also is not moving forward (cf. Hodgson 62).

This dilemma underlies the significance of the poem's structure and its serialization. The great good place in the poem is ultimately the middle, in which movement forward takes place but the end is not yet reached. The middle is the realm of life, situated between birth and death; it is also the realm of an ongoing, not-yet-finished tale. The poem several times equates endings of life and endings of tales.[23] "The Doom of King Acrisius" (the April classical tale), for example, explicitly equates narrative and human endings, especially since the passage below follows the happy, triumphant story of Perseus:

> Before the last words of his tale were done
> The purple hills had hidden half the sun,
> But when the story's death a silence made
> Within the hall, in freshness and in shade
> The trembling blossoms of the garden lay.
> (1:305)   Few words at first the elder men could say
> For thinking how all stories end with this,
> Whatever was the midway gain and bliss:
> "He died, and in his place was set his son;
> He died, and in a few days every one
> Went on their way as though he had not been."

The mariners can see uninterrupted steps forward leading only to death.

To resist the poem's movement toward an end, the whole *Earthly Paradise*'s structure postpones endings and expands the middle. In the 1868 prologue Rolf's tale of the Wanderers' quest becomes a prelude to a new phase of story. As his host tells him,

> ye [are] our living chronicle,
> And scarce can we be grieved at what befell
> Your lives in that too hopeless quest of yours,
> Since it shall bring us wealth of happy hours
> Whiles that we live, and to our sons, delight,
> And their sons' sons.
>   But now, sirs, let us go,
> That we your new abodes with us may show,
> And tell you what your life henceforth may be,
> But poor, alas, to that ye hoped to see.

(1:101)

Just as the Wanderers' tale served as prologue to the larger poem (unfinished when the prologue ended in 1868), so within the fictional frame the quest was a preliminary tale that became subsumed into the middle of the Wanderers' and Elders' ongoing story.[24]

Postponed endings and prolonged middles also characterize the body of *The Earthly Paradise*. "The Doom of Acrisius" is in fact two stories, the first a tale of Danae's imprisonment and release, and her story's ending inaugurates her son's adventures. Even Perseus's death ("And he, no god, must lie down by their side" [1:304]) is not the last word: it is followed by a recurrence to the frame tale, so that the announcement of Perseus's mortal end also reverts to the status of a middle.[25]

The same structural principle underlies the entire *Earthly Paradise*. At the end of the first August tale, "Pygmalion and the Image," the season brings an end to harvest and the fruition process developing since the poem's beginning in March:

> But o'er the same fields grey now and forlorn
> The old men sat and heard the swineherd's horn,
> Far off across the stubble, when the day
> At end of harvest-tide was sad and grey.

(1:615)

Yet this ending modulates into a new season that invigorates: "And all the year to autumn-tide did pass. / E'en such a day it was as young men love / When swiftly through the veins the blood doth move" (1:615). The frame tale of the Wanderers and Elders, then, along with the calendrical format, means that each verse tale, though having a beginning and an end, is ultimately a middle. Each is set within the ongoing story of the Wanderers and Elders, a part or middle of that larger story and the passage of the year.

The poem's parts publication also enlarged the middle of Morris's poem for his original audience. The volume issued in April 1868 contained the poem's first two (of four) parts and was (as many reviews noted) 676 pages long, an enormous accomplishment. An endpaper identified the last page as a middle, a lingering pause in an as-yet unfinished work: "In Preparation, The Second *and* Concluding Volume *of* The Earthly Paradise."[26] When that second volume appeared in December 1869 (though bearing the imprint of 1870), it, too, was unfinished (see figure 12); rather than moving on to the end, it also paused, hovered, and stepped back into the middle of an ongoing story. The second volume contained only three "months," September, October, and November, though it ran to 526 pages, making the third part almost as long as the first two parts published in 1868. The third and final volume (part 4: December, January, February) did not appear until December 1870. This truly was the last part, and yet even here, as in the 1869 volume, the poem resisted an ending and gestured toward an ongoing middle.

In the 1870 "Epilogue" Morris bids his tale to die yet immediately indicates that both poet and book will live on:

(3:437)

> And thou, O tale of what these sleepers were,
> Wish one good-night to them thou holdest dear,
> Then die thyself, and let us go our ways,
> And live awhile amid these latter days!

The poem is to step back into silence yet move onward through time. The poem at once closes (the function, after all, of an epilogue), yet it also persists into *L'Envoi,* which opens,

(3:438)

> *Here are we for the last time face to face,*
> *Thou and I, Book, before I bid thee speed*
> *Upon thy perilous journey to that place*
> *For which I have done on thee pilgrim's weed.*

Even here an apparent ending leads to a new beginning, the book's journey through time to the realm of lasting memory: *"thou goest forth to seek /* . . . *the Land of Matters Unforgot"* (3:438–39). Though the book may die before reaching this land, the poet hopes it will journey to greet his master, Geoffrey Chaucer, and Morris invites his own audience to imagine this rather than the finality of tales' or lives' endings.[27] *The Earthly Paradise* thus elevates the importance and appeal of the middle, and the work's appearance in parts extended the duration of the poem's own middle.[28]

Each time *The Earthly Paradise* paused between 1868 and 1870, Morris's audience had the opportunity to respond much as did audiences within the poem's frame tale. Quick to seize on Morris's characterizing the

Figure 12. Advertisement for uncompleted *Earthly Paradise* in the 13 November 1869 *Academy.* (*Alderman Library, University of Virginia*)

poet in the apology as an *"idle singer of an empty day,"* reviewers consistently referred to the dreaminess and otherworldliness of the poem. The 31 May 1868 *Sunday Times* praised the work's "fresh" and "unworldly . . . spirit in which the whole is conceived and executed, [so] that no thought of the length of the work remains after its perusal is completed"; and it compared reading the poem to "a walk by moonlight in some wide forest" that "seems peopled with strange phantoms, and [in which] dreams of faun and dryad half form themselves in the mind" (7). The 17 June 1868 *Guardian* called Morris "an accomplished story-teller, dreaming as it were his dream aloud, and vocal with a sweet garrulity," who had produced a book that "should be dreamed over rather than thought over; should be taken up from time to time, and not read continuously" (696). A similar comment appeared in the 20 June 1868 *Spectator,* in a review that opened, "Mr. Morris has revived the delightful art of dreaming the old dreamy stories in verse, so that they soothe and charm the ear and fancy without making any of the severe intellectual demands of most of our modern poets on the constructive thought and imagination of the reader" (737). This last can sound like censure to twentieth-century readers, and Morris scholars such as Florence Boos (*Design* 4–5, 28–31) and Carole Silver (56) have argued persuasively that Victorian readers misread his most popular work.

Yet insofar as Victorian reaction created the work's meaning for its first audience, that response has its own validity,[29] one connected to the pattern of the middle we have been tracing. Within the larger frame of *The Earthly Paradise* each inset tale is a moment of lingering, of postponing the onward journey to death in the outer frame. In its 28 January 1871 review of the poem's fourth and final part, the *Spectator* argued that "Mr. Morris's work is for seasons of rest, for such moods as, if they chance to find us on the water on a summer evening, bid us quit the oar and float awhile" (104). The inset tales also move forward within the onward stream of time and narrative so imperceptibly there is an impression of floating, of lingering, rather than moving ahead to the end. This dallying before arriving at the end would again have been extended by the poem's issuance in parts over a two-and-a-half year period.

If *The Earthly Paradise* shares the extended middles of all serial works and the pattern of a step forward followed by a pause, the sequence of twenty-four verse tales also forms a pattern of one step back for two steps forward related to the issue of doubt. The poem's oft-expressed fears of death derive from doubts about traditional religious assurances, as indicated in the December lyric: "O thou who clingest still to life and love, / Though nought of good, no God thou mayst discern" (3:2). In his famous review of *The Earthly Paradise* in the October 1868 *Westminster Review,*[30] Walter Pater obliquely referred to the poem's embedded scepticism, saying that "To regard all things and principles of things as inconstant modes or fashions has more and more become the tendency of modern thought" (89). Few others in 1868 saw dark notes in a poem that seemed so fresh, direct, and dreamy. After the second volume appeared in 1869 the 20 April 1870 *Guardian* remarked of Morris that "With all his love of beauty and rare power of depicting it, he is anything but a cheerful writer. . . . The several tales . . . are haunted by the feeling that the brightest flowers of life bloom and are gathered under the shadow of death" (468), yet this was again an uncommon response.

By the time the final volume was published, however, several reviewers commented on the hints of doubt in the poem (Gardner 53). The 24 December 1870 *Saturday Review* asserted that there were "passages breathing a spirit of unmistakable scepticism" (809). The 25 December 1870 *Sunday Times* reported that, "Looking through the passages marked for re-perusal and possible extract, the first thing that strikes one is how large a proportion of them bears on the solemnity of man's fate, the certainty of present sorrow, and the mistiness of the future towards which he steers" (7). And the January 1871 *Edinburgh Review* (248) and 8 February 1871 *Guardian* (161) seconded the *Saturday Review*'s charges of scepticism.[31] Hence the poem's movement forward toward completion was accompanied by readers' growing recognition that Morris's poem expressed doubts about the society's dominant religion and ability to create a better future.

An important pattern in *The Earthly Paradise,* then, is the movement toward hope or back into doubt in the individual installments of tales.[32] The tales of spring and summer are more often hopeful than not. In spring the three classical tales progress toward attainment of the hopes that inspired the Wanderers' quest. In "Atalanta's Race" the goddess Venus appears to Milanion to grant him his wish for victory in the race to win an earthly bride; in "The Doom of King Acrisius" Danae sexually unites with a god and produces a half-divine son, though both she and Perseus must still die; in "The Story of Cupid and Psyche" Psyche not only joins with a god, like Danae, but herself becomes immortal and escapes death forever in an earthly paradise. The northern spring tales, in contrast, unfold in the world of mortality. In "The Man Born to Be King" a poor but destined youth endures repeated malevolence from the reigning king but survives to wed the king's daughter and to become king himself. The title character in "The Proud King" becomes a more humane ruler after undergoing humiliation and deprivation. In "The Writing of the Image," the one visible king is dead, stuffed and on display in an underground crypt, and the tale is a stark account of greed and retribution. Thus, the classical tales inhabit the realm of the mythic and immortal and progress toward unalloyed victory: the northern tales inhabit the human world and exemplify a far more qualified attainment (cf. Calhoun 171; Boos, *Design* 89).

This pattern is modified in the summer tales, yet the volume ends affirmatively. In "The Love of Alcestis" Apollo lives amidst mortals, and the heroic Alcestis rescues her husband Admetus from death by dying in his place. "The Son of Croesus," unlike Admetus, enjoys no respite from fate and dies a young man despite his father's efforts to protect him. Yet in the culminating classical tale of the volume, "Pygmalion and the Image," Venus responds to Pygmalion's passionate prayer and grants life to the beautiful statue Pygmalion has carved. Thus, the summer classical tales begin with a step forward, a rescue from death at the cost of death; move back to a tale of fate and loss; then step forward and culminate in a fond, fantastic wish becoming reality through the active intercession of a goddess who heeds her devotees' cries.

The summer northern tales begin on the same dark note as "The Writing on the Image," but they, too, move forward to victory. In "The Lady of the Land" a young pirate fails to endure the frightening manifestation of a bewitched, beautiful woman in the guise of a dragon and dooms her to continued imprisonment in time, himself to permanent loneliness.[33] A king not content with great personal and political fulfillment loses all when he insists on enjoying the sexual pleasures of a sprite in "The Watching of the Falcon." But "Ogier the Dane" is blessed at birth by another sprite, Morgan le Fay, and after a full, glorious, heroic life on earth is given renewed youth and love in an earthly paradise; indeed, he returns to earth for a second stint of glory and then returns to paradise for everlasting bliss with Morgan. The northern tales that began by being rooted in mortality modulate into the realm of immortality; the classical tales that began in the realm of myth present a final victory when the timeless (the statue) becomes mortal.

The telling of these tales has a beneficent effect on the Wanderers, whose responses form a pattern of doubt and hope complementary to that of the stories themselves. At the end of the second March tale, "The Man Born to Be King," the mariners still feel the weight of "vain regrets," exhibit "wasted eyes," and can only begin to elude their woe: "as old men may do, whose hopes grew grey / Before their beards, they made a little mirth" (1:215). Yet by the telling of the first April tale, the mariners are progressing beyond their earlier doubt and dissatisfaction with existence. They flinch at hearing Perseus's inevitable descent into death, but they now find additional meaning in his story:

> Their hearts were softened,—far away they saw
> That other world, that 'neath another law
> Had lived and died; when man might hope to see
> Some earthly image of Divinity,
> And yet not die, but, strengthened by the sight,
> Cast fear away, and go from might to might,
> Until to godlike life, though short, he came,
> Amidst all losses winning hope of fame.
>   . . . . .
> So mused the Wanderers, and awhile might deem
> That world might not be quite an empty dream,
> But dim foreshadowings of what yet might come
> When they perforce must leave that new-gained home.

(1:305–6)

They do not rush to embrace faith, but they see grounds for hope and are less discontent at moving ahead in time.

As the Wanderers move into summer, they begin to accept mortality and its limitations, and hence find "The Love of Alcestis" (the first June tale) bittersweet:

> In spite of knowledge growing day by day
> Of lives so wasted, in despite of death,
> With sweet content that eve they drew their breath,
> And scarce their own lives seemed to touch them more
> Than that dead Queen's beside Boebeis' shore;
> Bitter and sweet so mingled in them both,
> Their lives and that old tale, they had been loth,
> Perchance, to have them told another way.

(1:503)

By the end of the August tales (and the first volume), the Wanderers remain poised between hope and regret, softened by their six months' sojourn on the isle and the genial seasons just past. They are now content to find some happiness in the very shadow of death:

> And now well nigh as much their pain was past
> As though death's veil already had been cast
> Over their heads—so, midst some little mirth,
> They watched the dark night hide the gloomy earth.

(1:676)

From bitter, disillusioned men the Wanderers have taken steps forward to become old men content to die and able to find some joy as they wait in the middle of life for the end to come. Their personal progress is intensified by the frequent strain of hope in the stories they tell and hear.

Reviewers emphasized the 1868 stories' freshness, innocence, and simplicity. In a comment seized upon eagerly for later advertisements of the poem, the 30 May 1868 *Saturday Review* praised Morris for fidelity to the details of classical legends while maintaining a purity and refinement suited to all members of the family. The 20 June 1868 *Spectator* perceived the connecting "thread" of the volume as "the importunate craving for some special isle of happiness amidst the cares of life, which all the tales more or less express, and the pathetic disappointments attaching to which all the tales more or less delineate" (738); yet the reviewer added that the book was a "delightful . . . escape from the problem-haunted poetry of the day" (737). The 2 January 1869 *Weekly Dispatch,* like other reviews, praised Morris for avoiding psychological analysis of character in favor of external description: "The poetry of our own generation has been the utterance of the mood of the time. The poet's eyes have been turned inwards rather than suffered to see the sights before them. . . . It is positively refreshing to listen to a living poet who talks with the simple truthful utterance so long unheard" (3). These several remarks insist on beauty combined with weightlessness, beauty that, like Psyche's own, sheds the burdens of mortal life; and they suggest a tendency to see *The Earthly Paradise* as a lovely, wholly affirmative work of art.[34]

Audiences' emphasis on affirmation was echoed not only by expressions of hope in the tales but also by the serial's promise of forward movement after a pause. The October 1868 *Tinsley's Magazine* remarked of the first volume, "It extends to 676 pages of close print, and if we had not read *The Life and Death of Jason,* it would be difficult to know where to find the courage to commence such an undertaking as the perusal of this volume. However, the astonishing fact is, that when we have arrived at the end of that task, we find ourselves convicted of a very strong desire to have in our hands the other volume of similar dimensions, which the plan of the work, as set forth in this one, necessitates, and which we are told is in preparation" (271–72). The 26 December 1868 *Daily News,* too, noted the length of pages in the first volume and remarked that "we are promised another volume, completing the series" (2c). Victorian readers seemed willing to rest in the lingering plenitude of a poem, yet looked forward, after a pause, to having the poem continue.

The movement toward happiness in the spring and summer tales was counteracted in the next, autumn installment of tales (part 3) that provided an altogether darker glimpse of life, love, and fate than had the first two parts. Even when there is triumph there is a sense of regret and irresolvable complexity, and the volume opens and closes with stories of tragic loss and wasted passion—and also, in "The Lovers of Gudrun," with a power and depth unanticipated in reactions to the first volume. "The Death of Paris," the September classical tale, opens with an arbitrary, virtually meaningless death, when amidst the banal latter days of the Trojan War a stray arrow shot from Troy fells a "well-tried warrior from the Cretan land" (2:6). The Greek Philoctetes randomly shoots a poisoned arrow in return, which wounds Paris. When Paris seeks help for his wound from his former lover Oenone, their encounter is a fierce, sad exchange of unyielding bitterness and unforgivingness on one side, obsessive and unsated lust on the other. "The Story of Acontius and Cydippe" is a far happier classical tale and ends with lovers overcoming barriers to unite; yet against the backdrop of their fulfillment the tale expresses doubt about love's permanence (see also Calhoun 183; Boos, *Design* 24n). The final classical tale, "The Story of Rhodope," at first seems even happier, with the beautiful but poor Rhodope leaving her homeland to become a king's bride; yet Rhodope's leading trait is an unquenchable restlessness reminiscent of the young Wanderers' discontent.[35] Favorable events occur in the last two classical tales, but good fortune seems underlain by an essential hollowness, an inevitable step back from hope and happiness.

The northern tales only grow darker as they progress. "The Land East of the Sun and West of the Moon," like "Ogier the Dane," features the attainment of earthly paradise, departure, then a recovery of paradise forever. But the recovery of paradise is more tenuous, more doubtful, than in "Ogier," and the tone of triumph is qualified by the hard human passions at the center of the tale, including the attempted seduction of the male hero by his brother's wife.[36] In the October tale, "The Man Who Never Laughed Again," Bharam finds an earthly paradise of love but loses it forever and lives a life of psychological torment. The final tale, "The Lovers of Gudrun," is a moving rendition of love and betrayal among the heroic Kiartan, his best friend Bodli, and Gudrun. There is perhaps consoling pleasure in the tale's very power, but it is a story of disaster following from potentially noble emotions.

After the brightness and hope of the spring and summer tales, then, these autumn tales focus on the loss, doubt, and failings of life. The Wanderers are also placed firmly within a framework of decay. In the time it takes for them to hear the tale of Acontius and Cydippe, we are reminded that "A short space more of that short space was gone, / Wherein each deemed himself not quite alone" (2:205). At the end of the October tales the mariners are situated in an ever-narrowing space of existence from which the only exit is death:

(2:272)

> For e'en as men laid on a flowery slope
> 'Twixt inaccessible cliffs and unsailed sea,
> Painless, and waiting for eternity
> That will not harm, were these old men now grown.

Yet despite the darkness of the tales themselves and the men's approaching death, the Wanderers go on. They have scant grounds for hope but (rather like Gudrun after all passion is gone) find a way to persist and to take small, limited joys that offer themselves. Even the tragedy of Gudrun and her lovers fails to quench the old men's cheerful stoicism, and they are surprised to find that sadness in a tale can yield pleasure to its auditors:

(2:526)

> The heavy grief that once their heads did bow,
> Had wrought so much for them, that they might sit
> Amid some pleasure at the thought of it;
> At least not quite consumed by sordid fear,
> That now at last the end was come anear;
> At least not hardened quite so much, but they
> Might hear of love and longing worn away
> 'Twixt birth and death of others, wondering
> Belike, amid their pity what strange thing
> Made the mere truth of what poor souls did bear
> —In vain or not in vain—so sweet to hear,
> So healing to the tangled woes of earth,
> At least for a short while.

The 1869 volume ended on a note of muted hope:

(2:526)

> yet behind
> That mask of pensive eyes, so unbeguiled
> By ancient folly any more, what wild
> Strange flickering hopes ineffable might lie,
> As swift that latter end of eve slipped by!

If the autumn tales presented a less hopeful, more doubtful perspective on life's events than those of spring and summer, the frame story as well as the year's advancing calendar suggested an ability to go on, to endure, and even to win some added pleasure amidst a darkening horizon.

The reception of the second volume of *The Earthly Paradise* acknowledged the tales' increasing somberness. "Sadness is, indeed, the key-note to all the poems" (7), the 19 December 1869 *Sunday Times* remarked. The 20 April 1870 *Guardian* uttered the "strong suspicion that there is no other abstract word that occurs in the volume before us so often as 'misery' " (468). Yet the reviews asserted Morris's growth in artistic complexity, especially his skill in psychological analysis. The 11 December 1869 *Pall Mall Budget* stated that "Gudrun" was "in its intention a half tragic, half epic study of fate and passion . . . having a quite modern subtlety and involution of emotion thrown into it" (26). The 25 December 1869 *Athenaeum* praised the "psychological truth with which his characters are informed" (868). G. A. Simcox, writing in the 12 February 1870 *Academy,* remarked that "there is less of naive adventure and blithe description in these stories, and more of psychological analysis, [though] we never cross the invisible line which divides the poetry of dream from the poetry of action" (121). The 12 March 1870 *Spectator* insisted even more than Simcox on the sustained dreaminess of the poems but still remarked of "Gudrun" that "the tragic passages of this tale disclose powers of which the author's former work had given no sign" (333). The increasing darkness in the tales was counteracted, in readers' eyes, by delight offered in the poet's more complex art.

The issues of doubt versus progression received articulation in yet another guise. The 11 December 1869 *Pall Mall Budget* remarked, amusingly, that "Length of wind in the narrators waxes with length of days. The wanderers tell each other longer stories as they grow older" (26). The decline of the mariners had been accompanied by an astonishing growth in the girth of the poem itself. The 20 April 1870 *Guardian* likewise commented on the serial growth of Morris's work, conveying a sense of earlier doubts followed by unexpected progression:

(467)

> *The very year after* The Life and Death of Jason, *came the first instalment of* The Earthly Paradise, *containing twelve narrative poems, supposed to be tales that were told in old time by certain gentlemen and mariners of Norway. . . . Mr. Morris was again to be congratulated, but with misgiving. The charm of his manner was unabated, yet there was reason to think that he might break down before the end of his task. In supplying tales for a month of the year he had visited in thought so many countries, touched on so many times, borrowed tradition and legend from such various sources, transposed and arranged so often those images of beauty, drawn from the world of sense, which are almost as essential to the*

poet as colour to the painter and sounds to the musician, that it might seem the months ranging from March to August had exhausted the plenitude of his powers, and left him, like a ruined spendthrift, to live for the rest of the year on the fragments saved from his former prodigality. The apprehension was needless. The portion of The Earthly Paradise *which Mr. Morris has lately published testifies to the development rather than the exhaustion of his genius.*

The poet and Wanderers alike, then, were noted for stepping back into doubt and dark visions yet emerging like the dying year in ongoing movement.

Though the first word of the final part and volume, published in December 1870, was *Dead* (in the lyric devoted to a still December midnight), the opening December tales in fact reverted to the hopeful patterns of the spring and summer narratives (Calhoun 199). In "The Golden Apples" men once again live in the company of gods and heroes, and the half-divine, half-mortal Hercules achieves his quest on the way to further glory and fame.[37] In the northern tale of December, "The Fostering of Aslaug," mythic fulfillment is also possible. The tale begins sadly enough, with the grim murder of Aslaug's protector and her subjection to brutish, tyrannical foster parents. But Aslaug's ability to endure silence and absence helps ensure a steadier future with her beloved Ragnar than that enjoyed by her mythic parents Sigurd and Brynhild. Death wrought by tragedy is the beginning, not the culmination of, a tale, and is followed by ongoing, fruitful life.

The January tales, however, regress from the possibilities established in the December tales. Bellerophon survives despite a series of disasters, and in this sense "Bellerophon at Argos" ends affirmatively. But the events of fratricide, suicide, sundered friendship, and betrayal dominate the story. "The Ring Given to Venus" is similarly a less happy tale than "The Fostering of Aslaug." Gods and goddesses appear, but the Greek gods are superannuated if not dead—though Laurence does unite with his bride after retrieving the ring he had placed on Venus's statue (see also Kirchhoff, *Morris* 83).

The final, February tales of the poem gesture equally toward the mixed hope and fear that have characterized the entire year's tales. "Bellerophon in Lycia" is a story of triumph, glory, and love that falls short of perfection only in that the wondrous hero who seems a very god to the Lycians is a mortal fated to grow old and die.[38] The atmosphere and tone of the spring stories, especially the adventures of Perseus, return in this tale. "The Hill of Venus," though, is a story of failed will and blasted passion. In this retelling of the Tannhäuser legend, Walter, already disillusioned with life (a step back), becomes Venus's lover (a step forward) and so recalls earlier mortal-immortal pairings. This sexual union, however, brings defeat and suffering, not joy. Walter travels to Rome to seek renewed life yet returns as he left, devastated with forever-unsated longing for the goddess, an ironic parody of the ever-renewed desire in Ogier's or Psyche's earthly paradises. But despite Walter's suffering (qualified by moments of rapture with Venus) there are signs of hope. As the entire *Earthly Paradise* approaches its end, the setting for the tale is the anticipated apocalypse at the end of the first millennium. As Walter journeys to Rome, pilgrims rush to meet the world's end amidst dire rumors, and the pope who sees Walter gives up on him. Yet out of such darkness and doubt the world *goes on:* the apocalypse never occurs. The pope even reconsiders and blesses Walter, and the dry staff blooms.[39]

The final, February tales seem attuned to the last month of winter, the decayed end of one year yet a time rife with signs of renewing life. The mariners, similarly, come closer to death, their personal apocalypse, with each month; yet they achieve a kind of psychic progress in this last installment. By December the Wanderers have largely forgotten their earlier doubts:

> Our elders sat within the guest-hall fair,
> Not looking older for the snow without;
> Cheery enough; remembering not old doubt,
> A gnawing pain once, grown too hard to bear,
> And so cast by.

(3:3)

Even after the dark January tale set in Argos the frame directs attention to the growth and hope that can take place amidst an unpromising time: "Yet mid the dead swoon of the earth, the days / 'Gan lengthen now" (3:178). The opening frame to the February tales in fact asserts that the mariners are more rather than less cheerful:

> little as the tide seemed made for mirth,
> Scarcely they lacked it less than months agone,
> When on their wrinkles bright the great sun shone;
> Rather, perchance, less pensive now they were.

(3:233)

After listening to the last tale, accordingly, their response is not to follow Walter's pattern of reversion but to imitate the Pope in blessing the beauty they find:

> But the old men learned in earth's bitter lore,
>
> . . . . .
>
>   wandered forth into the noonday sun,
>   To watch the blossoms budding on the wall,
>   And hear the rooks among the elm-trees call,
>   And note the happy voices on the breeze,
>   And see the lithe forms; making out of these
>   No tangled story, but regarding them
>   As hidden elves upon the forest's hem
>   Gaze on the dancers through the May-night green,
>   Not knowing aught what troubled looks may mean.

(3:433)

No review asserted a unified design in the completed poem,[40] but reviewers did often point to a dominant impression or theme. Sidney Colvin in the 15 December 1870 *Academy* identified hatred of death and a clinging to life as the poem's keynote (57), and G. W. Cox in the January 1871 *Edinburgh Review* similarly asserted that "This mournful sound of autumn-tide runs as a keynote through all the tales" (246).

Yet reviewers also discerned indications of progress or accomplishment in the poem. As Colvin asserted, "by degrees there have come other elements into some of the tales told,—deeper poetical motive, greater complexity of incident, greater force and subtlety of emotion, more of the conscious and sensitive modern self mingling with the ancient direct nature and all-adorning fancy" (57).[41] Colvin (57) as well as the 25 December 1870 *Sunday Times* (7) saw Morris as the hero of his own poem. As Colvin said, Morris had "in little more than three years carried his great undertaking safely through, and beyond all danger of falling, like so many poetical undertakings, into the category of things unaccomplished" (57). Where the poem qua poem was concerned, readers saw progress toward completion.

The *Sunday Times,* in fact, saw this step forward as the result of a cooperative venture between audience and poet, a hallmark of serial literature: "Lovers of poetry may be congratulated upon the accomplishment of Mr. Morris's noble task. An achievement of equal importance modern poetic annals do not chronicle. A rare and not to be expected combination of overflow of poetic fervour and creative power on the part of a singer, and a sudden and almost unprecedented display of sympathy and appreciation on that of the public, has brought about the completion of the task." The reviewer then asserted the importance of length in *The Earthly Paradise,* acknowledging the importance of a structure that resists ends in favor of an expanding middle, a structure emphasized by serialization:

(7)

> *Bulk is the last quality in a poem which we should, in ordinary cases, single out for praise. But bulk is in this instance a distinguishing and singularly valuable attribute. Who has not felt sorrow at the littleness, so far as regards mere dimensions, of the works of some poets, and longed for larger fields in which to disport. Our English woods have the fault that we are always reaching the verge and cannot, as in some countries, indulge in the hope of being lost in them. . . . we should hold the man who censured its dimensions about as reasonable as he who objected to a bequest of landed property on account of the extent of the estate. Often have we wished for what we here obtain, a work we could not master, a domain the manifold beauties of which we could not exhaust.*

From another standpoint the 24 December 1870 *Saturday Review* also hailed the poem's ability to resist an ending and to last into the future: "few readers will close the last portion of the *Earthly Paradise* without a sincere sigh of regret. Not that the sigh need be drawn too soon. There is a feast in store first, and, thanks to Mr. Morris's catering, one which ought to last, if husbanded well, right over the long winter nights and through the holiday season" (808). Most telling of all is the 28 January 1871 *Spectator,* which literally saw the poem as one to continue, a reaction possible only for those who had followed the work's installment publication:

(105)

> *Our last word is concerned not with anything that is in this part of the* Earthly Paradise, *but with certain things which were on the fly-leaf of the volume originally comprising the two first parts, and of which there is no sign in this. . . . the contents of the intended second volume were stated on the fly-leaf in question. The contents of the* Earthly Paradise *as it now stands completed are somewhat different from what Mr. Morris then told his readers to expect. There is assuredly nothing to complain of, for we have gained beyond the expectation then given "The Death of Paris" and "The Lovers of Gudrun," of which the former is not surpassed by any piece save one in the whole series, and the latter may fairly be singled out as that one which is the author's masterpiece. Yet one is irresistibly tempted to ask what has become of Theseus, and still less can one refrain from desiring to hear one day of Orpheus and Eurydice. . . . and we hope in time to have proof that he has not abandoned his choice.*

It is an enormous tribute to Morris that after presenting some fifteen hundred pages of poetry in three years his readers could ask for more. But the *Spectator* is also important because it is a reminder that for Morris's first readers, the circumstances of parts publication enabled audiences to envision the poem continuing beyond its apparent end. A terminal point without hope of renewal or continuation, a psychic step backward, first drove the Wanderers from home, and that and similar fears haunt the darkest moments and tales of the larger poem, a pattern that readers increasingly discerned as the three installments appeared. The design of the poem forms a structural resistance to endings, and the work's appearance in parts extended the pattern of doubt and hope, reversion and progression embedded in the book's forward growth over advancing time.

William Morris's later narrative poem, *The Pilgrims of Hope,* serialized in thirteen parts in *Commonweal* from March 1885 to 3 July 1886, more directly exemplifies doubt as a step backward for every two steps forward, and the poem's appearance in the Socialist League's official journal gives this serial work added interest. Unlike others discussed in this study, this work was not aimed primarily at a large middle-class audience. Because *Pilgrims* appeared only in *Commonweal,* not in a separately gathered volume during Morris's lifetime, and because the dominant periodicals were staunchly middle class and unlikely to review numbers of a radical Socialist paper, it is generally assumed that the poem's issuance took place within a deliberately confined audience and situation. Peter Faulkner's edition of *The Critical Heritage* thus contains no review of *Pilgrims of Hope.*

A larger segment of the Victorian literary audience than might be thought, however, followed the poem.[42] The *Commonweal* staff was intent on enlarging its readership. In the issue in which the last installment of *Pilgrims* appeared, Morris wrote in "A Letter from Scotland" that "our comrades are making most commendable efforts to puff the *Commonweal,* and with much success. The news-shops take it and sell it, too, and they are also getting newsboys to sell it; so that propaganda of some sort is going on" (3 July 1886: 106). While it is true that *Commonweal* hardly enjoyed the circulation of, say, the *Cornhill,* Morris's narrative poem received serious notice from other periodicals. The "Notes and News" column of the 25 April 1885 *Academy,* for example, listed the contents of the May 1885 *Commonweal* (containing the third part of *Pilgrims*) for its readers.

Even more revealing are two separate notices of *Pilgrims* in the *Athenaeum.* The 20 February 1886 notice came between the eighth and ninth parts of the poem (in the January and March 1886 numbers of *Commonweal*). While the larger design of the poem was not yet fully clear, its political orientation was. If the *Athenaeum* predictably discounted the political content, which, after all, was the poem's major impetus, the journal's notice in the "Literary Gossip" column indicated that *Pilgrims* was being read with attention and appreciation by many among the middle class:

(264)

> Mr. William Morris has had in hand for some time a poem called *"The Pilgrims of Hope,"* which deals with the Socialist propaganda, in which he is taking a share. Politics apart, the poem is full of the old qualities—perfect rapport with nature, admirable sketching of scenery, pathos, and simple diction. It is premature to criticize "The Pilgrims of Hope"; suffice it to say it is in the large anapaestic measure of "Sigurd the Volsung," and bids fair to be a work of capital importance. Portions of it have appeared in the Commonweal, *the organ of the Socialist League, and Mr. Morris is understood to be welding the parts together for publication as a whole.*

Some three months later, when it was clear that part of the hero's story involved his wife's falling in love with another man in the Socialist movement, the *Athenaeum* persisted in directing its readers' attention to the poem. The "Literary Gossip" column in the 29 May 1886 *Athenaeum* commented that "Mr. William Morris has recently issued in the *Commonweal* the eleventh section of his poem 'The Pilgrims of Hope,' in which the hero arrives at Paris with his wife and Socialist friend at the time of the Commune" (717). The poem may not have had the readership of *The Earthly Paradise,* then, but its audience was hardly negligible, or restricted only to regular subscribers of *Commonweal.*

That the poem, however, was both a serial and a Socialist poem might suggest points of strain between format and content, since the serial form was connected to dominant elements in middle-class ideology. In the 8 May 1886 *Commonweal* (41) Morris assailed "grovelling individualism" in favor of the united strength that promoted communal interests. Yet if one of the themes of *Pilgrims* is the need to place communal needs above individual needs (Holzman 381; Silver 108; Boos, "Narrative" 162), the poem is also about personal joy, pain, and commitment. The poem's political emphasis on communal efforts is not made at the expense of characterization.

Commonweal also challenged the middle-class commitment to gradualism by endorsing an apocalyptic, revolutionary break with capitalism rather than the meliorism advocated by Parliamentary liberals. But the moment of apocalypse was placed in the distant future; meanwhile, notions of gradual, evolutionary development and progress were in effect (Hobsbawm 267). Hence, Morris and E. Belfort Bax cowrote *Socialism from the Roots Up,* a developmental and causal analysis of history serially published in the *Commonweal* at the same time the later parts of *Pilgrims* were appearing. And in several columns Morris hailed the inevitable progress toward socialism, though the signs of progress to him might be the very depression of trade that inspired doubt in his middle-class countrymen (see, e.g., 22 May 1886: 57; see also Hobsbawm 259).

Morris's serial poem also made brilliant use of developmental modes, and of the time frame of serialization, at several key points. "The Message of the March Wind" (not yet indicated as a continuing poem when it appeared in the March 1885 *Commonweal*) identified manifold steps forward as the unnamed speaker connected the unseen yet steady growth of the "hope of the people," the "seed of midwinter, unheeded, unperished" beneath the snow, the dawning love shared with his lover, and "the babe 'neath [her] girdle that groweth unseen" (12). This progressive growth that took place unnoted, out of sight, was realized in literary terms in the next issue of *Commonweal,* when readers discovered that the short poem they read in March had germinated into a continuing poem that would persist into the future.[43] In the fourth part of *Pilgrims* (June 1885), some three months after "The Message of the March Wind" appeared, the babe growing unseen had reached full term and been born into the world, becoming the silent auditor of "Mother and Son." This child, always growing, continued to appear at intervals, as a child in the fields in the poem's eighth part (January 1886), and in the final installment (3 July 1886) as a son whose continued development would add one more man to fight for socialism.[44] Thus the poem was permeated by a sense of slow, steady growth, steps forward, that might not always have been visible but would inevitably develop and take effect in the future.

If serialization underscores developmental modes more often identified with bourgeois than Socialist thought, however, Morris's publishing the poem only in *Commonweal* constituted a kind of poetic decorum for socialism.[45] Leaving the poem in unassembled parts amidst the Socialist news and messages surrounding them implicitly paralleled the work's insistence on subordinating individualism to a larger, socially conscious group.[46] In the poem's penultimate part in the 5 June 1886 *Commonweal,* Richard, looking back on the days of the Commune, calls himself "an atom of the strife" (75), an essential but tiny part of a larger aggregate. Individual parts of *Pilgrims of Hope* might also be seen as "atoms" that melt into the larger numbers of *Commonweal.* Morris's decision to leave them there meant that the parts remained embedded in the matrix of a larger Socialist function and message rather than being separately bound as an individual aesthetic object or a commodity of the capitalist market.[47]

In addition to its political function, *Pilgrims of Hope* is also a significant treatment of doubt. Socialism itself is premised on doubts so intense about the future of capitalism that revolution is the only practical alternative; to get to that desired goal, however, the current, capitalist society must first worsen. Hence, there is an essential connection between socialism on the one hand and steps backward and forward on the other. Moreover, as members of a new political movement, Socialists were at once convinced of the inherent, inevitable progress toward socialism and sensitive to the opposition and even setbacks the "sect" would face, as evidenced by the fate of the Paris Commune that forms part of the poem's plot.[48] As Richard says to his wife in the poem's second part (April 1885), "Let us fear—and press forward where few dare to go; / Let us falter in hope—and plan deeds for the morrow" (20).

The poem is often criticized for a weak or unfocused plot (e.g., by E. P. Thompson 670–71, Holzman 375–76). Seen in the context of the steps backward and forward in socialism's progress, however, the poem's larger plot is a compelling story of a man whose commitment to socialism involves a series of personal steps backward on the way forward to the future, a rhythm extended by the poem's serialization.[49] In the second part he and his wife take a step forward, leaving the comfortable, safe haven of the beautiful countryside to join cause with the people in London for whom the city is a "prison" (part 2, April 1885: 20). Another step forward comes after the birth of his son, when Richard experiences a "New Birth" (the title of part 5) in a conversion to the Socialist cause. That step forward is itself the outcome of an earlier stage of doubt and retrogression. During a happy childhood Richard had met a survivor of the 1848 revolution in France (Holzman 382–83; Boos, "Narrative" 156); his "tale that never ends / [of] The battle of grief and hope with riches and folly and wrong" could not reach through the golden glow of Richard's serene youth. But when grown, Richard "saw things clear and grim," realizing that "the poor were poor, and had no heart or hope," until he "fell into bitter mood." Sharing his vision of social injustice won him a wife and renewed movement forward—"the tale told lifted the load / That made me less than a man; and she set my feet on the road" (August 1885: 68)—and at the end of the part he had arrived at the exalted joy of new commitment to the Socialist cause.

But the interval between the fifth and sixth parts (August and September 1885) brought no further advance or joy, only steps back into struggle and sorrow. Richard loses his inheritance to a lawyer's swindling, then his job to an oppressive master in "The New Proletarian."[50] Yet despite this step backward the part ended with a look to the future, absorbing Richard's loss into a lesson that, if taken to heart by others, could change the world: " 'Tis the lot of many millions! Yet if half of those millions knew / The hope that my heart hath learned, we should find a deed to do, / And who or what should withstand us?" (September 1885: 81). The seventh part (November 1885) brought the further loss of Richard's freedom and the sundering of his home while he stayed in prison; and the eighth part (January 1886) announced his wife's death. After this jump forward to the end of her life, the poem then backed up and gradually related the story of how she and their friend Arthur came to die.

In the ninth part (March 1886) Richard narrated a form of progress, the growth of the Socialist band and the gain of a personal friend in Arthur, blessed with wealth, education, personal charm, and a commitment to the Socialist cause. Yet Arthur, too, was now dead, and some other problem was indicated before the ninth part broke off: "He loved me; he grieved my soul: now the love and the grief are past" (March 1886: 22). The difficulty was announced in the tenth part (April 1886): Richard's wife and Arthur had, to their own dismay, fallen in love. When Arthur proposed that all three go to Paris for the last days of the Franco-Prussian War and aid the Socialist cause, Richard readily agreed, hoping to find death in battle.[51]

Yet in the eleventh number (8 May 1886) a step into the future arose out of what had seemed hopeless decline. Richard could think only that "toward the end [we] made speed" as they journeyed by train through France. But when they arrived in Paris, they encountered, not an end, but "A Glimpse of the Coming Day," the Commune that represented the future: "Paris was free; / And e'en as she is this morning, to-morrow all France will be" (8 May 1886: 45).[52] Amidst the profound communal joy that swept through Paris Richard saw this moment as the outcome of a slow developmental process that had long been preparing:

> For this was the promise of spring-tide, and the new leaves
>   longing to burst,
> And the white roads threading the acres, and the sun-warmed
>   meadows athirst.
(45)
> Once all was the work of sorrow and the life without reward,
> And the toil that fear hath bidden, and the folly of master and
>   lord;
> But now are all things changing, and hope without a fear
> Shall speed us on through the story of the changes of the year.

Yet the part did not swell to a simplistic, sentimental note of victory. It began with Richard's personal pain as an estranged husband, then shifted unexpectedly into a moment of profound joy for society; it ended with a regression to persisting personal anguish. Richard's wife, now working with the ambulances among the wounded, was "to all as a sister to be; / A sister amidst of the strangers—and, alas! a sister to me" (45).

The twelfth part (5 June 1886), conversely, presented a moment of muted personal triumph amidst political defeat. The Communards are overwhelmed by the bourgeois "war-machine" (75), but Richard, his wife, and Arthur are able to overcome personal competition and to share a love that transcends possession. In the final installment (3 July 1886), "The Story's Ending," the worst, culminating setback occurred: the Commune falls, and the wife and Arthur are killed. Even the significance of their deaths is already being lost:

                           they died;
Nor counted much in the story. I have heard it told since then,
And mere lies our deeds have turned to in the mouths of happy men,
And e'en those will be soon forgotten as the world wends on its way.

(107)

Yet just as the Commune was the result of nameless sacrifice and toil in the long years preceding (a point made in part 12), so Richard can see his wife's and Arthur's story continuing into the future with a new generation:

                      my soul is seeing the day
When those who are now but children the new generation shall be,
And e'en in our land of commerce and the workshop over the sea,
Amid them shall spring up the story.

(107)

After the seemingly hopeless step backward of nearly dying out, that is, their story will be reborn and lead toward progress in the future. At the end Richard sees no victory, no consolation:

         that is the last and the latest of the tale I have to tell.
I came not here to be bidding my happiness farewell,
And to nurse my grief and to win me the gain of a wounded life,
That because of the bygone sorrow may hide away from the strife.

(107)

I came to look to my son, and myself to get stout and strong,
That two men there might be hereafter to battle against the
     wrong;
And I cling to the love of the past and the love of the day to be,
And the present, it is but the building of the man to be strong
     in me.

Out of the worst possible setback has been born a determination to go on
and fight for the future.

This last installment, perhaps superfluously, is entitled "The Story's
Ending." Yet below the last line, where "*(to be continued)*" had so often
appeared before, there was now printed "*(to be concluded).*" Like the story
of Richard's wife and Arthur—like *The Earthly Paradise* and, we shall see,
Diana of the Crossways—the poem ceased, like some middle installment,
but did not end. No subsequent installment appeared, and one possible
implication was that the conclusion had to take place in the distant future,
the long, slow result of work by Richard and, more likely, the work of
readers willing to join in Richard's cause (see also Boos, "Narrative" 164–
65). Yet again, though now within a distinct political framework, *Pilgrims
of Hope* presented a paradigm of interrelated progress and doubt: steps
forward, succeeded by one step backward, ultimately leading to slow,
steady onward movement. As a serial the poem also participated in the
interplay of hesitation and development that characterized its plot.

George Meredith's composition of *Diana of the Crossways,* a novel that
established his popular reputation in late nineteenth-century England,[53]
provides yet another manifestation of doubt about Victorian values. The
story was written when neither Meredith nor his wife was well and yet
when writing was essential to meet financial obligations; thus personal
doubts affected him as he worked. When the editor of the *Fortnightly
Review* allowed him only two-thirds of the space necessary for the initial
publication of his tale, Meredith made cuts "on the proof-sheets of the first
edition" (Measures ix) to fit the story into six issues. (The first five parts,
appearing in June, July, September, October, and November 1884, were
each sixteen or seventeen pages; the last, in December, ran twenty-nine
pages.) The expanded three-volume edition appearing in February 1885
restored material cut for the serial version and included additional revisions. Thus, larger cultural doubts about the proper publication format for
fiction were also revealed in this novel's history.

The heroine of Meredith's story, Diana Warwick, lived out her romantic desires and pursued her career as a novelist making a number of
significant mistakes; thus, like many characters in *The Way We Live Now,*

especially Lady Carbury, she often moved toward fulfillment by taking one step backward for two steps forward. The last sentence of the serial version of Diana's story, appearing in December 1884 (see figure 13), underscored the hesitant movement of both heroine and novel: "Thus was the erratic woman stricken; and those who care for more of Diana of the Crossways will find it in the extended chronicle" (767). Diana, whose history had been "erratic," was at that moment in the story "stricken," stopped in a life-threatening illness. A number of signs throughout the serial version, including many in this last part, suggested that she would nonetheless resume her life in the future. Similarly, Meredith's story, *Diana of the Crossways,* was stopped at this moment in its serial publication, though it was "to be continued" in volume form. Meredith's doubts about personal development and about literary form were revealed in the methods by which his heroine found a place in her world and in which his novel found its audience in late Victorian England.

Just as we have examined other serial texts throughout this study, we wish to consider the *Fortnightly* version of *Diana* as a legitimate unit of Meredith's work. The existence of this original text, and the first response it created, shaped Victorian ideas about Meredith's *Diana of the Crossways.* Although subscription figures or personal accounts cannot prove conclusively that large numbers of readers followed Diana's story from June through December 1884, there is evidence that the concept of this new heroine in British literature achieved its basic contours during these months. And the later three-volume version tended to fill in additional detail of an already established portrait.

As Measures has reported, Meredith planned, in a text originally aimed at the *Cornhill,* for his heroine to die at the conclusion of the novel after revealing a state secret. The potential for a relationship with Mr. Redworth, however, was already present in the early chapters and was later heightened for the volume edition, which ended with his marriage to Diana. The serial, which concluded with Diana's near death after betraying Percy Dacier, thus conformed to the author's first complete vision of this story. The most famous statement about the serial version, however, has tended to obscure its merits. In an October 1884 letter to Robert Louis Stevenson, Meredith wrote: "Diana is out of hand, leaving her mother rather inanimate. Should you see the *Fortnightly,* avoid the section under her title. Escott gives me but eighteen pages in eight numbers—so the poor girl has had to be mutilated horribly' " (quoted in Measures 142). As Measures explains, however, the deletions from the longer version were

"Your servants love you," Emma said.

"Ah, poor good souls."

"They crowded up to me to hear of you. Madame of course at the first word was off to her pots. And we English have the habit of calling ourselves the practical people!—This bouillon is consummate.—However, we have the virtues of barbarians; we can love and serve for love. I never tasted anything so good. I could become a glutton."

"Do," said Tony.

"I should be ashamed to 'drain the bowl' all to myself: a solitary toper is a horrid creature, unless one makes a song of it."

"Emmy makes a song of it to me."

"But 'pledge me' is a noble saying, when you think of humanity's original hunger for the whole. It is there that our civilizing commenced, and I am particularly fond of hearing the call. It is grandly historic. So pledge me, Tony. We two can feed from one spoon; it is a closer bond than the loving cup. I want you just to taste it and excuse my gluttony."

Tony murmured, "No." The spoon was put to her mouth. She sighed to resist. The stronger will compelled her to move her lips. Emma fed her as a child, and nature sucked for life.

The first effect was a gush of tears.

Emma lay with her that night, when the patient was the better sleeper. But during the night at intervals she had the happiness of feeling Tony's hand travelling to make sure of her.

Thus was the erratic woman stricken; and those who care for more of Diana of The Crossways will find it in the extended chronicle.

GEORGE MEREDITH.

Figure 13. Concluding page of Meredith's *Diana of the Crossways* in *Fortnightly Review* referring to alternate version of the novel (December 1884). (*Alderman Library, University of Virginia*)

all done by Meredith himself, even when the allotted space was later reduced to six numbers.

The nature of some cuts improved the fiction. Measures notes that Meredith omitted from the serial "most of the heavily metaphorical digressive passages" (158): "This retention of almost all of the realistic detail of action makes the texture of the serial version much more concrete than the fuller version" (157). Meredith, as a veteran writer of five serials, several in the *Fortnightly,* also knew the limits and advantages of the form. Measures cites his "awareness of the demands of the serial form. The ideal serial unit is relatively close knit, with some interest of its own, and leaves the reader at a high point of expectation" (150). Indeed, all six installments are carefully crafted units, each focused on a clear subject, often beginning with unobtrusive references to previous events, and all ending on dramatic notes that throw interest forward. The *Fortnightly*'s established reputation[54] suggests that many would have read this version of Diana's story. Noting that this serial version received "a relatively wide circulation" (159), Measures also states: "The shortened version of the novel gained a wider circulation than Meredith would have wished. Three American publishers, the Federal Book Company, the F. M. Lupton Publishing Company, and the Munro Seaside Library, released pirated editions based on the serial version, without Meredith's final note, which may still be found on library and bookstore shelves and be read by the unwary as Meredith's novel" (163n).

When *Diana* began appearing in the *Fortnightly,* there were the customary notices in weekly newspapers. The 11 June 1884 *Guardian* announced to its readers that the first part of Meredith's latest was now available: "George Meredith commences a new tale, 'Diana of the Crossways,' of which he gives three chapters" (873). Several months later, the 7 September 1884 *Sunday Times* recognized the continuation of this serial: "Mr. George Meredith reappears this month with his pleasant 'Diana of the Crossways'" (2). The 8 June 1884 *Weekly Dispatch* also announced the beginning of Meredith's novel and indicated that it would be reading *Diana* as it appeared in the periodical in future months: "This *Fortnightly,* however, does not contain much of interest, except the opening chapters of a new novel, 'Diana of the Crossways,' by Mr. George Meredith, of which we shall defer speaking till we know more of its plot" (6). Other journals (the *Spectator,* the *Illustrated London News*) sometimes mentioned the *Fortnightly* in their regular magazine columns in the second half of 1884 without specifically commenting on *Diana:* the 9 July 1884 *Guardian,* for instance, drew attention to "an exceptionally good and varied number of the *Fortnightly Review*" (1036). Thus, regular subscribers to the *Fortnightly* and those who kept up with what was appearing in the periodical press in general were certainly aware of *Diana*'s beginning in June 1884.

Before considering both the structure of these individual installments and the complete serial form of *Diana of the Crossways,* we wish to note first the structure of Meredith's sentences and their embodiment of doubts similar to those identified in Trollope and Morris. Meredith's style, of course, was already famous in his time for its departures from traditional narrative patterns. W. E. Henley in the 14 March 1885 *Athenaeum* specifically wondered if *Diana*'s intensity would not prove too much for "this age of doubt" (quoted in Ioan Williams 261). He identified an element of Meredith's style that involved movement in more than one direction: "Here and there we are confronted with a metaphor in four dimensions (as it were), whose conquest appears to demand the instant and active exercise of all the five senses at once, and which even then emerges from the fight unvanquished" (quoted in Ioan Williams 261). Arthur Symons in the May 1885 *Time* similarly found that Meredith's style could not be described as linear: "His sentences are architectural, and every word is a plain or an adorned piece of masonry fitting into the general structure" (quoted in Ioan Williams 277).[55]

Meredith's unique style, often termed poetic by his contemporaries, frequently led to structures that took at least one step back for any movement forward. V. S. Pritchett writes: "He is concerned with the actions of his characters or their description; he wishes to push forward; but cannot resist striking an attitude or going off at a tangent, so that in fact his narrative often stands still. He is like a walker, continually stopping to enthuse instead of getting on" (41). For instance, in the first number (June 1884), where Diana is introduced to the reader, Emma Dunstane's thoughts move forward and back in a single sentence.[56] Redworth had just been startled by Diana's wit, and Lady Dunstane feared the "perplexity" visible in his face meant disapproval when it suggested surprise and dazzlement. Meredith comments: Emma's "reading of [Redworth's] mind was right, wrong altogether her deduction of the corresponding sentiment" (770). This sentence, which dangles a crucial element at the very end, raises a question, important to the whole novel, of whether one can see the true character in another's appearance and actions. As the sentence takes one step back (a wrong deduction about feeling) for its one forward (a right reading about thought), it fits a pattern for much of Meredith's prose in this novel.

Another construction in the second installment (July 1884) similarly moves forward and back at the same time. Redworth realizes that his adherence to traditional values (not marrying without sufficient income) has retarded his romantic life: "Yes, his principle, never to ask a woman to marry him, never to court her, without bankbook assurance of his ability to support her in cordial comfort, was right" (116). Here, an important character takes two steps back (never asking, never courting) for one step forward (adhering to a right principle); and the action is presented in a sentence whose completion or forward movement is delayed by a lengthy insertion in the middle, which recalls the construction of much of Morris's *Earthly Paradise*.

Meredith similarly describes the way of the world (or the way we live now) in the third installment (September 1884): "A woman doubted by her husband, is always, and even to her champions in the first hours of the noxious rumour, until they have solidified in confidence through service, a creature of the wilds, marked for our ancient running" (351). Redworth is with Diana at the Crossways here, as she contemplates flight from her husband Warwick, who has accused her of adultery. Using the word *doubt,* Meredith's sentence insists on two steps back (time must pass, service must be performed) before a step forward (faith restored) can be accomplished.

In the fourth installment (October 1884) the word *doubt* again appears in an ambivalent construction, questioning the power of love in a society committed to absolute standards of behavior. Percy Dacier thinks of Miss Aster, to whom he is "half engaged" and whom he will later marry, and then of Diana: "[Miss Aster's] transparency displayed to him all the common virtues, and a serene possession of the inestimable and eminent one outweighing all; but charm, wit, ardour, intercommunicative quickness, and kindling beauty, airy grace, were qualities that a man, it seemed, had to look for in women spotted by a doubt of their having the chief and priceless" (497). Here all the womanly virtues, including purity, urge Dacier to advance his relationship with Miss Aster, though her "serene possession" of innocence suggests a certain coldness, which causes him to hold back. In the case of women like Diana, Dacier must seek out good qualities in order to overcome a doubt inspired by the question of innocence. Since Diana has all the virtues of charm, wit, and so forth, though she is "spotted by a doubt," she can be a rival to Miss Aster. But it is not at all clear which woman Dacier will pursue in the future. Indeed, kept awake by the Bell at Rovio, "a little village below the Generoso" (495), Dacier will fall in love with Diana when he sees her in the morning; but her later betrayal of his state secret will inspire a speedy marriage to Miss Aster. In his complex sentence construction, then, Meredith raises doubts about reason as a guide in romance and about the possibilities for love in the context of strict Victorian moral codes.

The doubt expressed in many individual sentences of the *Fortnightly Diana* was also visible in the structure of individual installments and in the whole serial text. In each installment were signs of society's general progress consonant with basic Victorian ideology.[57] Redworth's ambition, for example, introduced in the first number (June 1884), was realized through his investment in the railroad. Even though he expressed some doubt in the second number (July 1884), that he "*might* be ruined" (113), he still could tell Diana he had invested "all I possess" (112) in this future. Like Paul Montague in *The Way We Live Now,* but more forcefully and effectively, he later traveled to America, where he was "engaged in carving up that hemisphere" (118) for progress. This commitment led him by the fourth number (October 1884) to such success that he was elected to Parliament "by a stout majority for the borough of Orrybridge" (490). Given the fact that the novel was set in the 1840s, but read in the 1880s after the evidence of history was in, Meredith's serial text had to confirm some of the advances of his own age, such as the growth of industry through the development of railroads, as well as political changes brought about by the Reform Acts and the repeal of the Corn Laws.

Still, this progress was not endorsed without reservations in the novel. In the same sequence of installments Diana moved, as Gordon has written (257), from the country to the city; this action confronted her with personal and political complexities she could not understand. The passion for Dacier she had denied in her own character and her marked ignorance about how a ministry functions led to her collapse at the end of the serial. Progress in this framework was, then, doubted rather than endorsed. Similarly, the novel's movement from face-to-face meetings and relationships in the early numbers to the larger stage of an urban landscape where political gossip, literary portraiture, and journalistic reporting determine identity suggested as much loss as gain. Dacier married the wrong person; Diana collapsed; the government was damaged. Meredith's doubt about the system retarded the plot of his narrative, although the final situation of his characters was still consistent with fundamental Victorian notions of progress.

Another of the ways in which the *Fortnightly Diana* manifested a fundamentally positive Victorian outlook was in its parts' structure: each installment presented a key unit of the story; and the series pursued a clear story line concluding in a finished plot. The third and sixth parts, however, slowed the action of the novel as they raised key questions about society's values. Thus, as in *Pilgrims of Hope,* faith and doubt were mixed in the complete structure of the literature.

The first number (June 1884) introduced three central characters, Diana, Emma, and Redworth, while also establishing the theme of Irish national identity. Its ending artfully stressed an important relationship and created suspense about the next installment. Redworth complimented Diana, and she recognized his discernment:

> *"That's the natural shamrock, after the artificial!" she heard Mr. Redworth say, behind her.*
>
> (780)   *She turned and sent one of her brilliant glances flying over him, in gratitude for a timely word well said. And she never forgot the remark, nor he the look.*

The second installment (July 1884) began with a reminder of what had happened ("A fortnight after this memorable Ball" [108]) and advanced the plot through Diana's unwise marriage to Warwick, a product of her affection for the Crossways, Sir Lukin's inappropriate conduct, and Redworth's delay in pursuing his suit. Emma vowed her eternal friendship even as rumors of Diana's relationship to Lord Dannisburgh began. The part ended dramatically "when the card of Thomas Redworth was fortuitously handed to" (125) Emma just as she finished reading Diana's letter announcing her decision to flee England.

Part 3 similarly presented an important element of the novel's plot, but its content also raised important doubts about Victorian values. Diana, accused of infidelity by her husband, was poised throughout the September 1884 installment between flight and confrontation, deciding on the last page that she would remain in England. This part of the text came after a two-month gap in the publication schedule, rather than the usual one. There was no part in the August issue, probably because of the operation undergone by Meredith's wife in June. The sense of the story's stopping or at least pausing here, then, taking a step back for its other steps forward, was heightened by the publication schedule of the novel's installments.

Halting the action at this crucial decision by the heroine, Meredith questioned the laws and customs of marriage in nineteenth-century England. Doubt about the institution of marriage had led to this crisis, in which Diana became the quarry rather than the hunter: "The doubt casts her forth, the general yelp drags her down; she runs like the prey of the forest under spotting branches; clear if we can think so, but it has to be thought in devotedness: her character is abroad" (351). She was literally at the Crossways and metaphorically at a crossroads in the third installment, wondering whether to go forward toward a new freedom denied by Victorian law (probably emigrating to America) or back to a relationship that was so flawed as to deny growth. Her role as Mrs. Warwick is described as "imprisonment": thus, "Diana, aroused by the later enlightenment as to the laws of life and nature, dashed in revolt at the laws of the world when she thought of the forces, natural and social, urging young women to marry and be bound to the end" (355). But Emma wisely characterizes flight as a "*second* wrong step" (346).

Meredith's picture of his society in the September installment, however, also included elements of faith to balance the doubt experienced by Diana, allowing her in the end to step forward rather than back: like Emma, "Redworth bore a strong resemblance to his fellow men, except for his power of faith in this woman" (351). The butterfly image, formerly suggesting Diana's freedom, was now used to remind readers of her ties to friends: when Redworth leaves her for the night, she feels "as a quivering butterfly impalpably pinned" (354). In a typical Meredith sentence, contrasting and confusing stability and change, Diana asks herself, "But was she holding the position by flight?" (357). Emma insists that flight would mean always "looking back" (359), and in the end Diana decides that staying is advancing: "So my field is London" (362). Thus her doubt is overcome by a faith that her friends and society at large will support her freedom.

No action except this decision had really taken place in the September installment; thus, that part might have seemed to take no step forward for the whole novel. But as the heroine resolved to defend her situation publicly, the novel progressed toward its resolution. Using one of his familiar metaphors, reading others as we do texts, Meredith concluded the monthly number: "by closely reading herself, whom she scourged to excess that she might in justice be comforted, she gathered an increasing knowledge of our human constitution, and stored matter for the brain" (362). The philosophy of the author revealed in this metaphor endorsed such fundamental Victorian notions of progress as the idea that increasing knowledge improves the condition of humanity.[58] Indeed, this sentence's prominent place at the conclusion of the number lent it additional resonance for Meredith's original serial audience.

The next part, October 1884, restored the plot's traditional forward movement, featuring Diana's new life in London during and after the trial, which had exonerated her and allowed her to live independently. Diana's faith in the "*common man*" (486), as opposed to the "gentleman [who] trades on his reputation" (487), suggests her and Meredith's alliance with progress in terms of political reform. The great enemy to her personal development is the "upper middle class" (487), which is "eminently persuasive of public opinion, if not commanding it" (487). In the new age represented by the London environment public morality can "brand a woman's character" (487). Traveling in Italy, removed from the power of the middle class's "printing-press" (487), Diana "reawakened, after the trance of a deadly draught, to the glory of the earth and her share in it" (493). Similarly, Victorian readers, meeting Percy Dacier on the next pages, could feel the novel resuming its forward movement, the pursuit of love. Although she is not yet ready to accept her passionate response to Dacier ("He seemed somehow to have dealt a mortal blow to the happy girl she had become again" [501]), Diana's future clearly once again involved romantic possibilities.

The fifth installment (November 1884) also sustained the swift progress of Diana's story. Now a successful author, Diana has adjusted to new rules in an urban, democratic society. She writes to Emma about her success with the middle-class novel reader: "*The Princess Egeria* . . . was conceived as a sketch; by gradations she grew into a sort of semi-Scudery romance, and swelled to her present portliness. That was done by a great deal of piecing, not to say puffing, of her frame. She would be healthier and have a chance of living longer if she were reduced by a reversal of the process. But how would the judicious clippings and prickings affect our 'pensive public?'" (656). If this was an indirect comment on his own novel, Meredith would seem to have been endorsing for posterity his serial text ("reduced" by "judicious clippings"), while acknowledging that the ("puffed") three-volume edition would be popular only for a time. As it provided her with an income, Diana's writing added to her social and personal development. But by questioning its quality and the values of its audience Meredith suggested a counterargument, as had Trollope for Lady Carbury throughout *The Way We Live Now:* there were doubts about whether Diana was truly moving forward.

Percy Dacier's continued interest in Diana, while she sits with Lord Dannisburgh's body (chapter 16) and then when Dacier asks her to run away with him (chapter 18), advanced the romantic plot in number 5 (November 1884). Her request that he "wait three days" (672) put her in between two worlds: "Her old world lay shattered; her new world was up without a dawn, with but one figure, the sun of it, to light the swinging strangeness" (674). Diana's hesitation again raised doubts about Victorian ideals, here the relation between reason and passion: "Thus she mused in the hum of her tempest of heart and brain, forgetful of the years and the condition preparing both of them for this explosion" (674). The issue was raised but not resolved in this installment, for, in another dramatic close, Meredith brought Redworth to her door in the last sentence of the number: "He said: 'You must come with me at once!' and he gave good reasons for the command" (674). The novel seemed headed for an acceptable romantic conclusion.⁵⁹

The last installment of *Diana of the Crossways* (December 1884) seemed to stop as much as conclude the plot, suggesting (like the third part) stasis, if not a step back, for both central character and novel. Doubts about the future, then, became a central theme in this sixth number and an important element of the whole. Meredith mixed life and fiction, living and writing, to suggest that a great danger in his world was that all activity and development might be undermined by doubt.⁶⁰

The crisis of Emma Dunstane's illness (the news Redworth was carrying to Diana at the end of installment 5) inspired doubts throughout number 6 (December 1884) in Emma herself, in Diana who nursed her, and in Sir Lukin who repented his infidelity. The operation, necessary to save Emma (producing "a new vision of the world and our life" [742]), nevertheless tried characters' faith by threatening an end: "All her dispositions were made for death" (741). By letting Diana decide that the heroine of her next novel must die ("I could not let her live" [743]), Meredith also continued to raise doubts about the profession she had chosen, doubts reinforced by the fact that reviewers had the power to shorten *Cantatrice's* life (743). Further, Diana, who would herself be near death at the end of this serial novel, soon found herself completely unable to write: "She stared at the opening sentence, a heavy bit of moralized manufacture. . . . The doubt reduced her whole MS. to a leaden weight, composed for sinking" (747). Her doubts about her own work would later inspire a traditional Victorian fear of being "bankrupt" (754), and she would tell Dacier that being unable to write meant "ruin coming" (761). Not only troubled as a writer, she also doubted her ability to understand another by reading character; she said to Dacier that "while you were reading me through, I was blind to you" (749).

Reduced to a "rag-puppet's state of suspension" (749) by Dacier's embrace and all these questions in the December installment, Diana was brought close to a state of paralysis that echoed similar crises of faith in Carlyle's *Sartor Resartus,* Mills's *Autobiography,* or Tennyson's *In Memoriam.* Her trip to Tonan occurred in a frozen season, "midnight and midwinter" (752), leaving Diana out of the ordinary flux of time, "where the morrow is manufactured" (754). The next "day" created by her news that the government planned to repeal the Corn Laws was hardly what she expected; thus, again, her role as writer or creator remained problematical. At Tonan's she also thought that the newspapers represented "the mirror of yesterday; we have to look backward to see forward in life" (754). Immobilized between looking back and moving forward, Diana was again at a crossroads in her life, assailed by many doubts. When her betrayal was revealed and understood, Diana collapsed ("The pallor and cold of death took her body" [763]), and Dacier took a step backward in marrying Miss Aster (764). Diana's forward movement in the novel's last chapter seemed only that of "a soul borne onward by the river of Death" (765).[61]

However, Emma Dunstane, her friend of longest standing, did in this December issue restore Diana to consciousness at least. That friendship appeared to be overcoming doubt, reaffirming Diana's most lasting relationship in an unconventional romantic conclusion to the serial novel: Emma says in the December 1884 installment, "We two can feed from one spoon; it is a closer bond than the loving cup" (767).[62] The installment text closed with the image of these two women: "Emma lay with her that night, when the patient was the better sleeper. But during the night at intervals she had the happiness of feeling Tony's hand travelling to make sure of her" (767). The bleakness of this scene almost seemed to carry over to some readers of Meredith's text, who struggled with his difficult style: the 25 February 1885 *Guardian* said, "He who skips [in reading] is sure to miss these indications [of Meredith's intention] and to fall into hopeless darkness" (311).

After the *Fortnightly Review* novel lingered at this almost static point of "hopeless darkness," Meredith restored its forward movement through the famous concluding sentence: "Thus was the erratic woman stricken; and those who care for more of Diana of The Crossways will find it in the extended chronicle" (767). Both his novel and his heroine were given additional life in another publication format of Victorian fiction, the volume edition of a serial story.[63] Both the three-volume novel that followed in February 1885, however, and the Diana described at greater length in that text are extensions of the audience's conception developed in the months of Meredith's serial, June–December 1884. As Louis James reminds us, periodicals like the *Fortnightly* shaped Victorian culture: "This genre mediated to the era much of its finest fiction and non-fiction, and helped give both their vitality, their sense of being a dialogue between writer and reader" (352). Audience response, thus, was central to the

Victorian literary experience, and, in this case, Diana's identity received its fundamental shape from author and readers in the last half of 1884.

No fundamental shift in Diana's character or world occurred when the story was continued beyond its serial ending in the longer edition. And some readers may have taken a step back (to the beginning of the story) in order to go forward (in the three-volume edition). Several early reviewers, in fact, asserted that Diana was a novel that needed more than one reading. James Ashcroft Noble said in the 28 February 1885 *Academy* that the first chapter "will be perused at least twice by every reader—once when he begins the story and again when he has finished it" (147). Lionel Stevenson reports that George Gissing advised his brother the novel was "to be read twice, or if need be, thrice" (259). Measures notes that the expanded version, which might encourage such a rereading by Meredith's contemporaries, did not alter the basic story: "Meredith's change in plan . . . in allowing his heroine to live and marry Redworth rather than to die after her relationship with Percy Dacier had ended, involved only the expansion of a situation already prepared for in the opening chapters" (11). And Gillian Beer describes the last third of the story added by the volume edition as a logical continuation of character and plot: "In the last section of the book we are shown the stages by which she moves to marriage with her faithful admirer, Redworth" (*Meredith* 150).[64]

The success of *Diana* was primarily a product of the nature of its central character, a woman who captured the imagination of her Victorian audience and whose essential identity was the same in both serial and volume format. The 25 February 1885 *Guardian* insisted that the strength of Meredith's fiction was "the depth, subtlety, and variety of the knowledge of human nature it betrays," concluding that in this novel, "All the light is concentrated on Diana, who stands, from the first chapter to the last, naked to the soul" (311). Judith Wilt calls Diana Meredith's "most famous novelist-heroine" (*Readable* 65); and Beer insists that here Meredith "succeeded in creating a vivid character who existed for his contemporaries beyond the bounds of the novel" (*Meredith* 156–57). The longer version of Diana's story may even have undermined some of the qualities established in the serial version, for a few readers found her marriage to Redworth conventional and unsatisfying. The 18 April 1885 *Spectator,* for instance, termed the ending "a somewhat commonplace *terminus ad quem* in the career of so magnificent a creature" (517).[65]

The power of *Diana of the Crossways* in 1884–85 must also be linked to the historical figure, Mrs. Caroline Norton, whose life might be viewed as an even earlier version of Meredith's novel. That story already had its place in the minds of Victorians, as the 28 March 1885 *Pall Mall Gazette* noted: Diana "and some of the other leading characters will be easily recognizable by every one who is well acquainted with the political society of the Thirties and Forties" (4). And the 28 March 1885 *Illustrated London News* noted that "this Diana is not an entire creation, but she was a social reality, mentioned often in the diaries of the day" (336). This familiarity with his subject allowed Meredith to begin his novel in June 1884 with an audience already eager to read. Stevenson notes that the appeal of Meredith's writing was augmented by "the hint that the book told the full story of Mrs. Norton's political and amatory adventures" (260).

This use of public interests, to whatever degree conscious on Meredith's part, linked subject and form of this fiction: both the protagonist and the novel profited from scandal. Diana's unconventional behavior made her a public figure, one whose name under the title of her books (*The Princess Egeria, Cantatrice*) attracted potential readers. For his subject, Meredith chose a genuine Victorian scandal, automatically drawing attention to his book. Further, the idea that the novel had been "mutilated" (as he wrote Stevenson) by the *Fortnightly* editor might have drawn additional notice from important figures in the literary world. The century was entering an era characterized by a split between artists and middle-class audiences and publishers; and to writers like Gissing, Moore, and James, a seriously reduced text of *Diana of the Crossways* might be a scandal.

Victorian serials were seldom so uncomplicated as to involve direct advances toward resolution and stability. Instead, retrogression and hesitation characterize major novels and poems of the age. Trollope questioned the reviewers and the publishing industry in *The Way We Live Now*, refusing to let his characters or his novel pursue a straight line to success. In *The Earthly Paradise* Morris chose a subject and form out of step with contemporary trends and a poetic structure that retarded forward movement in favor of retreat into an extended middle. In *Pilgrims of Hope* Morris challenged middle-class premises altogether, serializing his poem in a Socialist journal and suggesting that societal progress often depended on personal and even economic setbacks. Meredith wrote a successful installment novel at the same time he feared that the terms on which such fiction appealed to audiences were identical to those governing scandal. Such doubt about cultural principles were as essential a pattern in the Victorian serial as home, history, and empire.

VI

Prefiguring an End to Progress

There is more going on than meets the eye of a man walking through the streets. [Christminster] is a unique centre of thought and religion— the intellectual and spiritual granary of this country. All that silence and absence of goings-on is the stillness of infinite motion—the sleep of the spinning-top, to borrow the simile of a well-known writer.

Thomas Hardy, *Hearts Insurgent*

It is when we try to grapple with another man's intimate need that we perceive how incomprehensible, wavering, and misty are the beings that share with us the sight of the stars and the warmth of the sun.

Joseph Conrad, *Lord Jim: A Sketch*

SPIRIT OF THE PITIES
They are shapes that bleed, mere
    marionettes or no,
And each has parcel in the total Will.

SPIRIT OF THE YEARS
Which overrides them as a whole its parts
In other entities.

Thomas Hardy, *The Dynasts*

NEAR THE END of the nineteenth century Victorians were less confident about historical progress, personal growth, and natural development. Underlying celebrations of British home and empire at Victoria's 1887 and 1897 Jubilees were ominous signs of strain in the country's agricultural, industrial, and financial systems (Hobsbawm 188). As Richard Altick asserts in *Victorian People and Ideas,* the language and the literature of late

Victorians, as well as their material world, were changing: "Whether or not the age witnessed the decline of the English sentence, as is sometimes alleged, there was a world of difference between the expansive style of, say, a Ruskin or a Meredith and the economical one of an H. G. Wells or an Arnold Bennett, trained in the school of popular journalism" (97).[1] Significant opposition between literary theories was also evident in two publication formats of the time, installment issue (primarily in magazines) and the appearance of whole works in single volumes.

Many of these changes were related to new factors in the system of literary production, which were visible, as Cross has explained, in Gissing's famous novel of the 1890s: "Between 1880 and 1895 the world of publishing and journalism underwent a radical transformation: the introduction of syndication, the expansion of the popular press, the founding of the Society of Authors, the rise of the literary agent, the relaxing of mid-Victorian pruderies in fiction, the triumph of the adventure story and of the gossip column—all led to the climate and change and controversy that pervades *New Grub Street*" (205). Norman Feltes provides a more detailed analysis of the decline of the three-volume novel, which he terms "a radical transformation of the literary mode of production, the historical appearance of a new kind of structure, suited to, demanded, and provided by the larger structures of emergent monopoly capitalism" (*Modes* 79). The strains evident in a transition from old to new led to another primary determinant of late Victorian literature, the lingering structure of serialization overlying poetry and fiction conceived on new theoretical terms.[2]

In the last decade of the century serialization was the dominant form for the first appearance of major works by Stevenson, Hardy, Wells, Kipling, James, Conrad, and others. However, in these years novelists and poets were conceiving of stories that jarred with the fundamental dynamics of serial literature as we have outlined them in the previous four chapters. Instead of the patient creation of an idealized home, broken families often characterized the literary work; rather than steady historical progress, chaos or regression took over many plots;[3] instead of empire fostering growth and development, the will to power crushed individual identities; and skepticism replaced doubt about human potential, paralyzing society. Such narratives did not harmonize with the slow, sure growth and development of serial literature; instead the appropriate form for such visions of personal and social stagnation was the single volume, an autonomous whole, in which all parts found their places in a unity of theme and effect.

In the last decade of the century authors often wrote with two different formats in mind: composing their works to appear ultimately in single volumes, nonetheless they frequently issued such novels and poems first in installments, most often for financial reasons. In addition, authors either abridged and altered manuscripts to fit the editorial restraints of magazines or revised works initially published in periodicals for later whole-volume issue. While the audience for serious literature was breaking into small groups of specialized interests, who generally read works in volumes, subscribers to periodicals often represented the mass audience of the Victorian middle class. The existence, then, of two sets of literary works and two audiences marks a decline in the Victorian serial, both the publication format and the set of beliefs that had inspired it. Contradictory tendencies of serial and single-volume forms are evident in Hardy's *Jude the Obscure* (1894–95), Conrad's *Lord Jim* (1899–1900), and Hardy's *The Dynasts* (1904–8). These works' dual identities reveal the nature of the transitional period in English cultural history at the turn of the century.

It is usually assumed that the version of Thomas Hardy's last novel serialized in *Harper's New Monthly Magazine* from December 1894 to November 1895 is inferior to the fuller text published as a single volume on 1 November 1895. Michael Millgate makes the case concisely, noting that Hardy's manuscript was "severely and, in some respects, ludicrously watered down. Episodes such as the pig-killing and Arabella's seduction of Jude were modified or omitted altogether; Jude and Sue were obliged to live not together but 'near'; and the one child (instead of two) murdered by Father Time was Sue's by adoption only" (349). However, even if the serial version is inferior to the volume edition, it remains a fine work of fiction written by a major writer at the peak of his abilities.[4] Further, there is considerable reason to believe not just that *Harper's* had many subscribers at this time[5] but also that a substantial number of those customers were reading and discussing Hardy's serial novel as it appeared. As happened with Meredith's *Diana of the Crossways* (see chapter five), reaction to the volume edition in late 1895 was shaped by attitudes already formed and articulated by readers of the serial version.

The editor of *Harper's*, H. M. Alden, wrote to Hardy that he would include in his magazine "nothing which could not be read aloud in any family circle" (quoted in Millgate 349); since such businessmen did know what was good for circulation, it is likely that this periodical and its serial fiction were being read aloud by a significant segment of the population. Hardy's urging individuals to ignore the serial version ("Please don't read it in the Magazine, for I have been obliged to make many changes, omissions, & glosses" [Purdy and Millgate 70]) was necessary only if he expected people to follow *Harper's* regularly. In her vituperative attack on *Jude* Margaret Oliphant asserted such readers for Hardy's "last work, which has been introduced, as he tells us, for the last twelve months, into a number of decent houses in England and America, with the most shameful portions suppressed" (quoted in R. G. Cox 256). Enough reviewers, in fact, were keeping up with the serial to suspect that Hardy's narrative had skipped over important events (the illegitimate birth of Jude and Sue's child) in the version appearing in *Harper's* (Purdy 88).

Hardy also believed that, in addition to the periodical's regular subscribers, a significant number read serials in magazines supplied by the lending libraries. He wrote to John Lane on 23 February 1893, "The lending libraries are on the alert to trace stories in such cases, & pacify subscribers by handing over the periodical in which a tale in demand—or portion of it—has been issued, as I know from personal experience" (quoted in Purdy and Millgate 51). When the novel was later accused of being overly didactic (a "purpose" novel), Hardy admitted that the context of its serialization had influenced its meaning for his contemporaries: "I suppose the attitude of these critics is to be accounted for by the accident that, during the serial publication of my story, a sheaf of 'purpose' novels on the matter appeared" (letter of 10 November 1895 to Edmund Gosse, quoted in Purdy and Millgate 93). Robert Gittings points out that serialization "did not arouse much critical notice except some which pointed out inconsistencies caused by the cuts. What it did arouse was a different kind of reading public. . . . it spoke to the emerging, the new popularly-educated, the young. In the summer of 1895, its instalments were read avidly by the twenty-eight-year-old H. G. Wells" (76). Thus, to understand the place of Hardy's last major work of fiction in literary history—as well as to see what was happening at this time to a major Victorian publication mode, the serial—we need to examine the text read in installments from December 1894 to November 1895. This text established the basic terms under which the novel as a whole was judged in December 1895 and underscored the contradictory attitudes troubling England at the turn of the century.

Hardy began Jude's story under the title of *The Simpletons,* but changed to *Hearts Insurgent* (a title he had conceived even earlier) with the second installment after being reminded that Charles Reade had once published a story with the former name. Although a later choice for the serial's title was "The Recalcitrants,"[6] the name under which the text appeared in *Harper's* from January to November 1895 was *Hearts Insurgent.* Just as this title suggested themes appropriate to mid-century serials—

romantic fulfillment, ascension through social ranks, the expansion of a realm of influence—so the serial story of Jude for several months met some important audience expectations for conventional fiction. However, other fundamental elements of this novel, themes and techniques characteristic of more modern literature, eventually contradicted the initial impression, creating a crisis in literary experience that goes beyond the outcry at Hardy's frank treatment of sex and marriage.

The volume edition of *Jude* was controversial at the time of its publication and has continued to trouble critics, who frequently comment on its contradictory nature. A. Alvarez says: "There is something puzzling about *Jude the Obscure* as a work of art: in impact it is intensely moving; in much of its detail it is equally intensely false" (119). Penelope Vigar notes that scholars have found the work "possibly the most flawed artistically of all Hardy's novels" (190). Perry Meisel argues that Hardy's work is "a bridge between the old narrative sensibility and the dictates of the new" (145–46). Norman Page's observation suggests that the novel's contradictory style might be linked to publication format: "The book was published in a single volume at a relatively low price; it thus broke with the Victorian tradition of the expensive three-volume novel, the format in which most of Hardy's work had appeared" (x). Another central contradiction, the coexistence of serial techniques with themes of more modern fiction, added to the unique nature of both *Hearts Insurgent* and *Jude the Obscure*.

In his Preface to the first volume edition Hardy himself pointed to contradictory elements in his work. Calling it a "tragedy of unfulfilled aims" (5),[7] he suggested an opposition between personal ambition and social or natural limits. In the Postscript written some eighteen years later (1912) he identified those limits as "marriage laws" (6), finding the center of the novel's action in "the forced adaptation of human instincts to rusty and irksome moulds that do not fit them" (7). Another statement in the preface to the first edition, however, pointed more directly to the nature and effect of the serial version, *Hearts Insurgent*. Hardy called this story "simply an endeavour to give shape and coherence to a series of seemings, or personal impressions, the question of their consistency or their discordance, of their permanence or their transitoriness, being regarded as not of the first moment" (5). While it did not seem to matter to Hardy ("not of the first moment"), the "consistency" and harmony of this "series," the gradual coming together of these "seemings" or "impressions" into a recognizable, lasting shape, was important to his audience in *Harper's*. Conditioned by decades of periodical fiction (and larger social conventions) to expect a consistent, developing tale, readers found *Hearts Insur-*

gent going backward or standing still through the months of 1895 when it should, they thought, have been advancing.

The illustration for the first installment of *Hearts Insurgent* (see figure 14: "On the farther side of the stream three young women were kneeling"), for example, suggested to *Harper's* regular subscribers in December 1894 that this tale would continue along two familiar lines: adventure (the young man on the road with a pack slung over his shoulder) and romance (the three young women, with at least one of whom the protagonist presumably would establish some relationship).[8] Hardy's text in this first installment complemented the promises inherent in the initial illustration. Jude's delivering loaves of bread for his maiden aunt on "a creaking cart with a whity-brown tilt" (76) in and around Marygreen presented a traditional Victorian image of a determined young hero on the road to education at Christminster and, ultimately, success in life. Although the "unvoiced call of woman to man, which was uttered very distinctly by Arabella's personality" (80) at the end of the first installment, might be expected to distract Jude from his intended course, audiences could still anticipate the two forces of adventure and romance in the narrative to build a story worth reading.

The *Guardian's* response to the first installment of *The Simpletons* on 12 December 1894 showed traditional expectations for a "hero" with "aspirations" who might soon be "falling in love": "A new novel by Mr. Hardy, 'The Simpletons,' is begun in this number [of *Harper's*]. Jude Fawley, the hero, is a youth with a soul above his great aunt's bakehouse, but his aspirations after a life of study in the cathedral city near are somewhat checked by his falling in love with a pig-breeder's strapping if coquettish daughter" (1951). The 15 December 1894 *Illustrated London News* also recognized the beginning of Hardy's newest novel as significant for the literary world: "In fiction the most striking event is, of course, the beginning of Mr. Thomas Hardy's story, 'The Simpletons,' in *Harper's*" (762). This weekly focused on the romantic theme emerging at the end of the installment: "It is too soon to say anything definite of this except that the young woman of Wessex with the coming-on disposition already adorns the scene" (762). The first part was also noted, though only briefly, by *Saturday Review* (15 December 1894: 645).

Hardy was willing to raise such audience expectations through illustration and narrative at the beginning of *Hearts Insurgent;* but as the work continued, other techniques countered the sense of an ongoing story, confusing his audience and ultimately preparing the way for a rejection of the entire work. As early as the second installment, the tone of

Figure 14. "On the farther side of the stream three young women were kneeling," Hardy's *Simpletons / Hearts Insurgent* (first installment, *Harper's*, December 1894), suggesting earlier conventions of serial fiction. (*Alderman Library, University of Virginia*)

the *Guardian's* reaction altered. On 9 January 1895 the reviewer commented: "In Mr. Hardy's novel, the title of which is changed from 'The Simpletons' to 'Hearts Insurgent' (the one originally selected), comes a hasty marriage and almost as speedy repentance" (55). Although there seemed to be enthusiasm for the latest title and its associations, there was concern about the characters' failure to advance in life. The journal had picked up quickly on a central characteristic of the novel, oppositions (marriage and repentance) that reverse the direction of plot. The *Spectator,* reading the third installment on 9 February 1895, had reservations about Hardy's style in *Hearts Insurgent:* "Mr. Hardy's new story is evidently to be very interesting, and at least one of the characters in it, Jude Fawley, would seem to be a strong one. Yet this description of him in the February instalment is too obviously Meredithian" (206). By the time of the fourth installment the 6 March 1895 *Guardian's* reaction was terse: "The clouds over Mr. Hardy's 'Hearts Insurgent' grow blacker" (375). At this point in its serial publication, the story of Jude and Sue had so failed to meet audience expectations that, for traditional middle-class Victorian readers, only "clouds" and "blackness" characterized the fictional world. We can see Hardy's deliberate reversal of serial conventions throughout the text of *Hearts Insurgent,* but this one installment in particular, the fourth, included in the March 1895 *Harper's,* can be used to illustrate in detail this technique and its effects.

   Although it is a commonplace to say that each installment in a serial work had to stand on its own, few scholars have bothered to document the assertion, particularly for works appearing in periodicals. Hardy's March installment of *Hearts Insurgent,* however, can serve as an example of how successful some writers were in constructing individual parts that were consistent with the work as a whole but that also could be read alone, as self-sufficient short stories. (The reverse of this principle, by the way, is also true. Any modern short story can be read as one installment in a much larger work. Publication formats and literary theory in our century have favored the appearance of the short story over the long novel,[9] just as in the nineteenth century the opposite was the case.) What is distinctive about Hardy's installment compared to numbers in early or mid-century Victorian serials is that, rather than advancing a continuing story by adding to its linear development, it enacts in miniature the entire narrative. Thus, to use a phrase central to serialization, *Hearts Insurgent* is in the end a story *not* to be continued.[10] It is an early manifestation of modernist literary technique, in which the whole field of a work of art is presented, allowing a simultaneity of perception characteristic of single-volume reading.

The primary subject of the fourth installment is Jude's developing love for Sue, a version of the familiar Victorian domestic story. This March installment begins with an exposition in the form of his visit to his aunt's house, who recalls as a warning to Jude his cousin's unconventional behavior (567). When Jude receives "a quite passionate letter" (575) from Sue, the rising action begins, and he is soon living near her in Melchester. A climax occurs when they have a "grand day" touring Wardour Castle and spend the night at a shepherd's cottage. Sue's escape from the training school provides a traditional falling action; and the conclusion finds Sue asleep in Jude's room, with him "regarding her" as "almost a divinity" (582). The shock of students and school officials, that Sue "had waded through a depth of water reaching nearly to her shoulders" (581) on the way to Jude's room, recalls his aunt's still-outraged thought at the beginning of the installment, that Sue had once walked "into the pond with her shoes and stockings off" (567). This link is one of several tying the installment neatly together as a completed unit; yet the number in *Harper's* creates the suspense typical of serial fiction. The final sentence states that Jude's "reverie was interrupted by the creak of footsteps ascending the stairs" and is followed by the famous words "[TO BE CONTINUED]" (582).

This romantic story is complemented in part 4 by Jude's continuing effort to rise in society, which also involves familiar Victorian themes: often he would "stand opposite the house that contained Sue . . . and wish he had nothing else to do but to sit reading and learning all day what many of the thoughtless inmates despised" (581). A new direction to his ambition was inspired in the fourth installment when he wrote for help to a head of the college and was told to seek his fortune within his proper social sphere. Confessing his failures to Sue after a night of drunken sorrow, Jude was struck by a "new idea," pursuing "the ecclesiastical and altruistic life as distinct from the intellectual and emulative life" (574). This new goal sustains the second basic element of plot through the remainder of the installment: Jude works on cathedral repairs every day, and "his studies were recommenced" (577) at night as he reads and practices on a harmonium chants "single and double" (577). This earnestness naturally pleased many traditionalists, even Mrs. Oliphant, who wrote that in Jude's "early self-training there is much that is admirable" (quoted in R. G. Cox 257).

Despite this evidence of forward movement in both the love story and the success story, however, counterevidence in Hardy's serial text undermined any genuine sense of progress: a happy home for wife and family is an illusion to Jude; history does not place him on a line from a difficult past on the way to a better future; his world shrinks rather than expands; and his doubt is closer to absolute despair than to recovered faith.

The romantic plot is compromised by "matrimonial entangle- ment[s]" (576). Aware of Jude's "rough" hands (576), Sue has accepted Phillotson in part at least because marriage with an "old man" (576) does not threaten her. Although Jude is strongly drawn to Sue, he finds her "something of a riddle" (577), "one lovely conundrum" (578). There is also the continuing conflict in Jude's own personality, which led to his first marriage with Arabella and which would certainly affect any future ro- mance. His aunt reminded the March *Harper's* readers of a dangerous side to Jude's character: "Your marrying that woman Arabella was about as bad a thing as a man could possibly do for himself by trying hard" (567). In the end, any prospective home for Jude and Sue is likely to create disillusion- ment, as does the "nice little cottage" (578) the couple spends the night in; the owner tells them: "Oh, I don't know about the niceness. I shall have to thatch it soon, and where the thatch is to come from I can't tell" (579).

The pursuit of education, vocation, and social status in the March installment of *Hearts Insurgent* is also confused by naive confidence in human nature, in the social order, and in a divine being. When Jude arrives at Melchester, for instance, "He took it as a good omen that numerous blocks of stone were lying about, which signified that the cathedral was undergoing restoration or repair to a considerable extent. It seemed to him, full of the superstitions of his beliefs, that this was an exercise of forethought on the part of a ruling power that he might find plenty to do in the art he practised, while waiting for a call to higher labors" (575). Economic forces, of course, are also likely explanations of his good fortune here. Sue is similarly naive in her belief that progressive patterns can be seen in history. She tells Jude: "The Cathedral was a very good place [as the center of town] four or five centuries ago; but it is played out now" (577). Sue is also less the New Woman than she admits: alone in Jude's room at the end of the number, having changed her wet clothes for a set of his dry ones, she nervously says, "I suppose, Jude, it is odd that you should see me like this? Yet what nonsense! It is only a question of woven cloth and linen and the snip of a tailor's shears. I wish I didn't feel so ill and sick!" (582).

Sadly, too, Jude does not learn from experience that his ability to become a part of the larger British system is severely restricted. When he hopes to be a classical scholar, he discovers, after having devoted ten years to the project already, that the time involved is overwhelming: "at the rate at which, with the best of fortune, he would be able to save money, fifteen years must elapse before he could be in a position to forward testimonials to the Head of a College and advance to a matriculation examination. The undertaking was hopeless" (569). Yet his entering the priesthood means a similar commitment: in these studies he is soon "deep in the perusal of the Twenty-ninth Volume of Pusey's Library of the Fathers" (581). Entering the structure of England's empire, to say nothing of becoming an active agent in its expansion, is, then, beyond Jude's reach. Such success is beyond Sue as well, as shown in her inability to stay at the training school. When at the conclusion of the installment she is sitting in Jude's "only arm-chair," he sees "a slim and fragile being masquerading as himself on a Sunday, so pathetic in her defencelessness that his heart felt big with the sense of it" (582).[11]

Thus, the apparent overall pattern of movement toward success in March 1895 is contradicted by specific passages within this fourth install-ment. Perhaps the most telling evidence that Jude's progress is limited or illusory is the fact that he is continually relegated to small texts. No long stories, the major Victorian mode for achievement, are really available to him. One of his most famous writings is the brief inscription of his hopes carved on a milestone (573). In Marygreen, after he decides to pursue the priesthood, he occupies himself "with little local jobs in putting up and lettering head-stones about the neighboring villages" (574). Although he is eventually employed at cathedral repairs in Melchester, his "first work was some carving at the cemetery on the hill" (577). The realm Jude hopes finally to move in is repeatedly characterized by long works ("Pusey's Library of the Fathers" [581]) and reserved for a social class ("those who had passed their lives under trained teachers and had worked to ordained lines" [569]) in which he has no place. Even his own social class in town, which he sees at one point in the March number as "a book of humanity infinitely more palpitating, varied, and compendious than the gown life" (570), is, he concludes, but a "pack of fools!" (572). There is, then, no way in this world to satisfy Jude's deep need to rise above his origins and assume a new role in the larger system.

Sue's lack of faith in this installment foreshadows yet another future disappointment for the protagonist. Already further along in the study of religions, she prefigures, when they are touring Wardour Castle together, Jude's later despair. "Sue paused patiently beside him, and stole critical looks into his face as, regarding the Virgins, Holy Families, and Saints, it grew reverent and abstracted. When she had thoroughly estimated him at this, she would move on and wait for him before a Lely or Reynolds. It was evident that her cousin deeply interested her, as one might be interested in a man puzzling out his way along a labyrinth from which one had one's self escaped" (578). Although Jude had found himself "a poor Christ" after leaving Christminster (573), and felt after resting at his aunt's house "as if he had awakened in hell" (573), his doubt was met in this installment by the curate, Mr. Highridge. Hearing a confession of sorts from Jude, the priest encouraged him not to give up on his "call to the ministry" (574). Thus, Jude takes a new start toward a "true religion" (574); but that ambition matches too neatly his earlier one and is as likely to be frustrated: "He considered that he might so mark out his coming years as to begin his ministry at the age of thirty—an age which much attracted him as being that of his exemplar when he first began to teach" (575).

Jude's explanation of Christminster's special quality on the second page of the March installment can stand as a description of the entire text of *Hearts Insurgent,* for its ironic tone confirms and contradicts the speaker's own belief in progress. Jude answers a villager of Marygreen who did not see anything " 'going on' " in the famous university town: " 'You are wrong, John; there is more going on than meets the eye of a man walking through the streets. It is a unique centre of thought and religion—the intellectual and spiritual granary of this country. All that silence and absence of goings-on is the stillness of infinite motion—the sleep of the spinning top, to borrow the simile of a well-known writer' " (568). As this part and the entire novel come to assert, the city of Christminster is stagnant rather than spinning, and Jude's faith in its inner vitality unfounded. This mill grinds out no scientific knowledge or spiritual truth of use to such as Jude, who remains lost in the vast silence or stillness of timeworn similes. The closest thing to life and movement in the passage is what Jude discounts, "a man walking through the streets," that is, Jude himself, whose "eye" misses what is important. Although Jude seems to move in this fourth installment through the experience of disillusionment about his prospects as a scholar and a lover, he fails to arrive at any fuller understanding of fundamental principles: growth and development for him in this universe are not really possible.

Even readers used to Hardy's irony have found the downward spiral of Jude's fate unusually relentless. The *Athenaeum*'s review of the volume edition on 23 November 1895 articulated this fundamental contradiction between the traditional forms of Victorian fiction and Jude's experience: "It is not meant to be implied that an impossible theory of the universe is

necessarily incompatible with a good novel, although there is a considerable likelihood of this being so" (709). Just as Jude in the fourth installment
passes "the mile-stone at the top whereon he had carved his hopes years
ago" (573), characters in Hardy's world return to familiar places without
having advanced in life, and readers picked up new installments without
an adequate sense of a story's continuing. Although Jude at one point in the
installment feels himself in " 'the hell of conscious failure,' both in ambition and in love" (573), he foolishly, if humanly, starts off again and again
in hopes of romance and success.

Many of Hardy's serial readers resembled his protagonist in going
forward with experience, that is, reading *Hearts Insurgent* to its conclusion
even though they had little to say about it. The *Guardian* often commented
on *Harper's* after March 1895, the month of the fourth installment's appearance,[12] but did not specifically address Hardy's novel again until its
conclusion on 6 November 1895: "Mr. Hardy's 'Hearts Insurgent,' which
has received a new name in its book form, ends as gloomily if not so
violently as it might have been expected" (1732). When the *Guardian*
reviewed the novel as a separate book on 13 November 1895, it found this
work to be literature "of which it is not easy to discover the motive"
(1770). The paper could see virtue in Jude's youth, which it termed
"interesting and touching," but as a man he was thought "contemptibly
weak, unstable, and maundering" (1770).

The *Guardian,* as others, seemed aware of the lack of movement or
progress throughout the novel, explaining on 13 November 1895 that the
characters "are kept at a dead level of sordid commonness" (1770). The 23
November 1895 *Athenaeum* similarly complained about being subjected to
"one prolonged scolding from beginning to end" (709). Unhappy with a
realism that did not show characters advancing in life, the 15 February
1896 *Academy* insisted: "Mere imitation of nature is confessedly not syn-
onymous with art" (134). And the 16 November 1895 *Queen, the Lady's
Newspaper* explained Sue's static state through the metaphor of a wave:
"Unbalanced Sue was always balancing. On the crest of one wave she was
swept into her ill-starred and short-lived marriage with the schoolmaster;
the ebb of the wave swept her back from him. Throughout the years she
lived with Jude she was tossed to him and away from him on a choppy sea
of doubt; and then, when her mind was unhinged by the loss of her
children, a great storm-wave came and swept her away from him, and
flung her stranded high and dry beside her first husband, in a hopeless
wreck, soon to break up" (928). These images show the entire action of the
novel in a single moment, suggesting a simultaneity of perception charac-

teristic more of modernist than Victorian literature. This review also noted other failures to progress, citing "the long disappointment running through Jude's life" (928).

A few journals tried at the end of their reading experience to see the work in terms appropriate to the conventional serials of earlier decades. The 8 February 1896 *Saturday Review,* for example, thought there was development in the novel, seeing the main plot driven by "the fascination Christminster (Oxford) exercises upon [Jude's] rustic imagination, and . . . the climax of its development is the pitiless irony of Jude's death-scene, within sound of the University he loved—which he loved, but which could offer no place in all its colleges for such a man as he" (153). Edmund Gosse also found development in the novel, though in a downward direction. He said in the January 1896 *Cosmopolis* that the book is "irresistible . . . one of those novels into which we descend and are carried on by a steady impetus to the close, when we return, dazzled, to the light of common day" (quoted in R. G. Cox 268). And the 11 January 1896 *Illustrated London News* said: "He has carried you from one broken hope to another, through a series of painful climaxes; and such is the spaciousness which his grasp of elemental things imparts to the story that a tragedy of three lives seems to fill the world with sorrow, and invite irony from the heavens" (50). This emphasis on a "series" of events leading to a fuller vision of tragedy might, in fact, derive from the novel's having been read in *Harper's,* since this paper had mentioned *Hearts Insurgent* in December 1894. That is, the lingering form of serialization and a prolonged reading experience may have inspired some readers to see in the text change and process that were less evident to reviewers first encountering the story in a single-volume edition.

The 11 January 1896 *Illustrated London News,* finding what development there was in Hardy's story going in a direction it could not accept, insisted in the end that readers break with Hardy at a specific point in the text: "Now, up to this point, woe has been heaped upon woe, and the reader has accepted it all, with some reservations, as a natural evolution of the circumstances. The tragedy of the children strains his belief to snapping point; and then comes a perfectly superfluous touch [the doctor's assertion that a "universal wish not to live" is becoming common] which snaps it altogether" (50). Hardy's prefiguring an end to humanity's progress in the doctor's analysis of Little Father Time was clearly too much for this reviewer. The further widespread violent reaction to *Jude the Obscure* (Millgate 371) suggests that others shared the *Illustrated London News*'s reaction to Hardy's story, particularly to the death of the children. That review went on to claim that the readers' sensibility should and probably did then take over the novel after this event: "The immediate effect of this error in Mr. Hardy's scheme of all-embracing tribulation is that the reader renews his 'will to live' and be moderately cheerful, and is not at all disposed to take very seriously the final permutations of the conjugal tie which has played such pranks throughout the novel" (50). Thus, *Hearts Insurgent* for some readers ended in September 1895 (or even earlier) with the tenth installment in *Harper's*. Finding contradictions between author's text and their own expectations so fundamental and so absolute, much of Hardy's audience abandoned him in the middle of *Hearts Insurgent,* asserting their will to live against his pessimistic forecast.

This same crisis in literary form and philosophical outlook also occurred in the serialization of Joseph Conrad's *Lord Jim*. The story of *Lord Jim*'s composition has been told many times, by the author himself at one point to counteract a theory that "the work starting as a short story had got beyond the writer's control" ("Author's Note," June 1917, in Moser 1).[13] Conrad admitted that "my first thought was of a short story" (tentatively titled "Jim: A Sketch," then "Tuan Jim: A Sketch" [Najder 247]); but the early pages sketching out that idea were laid aside for a time, until "the late Mr. William Blackwood suggested I should give something again to his magazine" ("Author's Note," in Moser 1).[14] Conrad then resumed the story with "the pilgrim ship episode" as "a good starting-point," an event that he conceived could "colour the whole 'sentiment of existence' in a simple and sensitive character" ("Author's Note," in Moser 1). The work began appearing in the October 1899 *"Maga"* under the title of *Lord Jim: A Sketch* (see figure 15; the volume edition was later given the title *Lord Jim: A Tale*) and concluded in November 1900, having run fourteen rather than the three numbers initially forecast by the author. That the existing publication format allowed or even encouraged the continuation of Conrad's story far beyond his original intention underscores the power of the serial mode even in the last months of the nineteenth century.[15] But as with Hardy's *Hearts Insurgent,* Conrad's *Lord Jim: A Sketch* pursued a vision of man's aspirations frustrated or paralyzed by an unyielding reality, a vision appropriate to the twentieth century. The tension between an installment form (with its principles of process and progress) and a view of life as timeless and unchanging (which is linked to a belief in the work of art as an autonomous whole and the single-volume mode) reveals in additional detail the fault lines in British ideals a year before Queen Victoria's death.

Conrad's method did not match his audience's expectations because additional installments of *Lord Jim: A Sketch* failed to advance the plot in a

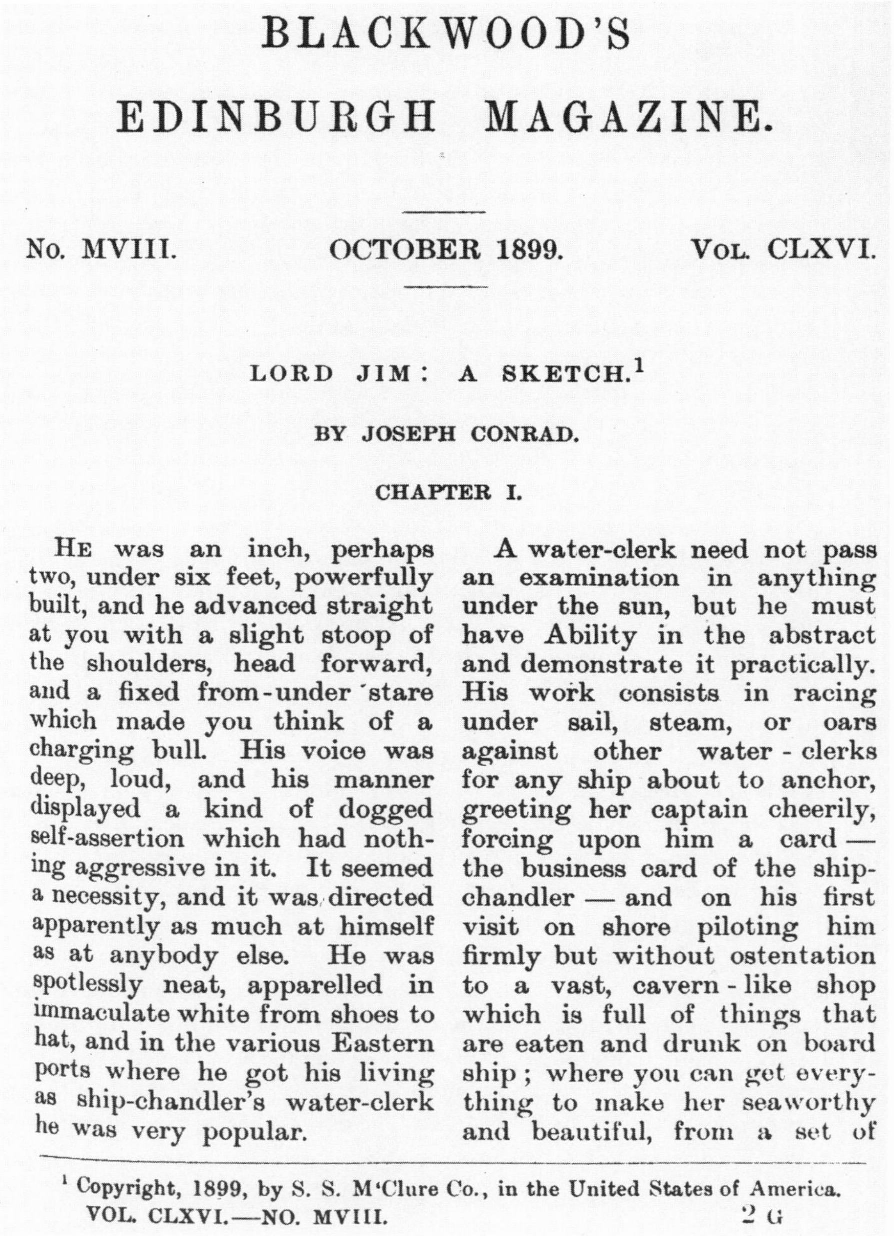

BLACKWOOD'S

EDINBURGH MAGAZINE.

No. MVIII.   OCTOBER 1899.   Vol. CLXVI.

LORD JIM: A SKETCH.[1]

BY JOSEPH CONRAD.

CHAPTER I.

HE was an inch, perhaps two, under six feet, powerfully built, and he advanced straight at you with a slight stoop of the shoulders, head forward, and a fixed from-under stare which made you think of a charging bull. His voice was deep, loud, and his manner displayed a kind of dogged self-assertion which had nothing aggressive in it. It seemed a necessity, and it was directed apparently as much at himself as at anybody else. He was spotlessly neat, apparelled in immaculate white from shoes to hat, and in the various Eastern ports where he got his living as ship-chandler's water-clerk he was very popular.

A water-clerk need not pass an examination in anything under the sun, but he must have Ability in the abstract and demonstrate it practically. His work consists in racing under sail, steam, or oars against other water-clerks for any ship about to anchor, greeting her captain cheerily, forcing upon him a card — the business card of the ship-chandler — and on his first visit on shore piloting him firmly but without ostentation to a vast, cavern-like shop which is full of things that are eaten and drunk on board ship; where you can get everything to make her seaworthy and beautiful, from a set of

---

[1] Copyright, 1899, by S. S. M'Clure Co., in the United States of America.

Figure 15. Opening page of Conrad's *Lord Jim: A Sketch* in *Blackwood's Edinburgh Magazine* (October 1899). (*Alderman Library, University of Virginia*)

traditional manner; that is, they did not add new episodes to Jim's history so much as they retold the essential features of his life in new ways.[16] This style of narrative, circling back to report again and again on a single important moment, is more characteristic of modern than Victorian fiction.[17] As Albert Guerard says, *Lord Jim* "appears at the turn of the century as the first novel in a new form" (*Conrad* 126). Each monthly number of this novel told the same story over again; at the heart of all fourteen installments was Jim's defining action, the jump. Even more consistently than *Hearts Insurgent, Lord Jim: A Sketch,* then, could be read as separate autonomous short stories about man's capacity for failure.

Conrad's audience seemed particularly aware of the unified nature of this novel as a whole. The 29 October 1900 *Manchester Guardian,* for instance, wrote: "The book is long, and even remarkably long, for it is written almost without a pause and with a concentration of purpose, a grasp of material, a deep energy which make it a great performance" (quoted in Sherry 113). The 24 November 1900 *Spectator* talked of "the sombre fascination of his narrative" and the reader's "thraldom" to its powerful style (753). The 10 November 1900 *Academy* said that minor characters and events matter "only and solely by virtue of their relation to Jim" and that Conrad's "story all the time is of Jim and his poor boyish conscience" (443). The 12 January 1901 *Illustrated London News* made a similar point: "for full two hundred pages Mr. Conrad sets Jim's action in every possible light" (48).[18]

The 3 November 1900 *Athenaeum* advised going slowly through Conrad's story: "Many will think it easier to enjoy the narrative as it appeared serially in *Blackwood's* magazine than in the form of a volume" (576). Although this reader was speaking specifically about the confusion of point of view in the novel (its "inverted commas"), the advice also suggests simply taking more time to assimilate the narrative in discrete units. Since Conrad's style was difficult, some, like the 10 November 1900 *Academy,* thought it would have been more accessible if it had retained some traditional narrative patterns: "why not have begun with page 3, at the words 'Originally he came from a parsonage'?" (443).[19] The 14 December 1900 *Daily News* felt that some excellent parts of the novel, like Stein's personal history, were "hidden, as are so many other good things, in the crowded pages of this tremendous and paragraph-less volume" (6d; quoted in Sherry 125). The serial *Lord Jim: A Sketch* gave more attention to such individual sections of the whole. In this chapter we will explore the April 1900 installment to determine how it affected the readers of *Blackwood's* in 1899–1900.[20]

Just as *Hearts Insurgent* was read in *Harper's*, *Lord Jim: A Sketch* was followed by a significant number of readers at the turn of the century. Noting the appearance of the volume edition one month before the last installment, the 20 October 1900 *Academy* commented: "This is the story which began in *Blackwood's Magazine* some months ago as a short story, and has grown into a long book" (362).[21] The serial's first numbers generated interest, as the *Illustrated London News*'s comment on 21 October 1899 suggested: "How well men write who have been to sea! They imprison in their sentences memories of the bigness and the mystery of the ocean. They have the steersman's keen vision, and their style is pungent with the Bible and Milton, the best schools for the young writer. I am thinking especially of Mr. Conrad, who has just begun a new story in *Blackwood's Magazine*" (565). And *Queen* stated on 3 November 1900 that, although the whole had been somewhat disappointing, "when the opening chapters of [*Lord Jim*] appeared in *Blackwood's*, readers thought they were face to face with one of the few novels which can be called great" (704).

Serial readers in general, like the *Queen* reviewer, may have lost interest in Conrad's expanding tale after reading a number of installments, just as the audience for *Hearts Insurgent* seemed to fall off after an initial enthusiasm for a new work by a well known author.[22] Najder notes that sales of the volume edition did not suggest a popular success: "in spite of the critics' praise, the popularity of *Lord Jim* was quite modest. True, the first impression, of 2,100 copies, was sold out in two months, but the next one, of only 1,050 copies, lasted four years" (271). Throughout the months of its serialization, however, Conrad did hear from readers. In a 19 May 1900 letter to David Meldrum the author, midway through the novel's composition, wrote: "*Lord Jim* brings me letters. From Spain to day! They take *Maga* in Madrid. Where is it they don't take *Maga*!" (Karl and Davies 273). Thus, the serial *Lord Jim: A Sketch,* widely distributed by the prominent *Blackwood's Magazine,* was a significant literary experience in the months of October 1899 through November 1900. Just as additional installments of *Hearts Insurgent* in 1894–95 had disappointed audience expectations of adventure and romance, however, so *Lord Jim: A Sketch* seemed to promise but never deliver a traditional story of love and success to late nineteenth-century readers. Conrad's style, telling one story many times many ways, was a cause for the Victorian audience's diminishing enthusiasm even for a major work by a recognized author.[23]

Before looking closely at one sample installment, it is helpful to see how all monthly parts of this novel included a key jump by one or more characters. That is, each installment of *Lord Jim: A Sketch* can be seen to a certain extent as the entire novel in miniature. While the central account of Jim's leap from the *Patna* is the culmination of installment 4 (January 1900),[24] Jim's failure to jump from the training ship into the rescue boat is at the heart of October 1899's part 1 (he is seen a moment later "on the point of leaping overboard" [444]). A drunken member of the *Patna* crew in installment 2 (November 1899) bursts out of a room in which he was restrained and "made one leap for dear life down the crazy little stairway" (654).[25] The apparently perfect Brierly takes a suicidal "leap into the sea" (809) in number 3 (December 1899). Jim, telling Marlow about his night in the boat after abandoning the *Patna,* "with a convulsive jerk of his elbow knocked over the cognac-bottle" (238) in number 5 (February 1900); he later corrects Marlow about his past action by saying he had "Jumped," not "cleared out" (246). The French lieutenant anticipates in installment 6 (March 1900) abandoning the *Patna* when he is towing her to port: " 'we had two quartermasters stationed with axes by the hawsers, to cut us clear of our tow in case she . . .' " (410). Number 7 (April 1900) recounts Jim's leap from the *Patna* in the court scene (discussed in more detail below), while Egstrom, recalling Jim's performance as a water clerk, mentions a "big jump" his employee took at an indirect reference to "sinking" (674) in the May 1900 *Blackwood's.*

These leaps, jumps, and impulsive acts all occur in the *Patna* portion of Conrad's tale, but involuntary responses occur as foundations for plot in the Patusan installments as well.[26] The central jump in numbers 9–14 occurs in installment 10 (July 1900) when Jim "leaped over" (93) the stockade in Tunku Allang's courtyard and then took a "second leap" (93) over the creek to reach Doramin's protection. Anticipating just such a chance at a new life, Jim had been ready in number 9 (June 1900) to "jump into the first gharry" (812) to Stein's house for instructions about Patusan. Number 11 (August 1900) shows another of Jim's foils, Cornelius, made to "jump and writhe" (260) when his daughter confronts him with his failures. Jim forces three assailants to "Jump!" (363) into the river in installment 12 (September 1900), and the appearance of another European, "Gentleman Brown," in number 13 (October 1900) recalls how Jim had "jumped" the "narrow creek" (561) near Tunku Allang's stockade. The final number (November 1900) narrates how Brown "jumped" (688) ashore into Patusan and how Dain Waris "jumped up and ran out upon the open shore" (703), where he was killed.

This structural principle of including at least one leap or jump in each installment underscores the novel's assertion that a key moment in life can reveal "the inner worth of a man, the edge of his temper, and the fibre of his stuff" (October 1899: 447). Also stressing this vision that a single impulsive act can "colour the whole 'sentiment of existence' in a simple and sensitive character" is the fact that each installment presents this theme fully. Number 7 of *Lord Jim: A Sketch* (April 1900), for instance, might be considered a single, complete short story with the title of "Walpole Reef." The *Athenaeum* gave special attention to this portion of the novel at its first reading, citing one passage from the installment as epitomizing Conrad's vision: " 'that faculty of beholding at a hint the face of his desire and the shape of his dream without which the earth would know no lover and no adventurer' " (576; the passage occurs in the first paragraph of *Lord Jim*'s chapter 16).

In this text Marlow is the protagonist who must decide whether to act in a specific case, and his weighing the possibilities through three chapters suggests that an individual must act ("leap") in this life, even though such action, a frightening responsibility at the moment, is ultimately found to be trivial in the larger scheme of existence. In arriving at this thematic resolution, "Walpole Reef" challenged a number of traditional Victorian themes, including empire, home, history, and doubt. Because this story's message was not one many British readers welcomed at the turn of the century, Conrad's audience did not grow with successive presentations. Because they still looked for a story "to be continued," the serial form of *Lord Jim: A Sketch* seemed attractive; but the modern content of each number disappointed and frustrated those expectations.

Installment 7 succeeds as a self-contained literary unit first of all simply because it provides sufficient information for the entire sequence of events to be comprehensible. That is, we learn in these pages that a character, Jim, abandoned "in the moment of danger" (513) people in his charge and that his punishment, "certificate cancelled" (514), cuts him off from any regular place in European society. Marlow's relationship to "James So-and-so" (514) is established when Chester asks if Jim has been "having grub with you in the Malabar" (517). Chester's proposal, that Jim "work" guano with "forty coolies" (518) on Walpole Reef, requires Marlow to act in his relationship to Jim: he must decide whether to relay this unsavory offer or propose an alternative to a young man in whom he has taken an interest.

A primary Victorian issue raised in this episode is empire, Chester's guano scheme recalling, for instance, Lopez's investments in *The Prime Minister* (see chapter four). The ideal of British colonialism is, of course, degraded by Chester, who pretends to be for "The making of Queensland!" but whose unscrupulous tactics include the exploitation of an already wasted "Holy-Terror Robinson" (515) and conclude in the ultimate "waste" (523) of all involved. Marlow also meets in this installment "a fellow fresh from Madagascar with a little scheme" (519) that resembles Chester's. This character's motto is "The minimum of risk with the maximum of profit" (519), and his presence in this part, along with the *Patna* officers convicted of "a breach of faith with the community of mankind" (511), suggests that few take seriously the Victorian ideal of empire as benevolent sponsor of growth and progress. Particularly at a time when Britain's realm was being challenged by the Boer War,[27] such revelations of greed at the heart of English colonialism would not have been likely to appeal to middle-class readers.

Another ideal called into question by the text of the April installment is home, for Marlow begins the number with a brief account of Selvin, his ship's chief mate. Selvin, "married thirteen years" (511), apparently loses control whenever he fails to receive an expected letter from his wife: "he would go quite distracted with rage and jealousy, lose all grip on the work, quarrel with all hands, and either weep in his cabin or develop such a ferocity of temper as all but drove the crew to the verge of mutiny" (511). After mentioning this regular danger to his ship, Marlow concludes that the "marital relations of seamen would make an interesting subject, and I could tell you instances. . . . However, this is not the place, nor the time, and we are concerned with Jim—who was unmarried" (511). This anecdote keeps the theme of romance for the protagonist alive, although minimally (to say he is now unmarried suggests he might later become involved);[28] and it insists that the Victorian ideal of home is strained by the Victorian imperatives of work and empire.

Although the ideals of empire and home seem to be directly compromised in Conrad's April installment of *Lord Jim: A Sketch*, the Victorian notion of history might at first appear intact. Jim, after all, later succeeds as "lover" and "adventurer" (522), according to Marlow: "The time was coming when I should see him loved, trusted, admired, with a legend of strength and prowess forming round his name as though he had been the stuff of a hero" (522). This apparent fulfillment, furthermore, comes after "a period of probation amongst infernal ship-chandlers" (523) and thus follows the traditional pattern of slow development in stages. But Marlow's reluctance to endorse fully Jim's achievements creates reservations about the course of history in this installment. Marlow insists, for instance, that he is "talking about [Jim] in vain" (522), either because his listeners do not grasp the importance of the tale or because Jim's story does not fit such a simple pattern: "I own that I was impressed, but I must admit to myself that after all this is not the lasting impression" (523). It is not "the image of his safety" but "him as seen through the open door of my room" (523) immediately after the trial that Marlow remembers. In fact, perhaps the most memorable image of Jim in this April installment is one that suggests an almost absolute insignificance: "At the moment of greatest brilliance the darkness leaped back with a culminating crash, and he vanished before my dazzled eyes as utterly as though he had been blown to atoms" (524).[29]

The narrator of this installment also follows a course of action that contradicts traditional nineteenth-century values. For instance, Marlow is often engaged in what ought to be a vital task for an emerging industrial middle-class world, writing; yet this production of words is mainly an empty gesture.[30] Marlow invites Jim back to his room after the court scene; then, trying to let the young man sort out his feelings, he busies himself at his desk as if Jim were "invisible": "I wrote and wrote; I liquidated all the arrears of my correspondence, and then went on writing to people who had no reason whatever to expect from me a gossipy letter about nothing at all" (521). That this effort is in the end merely "the scratching of my pen" (521) initiates this installment's questioning of the value of the written and the spoken word. Although he sees Jim in this scene as if he were "on the brink of a vast obscurity, like a lonely figure by the shore of a sombre and hopeless ocean" (521), Marlow does not at first seem aware of his own limited world: "There was not much in the room— you know how these bed-rooms are—a sort of four-poster bedstead under a mosquito-net, two or three chairs, the table I was writing at, a bare floor" (520). After some "industrious scribbling" (521), however, he admits to a "profound disturbance and confusion of thought . . . that mingled anxiety, distress, and irritation with a sort of craven feeling creeping in" (521).

Marlow, then, like Jude in *Hearts Insurgent* is in danger of slipping from doubt to despair about the human condition. Tested by Chester's plan for Jim, Marlow had been proud of the ability to remain calm early in this installment: "I was as mild as a curate" (516). Chester, however, forced a realization that if Jim did not belong on Walpole Reef, Marlow had to offer an alternative: "Oh! you are devilish smart. . . . See what *you* will do with him" (519). When Jim is later "shaken by his gasps" (521) of regret on the verandah, Marlow seems unable to meet Chester's challenge: "for a second I wished heartily that the only course left open for me were to pay for his funeral" (522). At this crisis point, Marlow finds himself unable to speak: "I found out how difficult it may be sometimes to make a sound.

There is a weird power in the spoken word. . . . And a word carries far—very far—deals destruction through time as the bullets go flying through space" (522). When Jim prepares to leave the room, the full hopelessness of the situation confronts Marlow: "It is when we try to grapple with another man's intimate need that we perceive how incomprehensible, wavering, and misty are the beings that share with us the sight of the stars and the warmth of the sun. It is as if loneliness were a hard and absolute condition of existence; the envelope of flesh and blood on which our eyes are fixed melts before the outstretched hand, and there remains only the capricious, unconsolable, and elusive spirit that no eye can follow, no hand can grasp" (524). This despair of communication and relationship marks the climax of this installment's plot.

At this point Marlow can assert the possibility of meaningful conduct in this world or accept a virtual nihilism. In reaching out to Jim, stopping him from going out into the world alone, Marlow performs the essential act of *Lord Jim: A Sketch*—he jumps, though here to rescue. Jim "pivoted on his heels, crossed the room, and had actually opened the door leading into the corridor before I leaped up from my chair" (526). At this moment, Marlow does nothing more than entreat Jim "to come in and shut the door" (526), but it is his affirmation and the resolution of the number.[31] He can do little for Jim, perhaps, but he will do what he can.

"Walpole Reef," then, pages 511–26 in the April 1900 *Blackwood's Magazine,* enacts in miniature the essential material of the entire novel, *Lord Jim: A Sketch.*[32] It affirms the value of a code of conduct at the same time that it suggests the code itself may be an artificial construction unrelated to the true identity, the "capricious, unconsolable, and elusive spirit," of individuals and of nature. Like a part of *Hearts Insurgent,* Conrad's installment seemed to offer traditional Victorian values of home, history, doubt, and empire; but ironic elements in the narrative undermined the solidity of these virtues, calling them into question.[33]

Despite the fact that each installment of *Lord Jim: A Sketch* creates the entire novel in miniature to a certain extent, the succession of parts does, of course, have a cumulative effect, one well identified in traditional Conrad criticism.[34] Victorian readers then and modern readers now see Jim in a different light at the conclusion of the novel, having considered the subject from many different vantage points. But the serial reading experience of 1899–1900 was characterized by a tension between the expectations of added knowledge and the repetitive nature of successive installments in *Lord Jim: A Sketch.* The serial form encouraged readers to find progress in the narrative because this had been the case with installment literature for sixty years. Conrad's more modern style, ultimately designed for the single volume rather than many installments, contradicted and frustrated those expectations.

Hardy's *The Dynasts* (1904–8), of course, differs from *Hearts Insurgent* and *Lord Jim* in genre. With its mixture of dialogue, verse, and prose, and its panoramic views, *The Dynasts* is sui generis. As a serial it differs from the two novels in having only three installments, though serial readers responded to each part, as they did with *Hearts Insurgent* and *Lord Jim: A Sketch,* as at once a self-contained whole and a part progressing toward a larger work. Appearing after Queen Victoria's death—part 1 in 1904, part 2 in 1906, and part 3 in 1908—*The Dynasts* faced the Victorian age in subject matter (the duke of Wellington is a major character) and the twentieth century in its publication dates. Hence, as a serial work it is poised, like *Hearts Insurgent* and *Lord Jim,* between Victorian and modernist conventions and themes.

Serial literature played a significant role in the origins of *The Dynasts.* At the age of eight, Hardy explains in the largely autobiographical account published under his wife's name, "He . . . found in a closet *A History of the Wars*—a periodical dealing with the war with Napoleon, which his grandfather had subscribed to at the time, having been himself a volunteer. The torn pages of these contemporary numbers with their melodramatic prints of serried ranks, crossed bayonets, huge knapsacks, and dead bodies, were the first to set him on the train of ideas that led to *The Trumpet-Major* and *The Dynasts*" (F. Hardy, *Early* 21). Susan Dean even suggests that the periodical's vivid illustrations helped shape Hardy's visual approach to materials in the drama (17–18). His first scheme for a poem devoted to the subject also shared elements of the serial form, a series of ballads "forming altogether an Iliad of Europe from 1789 to 1815" (F. Hardy, *Early* 140). Just as he complained about the restrictions imposed by the serialization of *Hearts Insurgent,* however, Hardy later stated that he regretted parts publication for the drama and contended he had resorted to it only because he was afraid he might otherwise never finish *The Dynasts* (F. Hardy, *Later* 105). If *The Dynasts* ultimately articulates a modernist perspective and aesthetic, its sequence and its reception by the reading community affirmed the continuing vitality of the serial tradition into the early twentieth century.

The drama's approach to its materials is likewise Victorian and modernist at once. As Henry Newbolt asserted in the March 1904 *Monthly Review* after the first part had appeared, "Of the Phantom Intelligences there are two to whom is especially committed the task of expounding Mr.

Hardy's theory of the universe. These two are . . . the Spirit of the Pities, which in general puts the question, and the Spirit of the Years, which gives the answer" (7). Others since have agreed that the Pities and the Years, which strongly differ in outlook, both represent Hardy's views. The Pities endorse assumptions that also underlay serialization, since the Pities hope for gradual progress toward a more beneficent universe and tend, as in the Fore Scene, to view the individual, the part, as cooperatively working toward a larger whole: *"They are shapes that bleed, mere marionettes or no, / And each has parcel in the total Will."* The Years, however, embody a modernist perspective also evident in *Hearts Insurgent* and *Lord Jim*. The Years discount the importance or viability of any part in favor of an omnipresent and instantaneous whole that dominates "parcels": "[The Will] *overrides them as a whole its parts / In other entities"* (1:6).[35] The Fore Scene, then, implicitly conveys alternative views not only of humankind and the universe but also of the art form that presents them—a serial drama that undercuts serial perspective.

Similar dualities are embodied in the work's publication format, which reveal Hardy using yet attempting to override the serial form. At the back of the first volume, immediately after the conclusion of act 6, scene 8, appeared "Contents of Second and Third Parts." (See figure 16.) Clearly Hardy wanted the wholeness of his design apparent despite his recourse to serialization (much as Browning forecast the contents of his four volumes at the end of the poem's opening monologue). Yet this assertion of established design is countered by the parenthetical "Subject to revision" just under the "Contents" heading, and even more by Hardy's note: "The Second and Third Parts are in hand, but their publication is not guaranteed." Again, one facet of the drama is oriented toward the future, to unclosed speculation about what the future will bring, while another facet urges the instantaneous glimpsing of the whole drama and its artistic design outside the workings of time.

The contingency and process inherent in serialization came to the fore when the second and third parts appeared and their contents did not match his outline of 1904. In addition, several reviewers remarked on Hardy's having left it up to his audience whether the succeeding parts would appear or not. As the 13 January 1904 *Morning Post* commented, "we trust the reception of this first part may be sufficiently warm to assure Mr. Hardy that if the rest of the drama does not appear it will be from no lack of desire on the part of [the] public" (3a). On 17 February 1908 the *Daily News* pronounced that "When Mr. Hardy issued the first volume of his colossal Napoleonic dramas he indicated that the completion of the design de-

SPIRIT SINISTER

Even Its official Spirit can show ruth
At man's fag end, when his destruction's sure!

SPIRIT OF THE YEARS

It suits us ill to cavil each with each.
I might retort.   I only say to thee
ITS slaves we are : Its slaves must ever be !

CHORUS (aerial music)

Yea, from the Vague we shape, like these,.
 And tarry till That please
To null us by Whose stress we emanate.—
 Our incorporeal sense,
Our overseeings, our supernal state,
 Our readings Why and Whence,
Are but the flower of Man's intelligence ;
And that but an unreckoned incident
Of the all-urging Will, raptly magnipotent.

A curtain of cloud overdraws.

END OF THE FIRST PART OF 'THE DYNASTS.'

CONTENTS OF SECOND AND THIRD PARTS

(*Subject to revision*)

PART SECOND

ACT FIRST

ACT SECOND

i

Figure 16. Concluding page of Hardy's *Dynasts,* part 1, and endpaper
projecting design of completed drama (1904).
(*Alderman Library, University of Virginia*)

pended upon the reception it had from the public. The second volume appeared in due course, and the third is now before us. We may assume, therefore, that the experiment, at once so daring, so original, and so vast, was received in a way that justified its completion. It would have been strange, indeed, if it had been otherwise" (4c). But the inevitability discerned by the *Daily News* in 1908 was only a distant hope in 1904— especially since Hardy was disappointed with the reviews of part 1, particularly the comments of the *Times Literary Supplement*.[36]

Hardy's assertion of both serial and instantaneous perspectives was paralleled by the divergent directives offered to readers throughout the drama's four-year publication process (see also Dean 32–33). Insofar as he declared to readers that future parts were subject to revision and dependent on readers' sympathy for their very appearance, he encouraged participation in serialization's suspense, anticipation, and provisional judgment. Insofar as Hardy stressed realism, contingency, and the importance of parts ("parcel[s] in the total Will"), he encouraged identification with the Pities, who oppose dynasts because a man like Napoleon "overrides"— i.e., dominates and uses—individuals as the Will uses Napoleon and all humanity to carry out an overarching design.[37] In the After Scene of part 3, the Pities invoke *"Thee whose eye all Nature owns, / Who hurlest Dynasts from their thrones"* (3:351) and idealize a cosmic presence that offers prospects opening onto the future and distant fulfillment:

> *We hold that Thy unscanted scope*
> *Affords a food for final Hope,*
> *That mild-eyed Consciousness stands nigh*
> *Life's loom, to lull it by and by.*

Above all, they invoke the vision of individuals, "parts" of humanity, leading gradually toward full participation in a beneficent whole:

(3:351–52)
> *And these pale panting multitudes*
> *Seen surging here, their moils, their moods,*
> *All shall "fulfil their joy" in Thee,*
> *In Thee abide eternally!*

The 17 February 1908 *Daily News* associated the Pities in this last scene with "the eternal cry of humanity," but ranged the Spirit of the Years with the "spirit of modern disillusion" (4d). Insofar as Hardy in his Preface to the 1904 volume directed readers to the "Eternal artistries" (1:ix) of the Immanent Will or "artistic unity" of his drama, insofar as he asked readers to bring "foreknowledge" of historical outcomes to the play and "fill in the curves" (Hardy also refers to "gaps") in the drama (1:ix), he appealed to the simultaneous perception consonant with modernist aesthetic principles. The *"scope"* of the Years *"is but to register and watch,"* as the Spirit comments in the Fore Scene (1:3), to stand apart and view the whole scene of earth from a detached and distant perspective that could serve as a gloss of the "aesthetic distance" vaunted in early twentieth-century formalist criticism:

> *Mercy? I view, not urge; nor more than mark*
> *What designate your titles Good and Ill.*
> *'Tis not in me to feel with, or against,*
> *These flesh-hinged mannikins Its hand upwinds*
> *To click-clack off Its preadjusted laws;*
> *But only through my centuries to behold*
> *Their aspects, and their movements, and their mould.*

(1:5–6)

Readers who brought knowledge of historical events to every scene helped create dramatic and cosmic irony that depended on their seeing different time frames and spaces all at once. In part 3, for example, readers were reminded of Ney's unjust death and the duke of Wellington's later pettiness even as Wellington was generously commenting on Ney's courage and daring. Such wholeness of perspective aligned readers with the perspective of the Years and clinched one of the great themes of Hardy's drama—the ultimate powerlessness of those who, to their peers, seem heroic and important figures who shape and direct the world.

In response to directives encouraging serial yet also simultaneous perspectives, Hardy's reviewers generally followed sequences of events, characters' developments, and unfolding of parts with delight—all traditional responses to serial literature—yet also seized on the themes of humankind as puppets and the insignificance of individuals, characteristic tenets of modern thought. To assess the place of *The Dynasts* in the Victorian serial, we will look at its reception in relation to three themes we have traced earlier in this study, home, history, and empire. Doing so will enable us to conclude our examination of the Victorian serial by revealing how far assumptions central to middle-class Victorian culture had eroded by the first years of the twentieth century. The contrast between Hardy's and earlier authors' treatments suggests that in addition to economic factors the serial owed its decline to the disintegration of the ideology that earlier underpinned it. Yet the tradition and assumptions connected with serialization were so well established that they also informed works (like those of Hardy and Conrad) that seemed bent on breaking with the tradition. We give particular attention to the treatment of history in *The Dynasts* because audience reaction to this issue most tellingly revealed the tension between perspectives appropriate to serial versus modernist frameworks, and because audience reaction to this theme was so deeply connected to the installment issue of the drama over a four-year span.

In relation to the issue of home, the Pities, not surprisingly, advocate family feeling and the slow, sustained development on which, as Patmore, Dickens, and Thackeray suggested (chapter two), key features of success-ful family life depend: *"We would establish those of kindlier build, / In fair Compassions skilled, / Men of deep art in life-development"* (1:4–5). In keeping with this interest in individuals and their development, intimate encoun-ters with selected characters, famous and obscure, were scattered through-out *The Dynasts* and often invited a compassionate, empathetic response.[38] In part 2, for example, the effect of being torn from the stable rhythms of life and precipitated into the dynasts' wars was conveyed through an unnamed deserter's contrast between the vile, burnt-out cellar in which he hides and scenes at home in Bristol: "Would that I were at home in England again, where there's old-fashioned tipple, and a proper God A'mighty instead of this eternal 'Ooman and baby;—ay, at home a-leaning against old Bristol Bridge, and no questions asked, and the winter sun slanting friendly over Baldwin Street as 'a used to do! 'Tis my very belief, though I have lost all sure reckoning, that if I wer there, and in good health, 'twould be New Year's day about now. What it is over here I don't know" (2:112).[39] Opposed to the empathy and community these "close-ups" encouraged (Wain ix–xiv) was Hardy's reliance on "panoramas," instantaneous per-spectives that promoted detachment in the observer.[40] And reviewers' comments suggest that readers seldom forgot the entanglement of the close-ups in a web of panoramas.[41]

Seen within the panoramic vantage of the Immanent Will or the ironies born of historical hindsight, the theme of family (or home) embod-ied in dynasties affords bitter commentary on ambitious, selfish, and ultimately futile desires to transcend time and perpetuate personal power through genealogy. Developmental sequences go awry with these royal families, since they are subject to rash reversals: old dynasties are toppled by new, but then old dynasties, like the Bourbon in France, can return (ironically signified by the raising of a mildewed flag), though they may just as easily topple again. Marriages, quite unlike those in Patmore's poem, often clash with notions of steady development over time and communal sensibility. Josephine is, then is not, Napoleon's wife; Napo-leon is, then is not, Marie Louise's husband (Buckler, "Hardy's" 223).

Readers' glimpses of the beginnings and endings of families and family aspirations within a single, whole perspective strike the familiar twentieth-century chord of families torn asunder through conflict, contrary needs, and the pressures of an increasingly chaotic age, just as they did in *Hearts Insurgent*.

But viewed serially, over a four-year course of reading (1904–8), the dynastic families assumed a modified aspect, though their stories were hardly the idealized stuff of *Angel in the House* or even the more complex but still benevolent depictions of families in *The Newcomes*. The foremost dynastic family is of course Napoleon's, and because Hardy dealt with this one at greatest length, it acquired special interest during the four years of the play's publication. In part 1 Napoleon is primarily a soldier, and women are banished to the periphery of action.[42] Josephine's single line only confirms her silence: "I spoke not, Sire" (1.56). In part 2, however, Napoleon turns his attention to founding a dynastic line. This was a clear development of part 1, since Napoleon sees an extended family line as a substitute for soldiers:

> When at the first clash of the late campaign,
> A bold belief in Austria's star prevailed,
> There pulsed quick pants of expectation round
> (2:188–89)   Among the cowering kings, that too well told
> What would have fared had I been overthrown!
> So; I must send down shoots to future time
> Who'll guard my standard and my story there.

The lines parallel the movement of the drama itself: as a serial work *The Dynasts* in 1904 had also sent "down shoots to future time" in its installment form.

Since Napoleon needed children, women became essential players in the world scene in part 2 (1906). The sequential, nonreversible flow of time, often linked with mid-Victorian serial treatments of domesticity, played an important role in the first parley of Napoleon and Josephine on a possible divorce. Napoleon, who in part 2 increasingly became identified with the Immanent Will, argued that the whole must override any part; or, as he said to Josephine,

> dwell not gloomily on this cold need
> Of waiving private joy for policy.
> (2:103)   We are but thistle-globes on Heaven's high gales,
> And whither blown, or when, or how, or why,
> Can choose us not at all!

Josephine, in contrast, invoked the slow patience of a Florence Dombey (and the anticipation that characterizes serialization) when she replied, "How—know you— / What may not happen! Wait a—little longer!" (2:100). Though Napoleon had a ready capacity for long prospects and slow planning, his entrapment in linear time cancelled patience where his dynasty was concerned.

Josephine was compelled to divorce, and Maria Louisa, whom Napoleon next married, also submitted to having her individual wishes overridden by the dictates of a larger whole, the Austrian Empire. When their son is born, there are two interpretations of the event; the male physician thinks the babe dead, but the female nurse, Madame Blaise, claims that the child is alive and shortly proves it.[43] The question is precisely whether this parcel of dynastic ambition is alive. For readers focused on the sequence of the unfolding parts, the child's life was paramount and his future a matter of suspense and anticipation left unresolved until the publication of part 3 two years later. The child was dead or at least a dead end as an heir, however, for readers who focused on knowledge of later historical events and who thus achieved an instantaneous perspective on the son's whole story from beginning to end.

In any case, part 2's treatment of domestic life was received enthusiastically by Hardy's professional reading audience. C. Lewis Hind, in the 12 February 1906 *Daily Chronicle,* praised Hardy's "vividness and characterisation" that brought to life, among other scenes, "the birth of Napoleon's son [as] a realistic domestic event" (3c–d), and Robert Ross in the 3 March 1906 *Academy* praised the scene in which Napoleon and Josephine discuss divorce as "the most beautiful and moving in the whole drama, though the motive (that of Napoleon's resolve to divorce Josephine) has often been treated before, but never with such direct simplicity" (207).

With the publication of part 3 in 1908 came the story of the empire's unraveling, and Napoleon's family, too, fell apart. At the end of part 3 Napoleon was utterly alone, not only because he had lost the battle of Waterloo and most of his army, but also because he had lost his dynasty: Marie Louise spurned her husband after being forced to flee Paris earlier, and eventually turned her eyes on Parma and the Count Neipperg; Napoleon's son, the king of Rome, assumed a new identity as the duke of Reichstadt.

In contrast to Napoleon's distortion of domestic relations because of his dynastic ambitions, at least one character in part 3 remained true to abiding affection. Josephine embodied sustained growth, development, and loyalty in love, since she revealed on her deathbed her continuing love for Napoleon, a persistence that complemented her plea for patience and waiting in part 2. While the absorbing interest and power of the Russian campaign and the battle of Waterloo attracted most attention in the reviews of part 3, several noted the death scene of Josephine, and the 11 March 1908 *Guardian* found it moving in the same way Dickens's readers might have done: "There is a depth of pathos which is quite admirable in the last words which she utters before she throws her arms around her children" (425). Readers' four-year-long involvement with the story of Napoleon would have deepened their intimacy with his, and Josephine's, lives and fates.[44] But Hardy's treatment of domesticity is in the completed *Dynasts* a source of irony. While the drama's four-year publication (as well as figures like Josephine) promoted the developmental and patient perspectives on home also fostered in mid-Victorian literature, the completed *Dynasts,* seen as a whole, emphasized the futility and even the reversibility of family lines and fortunes.

The serial versus "whole-volume" perspectives on the theme of history in *The Dynasts* are even more divergent, and hence more fully reveal the growing tension between the two publication modes at the turn of the century. Hardy explicitly adopted the materials of history and chose as his subject a story that made the Victorian story possible—without the triumphs at Trafalgar and Waterloo, the Victorian age as we know it is unthinkable. As G. M. Trevelyan asserted of the Napoleonic era in the 17 March 1906 *Speaker,* "It was the witches' cauldron of the bubbling hell-broth, out of which rose the child with the cap of liberty on its head and the engine and book in its hands—the nineteenth century" (577). In notable respects Hardy's treatment of history was also Victorian, not least in his use of a serial, sequential format to unfold his drama. His arrangement of materials drawn from history also furthered the notion that, as in Dickens's *A Tale of Two Cities* (chapter three), the flow of linear time is unidirectional and irreversible. Each of Hardy's scenes was carefully ordered to develop a sequence of cause and effect, as when George III's refusal midway through part 1 to bring the opposition into Pitt's cabinet hurries along Pitt's death, which occurs at the end of part 1. And the three parts of the drama that emerged with interruptions over time intensified the effect of sequence, since the first presented Napoleon's initial military triumphs, the second his dynastic schemes, and the third his military and dynastic defeats. Serialization, inevitably sequential and always embedded in linear time, would have reinforced the drama's emphasis on the unfolding of events over time.

Yet had Hardy stopped there, he would have written only an imitation of *War and Peace.* The drama's most famous figure is not Napoleon but the Immanent Will, and this challenges conceptions of sequence and the unidirectional flow of time. As the Ironic Spirit sings when Prussia is defeated in part 2,

(2:33)
> *So the Will plays at flux and reflux still.*
> *This monarchy, one-half whose pedestal*
> *Is built of Polish bones, has bones home-made!*
> *Let the fair woman bear it. Poland did.*

Readers aware of the ultimate outcome of events also experience "flux and reflux," since, while the "reel" of Hardy's drama runs forward, readers' memories run another film backward—e.g., running the later scene of Napoleon's defeat at Leipzig even as Napoleon lords it over the Prussians in part 2.[45] Time's reversibility is even more explicit in part 3, when the Pities who watch the French invasion of Russia see simultaneously the army's pathetic return: *"I see returning in a chattering flock / Bleached skeletons, instead of this array / Invincibly equipped"* (3:6).

Above all, however, the imagery used to body forth the Immanent Will contests the sequences of history, absorbing what may appear (to limited human vision) as linear cause and effect into the instantaneous, unified workings of an unconscious mind: "A new and penetrating light descends on the spectacle, enduing men and things with a seeming transparency, and exhibiting as one organism the anatomy of life and movement in all humanity and vitalized matter included in the display" (1:10). The Immanent Will is characterized not by a straight line but a web, as the Spirit of the Years remarks at Borodino (it is *"the will of all conjunctively; / A fabric of excitement, web of rage, / That permeates as one stuff the weltering whole"* [3:31]) and again at the drama's end:

(3:349–50)
> *Yet but one flimsy riband of Its web*
> *Have we here watched in weaving—web Enorme,*
> *Whose furthest hem and selvage may extend*
> *To where the roars and plashings of the flames*
> *Of earth-invisible suns swell noisily,*
> *And onwards into ghastly gulfs of sky,*
> *Where hideous presences churn through the dark—*
> *Monsters of magnitude without a shape,*
> *Hanging amid deep wells of nothingness.*

The coexistence of sequence and web in Hardy's drama may itself be a result of history, and a symptom of the serial's decline as a vehicle for the twentieth century's serious literature. Hardy's concept of the Immanent

Will as one enormous web pervading the cosmos resembles models of twentieth-century field theory developed around the same time as Hardy published his play. N. Katherine Hayles, in *The Cosmic Web*, explains that field theory grew out of work in quantum mechanics, relativity theory, and particle physics: "Characteristic metaphors [of the field model] are a 'cosmic dance,' a 'network of events,' and an 'energy field.' A dance, a network, a field—the phrases imply a reality that has no detachable parts, indeed no enduring, unchanging parts at all. Composed not of particles but of 'events,' it is in constant motion, rendered dynamic by interactions that are simultaneously affecting each other. . . . Its distinguishing characteristics, then, are its fluid, dynamic nature, the inclusion of the observer, the absence of detachable parts, and the mutuality of component interactions" (15). Hayles later elaborates this metaphor or model as a web. In the model individual parts subject to strict causality disappear in lieu of particles as an expression of "the field's conformation at a given instant, appearing as the field becomes concentrated at one point and disappearing as it thins out at another. Particles are not to be regarded as discrete entities, then, but rather . . . as 'energy knots' " (16).[46]

This is very close to the model or metaphor Hardy constructs of human beings within the grasp or "field" of the Immanent Will, who are likewise never detachable parts operating according to local, individualized intentions, and who cluster in multitudes (especially on battlefields) or thin out into small knots of groups according to the dynamics of history's "events."[47] This view of existence implicitly challenges an essential element in the Victorians' major scientific contribution, the theory of evolution. If theory allowed for the reversion and even the disappearance of species as well as their development, Victorian views of evolution stressed the sequence and gradualism on which the process depended rather than a simultaneous field. The jostling of these two perspectives, the evolutionary and the field view of the earth, intensifies at the close of *The Dynasts*. Immediately after the Spirit of the Years describes the cosmic web, the Pities, always aligned with a developmental and human perspective, invoke the idea of evolution:

(3:350)

> *Thou arguest still the Inadvertent Mind.—*
> *But, even so, shall blankness be for aye?*
> *Men gained cognition with the flux of time,*
> *And wherefore not the Force informing them,*
> *When far-ranged aions past all fathoming*
> *Shall have swung by, and stand as backward years?*

The Spirit of the Years, in response, concedes evolution in its own view-point (*"You almost charm my long philosophy / Out of my strong-built thought, and bear me back / To when I thanksgave thus"* [3:353]), and the play ends with the Chorus of the Pities anticipating an evolutionary development in the Will itself:

> But—*a stirring thrills the air*
> *Like to sounds of joyance there*
>   *That the rages*
>   *Of the ages*
> *Shall be cancelled, and deliverance offered from*
>   *the darts that were,*
> *Consciousness the Will informing, till It fashion*
>   *all things fair!*

(3:355)

Hardy appears to resolve the competition of two models of existence by absorbing the field view of the universe into an evolutionary model, a resolution to which the drama's serialization would have given added force since his own text developed slowly over an expanse of years.[48] In this modulation of the Will and in his use of the serial form, as much as in his historical materials, Hardy reveals how deeply rooted he was in the ideology of the Victorian age. Certainly the reviewers were quick to seize on the muted expression of hope (and evolution) and expressed a rush of enthusiasm for this concluding turn in the play's message. S. R. Lit-tlewood in the 12 February 1908 *Daily Chronicle* reported that "The last word, it is pleasant to know, for those who are mindful of the fatalistic shadow that hangs over nearly all Mr. Hardy's novels, is one of hope" (3c). And the 21 March 1908 *Spectator* closed its brief notice by commenting, "The philosophy, too, has taken a happier colouring. A hope of ultimate good relieves the fatalism of the early scenes, and the Pities speak the last word" (463).

The juxtaposition of the evolutionary and simultaneous also informs views of England's historical role in Hardy's drama. In his Preface Hardy stated that he aimed to redress "the provokingly slight regard paid to English influence and action throughout the struggle" (1:vi). English readers' familiarity with the outcome at Waterloo, even their awareness of the two great military leaders of the Napoleonic wars enshrined in the crypt of St. Paul's Cathedral, would have encouraged a view of the era as a sequence progressing toward Waterloo and of England as a privileged country whose special gifts enabled it to determine its free and unique course. In fact both Harold Orel ("What" 119) and F. R. Southerington

(192) term *The Dynasts* "a patriotic work," while Barton Friedman argues that Hardy "transform[s] the facts of the Napoleonic Wars into a heroic myth for Albion" (108). But if the Immanent Will determines all, then England would not be a privileged participant but merely an aggregate of beings that happened to fare well in the past and would be as likely to fare badly in the future. Reviewing Hardy's treatment of England's role in light of his simultaneous commitment to its importance and to the figure of the Immanent Will, and recovering the response of audiences to the successive parts of Hardy's drama, helps establish the presentation of history as sequence or as whole pattern.

Part 1 established the greatness of England and its role as Napoleon's true foe, a view fostered by Hardy's having Napoleon himself declare, "The English only are my enemies" (1:125). Above all, however, the brilliant and moving presentation of Trafalgar captured attention in part 1, so much so that Henry Newbolt declared in the March 1904 *Monthly Review* that the part's true end coincided with the death of Nelson (9).[49] The horrors of battle were never ignored amidst the depictions of valor, but the overall effect of the Trafalgar scenes was to emphasize Nelson's heroism and his importance in preventing an invasion of England. Above all, the Immanent Will's invisibility in the Trafalgar scenes made England seem a privileged nation capable of agency, unlike those depicted within the web of the Immanent Will at Austerlitz, where the lesser Continental forces suffered defeat.

Several reviews of part 1 focused on Nelson as hero. The 13 January 1904 *Standard* asserted, "Nelson's talk is very life-like, and the battle-scenes on the Victory are powerful and pathetic. The figure of Napoleon is less effective" (2b). Margaret Woods wrote in the 13 February 1904 *Speaker,* "The figure of Nelson is indeed the only romantic figure which fills any space in the foreground" (474). Henry Newbolt in the *Monthly Review* was likewise impressed with the scenes involving Nelson, and so distressed at Hardy's omission of the oft-quoted prayer Nelson spoke as his ship moved within firing range of the French that Newbolt printed the prayer in his columns to redress the missing documentation (March 1904: 12).

Several viewed *The Dynasts* essentially as the story of England. Henry Newbolt simply announced that Hardy's "hero [is] the English nation" (1). The 13 January 1904 *Morning Post* applauded Hardy's "courageous effort to present the greatest period of the modern history of Europe and of our own national story in the form of a drama" (3a). Margaret Woods in the *Speaker* wrote under the heading, "The Epic of England," and pronounced that "The subject which Mr. Hardy has chosen is the greatest which any writer has treated since Milton, and one of more complexity than 'the ways of God to man' as seen by a Puritan theologian. . . . It is a handling of a theme which deserved, which needed, handling: the great national drama of England's epic struggle with Napoleon" (13 February 1904: 474). And A. Macdonell made clear in the February 1904 *Bookman* that in its serial context this theme was seen as a sequence building to a well-defined but still distant whole: "To those likely to be mainly interested in it on its historical side, it should be said that one chief aim of 'The Dynasts' is to show the great controlling influence of England in the Napoleonic struggle. The statement of this can only be completed by the second and third parts, and until these appear we must suspend judgment as to the fulfilment of the purpose—though the portion before us does its fair share towards proving such a thesis" (221).

Yet despite this attention to England's role or some reviewers' placing the poem in the context of Hardy's Dorset past and *The Trumpet-Major,* most saw the work's major theme as the Immanent Will behind all. In this respect simultaneity won out over sequence. The 15 January 1904 *TLS* review that disappointed Hardy adopted this approach (11), but Henry Nevinson's reaction in the 13 January 1904 *Daily Chronicle* was also typical: "we are led through the tremendous happenings of ten short months, and the volume—the first part of the drama—ends with the death of Pitt. Tremendous happenings? It requires some courage to speak like that after watching Mr. Hardy's vision. . . . It is as though we took our stand upon some star to which the sun is but a firefly, and gazed upon this tiny dust-speck of an earth in which certain microscopic atoms were exploding with almost imperceptible noise" (3b).

Only Margaret Woods in the *Speaker* advocated an essentially sequential view of the entire drama. Several reviews, however, suggest that readers felt invited to both a sequential and a simultaneous perspective on history. The 13 January 1904 *Standard* in one breath observed that "The Captains and the Kings, Admirals, Statesmen, Emperors, the Great Conqueror himself, are seen moving in obedience to the mysterious laws of a Power too mighty for them to comprehend" (2b). But in the next breath it added that "Mr. Hardy's main object is to exhibit different phases and moments of the great contest between Napoleon and his opponents" and that the work was a "series of living pictures, flashing before the spectator one set of personages or events after another, with whose general outline and historical relations he is assumed to be familiar" (2b). Thus, the first part left reviewers particularly aware of the drama's impetus toward a panoramic rather than a sequential view of history, a whole pattern rather than a straight line or journey; yet both the materials of history and the serial format kept the viability of sequence before readers as well.

The most remarkable thing about part 2, the middle of Hardy's serial, is that the Immanent Will never appears. It is alluded to more than once, but never do the human characters suddenly melt into transparency and function as mere particles of a larger whole that overrides them.[50] The Immanent Will's visual absence coincides with increased emphasis on sequences, many having to do with Napoleon's dynastic designs, but others related to the progress (in more than one sense) of the English in the Peninsular campaign. True, the English suffer setbacks in part 2. Moore has all the courage and greatheartedness of Nelson and is also fatally wounded in battle, but no grand outcome ensues from his death. Talavera and Albuera are taken, but only with huge losses, and these victories are set against the disaster at Walcheren. Still, especially for readers with foreknowledge of Waterloo, the English drive toward overcoming the French could have appeared steady and progressive. The English are in fact explicitly associated with steadfastness and persistence in part 2. Parliament determines to pursue its course against France (2:226–27) despite losses, and earlier a Viennese citizen drinks to England's "consistency":

(2:141)

While we and all the kindred Europe states
Alternately have wooed and warred with him,
You have not bent to blowing hot and cold,
But held you sturdily inimical!

England is here clearly unique among the allies, even superior, and Sir Arthur Wellesley (who sets sail in act 2) is himself identified with the same steady progress and hard work as his country. The last act opens with a view of the defenses Wellington has had built in Spain, and as the French officer who encounters them observes, they have been built up over months and are "Lord Wellington's select device, / And, like him, heavy, slow, laborious, sure" (2:252). This celebration of the gradual and steady within a historical account that is itself serialized would have further authorized a sequential historical view.

Indeed, reviewers' attention to the Immanent Will and an instantaneous view of history declined markedly in 1906, though reviewers did not lose sight of the "puppet" theme in part 2. The notices focused most often on the theme of history and frequently noted the effects of the parts publication format.[51] The 9 February 1906 *Standard* praised Hardy for clarifying history to readers and noted that despite the format of " 'snap-shots,' apparently incoherent visions, and momentary revelations, a per-fectly logical sequence is secured" (4c). C. Lewis Hind in the 12 February 1906 *Daily Chronicle* stated, "I find the story itself as interesting as any historical novel" (3c). Robert Ross asserted in the 3 March 1906 *Academy* that "the great drama of *The Dynasts,* the second part of which has just been issued, proves him not merely a great novelist but an essayist, a poet and a dramatist and, I might add, an acute historical critic" (206). The 14 March 1906 *Guardian* contended that "it is impossible not to delight in the consummate artistic skill with which the poet has treated the most striking episodes of the Great War" (448).[52] The reviewer chosen for the 17 March 1906 *Speaker* was the historian G. M. Trevelyan, who termed Hardy's work "an historical play in three parts" and suggested that Hardy might pay even more attention to the lasting progress wrought by the era (577–78).[53] C. Lewis Hind in the *Daily Chronicle* pointed to England's impor-tance in the drama through a plot summary that placed England at the beginning and end of each part: "The first volume, published in 1904, began with England's alarm at the marshalling of Napoleon's army of invasion at Boulogne in 1805, and ended with the death of Pitt. The second volume, just published, opens with a scene in Fox's lodgings in Arlington street just before his death,[54] and closes with a gathering in Carlton House. . . . The third volume will carry this amazing play . . . to its conclusion—Waterloo" (12 February 1906: 3c). Part 2 and its reception, then, suggested that this second volume, much like Dickens's *A Tale of Two Cities* and Eliot's *Romola* (chapter three), interested and engaged readers in a sequential story with meaningful characters that, after follow-ing directly from a previous part, seemed to open onto the future with a note of hope and anticipation.

Part 3, published two years later in 1908, at once embodied and dissolved the sense of process and sequence associated with serialization and some Victorian views of history. The embedding of events in time and process, for example, would have intensified for Hardy's first readers several allusions back to passages read four or two years earlier. When Sergeant Young sings "Budmouth Dears" in the final part and thinks back to the fine time he and his men had in Wessex ten years ago, readers could echo the sergeant's sense of passing time as they harked back to the Wessex scenes in the 1904 volume—just as the reviewer did before citing the ballad of Trafalgar in the 14 March 1908 *Academy* ("Does the reader remember this from the first volume?" [556]). The scene in the old House of Commons, in part 3, likewise would have echoed the first such scene in part 1, and would also have emphasized the linear sequence of time both in and out of the text.

England's steadily growing importance was also confirmed in part 3's events: in his last appearance in the drama Napoleon credits English tenacity with undoing his ambitious schemes (3:347), and earlier England's role is highlighted when Wellington assumes primary responsibility for defeating Napoleon's forces at Waterloo because other allied troops are disabled or too far away. At Waterloo Wellington's entire strategy, moreover, consists of persistence and steadiness (plus holding a surprise store of reserves until the very end), just as his work in Spain had depended on "heavy, slow, laborious, sure" methods. When asked his commands, he replies, "These simply: to hold out unto the last, / As long as one man stands on one lame leg / With one ball in his pouch!" (3:323). This strategy won the day and secured a future for the duke and for Victorian England; in this case readers' knowledge of history would have intensified, not ironically countered, a steady and progressive outlook.

Wellington was a character from whom serial readers had waited four years to "hear" a spoken line; introduced as a figure seen only from afar in part 2, he utters his first line at the battle of Salamanca (3:16). Yet even as Wellington progresses from a peripheral to a central and victorious character, and from the periphery of Portugal to the center of battle with Napoleon, Hardy constructs a counterperspective to all. Instead of being only the opposing and victorious foe of Napoleon, Wellington emerges as his double. When these two leaders drew up battle lines across from each other at Waterloo, readers learned that the two men were the same age, and in the ensuing battle they both had to contend with officers who importuned for more reserves when none were to be had (Dean 199).

But above all they became doubles because, at the very climax of the English drive toward victory, Hardy revealed Wellington, like Napoleon, to have been in the control of the Immanent Will all along. Having imbued the English with the aura of heroism in the first two parts (four years' duration for Hardy's first readers), Hardy at the very end reabsorbed even this privileged nation into the machinations of an unconscious force that pervades the universe. Hence, in the two critical battles the English fought, first at Vitoria (3:74), then at Waterloo, the Immanent Will was bodied forth once again. The stage directions even made explicit Wellington's entanglement in the cosmic web at Waterloo: "The web connecting all the apparently separate shapes includes WELLINGTON in its tissue with the rest, and shows him, like them, as acting while discovering his intention to act" (3:320). Hence, a four-year glorification and extension of England (from 1904 to 1908) culminated in its sinking to the level of other nations; a line of progress became absorbed in a web; and a serial sequence modulated into a simultaneous perspective.[55]

In contrast to response to part 2, reviews of part 3 hardly mentioned the English role in the Napoleonic era, and few if any tried to read the drama as a historical novel. At the end a whole, simultaneous perspective seemed dominant. In the 12 February 1908 *Daily Chronicle* S. R. Littlewood asserted that "through all these kaleidoscopic scenes of jollity and horror . . . Mr. Hardy never loses sight of the profound philosophic purport, before which a blade of Wessex grass is as important as the fate of Europe" (3c). The comments of the 17 February 1908 *Daily News* were even more revealing, since this review explicitly articulated the image of a web and a simultaneous view of fifteen years by which temporality is transformed into a spatial trope. This reviewer found the drama's unity in its aerial views; in these spectators could see, "through the connecting descriptive passages, the web of events being woven into a piece" (4c); and the reviewer also called *The Dynasts* a "drama of suggestion to which the reader brings his knowledge to fill in the gaps. Then he may see those fifteen crowded years unrolled before him like a map" (4d).

Yet the serial reception of the play itself was not entirely effaced. Even before part 3 was out the *Daily Chronicle* commented in its "Writers and Readers" column on 29 January 1908, "Probably the most interesting book of February will be the third and closing part of Mr. Thomas Hardy's poem, 'The Dynasts.' The first volume rather bewildered people; the second filled them with admiration and anticipation; and the third—What will be the impression of it? It is concerned with the events which marked the decline and fall of Napoleon, and never surely was there in history a more dramatic chain of happenings. Moscow to Waterloo—that is the road along which Mr. Hardy here takes Napoleon" (3d). And if S. R. Littlewood recognized a "whole" philosophical outlook when reviewing the play in the same paper some two weeks later on 12 February, Littlewood also asserted, "it is only when one recognises the flower-like naturalness of the growth of 'The Dynasts,' that one begins to enjoy and value to the full the great work just completed" (3c). Even the 17 February 1908 *Daily News,* which offered such clear testimony that readers saw an instantaneous perspective dominating the work, reflected a developmental history of response to the drama: "The impression left on the mind by the first volume was that of bewilderment. One was overshadowed by the immensity of the conception. One needed the perspective of time and the relation of the parts in order to be able to say whether the structure was of granite or match-boarding. It would be hazardous even yet to offer a decisive verdict. And yet as one closes the book on that wan note of hope . . . one cannot resist the conclusion that this vast panorama of history is one of the great and enduring products of our time" (4c).[56]

Given the embedding of readers' interpretations in the serial reading process, it is perhaps not surprising that Walter de la Mare in the June 1908 *Bookman* could see the play's historical characters in two ways at once, both as agents pursuing meaningful lives and stories, and as puppets of a larger whole: "All are human, wilful, capricious, quite eminently 'masters of their fate'; much more the peasants and camp-followers—subtlest of thrusts—than Emperor and Prince Regent. All, too, how profoundly are mere puppets, motes of chance, the flitting phosphorescence of a wave that follows the moon. The temptation to dwell on this pervasive idea is irresistible" (111). Perhaps only when the serialization of *The Dynasts* is taken into account, however, a process that encouraged readers of the first two parts to see the drama as the epic of England's progress until part 3 appeared, can the interpretation offered by the 14 March 1908 *Academy* be understood. Few reading the drama as a whole volume would interpret it in the following terms:

> It is, we take it, plain that [Hardy] has not written three volumes simply in order to give us vivid pictures of crowded campaigns or a clear and sympathetic characterisation of Napoleon the Conqueror; though these things he assuredly has done. Beyond all this he gives us what is more valuable than thirty volumes of vivid pictures; he gives us a philosophical conception of the vast era, and suggests an interpretation of its national movements—indeed, of human progress itself. Here is the great theme. A finer background he could hardly have chosen, nor one more certain of appeal to thoughtful English readers. . . . Mr. Hardy tells us that
> (556)   Napoleon did not stand for himself only, nor for France only; he stood, as we may conceive, for man insurgent, awhile dominant, teased with glory, exposed, smothered. Mr. Hardy spares us the hateful gibe of supposing that lives vanished like smoke and tears fell like rain merely for the aggrandisement of an inordinately ambitious soldier. There is a Hand behind the Show. . . . The pervading idea of the Immanent Will. . . . affords a persistent clue to the meaning of the mystery of the heaving, bloody earth, that else were merely grotesque and grim. . . . The illumination of the Will itself is indicated, and the consequent redemption of the illimitable failure of the world.

If, then, a nonsequential, instantaneous view of history is an essential and even a dominant element of *The Dynasts,* the older view of history as emphatically linear and even progressive was made available to its first readers as well. The work's serialization, which gave to original audiences a reading history of four years' duration, enhanced the importance of sequential history both in and out of the text.

The treatment of empire in *The Dynasts* also shifts depending on whether it is viewed from within a serial or whole-volume context. If this theme is considered from the perspective of the whole play, irony will again dominate. Part 1 may culminate in the great victory at Austerlitz; part 2 may present the extension of Napoleon's empire into Prussia, Spain, and Austria, his alliance with Russia, and his parceling of the Ottoman Empire; but part 3 shows the utter unraveling of all that Napoleon so slowly built up. Indeed, Hardy underscores in part 3 the contraction (in contrast to earlier expansion) of French forces. The Semichorus of Rumours observe that at Leipzig Napoleon is *"Shrunk in power"* (3:101), while a citizen notes that the French "front has shrunk / From five miles' farness to but half as far" after the first day of fighting (3:105). Though Napoleon begins rebuilding his empire after escaping from Elba, he is still left utterly alone, emperor of nothing, in Bossu Wood at the play's end, an apt commentary on the human desire to build lasting monuments to its dubious magnificence.

This pattern of rise and fall can recall for us the rise and fall of Arthur's kingdom in *Idylls of the King.*[57] Napoleon himself gives his equivalent of "The old order changeth, yielding place to new" when he says to Mack in part 1, "All states must have an end, the weak, the strong" (1:125). Napoleon even undergoes a form of death, rebirth, and return (if not as romantic as Arthur's) when he attempts suicide at Fontainebleau, then vomits the poison, and eventually returns to his people to lead them once more. When he returns, moreover, he succeeds because he can rekindle loyalty and induce his soldiers to share his vision of a conquering France, just as the leaders (and writers) we examined in chapter four depended for success on extending a shared vision to others.

But of course the differences between the *Idylls* and *The Dynasts,* between Arthur and Napoleon, are more evident than their similarities. Arthur fails but does not decline as a leader; he upholds the same principles at the end as at the beginning, and serial publication of the *Idylls,* as we have argued, meant that the portrait of Arthur's leadership continued to grow even though each set of poems presented the realm's fall. Napoleon's capacity for leadership declines as his story progresses, and readers grow to understand only his failing powers in successive parts of the drama. His decline is especially apparent in Russia. Because of his persistent head cold and the whiskey he drinks to relieve it, he is drunk at the battle of Borodino, and his unimaginative battle strategy wins the day but slaughters a fourth of his men. When the retreat from Russia becomes too difficult, he abandons his men; and by the time he reaches Waterloo he actually lies to his soldiers to make them fight.

Napoleon differs from Arthur in another significant respect, one that suggests how far the image of growth and expansion in the *Idylls* is tied to liberal middle-class ideology. Arthur's leadership depends (invading heathens aside) not on compulsion but on inducing others to share his vision; he respects the autonomy of each individual, each part, but invites them to participate in a larger whole. Napoleon is an imperialist who conquers and compels; his rule is another instance of the whole overriding the part, whether it be the empire of France annexing other countries or Napoleon dominating fellow human beings as he does Josephine (see also Wilson).

Napoleon's imperialism is part of his decline: when he becomes emperor and attempts to start a new dynasty, he betrays the vision that he once shared with his compatriots—the overthrow of old dynasties and tyranny—and that brought him to power. His imperialism, moreover, aligns him in parts 1 and 2 with the Immanent Will, which also denies autonomy to parts and overrides them. Perhaps this shared attribute of Napoleon and the Will explains not only why Napoleon so often seems attuned to and aware of the Will, but also why Hardy draws back from a purely deterministic view at the drama's end. There the Pities express a faint hope for the amelioration of human lots with a regenerated Will that awakes into consciousness, more like an Arthur waking after sleep in Avilion than a Napoleon springing up from regurgitation.

Embedded in the serial issue of the three parts, however, was a pattern of growth and expansion that countered the emphasis on Napoleon's contracting empire in part 3. Two expressions of growth actually further the story of Napoleon's decline, since one pattern of growth is grim, the other ludicrous. As each part unfolds, more fighting occurs because of Napoleon's ambitions, and hence the carnage grows in each book, until— just before Waterloo—Napoleon's vision of those killed in his "cause" includes hundreds of thousands. The other form of growth, steady and sure, reflects Napoleon's personal decline: Napoleon gets fatter as the story progresses. We are directed to his stoutening figure in part 2, when "The light, crossed by the snow-flakes, flickers on his unhealthy face and stoutening figure" in Spain (2:117). Napoleon's girth continues to expand in part 3. We see his "puffed cal[ves]" in Russia (3:5); we learn that as he leaves Elba he "is much fatter than when he left France" (3:187); and at Waterloo he is fattest of all: "His stumpy figure, being just now thrown back, accentuates his stoutness" (3:289).

A more affirmative pattern of growth occurred in the poem itself.[58] Even in 1904 reviewers commented on the poem's great size. Henry Nevinson said in the 13 January 1904 *Daily Chronicle* that "Certainly there is nothing Lilliputian about the scheme of a work like that, and our poor little earthly stage managers must turn away in despair" (3b). Max Beerbohm made essentially the same point with his customary wit in the 30 January 1904 *Saturday Review:* "In England, during recent years, great writers in their autumn have had a rather curious tendency: they have tended to write either about Napoleon or about Mrs. Meynell. The late Mr. Coventry Patmore wrote about Mrs. Meynell. Mr. Meredith has written both about Mrs. Meynell and about Napoleon. Mr. Hardy now readjusts the balance, confining himself to Napoleon. So far, his procedure is quite normal: a new theme, through a new form. But I mislead you when I speak of Mr. Hardy as 'confining himself to Napoleon'. 'Excluding Mrs. Meynell' would be more accurate. He is so very comprehensive" (137).

In 1906 part 2 appeared with the same number of acts as part 1, but with forty-three rather than thirty-five scenes (thirty-six including the Fore Scene), and about a third again as many pages. Moreover, Hardy added scenes of domestic life to the earlier emphasis on political and military life as Napoleon sought his dynastic line, and the increasing role of women widened the scope and texture of the drama. And when part 3 appeared in 1908 it not only took up more pages than part 2 but also included a seventh act and fifty-three scenes. "As the action includes the campaigns of Moscow, Leipzig, Vittoria and Waterloo, and thus deals with more events of magnitude than occur in the earlier parts," the February 1908 *Book Monthly* remarked, "this one is somewhat longer" (321).[59]

Neither part 2 nor part 3 would have appeared had audiences failed to respond to part 1, a point noted by several reviewers in 1908. Further, Hardy's completed drama met with virtually universal praise after the final part was issued. We can, therefore, conclude that steady, progressive expansion of Hardy's poem over time was an expression of hope, appreciation, and community among writer and readers that provided an affirmative counterpart to the pattern of disintegration and futility embedded in Hardy's treatment of the French empire.

The Dynasts, then, like any middle installment of a Victorian serial, grew out of the past and anticipated the future of the Victorian serial. The drama's serial form, of course, reflected the Victorian past in both publication mode and the ideology associated with it: an assertion of the individual (or part), the developmental processes associated with family life, the sequences and pauses of history, the expansion of vision and growth embodied in empire, and the backtracking occasioned by doubt yet counterpointed by the forward motion of time and events. Like *Hearts Insurgent* and *Lord Jim: A Sketch,* however, *The Dynasts* also pointed to the future and to the aesthetics and ideology of the modernist tradition: the absence of progress, an elevation of the whole over the part, the dominance of simultaneous over linear perspectives, doubts about the integrity or identity of the individual.

Yet the fact that the two perspectives could coexist in Hardy's work perhaps suggests that they need not be seen as inherently inimical. After Einstein, simple notions of linear time for the cosmos seem unrealistic and reductive; yet we must all still live by the clock, meet deadlines, and go through the linear stages of childhood, youth, adulthood, and old age in sequence. To survive as a species we require the instantaneous vision of the global village, yet if we want the emotional richness of friendships and relationships we also need the localized framework within which we are individuals cooperating to build over time a larger whole. The work of twentieth-century linguistics and theorists indicates that language is a system, a web of syntactic, semantic, and grammatical interconnections always operating everywhere at once (J. Hillis Miller, *Linguistic* 306–9); yet to write about the operations of language in a given text one must proceed step by linear step, as we have done here. Finally, if criticism still tends (whether by Coleridgean, modernist, or postmodern standards) to judge a literary work by its effect as a whole, we think that our examination of Victorian serials from a variety of authors, decades, and thematic perspectives demonstrates the equal validity of engaging works experienced as a process of accumulating parts over time.

Conclusion:
Recovering
the Serial

VICTORIANS VALUED slow, steady development in installments over time, seeds planted in spring leading to harvest in distant autumn. In contrast, fast-forward visions of individual and communal life, plants growing from seed through blossom to death in the brief seconds of time-lapse photography, have figured prominently in modern literature and thought. Indeed, experience in our century has frequently insisted that life is short, frequently undermined by irony, marked by tragedy and failure. Yet many in this age have committed themselves to building coherent private and public lives, as well as consistent far-reaching theories about life itself. The frames of reference structuring these lives and many contemporary institutions are descendants, though often unacknowledged, of a nineteenth-century tradition, one important manifestation of which is the serial.

Certainly, serialization had in the nineteenth century the dangers of sensationalism, simplicity of outlook and form, padding that filled out pages. Yet the serials we have examined here did more in their time than avoid such temptations; they achieved their prestige by, among other things, taking advantage of the positive attributes of serialization, demanding from their audiences long-term commitment and sympathy, expanding structures of thought, the ability to connect distant pieces of a whole. These processes can be recovered in two major forums of contemporary life: literary scholarship and the classroom. As we have argued in this book's six chapters, twentieth-century audiences can come to understand neglected features of nineteenth-century life by studying the Victorian serial, whether through new critical methodologies like reception theory, reader-response criticism, and cultural studies or through the longer-established traditions of literary scholarship.

By teaching serials as serials in secondary-school, undergraduate, and graduate curricula, teachers can make available to students a whole range of significant literary works and ways of approaching them. Younger students who might once have thought *Middlemarch* intimidating in its very length can, by reading it in parts, find it suddenly manageable and even exciting. Graduate students situating the literary canon in its cultural context or assessing the impact of reading strategies on the production of meaning can also find the serial a form of interest and appeal.

Of course, academic semesters or quarters are not perfect patterns for teaching all installment literature. To teach serially one must sometimes group two, three, or more original parts together in one reading assignment. And the time between readings seldom can match the regular Victorian gap of a week or a month. Yet giving the full length of an academic term or year to the assimilation of a major work, with rests between parts to study shorter works and to let reaction to installments settle, allows modern students to recover the excitement, suspense, and involvement that characterized so much of the nineteenth-century literary experience. Those who have tried teaching serials in parts, particularly after years of teaching works as whole volumes read and discussed in essentially single sittings, say that not only is response changed, but the works themselves become different. New parts of the work demand and receive attention along the way of reading, and the questions asked about literature before it is completed turn out to vary in unexpected ways from established concerns.

Furthermore, the sense of a community, the class reading together rather than as isolated, separate individuals, generates associations and connections for students that are less easy to develop when whole works are read sequentially. One can begin a semester, in fact, reading the first installment or chapter of a work aloud as Victorians so often did; and later, students may wish to read or even present crucial scenes and passages in class. Questions raised by one student often become the concerns of others in subsequent reading and discussion, prompting the course to take new directions unanticipated even by the instructor. Excitement about what happens next usually becomes communal as well as private, and speculation frequently draws out students (and traits of students) held in reserve by traditional techniques of instruction.

Reading in parts does require regular, disciplined effort; and serialization places special demands on memory, sometimes requiring students to tie the conclusion of the course back to its beginning. However, many students avidly follow soap operas, movie sequels, or even a popular fiction series by writers of mystery or romance. And they can also get caught up in the ongoing stories of Dickens, Browning, George Eliot,

Tennyson, and Hardy. Although we would not want to champion all the movie and radio serials in the first half of this century, or the television soap operas, series, miniseries, and sequels in the second half, such popular entertainment has prepared students to engage more significant works of literature as serials. Furthermore, the fine BBC productions featured on "Masterpiece Theatre" and other public or cable television programs have provided excellent presentations of new and established works in an installment format.

There have also been significant twentieth-century artistic achievements in the traditional installment mode. Periodicals in England like *Blackwood's, Cornhill, Macmillan's,* and the *Strand* continued to publish fiction serially after 1900. Major novelists like Conrad, Wells, Joyce, Kipling, and Stevenson issued some of their works in parts, though most writers preferred the single-volume format. Many poets wrote long poems that were published in separate volumes over a number of years, including Ezra Pound, whose first *Cantos* appeared in three monthly parts; T. S. Eliot, each of whose *Four Quartets* first appeared as separate poems; and William Carlos Williams, whose *Paterson* was issued in five books from 1946 to 1958. Furthermore, a favorite modernist form, the trilogy or novel sequence, needs critical recognition and exploration as a descendant of the Victorian serial. Samuel Beckett, Joyce Cary, Lawrence Durrell, Ford Madox Ford, Robert Graves, Doris Lessing, Wyndham Lewis, George Moore, Paul Scott, and Eveyln Waugh, among others, composed trilogies or sequences of related narratives. These, too, constitute continuing stories in a Victorian tradition, a tradition most closely associated with Trollope's Barset and Palliser chronicles. Perhaps Anthony Powell's twelve-volume sequence, *A Dance to the Music of Time* (1957–75), most nearly recalls the giant reach of Victorian serialization.

In more recent years both English and American authors have attempted a recovery of the serial form. Norman Mailer serialized *An American Dream* in *Esquire* (January–August 1964). Tom Wolfe, announcing himself to be working in the tradition of Dickens, Zola, and Balzac, published a first version of the enormously successful *Bonfire of the Vanities* in the twice-monthly *Rolling Stone* (19 July 1984–29 August 1985). Fay Weldon serialized *The Hearts and Lives of Men* in the British weekly *Woman* before its volume issue in 1987. An even more promising effort was begun by Eric Kraft with the first installment of his ongoing *The Personal History, Adventures, Experiences, and Observations of Peter Leroy* in 1982. Eight 96-page parts of this modern *David Copperfield* appeared in the next few years from a small publisher in Boston. Then Warner Books reprinted numbers

1–4 and gave the work national distribution in 1986. In 1988 Kraft released with Crown Publishers a spin-off fictional biography of his protagonist Peter Leroy's grandparents; entitled *Herb 'n' Lorna,* it added to the author's growing reputation and audience. Kraft plans to continue telling the story of Peter Leroy and his world serially in a number of formats, like Laurence Sterne with his *Tristram Shandy,* into the indefinite future.

Other writers like William Faulkner have had a similar impulse to tell the story of an imagined world in parts over many years. More recently, novelist Donald Harington has been chronicling the life (and death) of Stay More, Arkansas, in *Lightning Bug* (1971), *Some Other Place, The Right Place* (1972), *The Architecture of the Arkansas Ozarks* (1976), and *The Cockroaches of Stay More* (1989). This last title suggests the immensity of time in the past, just as *Architecture* projected the time of Stay More into an as-yet undisclosed future. And of course the very name of Stay More embodies a serial sensibility with its invocation of a way of life and the close relation of storyteller and audience to continue and endure.

All these writers of continuing stories have found audiences in our time in part by taking advantage of qualities inherent in the installment format. And in other countries the serial form continues an important force in national cultural life. Even as this study of serial literature was being written, *Dr. Zhivago* made its first public appearance in the Soviet Union as a serial in the journal *Novy Mir.* And the newspaper serial is still a flourishing form in Egypt, whose Nobel Laureate, Naguib Mahfouz, has also published works in this form. Yet our existing academic framework discourages the teaching of works in installments; and literary criticism has often ignored or discounted the fact that many masterpieces established their places in culture with audiences who read them in parts over time. With the recognition that serialization means something in and of itself, scholars and teachers can retrace literary history not only by the single dates of volume publication but also through the expansive times of reading during which characters came alive and stories were set in motion for a community of interested readers. That story itself is one we have taken up here in the hope that others will pursue similar efforts, so that the entire story remains . . .

. . . to be continued

Notes

I. Introducing the Serial

1. A contrasting twentieth-century image might be Beckett's characterization of life in *Waiting for Godot,* a woman giving birth astride a grave.

2. The contrast between a compressed and an expansive time frame for assessing the meaning of events was one used a century and a half ago by Charles Lyell, whose *Principles of Geology* was issued in parts from 1830 to 1833. He remarked in his first volume:

   > How fatal every error as to the quantity of time must prove to the introduction of rational views concerning the state of things in former ages, may be conceived by supposing that the annals of the civil and military transactions of a great nation were perused under the impression that they occurred in a period of one hundred instead of two thousand years. Such a portion of history would immediately assume the air of a romance; the events would seem devoid of credibility, and inconsistent with the present course of human affairs. A crowd of incidents would follow each other in thick succession. Armies and fleets would appear to be assembled only to be destroyed, and cities built merely to fall in ruins. (1:78–79, quoted in Beer 8)

3. Our definition of the serial as a continuing story over time with enforced interruptions is intentionally inclusive. It might be fruitful to assess the differences occasioned by varying publication intervals (weekly versus monthly versus less regular issue), but such concerns lie outside the scope of this study, which seeks to establish the larger cultural and literary significance of the Victorian serial.

4. No available documentation indicates a poem appearing serially at the time of Arnold's sermon. Isaac Butt, however, editor of *Dublin University Magazine,* had serialized one of his poems in this monthly journal the year preceding Arnold's sermon. The poem was *The Rubi, a Tale of the Sea,* published in six installments from March through August 1838 (Wayne Hall 55).

5. Even Marryat's *Phantom Ship* had a two-month suspension in November and December of 1837, then a one-year hiatus occasioned by Marryat's travel to America (Vann 107). Irregular intervals between parts were common in serials generally characterized by periodic issue. Thus two two-month intervals occurred in the otherwise monthly appearance of Carlyle's *Sartor Resartus* in *Fraser's Magazine* from 1833 to 1834, and four one-month intervals elapsed between the parts of Alexander Smith's *A Life-Drama* otherwise appearing bimonthly in *The Critic* from 1 March 1852 to 15 January 1853.

6. Walter Houghton, in fact, asserts that "Arnold was not a writer of books; he was a writer of periodical literature" ("Periodical" 21). Houghton attributes

the existence of one of Arnold's major works, moreover, to the periodical's potential for expansion and growth: "It is fair to conclude that *Culture and Anarchy* would never have been written had there been no periodical to provide it with growing space. No doubt similar evolutions lie behind other books" ("Periodical" 22).

7. We have excluded a detailed examination of nonfiction prose works from this study, since our interest lies in fictive worlds built slowly over time. See, however, Maidment for a discussion of Ruskin's work.

8. Part 1 of *Hudibras* appeared in 1662, part 2 in 1664, and part 3 in 1678. James Thomson's *Winter* appeared in 1726, *Summer* in 1727, *Spring* in 1728, and *Autumn* in 1730. Byron's *Don Juan* appeared from 1819 to 1824, Tennyson's *Idylls of the King* from 1859 to 1885 (1842 to 1885 if one accepts his "Morte d'Arthur" as the beginning point), and Morris's *Earthly Paradise* from 1868 to 1870.

9. Graham Pollard traces the first serial fiction back to *Poor Robin's Intelligence,* issued in eighty-four weekly parts from 23 March 1676 to 20 November 1677 (253); R. M. Wiles considers Edward Ward's *The London Spy,* published in eighteen parts beginning November 1698, as the first original fiction issued serially (80). Ward also issued an original poem serially, *Hudibras Redivivus; or, a Burlesque Poem on Various Humours of Town and Country,* in twenty-four monthly parts from 1705 to 1707 (Wiles 82). Laurence Sterne's *Tristram Shandy* also appeared in separate volumes from 1759 to 1767, and Tobias Smollett's *Adventures of Sir Launcelot Greaves* first appeared in monthly parts in *The British Magazine* from January 1760 to December 1761 before being issued in volume form in 1762 (Graham Pollard 255–56). Serialization was common enough in the eighteenth century that, as R. M. Wiles records, in 1742 "Fielding, in the chatty introductory chapter in Book II of *Joseph Andrews,* had poked fun at the parcelling out of books" (7).

10. Our primary focus is the culture of the Victorian middle class, though serialization was also important in working-class newspapers (see, e.g., Altick, *English* 291–93; Ford 78–79; Louis James 358).

11. The serial was also an appropriate form for a society undergoing the radical dislocations of industrialization and urbanization. That Victorian literature inscribed urban experience in its texts is a critical commonplace. But since a serial part was always followed by an interruption during which individual readers were exposed to countless other stimuli before returning to the serial's continuing story, a solitary, sustained lyric or narrative voice was displaced in favor of multitudinous crosscurrents and voices, so typical of urban experience.

12. See also Gould, "Appendix" 99; Gould, *Time;* Chapple 89; and Collins, "Tennyson" 142.

13. The influence of Coleridgean aesthetics, it is true, caused many reviewers to cavil at serialization's fragmentation of the text, especially where poetry was concerned. That so many works nonetheless continued to be serialized suggests that parts publication posed no serious problems for readers. See also Levine, who views Wordsworth's poetry as more "uniformitarian," Coleridge's as more "catastrophic" ("Dickens" 263–64).

14. Beer notes that in the late eighteenth century *evolution* was a term tied to the history of the individual, since it referred to "the stages through which a living being passes in the course of its development from egg to adult" (15). Not until the 1830s, Beer states, was *evolution* used to apply to species' development. Beer identifies as key traits of Lamarckian evolution, the popular form of evolution in both the nineteenth and twentieth centuries, "continuity," "persisting development," and optimistic faith in "intelligent adaptation and intelligent succession" (25). Emphases on continuity, persisting development, optimism, and intelligent succession were common to serial literature as well.

15. See also our "Studying Victorian Serials." The issues we address in that preliminary study of serials and here are shared by a number of theoretical approaches developed in recent years, including reader-response and reception studies, which seek to establish the role of the reader or audience in constituting meaning; textual studies, which include publication format among a text's signifiers; and new historicist studies, which examine the material and ideological conditions underlying the production of literature.

16. David Carr's extended analysis of the narrative element of history is suggestive for this feature of serial reading. Carr distinguishes between two kinds of awareness of the past (retention and recollection) and two kinds of expectations of the future (protention and secondary expectation) to argue that awareness of the past and expectation of the future are essential to human consciousness rather than arbitrary cultural constructs. He also contends that storytelling, or narrative, is the medium by which human beings understand, report, and plan their lives. As Carr remarks at one point, stories "are told in being lived and lived in being told" (61).

17. Even when Victorians read volumes, they were not always reading complete texts. The standard library edition was three volumes. Many patrons at Mudie's Circulating Library, the industry leader through the second two-thirds of the century, were governed by the basic subscription, which allowed only one volume to be taken out at a time. Thus, no matter whether they were reading the three-decker *Jane Eyre* (1847) or the two volumes of Bulwer-Lytton's epic poem, *King Arthur* (1847–48), they could still read only a part—a single volume—at a time (Griest 103–4). Although the reading of these texts was less structured temporally than were actual serials, readers could not complete the literary experience without returning to the real world.

18. As Malcolm Woodfield suggests, these reviews could themselves reflect major elements of the culture in which they appeared. In his essay on Richard Holt Hutton's weekly reviews in the *Spectator,* Woodfield argues that the weekly review was an appropriate medium to Hutton because it accomodated a secular age yet also suggested that full understanding and belief were still possible: "for him, only the fragmented form of the weekly review provided a way of making sense of the 'real' nature of life in the second half of the nineteenth-century. What began as a necessity became a virtue in that the weekly reviewer's placing of the part before the whole seemed to him the only available mode of knowing what secular life was like, and in thus making sense of life he was resisting the most dangerous product of secularization, namely the belief that life made no sense. The weekly review was both peculiarly apt

for the tendencies of his time, and a means at the same moment of resisting those tendencies" (81). See also Schmidt 142.

19. See, e.g., Ricks, *Tennyson* 264–69.

20. Roger Hagedorn suggests that "the reification of scholastic disciplines has contributed to a failure on the part of scholars to recognize that since the 19th century the serial has been a dominant mode of narrative presentation in western culture—if not in fact the dominant mode" (5). Hagedorn asserts the serial's dominance primarily within a material and commercial framework.

II. Creating a Home

1. For a discussion of the cult of domesticity, see Altick (*Victorian*), Boone (*Tradition*), Gallagher (*Industrial*), and Houghton (*Victorian* 341–93). Kucich argues that Victorian repression actually enhanced the richness and importance of private, subjective life, but that this constructive element subverted possibilities for communal life and action.

2. As Kucich remarks, "twentieth-century culture . . . has been eager to view the Victorians as fearful, dishonest, silly, or coercive because of their refusals of emotional expression. Sometimes, the motive for the attack is only to see ourselves, by comparison, as part of a teleological movement toward freedom and authenticity" (4–5).

3. Patmore's Frederick Graham also suffers and endures disappointed love, but, characteristically, he suffers not in a home but out in the world, nursing his broken heart on a sea voyage to the Levant. Thackeray's *The Newcomes,* the least conventional treatment of domesticity among works discussed in this chapter, shows men suffering in the confines of the home when the Colonel and Clive are tyrannized by Mrs. Mackenzie, just as Clara Newcome earlier suffered the domestic tyranny of Barnes. If the men can escape, the Colonel to Grey Friars, Clive (though only temporarily) to his studio, so also does Clara, though she is stripped of reputation and the chance for future domestic happiness in the process.

4. For Col. Newcome, returning home and returning to literature amount to the same thing: "One of the great pleasures and delights which I had proposed to myself on coming home was to be allowed to have the honour of meeting with men of learning and genius, with wits, poets, and historians, if I may be so fortunate; and of benefiting by their conversation" (1:38).

5. Boone observes that in much Victorian fiction the love plot and the bildungsroman coincide, especially for female protagonists (*Tradition* 74).

6. *The Poems of Coventry Patmore,* ed. Frederick Page (London: Oxford Univ. Press, 1949). See Christ's "Victorian Masculinity and the Angel in the House" for an excellent feminist analysis of the 1886 poem.

7. As Basil Champneys records, Emily Patmore (from whom Patmore's fictive wife is drawn) knew Greek and Latin and was an author herself, although the titles of her published works—*Mrs. Motherly,* a book of children's verse, and *The Servants' Behaviour Book*—disappoint in their predictability (Champneys 1.120, 127). While Patmore's serial version invokes a living and speaking woman, his later, single-volume work removes this trace and insists on

woman as icon (Hughes, "Entombing"). Charles Rosen observes a similar shift in the serial versus whole-volume edition of Balzac's *The Unknown Masterpiece* (22, 24). Perhaps serial works' inherent involvement in temporal process predisposed authors to a greater insistence on life and process in serial versions.

8. An interesting precursor of *Angel in the House* is Samuel Richardson's *Pamela*, which also moved from betrothal in one volume to the aftermath of marriage in a subsequently issued volume. As Sheldon Sacks observes, the novel's first readers "rang church bells on learning of the fictional heroine's marriage to her would-be seducer" (239). The sequel, book 2, appeared in 1741, in which Pamela assumes the angelic role of perfect wife. Both Richardson and Patmore (in the last two installments of his poem) use the epistolary format. According to Wallace Martin, "Richardson said that one technical advantage of the epistolary form . . . was that in contrast to narration, letters use the present tense, thus inducing in readers a sense of immediate involvement and anticipation" (131). "Involvement and anticipation," of course, also characterize the serial-reading experience.

9. Edmund Gosse remarks that Patmore "saw no difference between marriage and poetry; the one was the subject of the other, the second a necessary interpretation of the first" (40).

10. The parody was printed as prose but used the meter of Patmore's poem. The concluding lines drew attention to the poem as serial: "From ball to bed, from field to farm, The tale flows nicely purling on.—With much conceit, there is no harm, In the love-legend here begun.—The rest will come another day If public sympathy allows;—And this is all we have to say, About 'The Angel in the House' " (76). Both Amy Cruse (226) and Edmund Gosse (75) have identified Chorley as the author of the "review."

11. So compelling was the sense of reality, in fact, that three different reviews assumed the poet himself was a clergyman living in or near Salisbury.

12. Weinig also notes the lack of closure at the end of *The Espousals* (76).

13. Nathaniel Hawthorne's private response to the poem indicates a sense of connection between life and poem, reader and poet. His 3 January 1858 journal entry records his and his wife's reaction to meeting Patmore, whose 1854 and 1858 volumes the Hawthornes had read "with unusual pleasure and sympathy. . . . It is a most beautiful and original poem—a poem for happy married people to read together, and to understand by the light of their own past and present life" (Champneys 1:99).

14. As Derek Patmore observes, the poem's popularity in America, partly the result of Emerson's efforts, helped win attention for it in England (83–84).

15. Boone also remarks that there are fewer "Wedlock versions of the love-plot" because "the narrative of wedded life lacks the teleological finality of courtship and seduction movements" (*Tradition* 113–14).

Brimley in the October 1856 issue of *Fraser's* had implicitly pitted the uniformitarianism of marital love against the catastrophism of romantic passion when he remarked that the interest of courtship could be compared to that of "watching the formation of a double star, and having all our interest concentrated upon the critical moment when the attraction of one for the other finally draws them within the inevitable vortex in which they are henceforth eternally to revolve. . . ." The metaphor he used for marital love was "the higher because more complex and mysterious region of chemistry" concerned with "the changes . . . constituent atoms undergo by combination, and by the action of the subtile elements—heat, light, electricity, and so forth" (478).

16. De Vere praised Patmore's strategy of centering the poem in ordinary, unexceptional life rather than in exotic, violent, or vehemently drawn circumstances. Both Basil Champneys (1:176–77) and Derek Patmore (84) note the role of De Vere's review in popularizing the poem.

17. At the outset Jane writes to her mother,

I see

(Faithful   How glad and thankful I should be
129, 130)   For such a husband. Yet, to tell
    The truth, I am so miserable!

. . . . .

    though he is often kind,
And never really cross, my mind
Is all so dull and dead with fear
That Yes and No, when he is near,
Is much as I can say. He's quite
Unlike what most would call polite,
And yet, when first I saw him come
To tea in Aunt's fine drawing-room,
He made me feel so common. Oh,
How dreadful if he thinks me so!

By the final letter of the volume Jane is writing to her mother-in-law to describe the serene, quietly happy celebration of Jane and Fred's wedding anniversary after twelve years of marriage:

We spent,—the children, he, and I,—
Our wedding anniversary
In the woods, where, while I tried to keep
The flies off, so that he might sleep,
(Faithful   He actually kiss'd my foot,—
233–34)   At least, the beautiful French boot,
Your gift,—and, laughing with no cause
But pleasure, said I really was
The very nicest little wife;
And that he prized me more than life.

Max F. Schulz argues that the couple's initial disaffection is indicated by their revealing their "inmost thoughts and feelings always by letter to a third party"; only in *Victories of Love* do we encounter a letter from Jane to Frederick, written when Jane is dying (242).

18. See, e.g., De Vere, quoted in Champneys 2:336; Burdett 80; and Frederick Page, *Patmore* 80.

19. In subsequent editions Patmore used the terms *preludes* and *cantos* and dropped the separate heading of *sentences* altogether. Ball argues that the abstract concepts of the preludes, paired with their embodiment in the experience

narrated in the cantos, comprise a parable of the "union of spirit and body" (193). Ball excludes any mention of *Faithful for Ever* and *Victories of Love* from her discussion, however.

20. Though of course Drayton's *Heroicall Epistles* and Pope's *Eloisa to Abelard* are also epistolary and hardly bourgeois.

21. Cf. Richard Garnett in a letter to Patmore: "I must own that I am a little confused by the difficulty I find in discovering whether Jane or Honoria is your heroine" (quoted in Champneys 2:343). Frederick Page is one of the few to insist that Frederick and Jane are crucial to the poem as a necessary balance to the overly idealized lovers Felix and Honoria and that "Honoria and Jane [are] equally his heroines" (73–74). See also Parins (50) for Patmore's overall philosophy of marriage.

22. E. J. Oliver, however, notes that Patmore's differed from "the Victorian ideal of love . . . in . . . that he was opposed to the romantic exaltation and insisted on the earthly roots of human affection" (55). Parins (51) makes a similar point.

23. See the *Guardian*, 19 December 1860: 1117, and the *British Quarterly Review* 33 (January 1861): 143–44.

24. "Book II" here refers to the second section of *Faithful for Ever,* entitled "Jane"; Book I is entitled "Honoria."

25. In its adverse review the 20 October 1860 *Critic* opened by objecting precisely to the continuing appearance of parts, here expressed in a domestic metaphor: "there certainly was just enough sweetness in 'The Angel in the House' to make such a composition pass for once in a way; but if we are to have angels in the house every year—cherubs, too, whose waxen rosiness and sweet unmeaning expression make them as like each other as cherries on a stalk—then we feel inclined to cry out with the unfortunate husband whose wife had presented him with a trio of blessings, 'Run and tell your mistress to stop'" (479). It was in response to this review that John Ruskin wrote a letter to the editor (printed the next week) defending the new volume.

26. Richard Garnett was one such reader. Note his assumption that another installment (and another round of interpretation) is yet to come:

> the most sensible impression we have derived from every reperusal of the "Angel in the House" has been one of astonishment at the amount of beauty which the last reading had left for us to discover. We may say of Mr. Patmore's book, as he says of his heroine, that we have found it "more to us"
>
>> "Yesterday than the day before,
>> And more to-day than yesterday."
>
> Any opinion, therefore, that we may express respecting the poem under consideration [*Faithful for Ever*] must be taken as subject to revision. (*Macmillan's Magazine,* December 1860: 125–26).

27.
(*Macmillan's Magazine,* October 1861: 442)

> You know my way
> Of feeling strong from twelve till two,
> After my wine. I'll write to you
> Daily some words, which you shall have
> To break the silence of the grave.

28. Lady Clitheroe's worldliness, and the prosaic nature of the letter, can be inferred from this passage:

> And as for getting old, my Dear,
> If you're but prudent, year by year
> He'll find some far-fetch'd cause the more
> To think you sweeter than before!
> My birth-day (for an instance take),
> As I was looking in the Lake,
> Studious if black would best subdue
> The red in my nose, or black with blue;
> Your Uncle, in his loftiest mode,
> Assured me that my face ne'er glow'd
> With such a handsome health!

(*Macmillan's Magazine,* November 1861: 35–36)

29. The review continued, "We doubt, indeed, the propriety of publishing a work like 'The Victories of Love' in monthly parts," yet only when Patmore did so was the paper moved to review it (in its column on "The Magazines"). Patmore's biographer, Basil Champneys, records a different reaction to the poem's serialization: "I had . . . read the 'Victories of Love,' as it appeared in *Macmillan's Magazine,* with the special interest which attached to it from the circumstances under which I understood it to have been written [during, that is, the illness of Patmore's wife, Emily], and had heard, from common friends, much about him personally" (1:351). See also Gosse 77.

30. Weinig also implies lack of closure when she notes that Jane's anticipating her son's marriage to Emily Vaughan "gives a new impetus to life in its sense of happy fulfillment of one kind of relationship, and in its expectation of good things to come for those Jane leaves behind" (78).

31. Horton, *Interpreting Interpreting,* illustrates the (many) possible readings of Alice Marwood, and much more, in *Dombey and Son* (130). That this is really a domestic novel and not a detailed analysis of the Victorian world of business is generally accepted. See, for instance, Russell (198) and Norman Feltes, "Realism, Concensus and 'exclusion itself': interpellating the Victorian bourgeoisie," who argues that Dickens did not possess the language necessary to reveal the true workings of a capitalist society.

32. Marcus notes that "the idea of growth or development" is "one of the chief conceptions" of the nineteenth- and twentieth-century world: "an idea of history; it asserts that all things have a history, that all things exist in history, and that our understanding of anything cannot be adequate until we regard it dynamically, from the moment of its origin" (319).

33. Florence's angelic nature has long been recognized, though different critics have responded to it in different ways. Marcus observes: "At the still point of the changing world stands Florence . . . the ability to feel affection, to respond to people with openness and fullness, to accede to the conditions of life, to sustain oneself through its changes, to be able to love" (351). Harry Stone comments that "Florence's recurrent angel-embraces, part of her dolorous ministerings, are translated into myth and at the same time are merged imperceptibly into the surrounding realism" (176).

Julian Moynahan links Florence's tears and Paul's waves with uncontrolled sentimentality (130). Juliet McMaster in *Dickens the Designer,* however, opposes Dombey's stiffness and coldness to Florence's softness and warmth, arguing that she is "convincingly dramatized as having movement and life" (131) in the novel. Alexander Welsh finds Florence's role as angel complicated, sometimes including her figuration as the angel of death; but he also acknowledges Florence's link to traditions of salvation (*City* 212).

34. Garis objects: "The simplest account of what is wrong with the suffering of Florence Dombey, Little Dorrit, and the rest is that one recognizes immediately and throughout that these heroines are doing proper 'woman's work,' as that was understood by a very inexperienced and undistinguished thinker on such matters" (239). Smith makes an interesting argument that Florence's role is necessarily melodramatic, since Victorian society is the first to face and attempt to understand what industrialization has done to human relationships (190).

35. The static role of Florence has been noted by a number of critics. Dyson says: "Florence is to remain unchanged until she can at last prove redemptive: a role simple, important, and only slightly embarrassing (more perhaps to the author than to his readers) in that it leaves her, for such long stretches, with so little to do" (112). Frank observes that Florence lives "incarcerated in an enchanted castle, cut off from time itself" (39); but in "the mirror of her mother's face, Florence sees herself as someone with the capacity to love and to evoke love in others" (39). Connor argues that Florence is "for long periods dormant and almost absent from the text" (39) because she does not count in the economic and paternalistic structures of society. Yelin notes "the unresolved tension between change and constancy which animates Dickens's portrayal of Florence" (312). Tobin's argument about the "genealogial imperative" in nineteenth-century literature would necessarily exclude a daughter from the main action in a novel about the family and its structure.

36. Adrian makes this point: "Having made a domestic situation a 'microcosm for a national one,' Dickens implies that a society dominated by greed, insular pride, and ruthless competition [Dombey] can be regenerated only through dedicated love [Florence]" (107). Harry Stone's position is similar: "The real villain . . . is the soullessness of the new business world" (149).

37. Barbara Hardy provides detailed discussion of Dickens's ability to direct emotional response, saying of *Dombey and Son* in particular, "He manipulated the emotions of his readers, making their flesh creep, making them laugh, cry, and wait. He created characters who forced him to meditate more finely and more analytically on the emotional life, as his art grew" (*Forms* 63).

38. Raymond Williams might be cited as one whose analysis is grounded in the notion of the text as a single, complete unit. For instance, in his introduction to the Penguin edition, he argues that Dickens's characters are immediately known in full at their first appearances: "It is not the slowly known, slowly learned personality, the steadily emerging relationships, of a smaller, more continuous, more knowable community" (28). Yet, we would argue, the serial appearance of Dickens's characters insists on gradual understanding, subtle shifts in personality over time. Zwinger has admitted that Florence "embodies the usual virtues of the hearth angel" (421) but also argues that criticism of her has been determined by masculine biases.

39. Ford reminds us that the novel's last two-thirds was felt by some to be a

letdown: "After the death of Paul, the later numbers of *Dombey* seemed anti-climactic" (59). As Kathleen Tillotson argues, however, "The relation between Mr. Dombey and Florence is the backbone of the whole book" (*Novels* 164).

40. Harry Stone sees Bunsby as linked to the magical world of fairy tales, to realms that give Dickens's text meaning (158).

41. Horsman points out that Dickens recognized Florence's part of the story as a challenge in the middle numbers, 9 to 15 (xxxiii). The tendency of most criticism is to see Florence primarily in her relation to her father, not on her own terms. Gold notes that Florence has her own special wisdom; for instance, it is "she only who makes sense out of what to do with [money]" (165). However, Gold also sees her as the feminine component missing in Dombey: "The female is embodied ideally in Florence and brings love, regeneration, gentleness and warmth to the human scene" (167). Qualls places the Dombey-Florence relationship within the tradition of religious experience (190). Kaplan mentions Florence in the context of Dickens's ability to "get closer to the formative mysteries that are hidden from the adult during his normal functioning" (142), a view that helps explain why she develops and grows offstage, unnoticed by Dombey.

42. We must confess that we are among those whom Susan Horton asks about in *Interpreting Interpreting:* "Who cares about or remembers the scenes in which Florence pores over the textbooks Paul is given at Dr. Blimber's Academy so that she may help Paul with his homework?" (106).

43. Susan Horton in *The Reader in Dickens's World* has analyzed the rhythm in *Dombey and Son*'s style (23). Donoghue has noted that "in fact Florence's feeling is not so monolithic as [some] readers say. There are gradations" (17).

44. In addition to the changes that occurred in Florence herself over these two months, Dickens provided indirect commentary on her developing life. Included in the August 1847 installment (number 11) were moving portraits of two of Florence's doubles: Harriet Carker (an "angel" [335] always busy "with her household tasks" [337]); and Alice Marwood (the text's "fallen angel" [347]). Dickens's use of analogy has been studied in detail by H. M. Daleski. Harry Stone sees Alice as "a transmutation of the innocent Florence, and a foil to upper-class Edith" (181). Sylvia Manning, who sees the major plot as "a flight from woman" (93), also notes: "Allied to Mr. Dombey's neglect of his daughter is the exploitation of their daughters by Mrs. Skewton and Good Mrs. Brown" (94).

   Garrett provides the definitive work on the effects of multiple plots in Victorian fiction: "From the perspective of the detached observer [the reader], these emerging relationships [like Florence and Alice's] offer an experience of increasing comprehension like that produced by the recognition of plot connections, a satisfying sense of combined unity and diversity, of a complex coherence" (49). Garrett goes on, however, to explore contradictions ultimately produced by such analogies.

45. Janice Carlisle observes how Dickens works "in a genre necessarily defined by time . . . and the reader who follows the story from page to page is necessarily, like Dombey, a being who 'lives in Time'" (70).

46. Herring notes that the Madeira is "used to indicate both the passage of time

and the increasing value Mr. Dombey places on Florence's love" (186). Carlisle comments about the symbolism of wine and cobwebs (92).

47. Harry Stone comments on the link between these numbers in terms of their use of fairy-tale motifs (189).

48. Carlisle discusses Dickens's use of present tense in this novel, an ability to "create, in short, the appropriate reverberating note at the end of an installment" (86). This technique, she argues, places reader, narrator, and characters in the same world. Auerbach finds the ending less optimistic than many: "The novel's narrator, who is himself the 'good spirit' hovering over the action and exposing it, reveals the pestilence hidden in 'home,' rather than reassuring us at the end with its glow" (96).

49. Critical tendency to place heavy emphasis on endings is evident in such works as Torgovnick's *Closure in the Novel:* "an ending is the single place where an author most pressingly desires to make his points" (19). This perspective is frequently used to argue that Dickens always, ultimately, finally retreats to the family and the hearth as an answer to social evils: "Dickens means to demonstrate that though private, small-scale responses to the social world may produce only local results, such responses are still more effective than larger, more organized movements" (49). But this emphasis on the end tends to undervalue the large middle of Dickens's (and other Victorian) novels, throughout which the author confronts head-on the major social problems of his times. To count only his happy endings, saying that he therefore gives up on changing society and retreats to an idealistic worship of "home," is incomplete. Critics need to look, as we have tried to do here, at what attitudes are being endorsed (patience, compassion, and an openness to process) in the long middles of his novels to change corrupt social institutions. The ending should perhaps be seen as a retreat, but a retreat only after a long and costly battle, with possible (probable) renewed engagement later (in other novels).

50. All references to *The Newcomes* are to the parts edition (London: Bradbury and Evans, 1853–55), which is paginated in two volumes.

51. Katherine Peters in her recent book on Thackeray has said it is "the ramifications and interconnections of a middle-class family network that are under examination, rather than the fortunes of any one of its members" (225).

52. Eve Sedgwick has placed one of these alternative homes, Pendennis's bachelor life, in the larger construct of cultural values: such a character inhabited "bohemia," or "the *temporal* space where the young, male bourgeois literary subject was required to navigate his way through his 'homosexual panic'— seen here as a *developmental* stage—toward the more repressive, self-ignorant, and apparently consolidated status of the mature bourgeois *paterfamilias*" (160–61).

53. Edward Burne-Jones, "Essay on the Newcomes," *Oxford and Cambridge Magazine,* January 1856: 50–60, quoted in Tillotson and Hawes 254.

54. Juliet McMaster says: "It is part of the intricate structure of the novel that the great world which it depicts in such painstaking detail is reflected in miniature in numerous little microcosms through the book" (*Thackeray* 162). Catherine Gallagher explores the contradictions evolving from novelists' use of metaphoric and metonymic representations of society (*Industrial* 120).

55. A tradition of domestic fiction, then, clearly shapes Thackeray's options in *The Newcomes*. Cross also notes, "No sooner had fiction writing become the most profitable form of literary activity, in the 1840s, than men began to outnumber women in the fiction publisher's lists. But by public demand, or publishers' edict, the subject matter of fiction seemed to have become more feminine. The new themes were 'anti-romantic, un-aristocratic, home and family centred' " (186).

Gallagher sees this genre developing in the popular fiction of magazines: "Elizabeth Gaskell was a pioneer of the working-class domestic tale. In 1837 she and her husband published a sketch of working-class life, 'rather in the manner of Crabbe,' which tried to illustrate that the 'poetry of humble life' exists 'even in a town.' Three short stories she published in *Howitt's Journal* share the intention of the sketch and are characterized by a wealth of domestic detail, illustrations of the charitable affection that the poor have for one another, and an emphasis on the trials and learning experiences of young women. All the women learn one thing: to do their duty, the duty obviously and immediately before them" (*Industrial* 78–79).

George Levine traces the tensions inherent in domestic realism throughout the nineteenth century, as the form struggles to accommodate an ever-changing and formless reality (*Realistic* 42).

56. The novel's world was frequently seen as the same as the readers': the 29 August 1855 *Times* said of Pen as narrator: "It is plain that he can fashion a world like the real world" (5). And Whitwell Elwin in the September 1855 *Quarterly Review* observed: "Just as the stream of life runs on through these volumes, so may it be seen to flow in the world itself by whoever takes up the same position on the bank" (351).

57. Jack P. Rawlins has discussed this extratextual focus, identifying "Thackeray's basic source of the realist illusion: admitting the lie of the novel, and thus asserting implicitly the reality of the novel's subject" (134). Polhemus also identifies this feature of Thackeray's style: "Thackeray's style is his message: life itself demands a style of consciousness that, like this prose, can incorporate and deal with contradictions" (*Comic* 165).

58. Ina Ferris comments on the letters of the novel: "Although [Thackeray] evokes vividly the rare moments when time fulfills rather than denies, emphasis even here tends to fall on transience and hence on loss. Clive and Ethel's happy days at Baden, for instance, are conveyed in part through gay letters written to Colonel Newcome in India, but the narrator interrupts to underline that their joy is long gone" (98).

59. Juliet McMaster enlarges on this point, discussing the use of sequels in Thackeray's career: "Thackeray needs that wide span of time [the two centuries his major works encompass] because of his vision of man as being not just himself, nor himself in his society, but a being partly determined by his past and his family's past" (*Thackeray* 151).

60. Similar enthusiasm for Thackeray's ongoing tale is evident in the 13 August 1854 *Weekly Dispatch:* "The same keen analysis of character and motives, the same mournful scorn over vice that is systemized, and the same yearning for the generous and the honest—all with which the author set forth—continue to

pervade the present [eleventh] number" (518). The 5 August 1854 *Weekly News and Chronicle* found Thackeray's slow development of plot especially fruitful: "There is a duel after the best esteemed fashion, but the remark we have made of previous numbers, that the story is a minor consideration and good stinging satire upon what is known as 'high life,' the chief object, applies to this last installment. The author each month gives just one little pull with his oars, and then, resting in his advanced position, satirizes all around" (490).

Edgar Harden (75–104) discusses the composition—and the many revisions made necessary by space and time (Thackeray is often abroad during these months)—for the numbers during which Thackeray gained his audience, specifically 4, 5, 6, and 10.

61. Rawlins identifies the relations "between Clive and Ethel" as "the center of sympathetic and thematic interest in the book" (92). Juliet McMaster notes of the novel: "its emotional appeal is greater [than *Vanity Fair's*], for ultimately we care less for the sirens and parasites like Becky and Amelia than for decent people like Clive, Ethel, and Colonel Newcome" (*Thackeray* 153).

62. John Loofbourow (68–70) has discussed this aspect of Ethel's character as developed by Thackeray's classical allusions. Robert Colby in *Thackeray's Canvass of Humanity* finds Ethel a summation of Thackeray's many heroines: "as clever as Becky, as tender-hearted as Amelia, as flirtatious as Blanche, and almost a match for Beatrix as a beauty" (379).

63. Robert Colby finds Ethel "unique among his young women in developing with the passage of time, in being 'improved' by her circumstances—as the moralists of Victoria's day would have it" (379). Barbara Hardy also notes important stages in Ethel's development (*Exposure* 82). Ina Ferris also stresses Ethel's development: "She does not spring full-blown upon the first page in which she appears but changes and grows in the course of the novel" (92). And Edgar Harden explains how in composition of the early numbers Thackeray "wanted to show this fundamentally loving aspect of [Ethel's] character—the root of her actions in the novel after the death of Lady Kew" (85).

64. This role is, of course, a Victorian ideal; but as Richard Altick stresses, it is frequently being scrutinized by major writers: "The revered cluster of Victorian domestic virtues served as a norm, a vulnerable assumption upon which writers frequently mounted an outright or covert attack on the unrealities and perversions of the prevailing womanly ideal, the myth of domestic accommodation and tranquility" (*Victorian* 56).

Robert Colby notes that Ethel's fate takes many months to unwind: Victorian serial readers "took it in gradually over a period of two years [and] were left in suspense as to whether Ethel was destined for the fate of the unfortunate Lady Clara, or of the Duchesse d'Ivry before her" (370). Mrs. Oliphant, before the novel was concluded, asked, " 'Is Ethel to consume what remnants are left to her of that fresh girl's heart she had when we first knew her—when she first fell in love with her good uncle—and be a great lady, and blaze her youthful days away in barren splendour?' " (quoted in Colby 370–71).

65. Juliet McMaster observes: Thackeray "likes to show, rather than the tragic agonies, the nagging twinges of existence, the little humiliations which can become so excruciating in their constant recurrence" (*Thackeray* 148).

66. Edgar Harden notes: "Ethel's maturing, educating herself, and devoting herself to others at the beginning of number twenty not only contrasts with Rosey's naive and destructive self-absorption at the beginning of number twenty-one but also leads directly to Ethel's discovery of the letter in the Colonel's beloved Orme at the end of the first half of the final installment— precisely because of her mature impulse to enter the feelings of others in loving sympathy" (136–37). Whitwell Elwin in the September 1855 *Quarterly Review* came to a similar conclusion, noting in Ethel "a charming example of the force of resolute virtue" (366).

67. Robert Colby says that some "modern readers feel that they get a little too much of Pen as model husband and especially of his angel in the house" (385). He also reminds us, interestingly: "The first part of that supreme paean to marriage, *The Angel in the House,* by Coventry Patmore came out in 1854. Its author was one of the most favorable reviewers of *The Newcomes*" (392n). Gordon Ray finds Pen's narrative acceptable early in the novel, but, particularly as the role of Laura increases, leading to "an atmosphere of domesticity at once cloying and factitious" (247).

    John A. Sutherland, however, makes a fine point about Clara's and Clive's sufferings at the hands of a member of the opposite sex, which shows how Thackeray is aware that patience and endurance do not always serve: "The Pendennis exchanges on the sanctity of marriage, which modern readers often find morally unctuous, thus emerge as a cunningly designed counterpoint to the Barnes-Clara wretchedness and the Highgate-Clara recklessness" (*Thackeray* 76). And Rawlins comments on how major characters from Thackeray's earlier novels reappear in minor roles in later works (129).

68. Barbara Hardy notes the "pastoral peace and harmony . . . in the Pendennis domestic chorus" (*Exposure* 155). Katherine Peters finds what happens to Ethel under this strain unfortunate: "In order to fit her for the descent into marriage, she has to decline disastrously, in the later chapters, into a pious and 'humble-minded' shadow of her earlier self . . . a clone of the egregious Laura Pendennis" (229–30).

69. Rawlins notes: "Pen often speaks in terms of a moral absolutism and simplicity that the experience of the novel belies" (139). Robert Colby sees this difference in circumstance revealed in Clive's career as artist: "Not the turbulent genius prized by the romantics, Clive, though temporarily deflected from his path by his ill-advised marriage, comes closer to the Victorian middle-class ideal of the artist. His conversion to 'the peaceful scenes of home' is most clearly signaled in that moment of illumination in Baden when his spiritual and human loves merge in his consciousness" (377).

70. Martin Meisel has analyzed Thackeray's indirect style, which avoids the dramatic scene for the slow accumulation of telling detail (349).

71. The 12 August 1855 *Weekly Dispatch* notes how Thackeray ties together this whole text, citing its "unity, coherence and consistency"; this paper, however, also finds these features "secondary, and subsidiary, to its matchless episodes and unapproachable illustrations of life's conventionalities" (6). The *Weekly Chronicle* for 4 August 1855 notes: "having gone carefully through each number, month by month, we believe it to be the most thoroughly natural work the author has yet produced" (490).

Gordon Ray has praised this scene, "the opening glimpse of the Colonel in the cave of Harmony, which one would choose before almost any other to illustrate the full range of his genius" (246).

72. Ethel appears to Rosey in the final double number as a loving sister, but the effect on the legitimate angel in Clive's house is deadly. Thus, when Ethel leaves Barnes's house she is not always "angelic," the qualities of patience and compassion not necessarily the ones called for.

73. Katherine Peters objects to the narrator as he appears at the end of the novel: "The voice of the Pendennis who tells the story of the Newcome family is now that of a middle-aged fogey, conventional in outlook, and dependent on the judgment of his wife Laura, who is presented as a model of moral rectitude" (224). Robert Colby, however, sees the narrative in a positive light, identifying one development in the novel as "another significant coming of age—that of the domestic novelist incarnated in the chronicler of the Newcome family" (377–78). Peters's comment was anticipated by Whitwell Elwin in the September 1855 *Quarterly Review*: "As long as he was kept in the back-ground he was neither an ornament nor a blemish, but when he comes forward as an actor in the story, as well as the narrator of it, we wish him away, and should prefer that Mr. Thackeray would tell his own tale without the unnecessary interposition of an Editor" (360).

74. Peter Garrett, for instance, finds this ending confusing: "Thackeray insists on the mediation that qualifies the authority of his long perspectives by keeping his patterns incomplete, as he does in the novel's end by his suspended resolution" (133). As Gordon Ray points out, Thackeray himself called the ending an "artistic blunder" (244). Ray also emphasizes the strength of readers' reaction to the ending's inconclusiveness: "A journalist named James Hain Friswell went so far as to write a supplementary chapter for *Sharpe's Magazine* 'in compassion for the many people who wished to share in the joys of Clive and Ethel'" (470n).

The success in Laura's and Pen's emotional life, we might add, is also consistently shown to derive from their ability to live outside London, the modern city. With the independence derived from inherited "property" (2:102) this couple does not face the challenges Clive and Ethel Newcome do.

75. Whether pleased or not with the ending, readers felt a long-term commitment to the characters by this point, as the 18 August 1855 *Spectator* demonstrates: "the public knows them as well as it does the faces of Disraeli and Lord John Russell, and has been much more interested about them for two years past. What can we say that has not been said over hundreds of dining-tables, in countless drawingrooms, students' chambers, under-graduates' rooms?" (859). The 29 August 1855 *Times* makes a similar comment: the Newcome family "are people with whose habits and motives we are familiar—about whom we have talked pleasantly for months—who have been more, perhaps, to each of us than many families of his or her acquaintance" (5).

76. The epilogue picks up some features of the overture, notably the fable motif: "the frog bursts with wicked rage, the fox is caught in his trap, the lamb is rescued from the wolf, and so forth" (2:422); thus the voice in the overture is presumably Thackeray's also.

77. Barbara Hardy has commented on the novel's conclusion: "It stands . . . as a

reminder of the unreality of novels and of the reality of unhappiness or moderate content outside novels" (*Exposure* 169).

78. Ina Ferris also points to how the ending moves from the world of fiction to that of real Victorian readers: "the sense of loss here is a measure of Thackeray's caring for his creations. Through them he convinces us that human lives do, after all, matter deeply" (99).

III. Living in History

1. Rosemary Jann notes that scientific discoveries, particularly the biological model, tended to shape historical awareness: "If change were in effect seasonal, even the most violent contrasts corresponded to a deeper regularity. If present were related to past as the man to the boy, the tree to the sapling, history could claim unity without uniformity. Manifestations of early stages of development were not scorned as backwards but appreciated as appropriate to their context and essential to growth" (210–11). Fleishman also comments that nineteenth-century historicism was inspired in part by the "doctrine of organic unity—the unity of historical phenomena in an evolutionary pattern of growth, and the unity of cultural phenomena in the unique identity of the nation" (*English* 19).

2. Welsh states: "The new idea of history was that of an endless sequence of events, one moment leading to the next from the limitless past to the limitless future. Primitive ideas of time as analogous to the returning seasons, dynastic ideas of time measured in the generations of kings, the Christian cycle of time from the creation of the world to the day of judgement, were eclipsed by historicism. Time was conceived to be irreversible" (*City* 217).

3. For a discussion of Victorian historicism and competing schools of Victorian historiography, see Altick (*Victorian*), Buckley, Culler, Dale, Jann, and Toulmin and Goodfield. Stephen Jay Gould (*Time's*), interestingly, also focuses on the straight line versus the cycle of time in his recent study of geological time.

   Historiography has received renewed attention in the twentieth century by, for example, Hayden White. The work of White and others reminds us that our perspectives on the Victorians are mediated, and limited, by our situation in twentieth-century America. But since our interest lies in the terms and approaches Victorians used to explain history to themselves, insofar as it is possible to recover them, twentieth-century challenges to Victorian historicism are not a major emphasis of this chapter.

4. Fleishman explains the emergence of the historical novel as an "outcome of the age of nationalism, industrialization, and revolution" (*English* 17). Wallace Martin explains how realistic fiction and historical writing are similar and why both increased in popularity in the nineteenth century: narrators in both genres "face the same problem: that of showing how a situation at the beginning of a temporal series leads to a different situation at its end" (72).

5. Buckley notes: "The Victorians, at least as their verse and prose reveal them, were preoccupied almost obsessively with time and all the devices that measure time's flight" (1–2).

6. Culler notes how literary forms were used to mirror human existence in the

nineteenth century: "Often the analogy [between their own age and a former period] was based upon a cyclical or undulatory conception of history, often on the supposed parallel between history and the course of human life" (vii).

7. Lund discusses this concept in *Reading Thackeray* (3). Iser provides a theoretical framework for such discussion (191–95).

8. Ford notes that *Tale* was "popular yet somewhat mechanical" (127).

9. Fleishman's definition of the historical novel fits Dickens's effort: "This, then, is the form of historical fiction: to interpret the experience of individual men— both actual or imaginary—in such a way as to make their lives not only felt by the reader as he would feel his own existence were he to have lived in the past, but understood as only someone who had seen that life as a completed whole could understand it" (*English* 12–13).

10. Sadoff explores Lucie's role in the novel: "Lucie Manette represents the daughter's ability to redeem time. Dickens's recurring metaphor in *A Tale of Two Cities* for daughterly redemption is the 'golden thread,' the phrase that provides Dickens the title for the novel's second book" (52).

11. The *Critic,* 17 December 1859, admired the "admirable" account of "the journey of the Dover Mail in the year 1775" (602). James M. Brown discusses Lorry on the road to Dover as a key opening scene (117).

12. The 17 December 1859 *Critic* commented unfavorably about the first chapter: "Read through, as it is evidently meant to be read, all in a breath, the effect is bewildering" (602). Culler observes that "most thoughtful Englishmen during the period of the 1820s and 1830s had a sense, far keener than they had ever had before, that they were living in the stream of history, that they were being swept by some great, irresistible force out of the past and into the future" (41). Such a feeling continued through the century, though 1859, the year of *Tale's* publication, seemed calmer to Victorians, as Michael Wolff explains (269–89).

13. Among the few critics to discuss the parts structure of *Tale,* Edwin Eigner notes: "Charles's marriage, in fact, occurs in the sixteenth of the thirty-one serial parts of the novel, that is to say, the very center, always the place of highest significance in a Dickens story" (154). That it was widely read as a serial before it appeared in volume form is underscored by comments like the following from the *Critic* (17 December 1859): "We have presumed our readers to be already acquainted with the 'Tale of Two Cities,' and have therefore attempted no sketch of its plot" (603). *Reynolds Newspaper* on 15 May 1859 anticipated wide readership of Dickens's serial, predicting that "a continuous tale from [Dickens's] own pen . . . ought to be alone sufficient to command success" for the new *All the Year Round* (2).

14. Discussing the relation of illustration to text, Martin Meisel argues that the author "rejects the fixed and material image as the equal partner of his art" (321), which is always in motion.

15. Brown presents Lorry as identical with Tellson's, a corrupt institution (116). Gallagher questions the implications of the "businesslike spying of Jarvis Lorry" ("Duplicity" 136). In "Nation and Generation," Hutter is less harsh in his analysis of "the ideal businessman" (453).

16. In this instance, Lorry resembles Darnay and other Dickens heroes, as described by McGowan: "The heroes of these three novels—Arthur Clennam,

Charles Darnay, and John Harmon—all confront a 'deadened' social world that seems likely to sustain itself unchanged forever. . . . To overcome the burden of the past, each of the heroes must perform a significant repetition in which a saving difference allows a new future to be born" (124).

17. Hutter makes this point in his fine analysis "The Novelist as Resurrectionist": "The overt and seemingly relentless subtext of this novel is to give meaning to death or to the past, to disinter the historical moment and make it come alive, to recover bodies and letters and everything that may presumably have disappeared and to resurrect them, to give them meaning" (25).

18. Baumgarten studies other works in 1859 with similar themes, many of which "explored what Asa Briggs calls a 'turning point in the late Victorian revolt against authority'—the crisis in the relations between older and younger generations" (165). Lorry's part of the story raises these same issues.

19. Baumgarten has described this style (166). Timko also sees two major strands in the narrative: "These two interwoven Carlylean ideas about history, so strong in the essays and in *Sartor,* figure strongly in Dickens' best-known 'historical' novel: history as prophecy and history as vignettes of the lives and characters of individuals" (179).

20. This experience of enforced pauses inspired by serialization had gone on, of course, as long as the novel. That Dickens's first readers did concentrate on the meaning of individual installments is suggested by the decision of *Lloyd's Weekly London Newspaper* on 1 May 1859 to recommend *Tale,* reprinting the entire third chapter for its readers. Victorian audiences thus sometimes had several places where Dickens's text could be studied in the pause before the story was continued.

21. On Manette's diary see Baumgarten (162) and Hutter, "Nation and Generation" (448–49). Garrett argues that Dickens's narration moves forward to discover significant action in the past, "a hidden origin" (55) such as this document.

22. Timko presents the traditional view about the importance of endings: "It is on the impact and effect of the final scenes, however, especially the tone and spirit of these, that one bases one's final assessment of the novel, especially its moral and aesthetic totality" (192).

23. Hutter discusses Lorry and Carton's relationship ("Nation" 451).

24. Welsh makes a similar point: "The rise of historicism fixed a temporal dimension on this tightening universe, by which not only moral acts but all events came to be seen as irreversible" (*City* 116).

25. The equation of form with content is also visible late in the novel as Darnay advances toward Paris and his place in history. His journey is along a single path marked by discrete stages, which contribute to a story whose meaning is clear, though Carton will later alter it.

26. Fleishman's assessment of Dickens's goal is similar: the author "aimed to induce his contemporaries to take a more profound view of their own condition—not by crude warnings of revolution but by a deepening of their historical imagination" (*English* 116).

27. Levine's determination that a major element of the novel is fable rather than realism has contributed to this trend. See also Bernard Paris. Gezari, however, argues that "any effort to transform Renaissance humanists into Victorian

rationalists and Renaissance religious reformers into Victorian religious re-
vivalists forces the main themes of *Romola* out of focus" (79).

28. The shape of Eliot's beliefs about history is generally acknowledged, if seldom
examined in detail or related to *Romola*'s form (see Fleishman, *English* 155–56).
Wilt identifies the broad background for Victorian interest in the historical
novel, which she terms "that arch-form of a century whose philosophical first
premise, from Hegel and Nietzsche to Darwin and Marx, was based on the
fact that the full understanding of history was equivalent to prophecy" (*Ghosts*
202).

29. For accounts of *Romola*'s composition and publication history, see Haight 360–
70; Redinger 445–54. Hamer argues that Eliot "took no practical account of
[installment structure] in writing her novel" (65), maintaining an independence from external restraint in her art. But the decisions on how to issue the
novel, first in twelve and later in fourteen parts, indicate that Eliot was
concerned with how the novel would be read by her first audience. For an
analysis of unconscious desire in shaping the fiction, see Sadoff (93).

30. Bonaparte identifies "the calendar as one of the book's most obvious and
striking features. It is in itself a complete symbolic structure, reflecting and
shaping the thematic movement throughout" (80). Shuttleworth notes that
the "fundamental question, of how far man should be bound by the culture of
the past, is present at every level of the text" (98), and then links this theme to
the author's role in writing: "Romola's dilemma concerning her relationship to
history is also that of her author [writing a historical novel]" (99).

31. Houghton (*Victorian* 1–23) describes this feature of Victorian life.

32. Wilt notes that "crowds" in *Romola,* "a powerful, jostling, occasionally irritating presence," late in the novel "become a mob, as if, lacking this element of
passionate upward striving [represented by Romola], the community tears
loose even from the exhilarating authority of Savonarola and the corroded
intelligence of Tito Melema to put itself under the guidance of the lowest,
most stupid element, the brutal Dolfo Spini" (*Ghosts* 196).

33. Welsh in *Eliot and Blackmail* comments about Eliot's decision to allow some
events to transpire offstage: "the narrative plays down two important events:
her marriage to Tito and her father's death" (179). Gezari carefully traces the
chronology of historical events in the novel, noting the passing of time
between books 1 and 2 (81) and between books 2 and 3 (82). Eliot uses the gaps
between installments to emphasize time passing in the narrative of other
novels. For instance, in *Daniel Deronda* three weeks pass in Gwendolen Harleth's life (the three weeks of her honeymoon with Grandcourt) between
books 4 and 5.

34. Wilt sees the Savonarola-Romola scene as structurally important, echoing the
waking of Tito at the novel's beginning and the later meeting of Romola and
Baldassarre at Tito's second home with Tessa (*Ghosts* 189–90). *Cornhill* readers
received a rather strong hint about Romola's future early in the next (the
February 1863) issue. An illustration facing the first page showed Romola
kneeling before Savonarola and was captioned "Father, I will be guided." As
explained here, however, the exact nature of Savonarola's guidance is not
presented until later in the installment.

35. Bonaparte discusses Romola's attempt to leave Florence, noting that it recalls

Paul's conversion on the road to Damascus (177–202). Witemeyer has shown that Frederick Leighton's illustrations to *Romola* underscored the protagonist's growth. For instance, Leighton included two pictures of Tito and Romola: "Presenting images of 'before and after,' the illustrations give an illusion of narrative growth and development, rather like two photographs of the same person in the same setting at different times in his or her life" (168).

36. Shuttleworth discusses the importance of language in this scene (111–12). McGowan links a faith in language to the tradition of realism (151–52).

37. Knoepflmacher links history to masculinity, romance to femininity in accounting for the drifting away from Florence ("Genre" 96). Fleishman also says that Romola's final flight takes her out of history (*English* 161). Donald D. Stone finds Romola's life of service in the village and later with Tessa and the children unsatisfying (*Romantic* 225).

38. Redinger notes that the publisher "had been overly optimistic about the attraction *Romola* would have for the *Cornhill* readers. For a while the name 'George Eliot' had worked its magic, but then reader interest slackened and was not significantly revived when Smith, Elder brought the novel out in three volumes" (451). As has been frequently remarked, commentators from the beginning have discussed Tito more than Romola, as did the 16 September 1863 *Guardian,* which focused its review on "the history of the growth of sin in the human soul" (875).

39. The reading public seemed to keep up with Eliot's story. The 25 July 1863 *Saturday Review* termed Romola "the central character of the work which bears her name, and the interest attaching to her increases as the book goes on" (in Carroll 211). The *Sunday Times,* which mentioned *Cornhill* installments of the novel consistently throughout its run, seemed more pleased with the last four monthly installments, finding the novel "greatly increase[s] in interest" (2) on 3 May 1863; calling it a "splendid story" on 7 June 1863 (2) and on 5 July 1863 (2); and declaring it "superbly clever but not entrancing" (2) at its conclusion on 2 August 1863. The *Weekly Dispatch* also referred fairly regularly to the last six months of the novel's appearance in *Cornhill,* saying, for example, on 5 April 1863 that it shows "undiminished power" (6).

40. Gezari comments: "The overriding theme of *Romola* is imaginative vision, and the novel is full of seers and prophets, both true and false" (91).

41. Neither Altick and Loucks nor Gibson ignore linearity, of course (see, e.g., Altick and Loucks 33–34; Gibson 10), but they ultimately privilege simultaneity over linearity in their readings of the poem. Mary Rose Sullivan, conversely, finds the poem's meaning in the process by which Browning first evolved truth and then the process that readers undergo in reading books 2–11 (176–78); she does not include the process of serialization in her discussion. Christ also omits any mention of serialization but gives equal emphasis to the time bound and the timeless (*Victorian* 115). Her assertion that "The fragmentation of narrative form [in Victorian and modern poetry] supplies the gap which allows historicism and ahistoricism contradictorily to occupy the same poetic space" (102) is especially suggestive for serial poetry.

42. Many connect the dramatic monologue in *The Ring and the Book* with circularity, since the speakers remain enclosed within their own worlds rather

than interacting with each other: in this respect there are twelve "rings" that comprise a book. But, as Loy D. Martin has explained, the dramatic monologue is a form "capable of fictionalizing the acts of speech and writing as never-complete, never-present, never-structural unfoldings of the world-in-discourse" (84) since the speaker's presentation in a given moment follows an unstated previous moment and precedes an unstated future. The dramatic monologue hence posits, like Victorian history, a line that runs from the past through the present and into the future. In some respects the monologue also resembles a serial installment: both are in one sense fragments, in another sense complete units in themselves; both ask readers to connect a given present moment to a past and an implied future; and both therefore dovetail with the questions of history insofar as history must construct meaningful sequences and relate part to whole.

43. Both Sue Lonoff and Anthea Trodd remind us that *The Moonstone* was serialized in the same year that Browning's poem, which Trodd calls his "great narrative of conflicting testimonies" (xi), began appearing. The immense popularity of *The Moonstone,* which concluded its serial run on 8 August 1868 (Vann 49), could have predisposed readers and reviewers to discern the trial motif in Browning's poem. Thomas notes Browning's exploitation of the middle-class vogue for "trial literature" (218); but Thomas refers to collected volumes of testimony rather than serial accounts.

44. Other reviews noting the resemblance of the poem to a trial appeared in the 24 March 1869 *Guardian* (344), the 27 March 1869 *Illustrated London News* (322), the April 1869 *Macmillan's Magazine* (550–51 [written by J. R. Mozley]), the October 1869 *North British Review* (117), and the November 1869 *Fraser's Magazine* (673 [written by Sir John Skelton under the pseudonym of Shirley]). These last two reviews indicate the persisting sense of linearity and periodicity even after the poem had appeared. The *North British Review* called the poem "cousin-german to a series of newspaper articles," while Skelton argued that "One reason . . . why the interest is kept up to the end is, that the poem is in effect a criminal trial, an investigation into the why and wherefore of a very dreadful crime, and we feel that in such an inquest a certain amount of repetition is inevitable, nay, that its absence would be disappointing and unsatisfactory." See also McElderry ("Victorian" 77–78).

45. The first edition supplied line numbers, an infrequent practice for Victorian publishers. To underscore here the poem's issuance in four separate volumes over an extended time period, we have prefixed to the conventional book and line citations the volume number in which passages appeared. Thus 1:1.21 in text refers to volume 1, book 1, line 21.

46. The 4 December 1868 *Daily Telegraph* recorded the sense of being in the midst of (confused) judgment after the first installment when it remarked that "the upshot certainly is to reproduce exactly the kind of feeling which must have prevailed in Rome at the time of the story. . . . Perhaps somewhere in the yellow book the poet has something to come, which will not leave London, like Rome, half thinking one thing of the matter, half another" (5).

47. *Saturday Review* closed its review of the first installment by stating that Browning's poem was hard to "understand all at once" (834). As Khattab

observes, "The disadvantage of reviewing part of *The Ring and the Book* was that the reviewers at first passed hasty judgments, which they drastically changed when the whole poem became available" (7). We consider the disparity between earlier and later reviews less a result of haste than of publishing format and reading process.

48. Cf. Harrold 166–67. The line that provides Harrold's study its title—"The variance now, the eventual unity" (1:1.1363)—is particularly applicable to a serial poem, which attains its unity only eventually, after the issuance of varied parts.

49. Cf. John Morley in the January 1869 *Fortnightly Review:* "Those who mark the construction of the poem will see a reason for its appearance in instalments, provided people read it as it is published; for it ensures that slow and prolonged absorption of the story which is essential to the success of the method in which it is composed" (126). Browning's 19 November 1868 letter to Julia Wedgwood also speaks of the poem's arrangement in terms of publication format: "The next book, Pompilia, is all white too: but then come the two buffoon lawyers, and, after the Pope, you have Guido's last display" (Browning and Wedgwood 146).

50. Browning remarked to William Allingham, "The *Athenaeum* notice is good" (Allingham 195).

51. Gridley notes the separation of "Tertium Quid" from the two preceding books by the month-long interval between installments (133–34) but omits discussion of effects on audiences' interpretation.

52. Altick and Loucks also note Tertium Quid's partisanship of Guido (45, 48, 136–40) and the shared social class of Caponsacchi and Guido. Gibson argues that Tertium Quid represents the corrupt aristocratic world from which Caponsacchi has escaped (134).

53. Cf. Tucker's assertion that Browning's poetry as a whole is "an art that resists its own finalities" (5).

54. E. Warwick Slinn (124) and Samuel Chell (100) also note the time-bound framework of Guido's monologue. Unlike Sydney Carton, whom we also last glimpse at the guillotine, Guido has no vision of an ongoing spiritual history or future narratives told to namesakes who live after him; the linear progress of history carries Guido only to death.

55. Gibson remarks that the German historian Burckhardt, whom she deems an influence on Browning, thought skepticism a necessary part of history "because historical beginnings and endings are all unknown" (162).

56. Morley here views the poem in terms of its publication triads (rather than the triads Altick and Loucks identify), just as he does later in the review: "In the second volume, Guido, servile and false, is followed by Caponsacchi, as noble alike in conception and execution as anything that Mr. Browning has achieved. In the third volume, the austere pathos of Pompilia's tale relieves the too oppressive jollity of Don Giacento, and the flowery rhetoric of Bottini; while in the fourth, the deep wisdom, justice, and righteous mind of the Pope, reconcile us to endure the sulphurous whiff from the pit in the confession of Guido, now desperate, satanic, and naked" (332).

57. Irvine and Honan equate the speakers of books 2–4 with "the 'noise of

Rumour's thousand tongues' in Carlyle's essay ['On History']" and identify their function as initiating "recorded history by offering along with gross illusions and petty prejudices ascertainable facts" (432). Cf. Wiener, who demonstrates that gossip as an element of journalism evolved around the same period that Browning published *The Ring and the Book* (265). Peckham asserts that the "fundamental appeal of history is identical with the appeal of gossip" (295).

58. Julia Wedgwood, to whom Browning also dispensed the poem in parts, wrote to Browning on 15 November 1868 after having read the first six books, "One's memory seems filled by the despicable husband, the vulgar parents, the brutal cutthroats; the pathetic child is jostled into a corner. I long for more space for her. In the third and fourth volumes I hope we shall have it" (Browning and Wedgwood 139).

59. As H. B. Forman commented in the July 1869 *London Quarterly Review,* the poem also delays our second encounter with Guido: "It is by artistically letting Guido speak last that the hardening of our hearts against one so ferocious is avoided. Had the harrowing details of the murder or any of the resultant miseries come after the picture of the poor cringing Count, as he realises for the first time the impending execution, it would have been hard to spare him the sigh we can now give for the wild desperation of his cry for life" (349). This effect, of course, would have been intensified by serial publication, which delayed the second encounter with Guido by two months.

60. The structure of the last book in part recapitulates the pattern of the entire poem insofar as it is a journey to and from Pompilia. Thus book 12 opens with the poet, followed by a total stranger to Pompilia; next come the letters of Arcangeli, who writes to someone who knew Guido well, and then of Bottini, who, having earlier defended Pompilia (apparently with no personal acquaintance of her) now takes issue against her. The book builds to Celestino who, of all those in the twelfth book, knew Pompilia best and was the immediate auditor of Pompilia's deathbed utterance; he thus had most proximity to her voice. After this Bottini comes forward again, and then the poet in his closing peroration. Hence, we move toward the closest advocate and companion of Pompilia and away yet again.

61. The Pope is also a kind of serial reader of history: "I will begin,—as is, these seven years now, / My daily wont,—and read a History" (4:10.2–3).

62. As Samuel Chell notes, "Pompilia's awakening in time cannot be complete until she establishes the continuity of her own experience in time, an effort demanding recognition of the past. Thus by bringing 'back reluctantly to mind' (633) her married life with Guido, Pompilia acts even in her dying moment to recover her true self in time" (113).

63. Zietlow notes the parallels Pompilia implicitly draws between her own and her mother's lives (196).

64. One of the major questions of the trial is what sort of straight line leads from the past through the journey: Guido's cruelty or Pompilia and Caponsacchi's illicit love. It is the pause on the journey at Castelnuovo that so complicates judgment, since this pause can be interpreted as a necessary reprieve to save the lives of mother and unborn child or as an occasion for adultery.

65. See also Gibson 33–34. The Pope is also much given to journeying in his life. Book 1 calls the Pope one "Who had trod many lands" (1:1.303).
66. Guido's pause in journeying after the murder, appropriately, also effects his downfall and eventual death.
67. The poem also asks readers to imagine Gaetano's future:

>   Did the babe live or die?—one fain would find!
>   What were his fancies if he grew a man?
>   Was he proud,—a true scion of the stock,—
>   Of bearing blason, shall make bright my Book—
>   Shield, Azure, on a Triple Mountain, Or,
>   A Palm-tree, Proper, whereunto is tied
>   A Greyhound, Rampant, striving in the slips?
>   Or did he love his mother, the base-born,
>   And fight i' the ranks, unnoticed by the world?

(4:12.814–22)

Browning never answers these questions, leaving them to readers' imaginations (see also Gridley 137, Harrold 178).
68. Buckler sees one positive outcome even of the pause at Castelnuovo: "It releases Pompilia from goodness to grandeur, from domesticity to epic heroism" (*Poetry* 153).
69. For another approach to the historiographic problems posed by the poem, see Gibson.
70. Altick and Loucks praise Browning's "unflagging attention to minute detail" and "a memory that could span thousands of intervening lines for the sake of providing the exactly suitable variation of an earlier figure at the exactly suitable moment" (228). Among Browning's contemporaries, however, J. R. Mozley concluded in the April 1869 *Macmillan's Magazine* that the poem was simply too long and remarked that a reader could too easily get lost (544).
71. The 3 April 1869 *Saturday Review* records the disparity between whole-volume and linear views of the poem: "the poem gains much in intelligibility by being studied as a whole. The introduction itself, which on the first reading seemed difficult and obscure, is illuminated by the light which is shed on it by what comes afterwards" (460).
72. Irvine and Honan argue that the title also alludes to the poem's "circular pattern of monologues" and "to its villain's 'round' of diabolic journeyings" (425).

IV. Building the Empire

1. Klancher sees such empire building in terms of dominance and submission: "the periodical writer both names and colonizes the social group to whom he writes, drawing into the public those still unincorporated into the universe of public discourse" (25); yet late nineteenth-century socialists and Fabians, who explicitly and passionately opposed colonialism, adopted a slogan also based on rhetorical and ideological expansion: "Agitate! Educate! Organise!" Their chosen format for education also included the periodical, especially *Commonweal*.
2. D. A. Miller argues that Trollope's style contains and controls contradictory

forces beneath the smooth surface of his fictional world. According to Miller, even unconventional sexual roles support rather than challenge a stable system: "The gentleman-woman and the lady-man in Trollope are not symptoms of a patriarchy in disarray; nor do they imply a critique of the established gender code or an invitation to transsexual experimentation. Rather, they are the raw material for that massive stereotyping which, turning them into reminders of the gender norms they seem to transgress, makes radical transgression impossible" (33).

3. Garrett notes: "The novel is organized by an antithesis of Palliser and Lopez, the man of honor and extreme scrupulousness living at the center of political power and social status set against the amoral, marginal adventurer" (216).

4. See, for example, McCormick (xvii).

5. Arthur Pollard comments: "Trollope was describing a condition of political flux, an old world dying and a new one struggling into what promised to be a violent infancy" (103). Edwards asserts: "In order to give his favourite political character, Plantagenet Palliser, now Duke of Omnium, the opportunity of leading the nation for three years, Trollope was obliged to invent a situation without any recent parallel [in England]" (*Trollope* 228); thus, it seems Trollope designed a political situation, a coalition government, for Palliser to illustrate certain principles of leadership.

6. Donald D. Stone has noted a similarity between Palliser and King Arthur: "Palliser is the Victorian novelist's equivalent to Tennyson's Arthur in the *Idylls of the King*—the unglamorous but selfless ruler of society" (*Novelists* 33). One of the best studies of Palliser is by George Butte, who argues: "The duke suffers through three years as a prime minister of a coalition government whose balance between liberalism and conservatism and consequent paralysis mirror the condition of his own mind" (219–20). John Halperin calls Plantagenet Trollope's "ideal statesman" (222) and explores the "interesting and unmistakable resemblances" between Palliser and Lord Palmerston (215).

7. Kincaid shares this view: "The Duke is Trollope's strongest character, according to his own judgement, a 'perfect gentleman' . . . but as Prime Minister he is miscast as badly as Mr. Harding would have been as bishop" (*Novels* 181). Klinger says of Palliser: "by accepting premiership he comes dangerously close to destroying the best qualities of his nature" (172); but he also terms this novel "one of Trollope's most significant achievements . . . successful not only in parts, but above all in its overall design and structure" (168).

8. Lansbury notes Trollope's use of analogy (214); and Kincaid adds, "The two controlling and linked images throughout [the Palliser novels] are those of marriage and politics" (*Novels* 179).

9. Juliet McMaster notes: "His Prime Ministership, then, is their second honeymoon" (*Trollope's* 124).

10. Hamer shows that Trollope placed important matters in key places, whatever the volume or serial format of the individual title (40–56).

11. Some of Palliser's anger here is probably directed at Glencora for failing to understand the limitations he faces; and his role would be easier if there were an easy program to initiate; but he is also frustrated that other politicians will not see that the best policy in this situation is to take no action.

12. Polhemus puts it more negatively: "Despite his virtue and idealism [Palliser] cannot preserve communal harmony, and that is the reason for the aura of defeat which hangs over his ministry" (*Changing* 207). Andrew Wright adds that the prime minister "is at a disadvantage on account of being unable to exert the leadership which magnetism makes possible" (108). Tracy comments: "To be ordinary, not outstanding, and to be able to make and retain friends—these are the requisites for political and social success in Trollope's world" (50); and he believes Palliser possesses the first but not the second quality.

13. apRoberts notes that Palliser in the end "must be content with having merely kept things going, in a coalition-y, compromise-y, *fainéant* sort of way" (146). Lansbury also notes that "Palliser, like Septimus Harding, is a study of failure that transcends the everyday criteria of success to achieve a special kind of triumph" (221).

14. Monk and the old duke, of course, can have their own motives for placating Palliser with such speeches; but even if insincere, such praise can be accurate.

15. We wish to thank here Robert May, whose expertise helped us avoid some errors in our discussion of decimal coinage and calculation. We are still responsible for any inaccuracies in this paragraph.

   Another fine example of Palliser's commonsense (we want to say "down to earth") philosophy is his interest in cork soles, a logical, uncomplicated way to keep one's feet dry in a damp climate. Trollope's unpretentious but effective style is also delightfully illustrated in this metaphor of cork soles as an indicator of the character of the duke and others. Banks has identified a number of similarities between the author Trollope and his character Palliser (178–81).

16. Sadleir says that a decline in Trollope's readership after 1870 was owing to a natural evolution in audience interests; but this "desertion was gradual and never, during Trollope's lifetime, complete" (312). That *The Prime Minister* was not a great popular success "shook him badly," according to Sadleir (313).

17. Levine says, "But the artist, at least the Trollopian artist, is not special. He is like other people in this compromised world, and his major responsibility is not to an ideal of art but to life itself" (*Realistic* 189). And Levine links the author's beliefs to those of his central character: "[Trollope's] creed is rather like the one he attributed to Palliser in *The Prime Minister* [the "'ideal is so distant that we need not even think it possible'"] (*Realistic* 202). R. D. McMaster says Trollope's account of how government appointments are filled "is convincing, and it matches the actual rivalries and jockeying for position one finds, for example, in the careers of such eminent legal figures as Lord John Campbell (1779–1861) and Alexander Cockburn (1802–80)" (*Trollope* 116). Kendrick insightfully says that Trollope developed "a theory not of the novel but of novel production, and a criticism whose paradigm is the lyric poem, a self-contained linguistic object, has not been able to see that it is a theory at all" (4).

18. The generic status of the *Idylls* has been much discussed, both in Tennyson's day and in our own. For recent views of the work's affinities with epic see Turner 163–64 and Buckler, *Man* 10–11, 302–4.

   All citations of the *Idylls* that follow are to the year of a given idyll's publication and to page number (not line number) of the relevant volume. Thus, 1885: 117 means page 117 in the volume published in 1885. Though published in December 1869, *The Holy Grail and Other Poems* was dated 1870 on the title page and is accordingly cited by the year 1870, though our discussion refers to "1869 idylls." Citations of "The Epic" and "Morte d'Arthur" are given from Tennyson's 1842 *Poems,* citations of "To the Queen" from the 1873 edition of Tennyson's collected poems. Again, citations are to publication date and page number.

19. This publication order also enhanced the poem's popularity. The 1859 volume was most frequently praised for the simplicity of the verse and, above all, for the vividness and humanity of the characters. Ten years passed before the 1869 installment introduced more explicitly metaphysical or didactic themes. Whereas later readers of the completed poem often resist what seems a bloodless allegory begun in "The Coming of Arthur," Victorian readers tolerated "The Coming" (which they did not especially admire) because it filled in the context for the characters (Arthur included) who had seemed so human and accessible in 1859. See Hughes, "Tennyson's," for a fuller discussion of this point.

20. Two key works in the Arthurian revival were also published in parts: Kenelm Digby's four-volume *Broad Stone of Honour: Rules for the Gentlemen of England* (the first edition issued from 1828 to 1829 and the second from 1844 to 1848), and Lady Charlotte Guest's translation of the *Mabinogian* (a source used by Tennyson), issued in seven volumes from 1838 to 1849 (Girouard 56, 60, 178). Kathleen Tillotson ("Tennyson's" 97, 97 n.1) notes additional serialization of Arthurian material in the *Monthly Packet,* edited by Charlotte Yonge. *King Arthur and His Knights,* by Ellen L. Millington, ran from 1859 to 1864, and an anonymous version of Galahad's grail quest appeared from 1852 to 1853.

21. The British orders of knighthood expanded in lockstep with the territorial expansion of empire (Girouard 228–29). In Girouard's view the end result of "moral chivalry" was World War I, in which young, idealistic men embarked to wage a war of honor and bravery and were blown, along with the chivalric ideal, to smithereens.

22. Victor Kiernan's "Tennyson, King Arthur, and Imperialism" explicitly examines links between the *Idylls* and empire. Kiernan does not situate the poem within the considerable body of literary criticism that has developed around the poem, but his essay is useful for establishing the actual events of empire, and especially imperialism, that occurred as the *Idylls* were appearing. See also Lang 1–4, 11–12, 15.

23. The July 1859 *National Magazine* was one of the few to anticipate later interpretations when it asserted that "It is the central idea or principle of the composition [that] Arthur stands for the 'Conscience of the Saint,' his knights for the 'warring senses' " (169). This review merely responded to lines all could read in "Guinevere," but in 1859 the lines were not seized upon as a concept governing interpretation. Occasionally 1859 reviews anticipated later commentaries by remarking that Arthur seemed a pallid, remote, or cold character, but this again was counter to the majority of reviews of the first installment, which stressed Arthur's humanity.

24. As Reed comments, Arthur and his knights "are mainly inarticulate because

their deeds speak for them"; hence they tend most to use language when their deeds lose efficacy (198).

25. Of course these lines, spoken by a governing male to a cowering female, hardly evoke the response among late twentieth-century readers that they did among Tennyson's contemporaries (even George Eliot wept— sympathetically—over "Guinevere"). See Weissman and Knight for effective feminist readings of this idyll. Thomas Huxley's response indicates, in contrast, how Victorians viewed the poem and how easily they linked it to thoughts of empire. When Huxley addressed the Royal Society in 1860 and argued that England's future as a world power depended on its allegiance to science, he used Arthur and Guinevere as a convenient metaphor:

> Cherish [science], venerate her, follow her methods faithfully and implicitly in their application to all branches of human thought, and the future of this people will be greater than the past. Listen to those who (quoted in would silence and crush her, and I fear our children will see the glory of Cruse 97– England vanishing like Arthur in the mist; they will cry too late the 98) woeful cry of Guinevere—
>
> It was my duty to have loved the highest:
> It surely was my profit had I known:
> It would have been my pleasure had I seen.

26. That three of the 1859 idylls added male to the original female names ("Geraint and Enid," "Merlin and Vivien," "Lancelot and Elaine") would have highlighted the absence of "Arthur" from "Guinevere," which alone retained the 1859 title. This idyll, of course, recounts the farewell of king and queen and the results of Guinevere's not joining with Arthur and sharing his vision, so the choice of title is appropriate on grounds other than Arthur's immersion in his table.

27. The 6 November 1869 *Spectator,* more than a month before the 1869 volume appeared, helped pave the way for the reception of the new idylls, in part by also extending backward the history of Tennyson's composition. The reviewer, obviously an intimate of the Tennyson household, notes the earlier expectation of an epic after the 1842 "Morte" and "Epic" were published, and adds, "We happen to have in our possession notes and memoranda made by him, and dating from about that period, which show how quickly the symbolic under-meaning to be given to or got from the legends flashed upon him. But the critics interposed, and for a whole generation the fragment of his *Morte d'Arthur* stood alone. The fire, however, was but checked, not quenched, and after long smouldering broke out again in his *Idylls of the King.* The immense acclamation which welcomed these may have helped to turn his mind back towards the completion of his old project, which is plainly indicated in the poems already published, though not so obviously but as to have escaped many readers. We are happy to believe that another volume of idylls is now about to be given to the world, and that in them the plan so long lain by (and rumour says resumed but twelve months since) is more fully and clearly shown" (1306).

28. Richard Holt Hutton's 2 December 1871 article in the *Spectator* was a notable exception to the many unfavorable reviews. As Hutton averred, Tennyson's

"Arthurian poem of many parts, is an elaborate picture of a great moral failure to subdue earthly circumstance to the highest will, but of a great moral failure in which there is more glory than in most success." Hutton had high praise as well for the poem's unity: "the power of this great series of poems consists entirely in the absolute unity of the imaginative centre to be traced in every piece from first to last" (1459). There are indications that many readers shared Hutton's enthusiasm. Patricia Srebrnik records that the issue of *Contemporary Review* in which "The Last Tournament" appeared went through several editions: "by 23 December, Strahan was able to advertise the third edition (ten thousandth) of that month's issue" (119).

29. The comments of the 21 December 1872 *Chambers's Journal* represent the tone of the negative reviews: "It is a pity that our Laureate has been witched by Merlin, and pours his genius out so lavishly on such a worn-out theme as Arthur and his knights. Well as he has treated it, we own ourselves fairly tired of the 'table round;' he has never beaten that magnificent epic fragment, his *Morte d'Arthur;* and all that he has told us subsequently about the blameless king wears of necessity an air of bathos" (813). See also the *Examiner,* 26 October 1872: 1056–57; *Bell's Weekly Messenger,* 2 November 1872: 4; *News of the World,* 3 November 1872: 6; *Blackwood's Edinburgh Magazine* 112 (December 1872): 760–65; *London Quarterly Review* 39 (January 1873): 394–405; and *Westminster Review* 100 (July 1873): 153–54.

30. Hutton's review also reflects the notion of the *Idylls* as a serial work that grows not only in extent but in design and effect: "as the poem put forth new shoots in both directions, backwards and forwards, and the noble portions on 'The Coming of Arthur,' 'The Holy Grail,' and 'The Passing of Arthur,' appeared,—poems in which the gradual growth and fall of the ideal kingdom of the spiritual chivalry were depicted,—I found the grandeur of the new poem eclipsing in interest, for me, almost everything that Mr. Tennyson had written, and the first published Idylls themselves growing in their intellectual fascination" (157). Hutton also found "Gareth and Lynette" "amongst [Tennyson's] happiest efforts" (163).

31. Barbara Hardy attributes this aspect of the novel in part to Eliot's range of experience ("Introduction" 29).

32. These three works share many specific similarities in addition to the theme of empire. In pursuing a subject (Jewishness) foreign to her audience's traditional interests, Eliot resembles Tennyson's taking up the myth of Arthur at a time when conventional wisdom dictated contemporary society as the proper subject for art. The 16 September 1876 *Saturday Review,* for instance, commented: "And not only are these personages outside our interests, but the author seems to go out with them into a world completely foreign to us" (357). The presence of many individual tales in the *Idylls,* some early stories continued or expanded in later poems, also resembles the multiplot construction of so many nineteenth-century novels like *Deronda* and *The Prime Minister.* The question of origin or paternity also links Tennyson's King Arthur with Eliot's Deronda.

Parallels between Eliot's and Trollope's fictions are even more striking when we realize that they were being composed and published almost simultaneously (Hamer 185; Haight 477). The eight-part publication format had been initiated by Eliot with *Middlemarch* (1871–72), though in that case the first six volumes came out at two-month rather than monthly intervals. *Deronda,* like *The Prime Minister,* appeared in eight monthly half-volumes, matching as a completed work the fairly familiar four-volume form. (Pagination in *Deronda,* as in *The Prime Minister,* matches the four-volume format, books 1 and 2, 3 and 4, 5 and 6, 7 and 8 making up the four volumes, each paginated separately. Citations in the text that follows include the month of the book and the page number.) Both novels explicitly took up political issues, with characters like Sir Hugo Mallinger and Phineas Finn sitting in Parliament; and each explored questions of power and authority in personal relationships through an extended study of marriage. These structural and thematic similarities underscore, of course, common authorial interests as well as shared concerns of readers.

33. In Victorian literature leaders are male. Gilbert and Gubar explain, however, how women like Gwendolen and Mrs. Glasher, who are subservient, gain subtle strength: "What distinguishes the heroine from her double is her deflection of anger from the male she is shown justifiably to hate back against herself so that she punishes herself, finding in self-abasement a sign of her moral superiority to the man she continues to serve. . . . she is considering how the injustice of masculine society bequeaths to women special strengths and virtues, specifically a capacity for feeling born of disenfranchisement from a corrupt social order" (198).

34. The 16 September 1876 *Saturday Review* discussed heroes in its review of *Deronda:* "It is not often that the poet or novelist sets himself to draw a perfect man. . . . Tennyson's *King Arthur* and Wordsworth's *Happy Warrior* have perpetuated some grand ideas with this aim" (357).

35. Myers points out that in the novel Grandcourt is "the locus of a brutality no less real and active than 'the tread of an invading army' " (214). Juliet McMaster, discussing Victorian novelists and sexuality, notes "the horrible interaction of frigidity and sadism in the Grandcourt marriage" ("George Eliot" 25). Shuttleworth examines the "assertive power in colonial rule" evident in Grandcourt's speech (182) and explains that Eliot offers "two alternative languages" (183) to that of the English ruling class—those of Klesmer and Mordecai. Hester links the themes of government and marriage: "The chief historical events mentioned in the novel—the American Civil War, the native uprising in Jamaica, and the Austro-Prussian War—all involve a struggle for independence and thus provide approximate historical parallels to Gwendolen's contention with Grandcourt" (116).

36. Criticism that *Deronda* is made up of two separate plots and is therefore a failure as a single novel began with the work's first publication. Haight, however, notes: "The Jewish elements, which careless readers used to think separable from Gwendolen's story, made part of her plan almost from the start" (469). R. T. Jones cautions against rejecting the Mordecai-Mirah plot: "If we are inclined to say that this large part of the book is a failure, we must be careful to ensure that we are . . . not merely expressing a version of the commonplace scepticism of our time" (112). Garrett explores some "surprising similarities between the novel's two worlds" (174).

37. Ermarth points out: "The thought that ideas and enactments are one, has a special place in George Eliot's conception of the social and human world" (131). Knoepflmacher has argued that the novel is "more than a plea for toleration of the Jews and the establishment of a Jewish nation. . . . [it is] Eliot's attempt to define a new climate for religious belief" (*Religious* 135). Shuttleworth places the novel within scientific theories of interest to Eliot and Lewes.

38. Books 5 and 6 will also open appropriately with representations of Deronda's thoughts rather than description of characters and events. McGowan finds Eliot's interest in ideas and thoughts subordinate in the end to a theory of realism: "Reality exists prior to any act of imagination, which is limited to generating new modes of perceiving the real" (155).

39. Welsh, for instance, comments: "George Eliot implants in her hero an early discontent with some customary ways of carving a career from knowledge in England" (*George Eliot* 301). Smith also states: "The novel's analysis and definition of England and Englishness embodies, in my view, something like a total rejection by George Eliot of her society, certainly at the imaginative level" (209). Graham Martin concludes: "In sum, English society is so constituted that Deronda has to leave it, not because it rejects him, but because, threatening to condemn him to a meaningless life, he rejects it" (146–47).

40. Myers explains how Eliot was moved by the Franco-Prussian War of 1870, which underscored the importance of movements toward national unity in nineteenth-century Europe (211–14).

41. One key word here is repeated in chapter 51. When he comes to meet his mother, Deronda is a "striking young gentleman whose appearance gave even the severe lines of an evening dress the credit of adornment" (August: 16).

42. *Bell's Weekly Messenger* on 5 February 1876 paid special attention to Rex Gascoigne, quoting the passage that describes his falling from his horse (6). The 29 January 1876 *Examiner* also stated: "The various members of the Gascoigne family, too, are studies on which we dwell with increasing admiration" (125). Sudrann (436–38) explains why the conventional Gascoignes would appeal to middle-class readers.

43. Myers identifies Rex and Anna's story as a "mildly Trollopian novel in which they might have been central characters," noting that it "is not developed in the text because it does not need to be" (225). Graham Martin also notes that Rex "illustrates the educated middle class of genteel origin, but without fortune, who turn to the professions for support" (145).

44. Barbara Hardy commented in 1967 that *Daniel Deronda* "suffered in its own day and perhaps in ours too by the inevitable comparison with its immediate predecessor, *Middlemarch* [which] is, in everyone's opinion, George Eliot's greatest novel" ("Introduction" 8–9). In the last two decades, however, her last novel has received increasing recognition and appreciation. Swann provides an enthusiastic defense of the central character as a genuine religious leader (49). Carol Martin recreates the month-by-month response to Deronda, noting: "occasional early reviewers clearly found [Deronda] quite satisfactory as long as it appeared that he would be a love interest in Gwendolen's life" (95).

45. The April 1876 *New Quarterly Magazine* stated: "The hero, Daniel, is quite a new creation in fiction and the novelty of the conception makes amends for the

absence of some of the sterling qualities of the old-fashioned type of novel hero. . . . The young man is of the type that fond mothers dote upon, which sisters adore, but which other women, as a rule, are apt to be contemptuous about" (275). For a discussion of how in the novel Deronda works out his private rather than his political identity, his relationship to his parents, see Mann (127–29). Newton praises Eliot's efforts with this character (188).

46. Witemeyer underscores Deronda's development through Eliot's allusions to two works by Titian: the secular painting "The Young Man with a Glove" and the religious painting "The Tribute Money" (101). Witemeyer explains that Deronda "moves from a secular to a religious life, from a poised sitter in a portrait to a dramatic actor in a sacred history painting" (104).

47. The 4 March 1876 *Examiner,* for example, was sympathetic even to Gwen's desire to appear favorably before others, though not to her desire to rule over them: "Still there were possibilities of good left even in this desire to produce an impression on the impassive witnesses of human action because it might imply a thirst for approbation as well as for empire" (265).

48. An exception to this general lack of interest in Mirah might be the 19 March 1876 *News of the World:* "Of the new characters introduced the last comer is a poor Jewish girl, with wondrous eyes and dainty face and figure, who has wandered all the way from Prague in search of some friends, and not finding them in the wilderness of London is about to drown herself when Daniel Deronda comes to her rescue" (6).

49. See also George Eliot's Journal, 3 June 1876: "Book V published a week ago. Growing interest in the public and growing sale, which has from the beginning exceeded that of *Middlemarch.* The Jewish part apparently creating strong interest" (quoted in Carroll 365).

50. Ashton argues that Deronda's "'life' in the novel depends on his relationship with Gwendolen, who is so much more realised than he is that the difference strikes us forcefully" (88). Newton suggests, however, that, "In his efforts to help her overcome her alienation and to prevent her being engulfed by her inner demons, he becomes more aware of his own need for what he prescribes for her" (197); and Paris notes that Deronda's life "took a more definite shape when his actions were guided by the responsibilities he felt in his relations with Mirah and Gwendolen" (206).

51. Alley has discussed chapters 35 and 36 as the crucial midpoint of the novel, calling them "Janus-faced, since they look back on the old Gwendolen, the spoiled child, and then ahead, to the new, tragically penitent heroine; back, again, on the stiff and abstaining Deronda, the observer of society, and ahead to the new hero, ardently involved in mankind's religious and social destiny" (147). Carpenter also stresses the importance of the meeting at the abbey (152). And Kearney provides an analysis of these scenes at the midpoint of the novel, calling chapters 35 and 36 "among the finest achievements of George Eliot's fiction" (288). Liddell, who dislikes Deronda, admits: "This is his best moment with her" (179).

52. For readers of book 5, Rex Gascoigne remained available as a suitor to Gwen, should anything happen to Grandcourt. Hans tells Deronda of meeting him at Cambridge. And Hans's own comic pursuit of Mirah allowed Eliot's audience to continue to discount Deronda as a match for Mirah.

53. Richard Holt Hutton had been disappointed with Deronda in his 10 June 1876 *Spectator* review of book 5, finding him "a wreath of moral mist. . . . Possibly, however, Mordecai's teaching is intended to crystallize the young man's mind into clear and vigorous purpose" (quoted in Holmstrom and Lerner 133). Hutton seemed more pleased with book 6, stating in the *Spectator* on 29 July 1876 that none other of her works "has been so powerfully constructed in point of plot" (quoted in Holmstrom and Lerner 135).

    Welsh acknowledges Eliot's aversion to doctrine, but sees in this novel the advocacy of a specific set of beliefs that strengthens the leader: a "recourse to ideology actually restores a partial opening for heroism among the leadership" (*George Eliot* 316).

54. See also the 1 July 1876 *Bell's Weekly Messenger:* While "the second plot, if it may be so called—by means of which the reader is introduced to many singular phases of Jewish life and manners—is the more satisfactory portion of the work by far, we, nevertheless, cannot deny that there is a fascination about the former, which holds us, as it were, spellbound" (6).

55. Among the milder and more indirect reviews was the 5 August 1876 *Examiner,* which noted "the bewilderment [George Eliot] has caused among the 20,000 readers of 'Daniel Deronda,' some of whom must be simple folk who read her as a social duty, by giving them such a nut to crack as the wonderful Jew Mordecai" (885).

56. Cynthia Chase has argued that Deronda ought to have known his race: "evidence of circumcision amounted to evidence of Jewish origin. For Deronda not to have known he was Jewish until his mother told him means, in these terms, 'that he never looked down,' an idea that exceeds, as much as does magical metamorphosis, the generous limits of realism" (222).

57. Deronda accepts his grandfather's tradition despite the fact that, as his mother explains, the old order involved domination: "such men turn their wives and daughters into slaves. They would rule the world if they could; but not ruling the world, they throw all the weight of their will on the necks and souls of women" (August: 30–31).

58. The 9 September 1876 *Spectator* made the same point: Deronda is gone "to preach ideas which have only been hinted, and which must rest on a creed that has hardly been hinted at all" (1133). The 4 October 1876 *Guardian* added that it could not find "the faintest idea of the practical work to which Deronda's life is henceforth to be dedicated, and, in spite of all his predilections and anticipations, we cannot but fear that he will make a very indifferent Jew" (1312). Of course, some of the complaint about Deronda disguises a Victorian resistance to Eliot's view of the world, as Carpenter describes it: "The narrative solidly identifies the downward progress of worldly empire with the English 'half' [of the novel], whereas the Jewish 'half,' dominated by Daniel, Mordecai, and Mirah, represents visionary growth and progress" (135).

59. Eliot's empire at this stage is unusually nonaggressive, since it involves regaining a lost unity, Jews reclaiming their national identity rather than one culture's overcoming another. In this sense, the novel's treatment of empire is a special case and sidesteps some difficult issues, even the novel's own equation, taught to Gwendolen by Deronda, that "our gain is another's loss." When that Jewish cultural identity begins in the future to have more of an

effect on English thinking, greater difficulties would be encountered, as Edward Dowden suggested in the February 1877 *Contemporary Review:* "that some should find [Deronda] incredible proves no more than that clever critics in walking from their lodgings to their club, and from their club to their lodgings, have not exhausted the geography of the habitable globe" (355). Dowden's insightful article also links the theme of national development to the nature of literary form: "It might indeed be contended that at a period when on the continent of Europe the idea of nationality—unity of Italy, pan-Teutonism, pan-Slavism—has played and is playing so important a part, there were a historical justification and a historical propriety in its employment as a poetical motive in a work of art" (364).

60. Gwendolen's trials at this time, by the way, were extended in the audience's experience of them in a way that resembles what happened with Emily Lopez's story in *The Prime Minister.* Gwendolen fears having a child who would extend Grandcourt's crippling empire over herself and Lydia Glasher's family: "She was reduced to dread lest she should become a mother" (August: 107). Victorian readers suffered a similar fear longer than modern single-volume readers because of the novel's installment publication. After the suggestion of motherhood was raised in book 7 (August 1876), serial readers had to wait at least a month to learn whether this would be her fate. In book 8 (September 1876), after the accident, Mr. Gascoigne in England worries "there may possibly be an heir yet to be born" (September: 180). Later, when he and Mrs. Davilow have been several days in Genoa looking after Gwendolen, Deronda is able to tell Sir Hugo that no heir is likely.

61. Rex also, like Arthur Fletcher, continues to wait patiently for a possible revival of marriage hopes. Eliot keeps his name before the reader in book 7 by having Hans Meyrick live near him in London.

62. In a letter to Mrs. Harriet Beecher Stowe, 29 October 1876, Eliot said: "There is nothing I should care more to do, if it were possible, than to rouse the imagination of men and women to a vision of human claims in those races of their fellow-men who most differ from them in customs and beliefs" (quoted in Holmstrom and Lerner 155). Gallagher sees the novel more as narrowing down toward a revived English nationalism than as opening out to larger traditions ("George Eliot" 58–59). Sudrann explains that George Eliot's characters must learn to go into exile in order to discover new ways of living (439). Vargish, on the other hand, stresses an ultimate unity toward which Eliot is moving: "*Daniel Deronda* really is about the heart of the social matter—what it is that holds human beings together, what unites a family, a nation, a people, the human species, and what the true value of these identities can be for the individual constituents" (229).

63. The 4 October 1876 *Guardian* found fault with a hero who had been praised in the early books of *Deronda*: "It is impossible to say much for the nominal hero, Deronda. . . . altogether vague, shadowy, and unreal" (1312). This review also noted a change in tone with the last book: "it is probably the pure indulgence of a personal fancy which has induced her to bring the Jews so prominently forward in this last [eighth] book" (1312).

64. *Bell's Weekly Messenger* presented a different evaluation on 2 September 1876:

"The conclusion, in fact, is painfully inconsistent and incomplete, and is made so much the more to appear so, because the opening and the development of the purpose, up to the end of Book VII, are amongst the most brilliant evidence of superior talent, which George Eliot, in any former work, has made apparent" (6).

65. Eliot, for instance, opens this book with a description of the English countryside rather than presenting a foreign location or narrating the thoughts of Deronda.

66. Rex Gascoigne, an audience favorite throughout the novel, is still in book 8 a possible figure in her future, seen starting "up as if a missile had been suddenly thrown into the room" (775) when he learns of Grandcourt's death. R. E. Francillon in the October 1876 *Gentleman's Magazine* even speculated that Gwendolen "is married to Rex and corresponds with Deronda" (quoted in Carroll 388). Deronda himself, as Graham Martin notes, presents the ideal pattern of growth and development: "searching for his true identity, [he] moves outwards from the Mallingers, to the Meyricks, the Cohens, Mirah and Mordecai, and finally the unknown millions of the Diaspora" (142).

67. As Haight observes, her appeal to Jewish readers was far-reaching, and her novel even provided a significant stimulus to the Jewish national spirit (488). The 15 December 1876 *Jewish Chronicle* represents this reaction: "And now let us stop for a moment and consider the aspirations, to the realization of which Deronda vowed to devote his life. Such an enquiry is the more opportune, when it is instituted at a period pregnant with great events apparently bearing on the subject" (quoted in Holmstrom and Lerner 153).

V. Expressing Doubt

1. Tanner argues that the concept of adultery was central to an age that publicly stood for fidelity and the hearth (*Adultery* 13).

2. See also Perkin 425–54; Gross, *Rise* 131–32; and Beer, *Darwin* 145—all of whom discuss the weakening confidence in progress and growing doubt about the future among the dominant Victorian cultures in the 1870s and 1880s.

3. Tobin has noted how the linear shape of nineteenth-century fiction inevitably endorsed ideas of progress: "No matter how severe an indictment the novelist might bring against his real world, no matter how devastating a picture he might paint of social disintegration, his novel with its ordered progress in time offered a disproof of his vision of disorder" (36).

4. Donald D. Stone connects Trollope's self-reflective mood in the 1870s to the tone of *The Way We Live Now* (*Romantic* 33). Harvey has linked that novel to its successor in Trollope's career, *The Prime Minister:* "there are grounds for thinking that Trollope regarded [*The Way We Live Now* and *The Prime Minister*] as contiguous and complementary studies of the major sources of power in the modern age, presenting from different perspectives a coherent judgement of Victorian society" (125–26).

5. Robin Gilmour also explores contradictory elements in the novel: "*The Way We Live Now* can be made to seem an impressively unified work, with a thematic coherence and satirical power not unworthy of comparison with the

great satires of Dickens and Thackeray [but] such a reading . . . knits a net with so wide a mesh that much of what is most interesting in the novel slips through" (187–88).

6. Garrett sees this multiplot novel as less diverse than others in Trollope's canon (217).

7. Brooks defines the traditional form of much nineteenth-century fiction in terms of its plot and the expectations it arouses: "The Balzacian novel is constructed precisely on a dramatic, even a theatrical, model, by which will and action are plotted toward major 'showdowns,' scenes of confrontation in which characters act out, give full expression to the issues in conflict, and where the dramatic moment produces changed relations, a significant outcome to the problems posed" (176). In this novel Trollope extends such linear progress toward resolution by having characters occasionally retreat before advancing to these "major showdowns," making use of certain installments to take steps away from key dramatic moments.

8. Kendrick has insisted on seeing Trollope's style as dynamic: "The realistic novel, for Trollope, is never a static structure to be contemplated or reflected upon. It is always dynamic, a process rather than an object" (4).

9. This style, statement followed by qualification, is found in much of Trollope's work; it is also present, for instance, in *Can You Forgive Her?* (1864–65). Such a style can be attacked as the product of the serialist's need to fill up an installment, mere padding inspired by format. A style in Trollope and other Victorians that sometimes seems repetitive or hesitant may also be a reflection of fundamental doubts about nineteenth-century ideology.

   Published in twenty monthly parts, *The Way We Live Now* was paginated in the manner of a two-volume edition.

10. In one aspect of contemporary society, Trollope clearly did see decline. Roger Carbury and the landed aristocracy seemed to be leading society forward but were actually themselves falling behind new standards: "the Carbury property has considerably increased in value. . . . But the income is no longer comfortably adequate. . . . [Thus,] the Squire of Carbury Hall had become a poor man simply through the wealth of others" (1:33).

11. Hamer argues that by the time of *Phineas Finn* Trollope had become a master of the multiplot novel (176). Trollope himself felt *The Way We Live Now* uneven: "the young lady with her two lovers is weak and vapid. I almost doubt whether it be not impossible to have two absolutely distinct parts in a novel, and to imbue them both with interest" (from Trollope's *Autobiography,* quoted in Smalley 395).

12. Roger L. Slakey, for instance, traces the general progress from empty words to substance in this novel: "The novel closes on word-act, not on mere words, on family, not on estrangement, on a giving of one person to another, not on a seeking for self" (259).

13. R. D. McMaster has noted this element of the novel: "Marie Melmotte, perhaps, provides the clearest example in the book of evolving identity, authenticity, and resistance to the way of the world" ("Women" 70). Marie's development in the second half of the novel goes on more offstage than before

the reader; thus, her commitment to choosing her own life in the first volume is studied in detail here.

14. John Hall reports that little can be concluded about the thematic importance of illustrations in this novel, as "we simply do not know how active a role [Trollope] played" with the illustration of *The Way We Live Now* (140). Hall also notes, however, that Trollope approved of illustrating his novels in general. He wrote to Mary Holmes during the serialization of *The Way We Live Now:* "I desire, of course, to put my books into as many hands as possible, and I take the best mode of doing so" (Hall 145).

15. Mrs. Hurtle evoked a divided, intense response from Victorians. The 28 August 1875 *Examiner* found that she "combines with a Southern ardour of passion and a Northern energy and force of will, a certain degree of feminine gentleness of nature" (971). The 26 June 1875 *Spectator,* however, found her "base," saying "the bright American . . . is really in love with Paul Montague, but admires big dishonesty" (825). The 17 July 1875 *Saturday Review* stated: "Mrs. Hurtle, the American beauty, who has killed her man, and divorced herself from her husband, has no doubt something to say for herself as to both acts, but her line altogether is at war with our prejudices" (88). The 24 August 1875 *Times* review, probably the most favorable to the novel, found "the episode of the pretty American widow . . . scarcely necessary to the construction of the story" (4).

16. Russell notes that Victorian authors in general "cannot entirely stifle their admiration" of great and powerful men (130). Edwards explains that Trollope originally planned for Melmotte's trial to be narrated, which would have extended the narrative of his fall but also resolved it more neatly for his audience ("Trollope" 91). Wall makes an interesting observation about authors that we would also apply to readers, that they come to like characters they intended on first meeting to dislike: "The acquaintance with Lady Carbury that writing the novel has deepened has nurtured a fellow-feeling [in Trollope] which inhibits censure" (46). The same kind of affection, according to Wall, grew in Trollope as he wrote about Melmotte. Gilmour identifies the dinner party as a point at which readers begin to reverse their feelings about Melmotte (194) and concludes: "Trollope and his reader become involved in the sympathetic understanding of those very outsiders who seem to offer the most dramatic threat to what one senses to be his own values" (200).

17. Gilmour identifies several financiers whose careers are recalled by Melmotte (193). Robert Lee Wolff provides a detailed account of the novel's historical background and its place in Western literary tradition.

18. Juliet McMaster has noted the importance of letters as "action" in Trollope (*Trollope* 29). Lady Carbury's reform (in Victorian terms) was frequently cited as one of the few clear signs of progress in the novel. Harvey is one of the more recent critics to see positive development in the novel, arguing that Marie "matures" (139), that Mrs. Hurtle becomes a "woman distinguished by her capacity to care" (140), and that Lady Carbury exhibits a "rare naturalness" (140) in loving her son. R. D. McMaster identifies another area where decline characterizes Trollope's world, the legal profession as represented by Mr. Squercum (*Trollope* 571).

19. Woolford, for instance, reminds us: "Victorian aesthetic theorists had, by the 1850s, arrived at the firm belief that popular acceptability formed a test not only of success but even of artistic *merit*" (114). Ikeler explains the differences between nineteenth-century and twentieth-century appraisals of this novel.

20. There is still some evidence that the novel was being read in parts, despite a shaky beginning. The 31 January 1874 *Saturday Review* carried an ad for the first installment indicating that it was "To be Completed in Twenty Monthly Parts." The 7 February 1874 *Academy* commented in a review of *Phineas Redux* (published in volume form in December 1873) that the first part of *The Way We Live Now* "is cruelly beset with claimants and plaintiffs of most seductive ingenuity" (143), suggesting that readers would be following this tale. John Sutherland argues that the novel "did not prosper as a monthly serial" but finds that "for Chatto, its principal owner over the years, *The Way We Live Now* was not a commercial disaster" ("Success" 467). R. H. Super concludes, however, that we cannot say whether the novel was a commercial success or failure. In "Trollope at Work on *The Way We Live Now*" Sutherland recreates, from detailed authorial notes, the stages of the novel's composition.

21. Cf. Florence Boos's assertion that through disillusionment the Wanderers master the virtues of "persistence, modesty, and self-abnegation" (*Design* 60). In "each of the work's three levels of narration [the lyrics, frame, and tales]," she discerns "a near-parallel emotional progress, from unresolved anxiety, to historical contemplation, identification, and acceptance" (*Design* 25).

    All citations of *The Earthly Paradise* are given by volume and page number.

22. A number of critics view the Wanderers' quest as an act of hubris, a desire to escape mortal limits. Yet the Wanderers live because they leave, and their quest "produces" the poem: "[their] bitter hope hath made this book" (3.434). See also Frederick Kirchhoff (*Morris* 60, "Aesthetic" 233), Amanda Hodgson (54), and Florence Boos (*Design* 39–60) for affirmative elements in the Wanderers' quest.

23. Blue Calhoun identifies Spenser's *Shepherd's Calendar* and that work's "suggested source, the old *Kalender of Shepherdes*," as precedents for associating the journey through time and narrative with the journey to death (68).

24. Cf. Frederick Kirchhoff: "all twelve stories told by the Wanderers are merely extensions of their own story: attempts to define narrative conventions through which the events of their own lives can be interpreted" ("Aesthetic" 234).

25. Blue Calhoun argues for an opposite effect, the emphatic closure of each tale with an enclosing frame: "The framework story itself, which provides meditative continuum, also serves to interrupt, arrest, and distance heroic motion [in the tales themselves]" (118–19). In the serial tradition, however, interruption and arresting of the narrative were most often associated with continuum, with, that is, an ongoing and ultimately coherent story.

26. Following was a list of tales to be included in the second volume. As with *The Dynasts* (to be discussed in chapter six), the planned table of contents published by the poet did not coincide with the actual contents of the completed work. The 1867 *Life and Death of Jason* had also included a proposed table of contents

of *The Earthly Paradise* among its endpapers. See May Morris, Introductions 3:xi–xii, for the *Earthly Paradise* table of contents appearing in *Jason* and the disparities between this list and the actual *Earthly Paradise* volumes.

27. Amanda Hodgson argues that since "there is no reason why the narrators should not start again on another twenty-four stories[,] There is no finality in the poem, no necessary end" (69).

28. Interestingly, the first popular edition of *The Earthly Paradise* was issued serially in ten monthly parts in 1872 (May Morris, Introductions 3:xxx).

29. E. P. Thompson argues that reviewers praised *The Earthly Paradise* because its perceived escapism effectively marginalized the poetry, divorcing it from any difficult questions about the status quo (144–45). Oscar Maurer, in contrast, asserts that the poem "was received with approval because it furnished escape of another and purely literary sort," particularly from "the obscurity of Browning" (257). As Maurer observes, the appearance of *The Earthly Paradise* and *The Ring and the Book* overlapped in 1868–69.

30. It was in this review that Pater first asserted, "To burn always with this hard gem-like flame, to maintain this ecstasy, is success in life" (91).

31. As Peter Faulkner records, the March 1870 *Christian Observer* also "noted the lack of religious feeling" in the poem but connected this to the time's prevalent " 'Epicurean indifference . . . which would fain make the most of the world, and over which the consciousness of a world to come does but cast a dark shadow and a chilling fear' " (*Against* 56).

32. Most scholars agree that the autumn tales are darker than those of the spring and summer, but opinion diverges on the final, winter tales, with some arguing for a further darkening of outlook, others for a recurrence of hope. Among the latter, Florence Boos argues that in the final winter tales "labor and endurance do achieve some good results" (*Design* 149).

33. Frederick Kirchhoff remarks of this tale, "For the first time in the stories, the hero fails to rescue the virgin. For the first time, too, the tragic implications of her state are fully realized" (*Morris* 71).

34. The book itself was identified with an earthly paradise, first by Walter Pater, who shrewdly based his assertion on the poem's very artificiality: "this new poetry . . . is literally an artificial or 'earthly paradise.' It is a finer ideal, extracted from what in relation to any actual world is already an ideal" (79–80). This was a point taken up by the October 1868 *Tinsley's Magazine:* "The book *is* an earthly paradise as far as a book can be; and it is not an enervating bower of Armida, as such a work might easily be, but a fine, wholesome, open-air atmosphere of pleasantry and enjoyment" (272).

35. As the May 1870 *Blackwood's Magazine* observed, "Rhodope must have been brought into this world somewhere in the eighteen-thirties, we should say, at the very earliest, and questions herself about herself as much as one of Miss Brontë's young ladies, or any of their free-spoken successors" (quoted in Maurer 264). May Morris similarly notes the modernity and restlessness of Rhodope (*Morris* 1:422).

36. Similar points are made by May Morris (*Morris* 1:411–12), E. P. Thompson (132), and Florence Boos (*Design* 121–29).

37. As Amanda Hodgson observes, Hercules "sees the world not as controlled by

a cyclical process of repetition but as progressing towards an ultimate end. This linear movement requires his heroism. . . . he stands for progress and change rather than the passivity which can lead to death-in-life" (77–78).

38. As Charlotte Oberg notes, "More than any other hero in *The Earthly Paradise,* Bellerophon is envisaged as a godlike figure and is identified with the sun as life principle" (45–46). His glory is emphasized since a third tale of Bellerophon is omitted ("no third tale there is, of what befell / His fated life, when he had won his place" [3:89]). Oberg comments that the suppressed third tale is the story of Bellerophon's attempt to scale Mount Olympus on Pegasus, which resulted in his blinding (46–47).

39. May Morris calls both "The Hill of Venus" and "The Man Who Never Laughed Again" "stories of wild, barren passion . . . built up in an atmosphere of such an unquenchable melancholy that if my Father had written little else of note, . . . you would say, Here is an inward-looking being with scarcely a hope in his life" (*Morris* 1:433). Yet she calls the pope's meditation and death in the garden at the tale's end a scene of "human tenderness and piety" (1:435), all the more significant because the pope's reconsideration and blessing of Walter were not in Morris's medieval sources (Introductions 6:xxvi).

40. G. W. Cox argued in the January 1871 *Edinburgh Review,* "as we read tale after tale, it would be vain to attribute to [Morris] the fixed design by which Mr. Tennyson has worked the several parts of the Arthurian story into one magnificent whole" (243). See Cruse 377 for another contemporary comparison of *The Earthly Paradise* and the *Idylls.*

41. At the same time, Colvin saw this very intensification of the poem as a problem, since he considered these more complicated stories less well-suited to the form Morris had adopted (15 December 1870 *Academy:* 57).

42. Mackail (2:148) and Thompson (414) discuss *Commonweal*'s circulation figures. Mackail also comments on the accessibility and appeal of *Pilgrims of Hope,* asserting that "this series of poems is perhaps the only contribution to the first year's issue of the *Commonweal* which appeals to a wide circle or has any permanent value as literature" (2:148). Indeed, Gardner notes that when three excerpts from *Pilgrims* appeared in *Poems by the Way* (1891), commentators often praised them, failing to recognize their Socialist underpinnings (93).

Citations of *Pilgrims of Hope* are by date and page number. *Commonweal* began as a monthly periodical, then switched to a weekly format. Month and year are given for parts of the poem appearing in monthly issues of *Commonweal,* but those parts of the poem appearing in weekly issues of the periodical are cited by day, month, and year.

43. A parenthetical note under the title of the second part, "The Bridge and the Street," identified what followed, "*(Being a continuation of 'The Message of the March Wind').*" A footnote announced, "It is the intention of the author to follow the fortunes of the lovers who in the 'Message of the March Wind' were already touched by sympathy with the cause of the people" (*Commonweal* April 1885: 20).

44. Similarly, there was a seven-month delay between Richard's announcing the fact of his wife's death in the eighth part (January 1886) and his final narration of the immediate cause of her death in the poem's last part (3 July 1886). Since

he stated in the eighth part that he could not yet talk about her death because of grief, this seven-month term of silence was an index of Richard's grief as well as a means of intensifying the mystery of her death.

45. Morris considered revising *Pilgrims* for separate publication. As May Morris records, her father asserted in a 29 October 1886 letter that " 'I am going to start getting my *Pilgrims of Hope* in order, so as to make a book of it: I shall add and alter a good deal though' " (May Morris, Introductions 19:xxxvii). For unknown reasons (several suggest lack of time) Morris abandoned this plan, and Buxton Forman reports, "I could not persuade its author to reprint it" (125).

46. Michael Holzman, who provides an installment-by-installment account of the relationship between *Pilgrims'* parts and articles in *Commonweal* (378–91), remarks that the poem, "like Morris's other serialized work in *Commonweal*, was firmly bound up with the news of the day, both literally—as it appeared in the columns of the newspaper—and in content, the literary work constantly referring to current events of agitational interest" (385).

47. Morris did print another series of Socialist poems in volume form, his *Chants of Socialism*, issued in 1885. The chants did not, however, form a continuing story over time, nor were they a capitalist commodity. According to Buxton Forman, Morris himself printed the volume, which included the *Commonweal* imprint and hence a Socialist context.

48. Cf. Morris's "Our Policy" in the March 1886 *Commonweal*: "Education towards Revolution seems to me to express in three words what our policy should be: towards that New Birth of Society which we know must come, and which, therefore, we must strive to help forward so that it may come with as little confusion and suffering as may be" (17).

49. See Isabel Murray 23–25 and Florence Boos's "Narrative" for other accounts of the poem's unity.

50. Five months after Morris published this sixth part of the poem in September 1885, Morris's "Notes" for the February 1886 *Commonweal* reported a parallel instance from real life: "a comrade at Oldham, a good workman and an earnest Socialist, has been dismissed from his employment on account of his principles, and is now out of work. His case is a hard one as he and his wife and children are in great distress" (12).

51. Unlike the Wanderers in *The Earthly Paradise*, then, Richard hastens to death. See Holzman 380 for another contrast between *The Earthly Paradise* and *Pilgrims of Hope*.

52. Boos notes that in his March 1887 essay in *Commonweal*, "Why We Celebrate the Commune of Paris," Morris also asserted the heroism and affirmation embodied in an episode that might seem merely tragic to others ("Narrative" 148).

53. Calder sees Victorian questioning of sexuality and marriage as a significant reason for *Diana's* success (43). Citations of *Diana of the Crossways* are to the pages of *Fortnightly* in the June, July, September, October, November, and December 1884 issues.

54. The editors of the *Wellesley Index* include *Fortnightly* in volume 2 because it meets their criteria as a "principal" journal: "of relatively high calibre in the

writing and editing, and of considerable reputation in educated circles" (2:xiii). Of the 1880s, they note: "Although many of Escott's literary and political articles were worthy of the *Fortnightly's* tradition, by and large the *Review* declined in quality and circulation" (2:179).

55. Other comments on Meredith's unusual style include the 25 February 1885 *Guardian:* his sentences "follow one another in such rapid and dazzling succession that the brain reels at the end of half-a-dozen chapters" (311); W. L. Courtney in the *Fortnightly Review* for June 1886: "Of all introductory chapters to an interesting novel, surely that which prefaces the history of *Diana of the Crossways* is the most irritating. It may be presumed that many a reader brought face to face with such a bristling rampart of phrases has sadly gone back and walked no more with an author of so appalling a cleverness" (773); the 1 June 1885 *Times:* Meredith could be called "the Carlyle of fiction, so rugged is his style, so uncouth his ellipses, so powerful the collocation of his words. Such a mannered style does not sit well on a novelist, especially in dialogue, where the speakers are made to appear uniformly *bizarre* of speech" (4); the 28 March 1885 *Pall Mall Gazette:* Meredith's "perverse" style keeps him "an unknown name to the 'reading public' " (4); F. V. Dickens in the 18 April 1885 *Spectator:* his are "epigrammatic sentences, phrases stuffed to bursting with meaning" (518); and C. Monkhouse in the 21 March 1885 *Saturday Review:* the book is "somewhat overcrowded" with [Diana's] "laboured 'sayings' " (389).

56. Muendel notes that the first chapter is "notoriously difficult" (101). Glock analyzes the style of this novel in detail, arguing that "Meredith's chief quality is stylistic; that the intellectual content of the novel may be found in the metaphoric action depicting, and at the same time paralleling, the main theme" (68).

57. Deis, for instance, notes that "Diana's slow, painful growth into a balanced, clear-sighted individual is emblematic of the gradual evolution of society" (19). Glock also accepts the notion of progress, citing Diana's "gradual increase of knowledge and experience in the social world, and her painfully slow growth of insight into the nature of reality" (71). And Beer sums up Meredith's complex presentation of development: "Meredith records the diffused eddying of feeling and action; he insists on the protracted growth of relationships; he eschews the heightened scene; he rejects novel conventions which tighten and simplify the deviousness of human feeling" (*Meredith* 164).

58. Later in the century, doubt about such Victorian certainties had turned nearly to despair, as we show in discussing Conrad's *Lord Jim* in chapter six.

59. The story, probably untrue, that Caroline Norton, while Melbourne's mistress, had disclosed plans to repeal the Corn Laws, was known to Meredith's audience. This knowledge might have forecast a mistake by Meredith's heroine, revealing a state secret, but hardly the reactions of Dacier and Diana herself presented in the last installment.

60. Deis makes a similar argument: "All of Meredith's novels argue (and often demonstrate in their tortured style and hectic structure) that bringing opposing elements together into a harmonious whole is a difficult, well-nigh impossible task" (17).

61. Janet Murray, whose book provides a detailed feminist reading of Diana as a victim of men (121–72), pays special attention to this entry into the world of male power, the city and the newspaper at night. Wilt has discussed some of Diana's failures to "read" her own character (*Readable* 71), which contribute to this final collapse.

62. Beer notes that Diana's relationship to Emma is "Meredith's most extensive fictitious addition to his source material," the career of Caroline Norton (*Meredith* 150). Thus, he clearly felt it a significant element of the work.

63. Stevenson discusses the novel's popularity, arguing that tastes in fiction were changing to Meredith's advantage in the 1880s. Such events as the establishment of women's colleges at Oxford and Cambridge, the Married Women's Property Act (1882), and near success in achieving female suffrage through the Reform Bill of 1884 encouraged a reexamination of the position of women in Victorian society (261). The popularity of *Diana* led to the reissue of nine volumes of Meredith's previous writings at monthly intervals in 1885, which "made his work available to many readers" (264).

64. Measures also notes that "marginal and interlinear inserts expand elements already in the manuscript to a much larger extent than they add new elements, or new tones" (111). She also reports that Escott claimed Meredith's popularity was " 'not fully established on a lasting basis until *Diana* completed its appearance in the *Fortnightly Review* during the years of his connection with that periodical' " (143n).

65. Lindsay is also unhappy with the volume edition's conclusion, "a conventional marriage," which he argues was "acceptable to the middle-class public" (268).

VI. Prefiguring an End to Progress

1. Related changes manifested themselves in a more radical women's literature (Showalter 28–29), in explorations of male sexual roles (Sedgwick 176), in challenges to the accepted conventions of realism (Levine, *Realistic* 49–53; Tanner, *Adultery* 52), and in the battle between those who saw art serving a social or moral purpose (Besant's 1884 *Art of Fiction*) and those (James's 1884 *Art of Fiction*) who argued for a literature responsible to its own inner dictates (Cross 218).

2. Martin Meisel sees the disappearance of illustration as a part of the decline in serialization: "Fiction turned, and not only in its monumental works, to the representation of inner landscapes [by the turn of the century]. Symptomatic of the change was the disappearance of pictorial collaboration. Pictures were now a nuisance, and the illustration of fiction was relegated to elegant editions of older work, magazine stories, and children's literature" (435).

3. For a discussion of these changes' relation to a transition in scientific ideas about order, see our "Linear Stories and Circular Visions: The Decline of the Victorian Serial."

4. Although the editor required changes in the manuscript, Hardy himself made the decisions about what was to be printed.

5. Wood notes that *Harper's* was in the 1890s "at the height of its excellence as a literary magazine" (75).

6. For a more detailed account of the writing and publication of *Hearts Insurgent,* see Mary Ellen Chase (115–77) and Ingham. Ingham argues that "Hardy in practice by no means chose to reject all the alterations that he made for the serial" (31). Lodge examines how "the form of *Jude* works to articulate and reinforce the pessimism of its vision of life. I use the word *form* in its widest sense to include . . . the design of the plot, the point of view of the narration, the tone of the narrator, symbolic action, figurative language, right down to the construction of the simplest sentences" (195). Lodge, however, never mentions the novel's installment structure. Patricia Alden's study suggests a short-story origin for *Jude* ("A Tragedy of Two Ambitions," 1888), a situation repeated with Conrad's *Lord Jim.*

7. The Preface is included in Norman Page's Norton Critical Edition of *Jude the Obscure.* References to *Hearts Insurgent* in this chapter are to the page numbers in the serial version in *Harper's Magazine;* references to *Jude the Obscure* are to the Norton Critical Edition.

   Casagrande points out that *Jude* is a special case in Hardy's work, featuring a protagonist trapped by "the deathward tendency in things" (210), and ought to be considered in conjunction with other works, particularly *Tess.* Benvenuto has argued that two modes of perception account for the novel's contradictory tone (33).

8. Feltes has shown how magazine editors more than authors often controlled the content of illustrations in these years and discusses in detail how such publication forces shaped Hardy's *Tess* (*Modes* 57–75). Hardy was, however, apparently unusually satisfied with William Hatherell's efforts in the case of *Hearts Insurgent* (see 10 November 1895 letter to Hatherell, quoted in Purdy and Millgate 94). Kramer has paid special attention to early scenes of the novel (141). Fischler explains how, though Jude appears to be moving up in the world in this installment, there are also hints that he is trapped in his place.

9. Contemporary novelist Anne Tyler, for instance, found the publication industry's desire for short stories acting on her novel *Breathing Lessons* (1988). The novel's second chapter appeared in the 4 July 1988 *New Yorker* under the title of "Rerun" without reference to the complete work, which had not yet been published. Tyler responded to our inquiry: "it was the *New Yorker* that thought of making the piece stand alone—I was doubtful it would work, since that scene was just part of a much larger picture in my head." She allowed the story to appear, however, "since it didn't violate any particular principles of mine." Tyler resembles many Victorian novelists in growing fond of her characters and in wanting to know their complete stories: "what makes a book come to an end, for me, is the feeling that I've brought my characters to a point where I can feel fairly sure of their destinies from there on out. So I have nothing more to say about them, even though I may miss them personally."

10. Mary Ellen Chase notes that the only change of plot in this installment from serial to book involved Hardy's having Jude write to five scholars at Christminster, rather than one. She terms this an "interesting, though perhaps not particularly significant change in the serial version" (141). Of the overall composition of the novel, Ingham says: "the evolution of *Jude the Obscure* is not linear: from the beginning it had an obsessive core to which other elements were attracted and by which they were transmuted" (169).

Guerard explains that the "fury aroused by *Jude the Obscure* was the fury of outraged optimism, not of outraged prudery" (*Hardy* 37). Thus, Hardy's sexuality, the major object of editorial restraint, is a minor affront to Victorian ideology compared to the contradiction of larger cultural assumptions embodied in his serial text. Knoepflmacher says that Hardy broke with a long tradition of author-audience relationship: "For all their pessimism, the earlier Victorian novelists refused to make negation the essence of their work. To resist despair became for them not only a deep personal need but also a kind of public task that was sure to be sanctioned by their readers" (*Laughter* 203).

11. The similarities between Sue and Jude have been discussed by many critics, Barry Schwartz, for instance, noting: "She is frigid, she is lonely, she is also obscure, and Jude is an extension of her" (803).

12. The *Saturday Review* also frequently mentioned *Harper's,* but commented specifically (13 July 1895) only on the July number, in which Father Time appears: "Mr. Thomas Hardy contributes four chapters of his 'Hearts Insurgent' " (56). The *Illustrated London News* also discontinued specific reference to *Hearts Insurgent* after December 1894.

13. References to *Lord Jim: A Sketch* are to pages of the serial version published in *Blackwood's Magazine,* October 1899 to November 1900.

14. Conrad wrote to William Blackwood on 14 February 1899 that he had "a story *Jim* half-written or one-third written (10,000 words)" (Karl and Davies 166).

15. Watt says that in the novel since Flaubert there is "a tendency towards what may be called the method of the scenic present, towards a narrative form which makes the novel progress as much as possible through a succession of compositional units" (286–87). Although he does not equate these "compositional units" with serial publication, Watt does point out that this technique is related to larger cultural ideas: "in their different ways Darwin, Marx, and Freud all suggested that the individual life must be understood in the context of a process of chronological development—biological, economic, or psychic" (288–89). Guerard studies the reader's paragraph-by-paragraph experience of *Lord Jim* (*Conrad* 136–39).

16. Eloise Knapp Hay argues, "Knowing how Conrad worked in his first two novels and the unfinished *Rescue,* which must have been outlined in his mind at the time, we could safely predict that 'Tuan Jim' already foreshadows that Jim's fatal flaw will be active to the end of the story" (18). Conrad wrote to William Blackwood on 18 July 1900, after he had finished *Lord Jim,* that the novel consists of "the development of *one* situation, only *one* really from beginning to end" (Karl and Davies 282). He also wrote a month later to Blackwood on 22 August 1899: "I devote myself exclusively to *Jim.* I find I can't live with more than one story at a time. It's a kind of literary monogamism" (Karl and Davies 194).

17. C. B. Cox has noted of the narrative in general: "Marlow is not sure in what genre he is composing his story" (21).

18. The 6 February 1901 *Guardian* admitted the novel's difficult style ("A large part of the book consists of a narrative in inverted commas" [189]) but also praised its "force and colour and spirit" (189). The 14 November 1900 *Sketch* complained: "It is a short character-sketch, written and re-written to infinity,

dissected into shreds, masticated into tastelessness" (quoted in Sherry 118). And the 5 December 1900 *Pall Mall Gazette* called the novel "over-elaborated" (4), "a very broken-backed narrative" (5). *Bookman* in February 1901 said: "The book is all Jim—there is nothing else in it that counts" (161). Modern criticism has sustained this opinion. Baines, for instance, notes: "Every character and every incident is subordinated to and intended to develop this theme [guilt and atonement]" (35).

19. Raval concludes: "The narrative of *Lord Jim* therefore pulls and strains in ways that reveal contradictions as conjunctions, success as failure, and ideals as perversion" (391). See also Teets's poststructuralist reading of the novel.

20. Conrad frequently spoke of the novel's weaknesses, but Watt observes that the " 'massacre' of Conrad's 'good intentions' seems to have had no connection with the conditions of serial publication" (262).

21. The 14 December 1900 *Daily News* also noted that the book "has recently run through many pages of 'Blackwood's Magazine' " (6d).

22. The *Queen* reviewer of 3 November 1900 went on to say that the rest of the novel "drags": "The paragraphs, for one thing, are far too long. They sometimes wander on for pages. The book wanders on in the same way" (704). The *Pall Mall Gazette* also noted on 5 December 1900 that "the various fragments of narrative do not hold the interest, or rather pass it on from point to point" (84). Conrad might well have anticipated his loss of readers when in the October 1900 part he posited that only one of Marlow's listeners "showed an interest in [Jim] that survived the telling of his story" (548).

23. Although we examine in detail only the April 1900 part of the novel, many other installments of *Lord Jim: A Sketch* are self-sufficient. The fourth part (January 1900), which ended with Jim in the water, "the ship he had deserted uprising above him" (73), had begun with his standing "stock-still by the hatch expecting every moment to feel the ship dip under his feet" (60). The three chapters of this number established all pertinent information (the existence of the pilgrims, the crew, Marlow and his audience) and traced events in fairly clear chronological sequence. Number 9 (June 1900) also stood on its own, beginning, " 'I don't suppose any of you had ever heard of Patusan?' Marlow resumed, after a silence occupied in the careful lighting of a cigar" (803) and ending, "He [the master of the brigantine taking Jim to Patusan], too, raised his arm as if for a downward thrust. Absit omen!" (817).

24. For four months readers of *Blackwood's* had, like Jim, anticipated the possibility of the *Patna*'s sinking. Particularly through the April 1900 installment the text encouraged readers to imagine the bulkhead collapsing and the ship going down in a whirlpool. But Conrad's masterful conclusion of the number, his cliff-hanger, depicted Jim going down "an everlasting deep hole" when he jumps and the ship floating up above him: Jim "saw vaguely the ship he had deserted uprising above him" (73). The reversed position of ship and sailor is both a skilled use of the Victorian serial mode and an example of modern irony.

25. Tanner ("Butterflies") explains how this same character implicates Marlow in spontaneous involuntary action when in the November 1899 installment he asks him to look under his bed for "Millions of pink toads" (655). Marlow's response is very nearly a leap.

26. Fleishman has discussed Jim's success in the Patusan narrative (*Conrad's* 106–11). Davidson argues that Jim does not finally succeed in Patusan.

27. As Najder notes, Conrad himself was much troubled by events in South Africa as he wrote *Lord Jim: A Sketch* (261). Gillon discusses how Conrad's feelings about his native Poland affected his writing about England and the empire (96–98).

28. Tennebaum has discussed the romantic theme of the novel, arguing that Jewel is Stein's illegitimate daughter, though neither she nor Jim knows this fact.

29. C. B. Cox stresses the importance of this scene on the verandah (30).

30. Roussel argues that Conrad's stories are often about an author's creative challenges. Seidel has discussed the characters of Robinson and Chester and the scene in which Marlow writes (83).

31. Conrad's audience also felt a need for affirmation. The 24 November 1900 *Spectator* listed as Jim's great achievement the fact that "he wins the devoted love of the only white woman in Patusan, the stepdaughter of a Portuguese half-caste" (753). Jim's desire to remain true to a code of conduct was another convention readers clung to in this novel, as suggested by the same review: "throughout all his long exile [Jim] never loses touch with the sentiment, the ideals, the essential *ethos,* of his race" (753).

32. Conrad himself was not pleased with the form of this particular installment, writing to David Meldrum on 3 April 1900: "I've been horribly disappointed by the shortness of the inst[allmen]t in the Ap[ril]. No the more so that the break just there destroyed an effect. If one only could do without serial publication!" (Karl and Davies 260).

33. We explain in "Linear Stories and Circular Visions" that in installment 11 (August 1900) Conrad's text challenged not only these values but also the established convention of narrative itself. His circling, repetitive style flirted with negating one of the most basic principles of storytelling, that more narration will ensure greater understanding.

34. An end to one strain in that scholarship might be J. Hillis Miller's assertion in *Fiction and Repetition* that because Marlow cannot conclude his narrative with a final definitive explanation, the work itself cannot have a determinate meaning (39). Saldivar pursues a similar argument about Hardy's *Jude the Obscure.* While such assertions are possible when we read texts as static wholes, the original serial reading of *Lord Jim: A Sketch* (and *Hearts Insurgent*) adds a temporal frame of reference to the novel's meaning, revealing that there is value in the process of Marlow's sustained questioning.

   Daniel Schwarz suggests what criticism has neglected in studying *Lord Jim:* "The criticism of fiction has tended to be more comfortable with address-ing the completed 'event,' as if a novel could be perceived in its totality like a painting or sculpture. But fiction is the most linear of art forms and exists for the reader primarily within the duration required to complete the act of reading. . . . It is not enough to discuss a novel in its moment of stability after its ending has apocalyptically clarified every preceding detail with proleptic (and prophetic) meaning" (76).

35. Citations of *The Dynasts* are by volume and page number. Thus, "1:6" indicates a citation from page 6 of volume 1, published in 1904.

36. The negative reaction noted by Hardy and numerous scholars was not perva-

sive. Even *TLS,* while flatly stating its disappointment in the form Hardy used for his subject, asserted, "For the present, judgment must be reserved" and expressed some hope for future parts: "it may be that the publication of the second and third parts will knit up what now is scattered and piecemeal, and display an artistic whole which at present can only be guessed at" (15 January 1904: 11, 12). The cold response of *TLS,* moreover, was not generally shared by the less prestigious daily papers. When part 2 was published in 1906 several excerpts from dailies' reviews of part 1 were printed at the end of the volume. Hardy was much more pleased with the reception of part 2 (F. Hardy, *Later* 117).

37. Child (so identified by R. G. Cox) in the 27 February 1908 *TLS* had also noted the simultaneous assertion and contesting of the individual's importance: "After reading the first part of the drama we hazarded a guess that the complete work would prove to be a drama, not of men, but of nations. The guess was at once too wide and too narrow. *The Dynasts* is a drama not of nations only, but of human life; it is also a drama of individual persons. . . . Each and all are the puppets of the blind, senseless, Immanent Will. . . . [but] each one contributes his share without knowing it; and each one, therefore, by a strange perversion, as it might seem, wins dignity and being, not their opposites" (65).

38. As Henry Newbolt commented in the March 1904 *Monthly Review,* "the scene of Nelson's death, though given with many details of studied accuracy, is enriched by passages of great poetical beauty, unlike anything in the authentic prose narratives of the time. Hardy, in whom we cannot help seeing a sympathetic reflection of his namesake's mind, stands by Nelson's side in the cockpit, and for a moment, like the dying Blake, dreams of the West Country" (4).

39. C. Lewis Hind in the 12 February 1906 *Daily Chronicle* thought this the "most imaginative" scene of part 2, though part of the reason for Hind's enthusiasm was that "In the talk of the deserters, as elsewhere in the volume, we have welcome gleams of the novelist Hardy" (3d).

40. It is, of course, too simple to say that the close-ups promote community while the panoramic sweeps undermine it. If aerial perspectives, which make whole armies look like molluscs on a leaf, banish human beings as meaningful elements in the landscape or cosmos, they also promote the global perspectives (more familiar to twentieth-century than Victorian readers) that suggest the idiocy of warfare among kindred peoples who share the same planet, as when French and English soldiers, exhausted after fighting at Talavera, are forced by thirst to share water from the same river (2:173). See also F. Hardy, *Early* 294 and *Later* 174, 227; Wickens 104–5.

41. In perhaps the single funniest reaction to *The Dynasts,* Max Beerbohm indicated in the 30 January 1904 *Saturday Review* how the two perspectives might occasionally jostle:

> It is easy to smile at sight of all these great historic figures reduced to the size of marionettes. I confess that I, reading here the scene of the death of Nelson, was irresistibly reminded of the same scene as erst beheld by me, at Brighton, through the eyelet of a peep-show, whose proprietor strove to make it more realistic for me by saying in a confidential tone " 'Ardy,

'Ardy, I am wounded, 'Ardy.—Not mortially, I 'ope, my lord?—Mortially, I fear, 'Ardy." The dialogue here is of a different and much worthier kind; yet the figures seem hardly less tiny and unreal. How could they be life-sized and alive, wedged into so small a compass between so remote and diverse scenes? Throughout this play the only characters who stand to human height, drawing the breath of life, are the Wessex peasants. . . . For my own part, I wish these Wessex peasants had been kept out of "The Dynasts." They mar the unity of an effect which is, in the circumstances, partially correct. (137)

42. The 23 January 1904 *Athenaeum* in fact complained that Hardy "foregoes . . . all feminine interest and influence—at least so far as the present portion is concerned, though such may, perhaps, be obtained when in a subsequent instalment he has to depict the unparalleled sorrows of Queen Louisa" (123).

43. This detail derives from Hardy's memory of the story surrounding his own birth; see F. Hardy, *Early* 18.

44. To the degree, however, that part 2's focus on the family raised expectations of further domestic portraiture in the succeeding part, expectations quashed in 1908, the drama's serial format would have reinforced the cosmic irony of human expectations coming to naught. Perhaps this disappointment lay behind the *Guardian*'s comment that "the third portion of Mr. Hardy's dramatic poem lacks to some extent the intensity of interest centred in those which preceded it" (425).

45. Kern remarks on the cinema's role in undermining linear notions of time, since film could be played backward as well as forward (29–30).

46. See our "Linear Stories" for a fuller discussion of this argument. Susan Dean points out that Hardy's careful use of words such as "like," "perchance," etc., in descriptions of the Immanent Will indicates that the image of a brain is presented as a model, not the substance. As Hayles notes (21), field models are always carefully distinguished as models, as conceptualizations of reality rather than its embodiment. See also J. Hillis Miller, *Linguistic* 310–11 and *Hardy* xi.

47. At Austerlitz in part 1, the presence of the Immanent Will within and behind all is described thus: "a preternatural clearness possesses the atmosphere of the battle-field, in which the scene becomes anatomized and the living masses of humanity transparent. The controlling Immanent Will appears therein, as a brain-like network of currents and ejections, twitching, interpenetrating, entangling, and thrusting hither and thither the human forms" (1.197). As Dean comments, at Leipzig the dumb show embodies "what in this poem lives are at their base—temporarily charged bits of matter" (81).

48. Dean also sees a progression in the way the Immanent Will—as—brain is imaged and perceived as the drama moves forward (50–55).

49. Hardy approved of Newbolt's review and later stated that the meliorism expressed in the drama's final lines was partly influenced by Newbolt's commentary (see Walter F. Wright 119, 121). Chakravarty also notes the elevation of Nelson as representative of a "saner order" (57).

50. One effect of this patterning is to further identify Napoleon with the Immanent Will in part 2. Here Napoleon's desires and the Will's designs are con-

gruent, and Napoleon subsumes the Will's traits unto himself. For further discussion of Napoleon as analogue of the Will, see Bailey 187–88, 212–13. Bailey also notes that the Will is not visually present in part 2 and seems puzzled by the omission (97).

51. Harold Orel is one of the few to discuss the effects of individual parts (*Hardy* 56–61). He finds the "artistic unity" of part 2 least satisfactory because Napoleon "is involved in too many schemes" (*Hardy* 58). For a different opinion of part 2, see Howarth 102.

52. So successful was Hardy's blend of poetry, historical realism, and epic scope, in fact, that the 23 March 1906 *Daily News* reported that "the epic is becoming a fashion. I have not read the first instalment of Mr. Alfred Noyes' epic poem, which appears in 'Blackwood's Magazine,' but I hear that in twelve monthly parts, which will afterwards become three volumes, this competent poet is to set forth the exploits of 'Drake' and the English Navy of his time. This is a second instance in which the poet, once accustomed to rejoice in legend, now finds his theme in the accurate facts of modern history" (4). Noyes's work, however, failed to kindle the response enjoyed by *The Dynasts*, and the serialization of *Drake: An Epic* was suspended after the first three parts had appeared, though the poem was eventually completed and published in its entirety in 1908.

53. Trevelyan's entire review is testimony to the staying power of Whig notions of history popularized by Trevelyan's great uncle, Macaulay: "there is another element in the period, well fitted for poetic treatment, which Mr. Hardy has omitted. He detects no subterranean growth towards better things, in the Napoleonic epoch—he sees only cosmopolitan massacre, organised apparently for no end save the ambitions of little 'Dynasts' . . . but really at the haphazard dictate of the 'Immannet [*sic*] Will.' . . . the history of the Napoleonic period did really mean something for poor humanity. . . . It broke up the *ancien régime*. . . . It founded the German and Italian nations. It made room for the new industrial world to grow, by sweeping away the feudal and clerical. . . . we cannot expect Mr. Hardy to adopt an optimistic philosophy, but he might see that historically the Napoleonic period did *happen* (let us say) to mean something for the descendants of the wretched millions which it slew" (577). Trevelyan's framework of progressive history also disposed him to proclaim that "Nelson (or rather in this second part Nelson's invisible, ubiquitous ghost) is the real hero of Mr. Hardy's Napoleonic drama" (578).

54. Hind's comments remind us that serialization would have created a handling of Pitt's and Fox's deaths different from that associated with single-volume reading. While Fox's reign is much shorter than Pitt's in either publication format, the spacing of their deaths is different. In single-volume reading Pitt's death is succeeded almost instantly by Fox's. In serial reading, which provided a two-year pause between Pitt's death and readers' first sight of Fox, the sequencing is less catastrophic, more gradual.

55. To the degree that England was "demoted" to the level of other nations in part 3, controlled like them by the Immanent Will rather than by a special destiny, those who hoped to read the play as a testament to the nation's greatness would have been disappointed in 1908. Serialization could have intensified readers'

disappointment, since a four-year habituation to the heroic treatment of England would have made a shift in perspective more startling and difficult.

56. The 21 March 1908 *Spectator* also revealed a changing and developing course of judgment: "We congratulate Mr. Hardy on the completion of what, with all its strangeness and imperfections, is a very remarkable poem. Four years ago, when the first part appeared, we stated very frankly the objections on the score of art both to the form Mr. Hardy had chosen and to his method of treatment. . . . To many of these criticisms, especially those on the score of form, we adhere; but the subsequent volumes have led us to revise our judgment on one important point. We wrote in 1904 that Mr. Hardy's reach seemed to exceed his grasp. After laying down the last volume we admit that we were wrong" (462–63).

57. Interestingly, Hardy alludes to Camelot in his note discussing the mysterious location of the Brussels ball on the eve of Waterloo (3.231).

58. F. R. Southerington offers another instance of growth, cogently arguing that the varied nations' increasing ability to cooperate—a trait needed if the Will is ever to become conscious—is directly related to Napoleon's pattern of decline. In this argument Southerington also offers a model whereby individual parts merge gradually into a larger whole, which then has a positive effect. See 187–88, 203.

59. Barton Friedman suggests that Hardy's breaking the pattern of six acts in earlier parts invests the seventh, "Waterloo" act here with apocalyptic overtones; hence the Waterloo material cannot be absorbed into preexisting patterns. Friedman further suggests that Shelley's fourth act in *Prometheus Unbound* served as a model for this structural device (119).

Bibliography

Adrian, Arthur A. *Dickens and the Parent-Child Relationship*. Athens: Ohio Univ. Press, 1984.

Alden, Patricia. "A Short Story Prelude to *Jude the Obscure:* More Light on the Genesis of Hardy's Last Novel." *Colby Library Quarterly* 19 (1983): 45–52.

Alley, Henry. "New Year's at the Abbey: Point of View in the Pivotal Chapters of *Daniel Deronda.*" *Journal of Narrative Technique* 9 (1979): 147–59.

Allingham, William. *A Diary,* edited by Helen Allingham and D. Radford. London: Macmillan, 1907.

Altick, Richard D. *The English Common Reader: A Social History of the Mass Reading Public, 1800–1900*. Chicago: Univ. of Chicago Press, 1957.

———. "Varieties of Readers' Response: The Case of *Dombey and Son.*" *Yearbook of English Studies* 10 (1980): 70–94.

———. *Victorian People and Ideas*. New York: W. W. Norton, 1973.

———, and James F. Loucks II. *Browning's Roman Murder Story: A Reading of "The Ring and the Book."* Chicago: Univ. of Chicago Press, 1968.

Alvarez, A. "Jude the Obscure." In *Hardy: A Collection of Critical Essays,* edited by Albert J. Guerard. Englewood Cliffs, N.J.: Prentice-Hall, 1963. Pp. 113–22.

apRoberts, Ruth. *The Moral Trollope*. Athens: Ohio Univ. Press, 1971.

Arnold, Thomas. *Christian Life, Its Course, Its Hindrances, and Its Helps: Sermons, Preached Mostly in the Chapel of Rugby School*. 4th ed. London: B. Fellowes, 1845.

Ashton, Rosemary. *George Eliot*. Oxford: Oxford Univ. Press, 1983.

Auerbach, Nina. "Dickens and Dombey: A Daughter After All." *Dickens Studies Annual* 5 (1976): 95–114.

Bailey, J. O. *Thomas Hardy and the Cosmic Mind: A New Reading of The Dynasts*. Chapel Hill: Univ. of North Carolina Press, 1956.

Baines, Jocelyn. "Guilt and Atonement in *Lord Jim.*" In *Twentieth Century Interpretations of Lord Jim,* edited by Robert E. Kuehn. Englewood Cliffs, N.J.: Prentice-Hall, 1969. Pp. 35–45.

Ball, Patricia M. *The Heart's Events: The Victorian Poetry of Relationships*. London: Univ. of London, Athlone Press, 1976.

Banks, J. A. "The Way They Lived Then: Anthony Trollope and the 1870's." *Victorian Studies* 12 (1968): 177–200.

Baumgarten, Murray. "Writing the Revolution." *Dickens Studies Annual* 12 (1983): 161–76.

Beer, Gillian. *Darwin's Plots: Evolutionary Narrative in Darwin, George Eliot, and Nineteenth-Century Fiction*. London: Routledge & Kegan Paul, 1983.

———. *Meredith: A Change of Masks*. London: Univ. of London, Athlone Press, 1970.

Benvenuto, Richard. "Modes of Perception: The Will to Live in *Jude the Obscure.*" *Studies in the Novel* (North Texas State Univ.) 2 (1970): 31–41.

Bonaparte, Felicia. *The Triptych and the Cross: The Central Myths of George Eliot's Imagination.* New York: New York Univ. Press, 1979.

Boone, Joseph A. *Tradition Counter Tradition: Love and the Form of Fiction.* Chicago and London: Univ. of Chicago Press, 1987.

———. "Wedlock as Deadlock and Beyond: Closure and the Victorian Marriage Ideal." *Mosaic* 17 (Winter 1984): 65–81.

Boos, Florence S. *The Design of William Morris' The Earthly Paradise.* Lewiston, N.Y.: Edwin Mellen Press, 1990.

———. "Narrative Design in *The Pilgrims of Hope.*" In *Socialism and the Literary Artistry of William Morris,* edited by Florence S. Boos and Carole G. Silver. Columbia: Univ. of Missouri Press, 1990. Pp. 147–66.

Bradbury, Malcolm, and David Palmer. Preface. *Victorian Poetry,* edited by Malcolm Bradbury and David Palmer. Stratford-upon-Avon Studies, no. 15. London: Edward Arnold, 1972.

Brooks, Peter. *Reading for the Plot: Design and Intention in Narrative.* New York: Vintage Books, 1984.

Brown, James M. *Dickens: Novelist in the Market-Place.* Totowa, N.J.: Barnes & Noble, 1982.

Browning, Robert. *The Ring and the Book.* 4 vols. London: Smith, Elder & Co., 1868–69.

———, and Julia Wedgwood. *Robert Browning and Julia Wedgwood: A Broken Friendship as Revealed by Their Letters,* edited by Richard Curle. New York: Frederick A. Stokes, 1937.

Buckler, William E. *Man and His Myths: Tennyson's Idylls of the King in Critical Context.* New York and London: New York Univ. Press, 1984.

———. *Poetry and Truth in Robert Browning's The Ring and the Book.* New York and London: New York Univ. Press, 1985.

———. "Thomas Hardy's 'chronicle-piece' in 'play-shape': An Essay in Literary Conceptualization." *Victorian Poetry* 18 (1980): 209–27.

Buckley, Jerome H. *The Triumph of Time: A Study of the Victorian Concepts of Time, History, Progress, and Decadence.* Cambridge: Harvard Univ. Press, 1966.

Burdett, Osbert. *The Idea of Coventry Patmore.* London: Oxford Univ. Press, 1921.

Butte, George. "Trollope's Duke of Omnium and 'The Pain of History': A Study of the Novel's Poetics." *Victorian Studies* 24 (1981): 209–27.

Calder, Jenni. "Cash and the Sex Nexus." *Tennessee Studies in Literature* 27 (1984): 40–53.

Calhoun, Blue. *The Pastoral Vision of William Morris: The Earthly Paradise.* Athens: Univ. of Georgia Press, 1975.

Carlisle, Janice. *The Sense of an Audience: Dickens, Thackeray, and George Eliot at Mid-Century.* Athens: Univ. of Georgia Press, 1981.

Carlyle, Thomas. "On History." *Fraser's Magazine,* 1830. Rpt. in *Critical and Miscellaneous Essays.* Vol. 2. Centenary Edition. New York: Charles Scribner's Sons, 1899. Pp. 83–95.

Carpenter, Mary Wilson. *George Eliot and the Landscape of Time: Narrative Form and Protestant Apocalyptic History.* Chapel Hill: Univ. of North Carolina Press, 1986.

Carr, David. *Time, Narrative, and History*. Bloomington: Indiana Univ. Press, 1986.

Carroll, David, ed. *George Eliot: The Critical Heritage*. London: Routledge & Kegan Paul, 1971.

Casagrande, Peter J. *Unity in Hardy's Novels*. Lawrence: Regents Press of Kansas, 1982.

Chakravarty, Amiya. *The Dynasts and the Post-War Age in Poetry: A Study in Modern Ideas*. 1938. Rpt., New York: Octagon Books, 1970.

Champneys, Basil. *Memoirs and Correspondence of Coventry Patmore*. 2 vols. London: George Bell & Sons, 1900.

Chapple, J. A. V. *Science and Literature in the Nineteenth Century*. Houndsmill, Basingstoke, Hampshire, and London: Macmillan Education, 1986.

Chase, Cynthia. "The Decomposition of the Elephants: Double-Reading *Daniel Deronda*." *PMLA* 93 (1978): 215–27.

Chase, Mary Ellen. *Thomas Hardy from Serial to Novel*. Minneapolis: Univ. of Minnesota Press, 1927.

Chell, Samuel L. *The Dynamic Self: Browning's Poetry of Duration*. English Literary Studies, no. 32. Victoria, B.C.: Univ. of Victoria, 1984.

Christ, Carol T. *Victorian and Modern Poetics*. Chicago: Univ. of Chicago Press, 1984.

———. "Victorian Masculinity and the Angel in the House." In *A Widening Sphere: Changing Roles of Victorian Women*, edited by Martha Vicinus. Bloomington: Indiana Univ. Press, 1977. Pp. 146–62.

Colby, Robert. *Thackeray's Canvass of Humanity: An Author and His Public*. Columbus: Ohio State Univ. Press, 1979.

Colby, Vineta. *Yesterday's Woman: Domestic Realism in the English Novel*. Princeton: Princeton Univ. Press, 1974.

Collins, Philip. "Tennyson In and Out of Time." In *Studies in Tennyson*, edited by Hallam Tennyson. Totowa, N.J.: Barnes & Noble, 1981. Pp. 131–54.

———, ed. *Dickens: The Critical Heritage*. London: Routledge & Kegan Paul, 1971.

Connor, Steven. *Charles Dickens*. New York: Basil Blackwell, 1985.

Conrad, Joseph. *Lord Jim: A Sketch*. London: *Blackwood's Magazine*, 1899–1900.

Cox, C. B. *Joseph Conrad: The Modern Imagination*. London: J. M. Dent, 1974.

Cox, R. G., ed. *Thomas Hardy: The Critical Heritage*. London: Routledge & Kegan Paul, 1970.

Cross, Nigel. *The Common Writer: Life in Nineteenth-Century Grub Street*. Cambridge: Cambridge Univ. Press, 1985.

Crowell, Norton B. *The Convex Glass: The Mind of Robert Browning*. Albuquerque: Univ. of New Mexico Press, 1968.

Cruse, Amy. *The Victorians and Their Reading*. 1935. Rpt., Boston: Houghton Mifflin, 1962.

Culler, A. Dwight. *The Victorian Mirror of History*. New Haven: Yale Univ. Press, 1985.

Dale, Peter Allan. *The Victorian Critic and the Idea of History: Carlyle, Arnold, Pater*. Cambridge: Harvard Univ. Press, 1977.

Daleski, H. M. *Dickens and the Art of Analogy*. New York: Schocken Books, 1970.

Davidson, Arnold E. *Conrad's Endings: A Study of the Five Major Novels*. Ann Arbor, Mi.: UMI Research Press, 1984.

Dean, Susan. *Hardy's Poetic Vision in The Dynasts: The Diorama of a Dream.* Princeton: Princeton Univ. Press, 1977.

Deis, Elizabeth J. "Marriage as Crossways: George Meredith's Victorian-Modern Compromise." In *Portraits of Marriage in Literature,* edited by Ann C. Hargrove and Maurine Magliocco. Macomb, Ill.: Essays in Literature, 1984. Pp. 13–30.

DeVane, William Clyde. *A Browning Handbook.* 2d ed. New York: Appleton-Century-Crofts, 1955.

Dickens, Charles. *Dombey and Son.* London: Bradbury and Evans, 1846–48.

———. *A Tale of Two Cities.* London: *All the Year Round,* 30 April–26 November 1859.

Donoghue, Denis. "The English Dickens and *Dombey and Son.*" *Dickens Centennial Essays,* edited by Ada Nisbet and Blake Nevius. Berkeley: Univ. of California Press, 1971. Pp. 1–21.

Dyson, A. E. *The Inimitable Dickens.* London: Macmillan, 1970.

Edwards, P. D. *Anthony Trollope: His Art and Scope.* New York: St. Martin's Press, 1977.

———. "Trollope Changes His Mind: The Death of Melmotte in *The Way We Live Now.*" *Nineteenth-Century Fiction* 18 (1963): 89–91.

Eigner, Edwin M. "Charles Darnay and Revolutionary Identity." *Dickens Studies Annual* 12 (1983): 147–59.

Eliot, George. *Daniel Deronda.* London: Blackwood, 1876.

———. Letter to Mrs. Harriet Beecher Stowe, 29 October 1876. Rpt. in *George Eliot and Her Readers: A Selection of Contemporary Reviews,* edited by John Holmstrom and Laurence Lerner. New York: Barnes & Noble, 1966. Pp. 155–56.

———. *Romola.* London: *Cornhill Magazine,* 1862–63.

Ermarth, Elizabeth Deeds. *George Eliot.* Boston: Twayne, 1985.

Faulkner, Peter. *Against the Age: An Introduction to William Morris.* London: George Allen & Unwin, 1980.

———, ed. *William Morris: The Critical Heritage.* London and Boston: Routledge & Kegan Paul, 1973.

Feltes, Norman N. *Modes of Production of Victorian Novels.* Chicago: Univ. of Chicago Press, 1986.

———. "Realism, Concensus and 'exclusion itself': Interpellating the Victorian Bourgeoisie." *Textual Practice* 1, no. 3 (Winter 1987): 297–308.

Ferris, Ina. *William Makepeace Thackeray.* Boston: Twayne, 1983.

Fischler, Alexander. "Gin and Spirits: The Letter's Edge in Hardy's *Jude the Obscure.*" *Studies in the Novel* (North Texas State Univ.) 16 (1984): 1–19.

Fleishman, Avrom. *Conrad's Politics: Community and Anarchy in the Fiction of Joseph Conrad.* Baltimore: Johns Hopkins Univ. Press, 1967.

———. *The English Historical Novel: Walter Scott to Virginia Woolf.* Baltimore: Johns Hopkins Univ. Press, 1971.

Ford, George H. *Dickens and His Readers: Aspects of Novel-Criticism since 1836.* Princeton: Princeton Univ. Press, 1955.

Forman, H. Buxton. *The Books of William Morris.* 1897. Rpt., New York: Burt Franklin, 1969.

Frank, Lawrence. *Charles Dickens and the Romantic Self.* Lincoln: Univ. of Nebraska Press, 1984.

Friedman, Barton R. "Proving Nothing: History and Dramatic Strategy in *The Dynasts.*" *CLIO* 13 (1984): 101–22.

Fulweiler, Howard W. "Tennyson's 'The Holy Grail': The Representation of Representation." *Renascence* 38 (1986): 144–59.

Gallagher, Catherine. "The Duplicity of Doubling in *A Tale of Two Cities.*" *Dickens Studies Annual* 12 (1983): 125–45.

———. "George Eliot and *Daniel Deronda:* The Prostitute and the Jewish Question." In *Sex, Politics, and Science in the Nineteenth-Century Novel,* edited by Ruth Bernard Yeazell. Baltimore: Johns Hopkins Univ. Press, 1986. Pp. 39–62.

———. *The Industrial Reformation of English Fiction, 1832–1867.* Chicago: Univ. of Chicago Press, 1985.

Gardner, Delbert R. *An "Idle Singer" and His Audience: A Study of William Morris's Poetic Reputation in England, 1858–1900.* The Hague: Mouton, 1975.

Garis, Robert. *The Dickens Theatre: A Reassessment of the Novels.* Oxford: Clarendon Press, 1965.

Garrett, Peter K. *The Victorian Multiplot Novel: Studies in Dialogical Form.* New Haven: Yale Univ. Press, 1980.

Gent, Margaret. " 'To Flinch From Modern Varnish': The Appeal of the Past to the Victorian Imagination." In *Victorian Poetry,* edited by Malcolm Bradbury and David Palmer. Stratford-upon-Avon Studies, no. 15. London: Edward Arnold, 1972. Pp. 11–35.

Gezari, Janet K. "*Romola* and the Myth of Apocalypse." In *George Eliot: Centenary Essays and an Unpublished Fragment,* edited by Anne Smith. London: Vision Press, 1980. Pp. 77–102.

Gibson, Mary Ellis. *History and the Prism of Art: Browning's Poetic Experiments.* Columbus: Ohio State Univ. Press, 1987.

Gilbert, Sandra M., and Susan Gubar. *The Madwoman in the Attic: The Woman Writer and the Nineteenth-Century Literary Imagination.* New Haven: Yale Univ. Press, 1979.

Gillon, Adam. *Joseph Conrad.* Boston: Twayne, 1982.

Gilmour, Robin. "A Lesser Thackeray? Trollope and the Victorian Novel." In *Anthony Trollope,* edited by Tony Bareham. New York: Barnes & Noble, 1980. Pp. 182–203.

Girouard, Mark. *The Return to Camelot: Chivalry and the English Gentleman.* New Haven and London: Yale Univ. Press, 1981.

Gittings, Robert. *Thomas Hardy's Later Years.* Boston: Little, Brown & Co., 1978.

Glock, Waldo Sumner. "Theme and Metaphor in *Diana of the Crossways.*" *Dalhousie Review* 65 (1985): 67–79.

Goetz, William R. "The Felicity and Infelicity of Marriage in *Jude the Obscure.*" *Nineteenth-Century Fiction* 38 (1983): 189–213.

Gold, Joseph. *Charles Dickens: Radical Moralist.* Minneapolis: Univ. of Minnesota Press, 1972.

Gordon, Jan B. "*Diana of the Crossways:* Internal History and the Brainstuff of

Fiction." In *Meredith Now: Some Critical Essays,* edited by Ian Fletcher. London: Routledge & Kegan Paul, 1971. Pp. 246–64.

Gosse, Edmund. *Coventry Patmore.* London: Hodder & Stoughton, 1905.

Gould, Stephen Jay. "Appendix A: Stephen Jay Gould's Extemporaneous Comments on Evolutionary Hope and Realities." In *Darwin's Legacy* (Proc. Nobel Conference 18, Gustavus Adolphus College), edited by Charles L. Hamrum. San Francisco: Harper & Row, 1983. Pp. 97–103.

————. *Time's Arrow, Time's Cycle: Myth and Metaphor in the Discovery of Geological Time.* Cambridge: Harvard Univ. Press, 1987.

Gray, J. M. *Thro' the Vision of the Night: A Study of Source, Evolution, and Structure in Tennyson's Idylls of the King.* Montreal: McGill-Queen's Univ. Press, 1980.

Griest, Guinevere L. *Mudie's Circulating Library and the Victorian Novel.* Bloomington: Indiana Univ. Press, 1970.

Gridley, Roy E. *Browning.* London and Boston: Routledge & Kegan Paul, 1972.

Gross, John. *The Rise and Fall of the Man of Letters: A Study of the Idiosyncratic and the Humane in Modern Literature.* New York: Macmillan, 1969.

————. "*A Tale of Two Cities.*" In *Dickens and the Twentieth Century,* edited by John Gross and Gabriel Pearson. Toronto: Univ. of Toronto Press, 1962. Pp. 187–97.

Guerard, Albert J. *Conrad the Novelist.* Cambridge: Harvard Univ. Press, 1966.

————. *Thomas Hardy: The Novels and Stories.* Cambridge: Harvard Univ. Press, 1949.

Hagedorn, Roger. "Technology and Economic Exploitation: The Serial as a Form of Narrative Presentation." *Wide Angle* 10, no. 4 (1988): 4–12.

Haight, Gordon S. *George Eliot: A Biography.* New York: Oxford Univ. Press, 1968.

————, and Rosemary T. VanArsdel, eds. *George Eliot: A Centenary Tribute.* Totowa, N.J.: Barnes & Noble, 1982.

Hall, N. John. *Trollope and His Illustrators.* London: Macmillan, 1980.

Hall, Wayne E. "The *Dublin University Magazine* and Isaac Butt, 1834–1838." *Victorian Periodicals Review* 20 (1987): 43–56.

Halperin, John. *Trollope and Politics.* London: Macmillan, 1977.

Hamer, Mary. *Writing By Numbers: Trollope's Serial Fiction.* Cambridge: Cambridge Univ. Press, 1987.

Harden, Edgar. *The Emergence of Thackeray's Serial Fiction.* Athens: Univ. of Georgia Press, 1979.

Hardy, Barbara. *The Exposure of Luxury: Radical Themes in Thackeray.* Pittsburgh: Univ. of Pittsburgh Press, 1972.

————. *Forms of Feeling in Victorian Fiction.* Athens: Ohio Univ. Press, 1985.

————. Introduction and Notes. *Daniel Deronda,* by George Eliot. New York: Penguin, 1967.

Hardy, Florence E. *The Early Life of Thomas Hardy: 1840–1891.* New York: Macmillan, 1928.

————. *The Later Years of Thomas Hardy, 1892–1928.* New York: Macmillan, 1930.

Hardy, Thomas. *The Dynasts. A Drama of the Napoleonic Wars, in Three Parts, Nineteen Acts, and One Hundred and Thirty Scenes.* London: Macmillan, 1904–8.

————. *Hearts Insurgent*. New York: *Harper's New Monthly Magazine*, 1894–95.

Harrold, William E. *The Variance and the Unity: A Study of the Complementary Poems of Robert Browning*. Athens: Ohio Univ. Press, 1973.

Harvey, Geoffrey. *The Art of Anthony Trollope*. New York: St. Martin's Press, 1980.

Hassett, Constance W. *The Elusive Self in the Poetry of Robert Browning*. Athens: Ohio Univ. Press, 1982.

Hay, Eloise Knapp. "*Lord Jim:* From Sketch to Novel." In *Twentieth Century Interpretations of Lord Jim,* edited by Robert E. Kuehn. Englewood Cliffs, N.J.: Prentice-Hall, 1969. Pp. 14–34.

Hayles, N. Katherine. *The Cosmic Web: Scientific Field Models and Literary Strategies in the Twentieth Century*. Ithaca, N.Y.: Cornell Univ. Press, 1984.

Herbert, Christopher. *Trollope and Comic Pleasure*. Chicago: Univ. of Chicago Press, 1987.

Herring, Paul D. "The Number Plans for *Dombey and Son:* Some Further Observations." *Modern Philology* 68 (1970): 151–87.

Hester, Erwin. "George Eliot's Use of Historical Events in *Daniel Deronda.*" *English Language Notes* 4 (1966): 115–18.

Hobsbawm, E. J. *The Age of Empire: 1875–1914*. New York: Pantheon, 1987.

Hodgson, Amanda. *The Romances of William Morris*. Cambridge: Cambridge Univ. Press, 1987.

Holmstrom, John, and Laurence Lerner, eds. *George Eliot and Her Readers: A Selection of Contemporary Reviews*. New York: Barnes & Noble, 1966.

Holzman, Michael. "Propaganda, Passion, and Literary Art in William Morris's *The Pilgrims of Hope.*" *Texas Studies in Literature and Language* 24 (1982): 372–93.

Homans, Margaret. "Tennyson and the Spaces of Life." *ELH* 46 (1979): 693–709.

Horton, Susan. *Interpreting Interpreting: Interpreting Dickens's Dombey*. Baltimore: Johns Hopkins Univ. Press, 1979.

————. *The Reader in the Dickens World: Style and Response*. Pittsburgh: Univ. of Pittsburgh Press, 1981.

Horsman, Alan. Introduction. *Dombey and Son,* by Charles Dickens, edited by Alan Horsman. Oxford: Clarendon Press, 1974.

Houghton, Walter E. "Periodical Literature and the Articulate Classes." *The Victorian Periodical Press: Samplings and Soundings,* edited by Joanne Shattock and Michael Wolff. Toronto: Leicester Univ. Press and Univ. of Toronto Press, 1982. Pp. 3–27.

————. *The Victorian Frame of Mind, 1830–1870*. 1957. Rpt., New Haven: Yale Univ. Press, 1971.

Howarth, Herbert. "The Poor Man and the *Dynasts.*" *Mosaic* 3, no. 1 (1969): 102–15.

Hughes, Linda K. "Entombing the Angel: Patmore's Revisions of *Angel in the House.*" In *Victorian Authors and Their Works: Revision Motivations and Modes,* edited by Judith Kennedy. Athens: Ohio Univ. Press, 1991. 140–68.

————. "Tennyson's Urban Arthurians: Victorian Audiences and the 'City Built to Music.' " In *King Arthur through the Ages,* 2 vols., edited by Mildred Leake Day and Valerie Lagorio. New York and London: Garland, 1990. 2:39–61.

———, and Michael Lund. "Linear Stories and Circular Visions: The Decline of the Victorian Serial." In *Chaos and Order: Complex Dynamics in Literature and Science,* edited by N. Katherine Hayles. Chicago: Univ. of Chicago Press, 1991.

———, and ———. "Studying Victorian Serials." *Literary Research* 11 (1986): 235–52.

Hutter, Albert D. "Nation and Generation in *A Tale of Two Cities.*" *PMLA* 93 (1978): 448–62.

———. "The Novelist as Resurrectionist: Dickens and the Dilemma of Death." *Dickens Studies Annual* 12 (1983): 1–39.

Hutton, Richard Holt. Review of *Middlemarch. Spectator,* 7 December 1872, rpt. in *George Eliot: The Critical Heritage,* edited by David Carroll. New York: Barnes & Noble, 1971. Pp. 305–6.

Ikeler, A. Abbott. "That Peculiar Book: Critics, Common Readers, and *The Way We Live Now.*" *College Language Association Journal* 30 (1986): 219–40.

Ingham, Patricia. "The Evolution of *Jude the Obscure.*" *Review of English Studies,* n.s. 27 (1976): 27–37, 159–69.

Irvine, William, and Park Honan. *The Book, The Ring, and the Poet: A Biography of Robert Browning.* New York: McGraw-Hill, 1974.

Iser, Wolfgang. *The Act of Reading: A Theory of Aesthetic Response.* Baltimore: Johns Hopkins Univ. Press, 1978.

James, Henry. "The Novel in 'The Ring and the Book.' " *Quarterly Review* 217 (1912): 68–87.

James, Louis. "The Trouble with Betsy: Periodicals and the Common Reader in Mid-Nineteenth-Century England." *The Victorian Periodical Press: Samplings and Soundings,* edited by Joanne Shattock and Michael Wolff. Toronto: Leicester Univ. Press and Univ. of Toronto Press, 1982. Pp. 349–66.

Jann, Rosemary. *The Art and Science of Victorian History.* Columbus: Ohio State Univ. Press, 1985.

Jones, Howard Mumford. "1859 and the Idea of Crisis: General Introduction." In *1859: Entering an Age of Crisis,* edited by Philip Appleman, William A. Madden, and Michael Wolff. Bloomington: Indiana Univ. Press, 1959. Pp. 13–28.

Jones, R. T. *George Eliot.* Cambridge: Cambridge Univ. Press, 1970.

Jordanova, L. J. Introduction. *Languages of Nature: Critical Essays on Science and Literature,* edited by L. J. Jordanova. New Brunswick, N.J.: Rutgers Univ. Press, 1986. Pp. 15–47.

Kaplan, Fred. *Dickens and Mesmerism: The Hidden Springs of Fiction.* Princeton: Princeton Univ. Press, 1975.

Karl, Frederick, and Laurence Davies, eds. *The Collected Letters of Joseph Conrad.* Vol. 2, *1898–1902.* Cambridge: Cambridge Univ. Press, 1986.

Kearney, John P. "Time and Beauty in *Daniel Deronda.*" *Nineteenth-Century Fiction* 26 (1971): 286–306.

Kendrick, Walter M. *The Novel Machine: The Theory and Fiction of Anthony Trollope.* Baltimore: Johns Hopkins Univ. Press, 1980.

Kern, Stephen. *The Culture of Time and Space, 1880–1918.* Cambridge: Harvard Univ. Press, 1983.

Khattab, Ezzat A. *The Critical Reception of Browning's The Ring and the Book: 1868–1889 and 1951–1968.* Salzburg Studies in English Literature, edited by James Hogg; Romantic Reassessment, no. 66. Salzburg: Institut für Englische Sprache und Literatur, Universität Salzburg, 1977.

Kiernan, Victor. "Tennyson, King Arthur, and Imperialism." In *Culture, Ideology, and Politics: Essays for Eric Hobsbawm,* edited by Raphael Samuel and Gareth Stedman Jones. London: Routledge & Kegan Paul, 1982. Pp. 126–48.

Kincaid, James R. *The Novels of Anthony Trollope.* Oxford: Clarendon Press, 1977.

———. *Tennyson's Major Poems: The Comic and Ironic Patterns.* New Haven: Yale Univ. Press, 1975.

Kirchhoff, Frederick. "The Aesthetic Discipline of *The Earthly Paradise.*" *Victorian Poetry* 18 (1980): 229–40.

———. *William Morris.* Boston: Twayne, 1979.

Klancher, Jon F. *The Making of English Reading Audiences, 1790–1832.* Madison: Univ. of Wisconsin Press, 1987.

Klinger, Helmut. "Varieties of Failure: The Significance of Trollope's *The Prime Minister.*" *English Miscellany* 23 (1974): 167–83.

Knight, Stephen. *Arthurian Literature and Society.* New York: St. Martin's Press, 1983.

Knoepflmacher, U. C. "Genre and the Integration of Gender: From Wordsworth to George Eliot to Virginia Woolf." In *Victorian Literature and Society: Essays Presented to Richard D. Altick.* Columbus: Ohio State Univ. Press, 1984. Pp. 94–118.

———. *Laughter and Despair: Readings in Ten Novels of the Victorian Era.* Berkeley: Univ. of California Press, 1971.

———. *Religious Humanism and the Victorian Novel: George Eliot, Walter Pater, and Samuel Butler.* Princeton: Princeton Univ. Press, 1965.

Kramer, Dale. *Thomas Hardy: The Forms of Tragedy.* Detroit: Wayne State Univ. Press, 1975.

Kucich, John. *Repression in Victorian Fiction: Charlotte Brontë, George Eliot, and Charles Dickens.* Berkeley: Univ. of California Press, 1987.

Lang, Cecil Y. *Tennyson's Arthurian Psycho-Drama.* Tennyson Society Occasional Paper, no. 5. Lincoln, England: Tennyson Society, 1983.

Lansbury, Coral. *The Reasonable Man: Trollope's Legal Fiction.* Princeton: Princeton Univ. Press, 1981.

Letwin, Shirley Robin. *The Gentleman in Trollope: Individuality and Moral Conduct.* Cambridge: Harvard Univ. Press, 1982.

Levine, George. "Dickens and Darwin, Science, and Narrative Form." *Texas Studies in Literature and Language* 28 (1986): 250–80.

———. *The Realistic Imagination: English Fiction from Frankenstein to Lady Chatterley.* Chicago: Univ. of Chicago Press, 1981.

———. " 'Romola' as Fable." In *Critical Essays on George Eliot,* edited by Barbara Hardy. New York: Barnes & Noble, 1970. Pp. 78–98.

Liddell, Robert. *The Novels of George Eliot.* New York: St. Martin's Press, 1977.

Lindsay, Jack. *George Meredith: His Life and Work.* London: The Bodley Head, 1956.

Lodge, David. "*Jude the Obscure:* Pessimism and Fictional Form." In *Critical*

Approaches to the Fiction of Thomas Hardy, edited by Dale Kramer. New York: Barnes & Noble, 1979. Pp. 193–201.

Lonoff, Sue. "Multiple Narratives and Relative Truths: A Study of *The Ring and the Book, The Woman in White,* and *The Moonstone.*" *Browning Institute Studies* 10 (1982): 143–61.

Loofbourow, John. *Thackeray and the Form of Fiction.* Princeton: Princeton Univ. Press, 1964.

Lund, Michael. *Reading Thackeray.* Detroit: Wayne State Univ. Press, 1988.

McCormick, John. Introduction. *The Prime Minister,* by Anthony Trollope, edited by Jennifer Uglow. New York: Oxford Univ. Press, 1983.

MacDonald, Susan Peck. *Anthony Trollope.* Boston: Twayne, 1987.

McElderry, B. R., Jr. "The Narrative Structure of Browning's *The Ring and the Book.*" *Research Studies* (State College of Washington) 11 (1943): 193–233.

———. "Victorian Evaluation of *The Ring and the Book.*" *Research Studies* (State College of Washington) 7 (1939): 75–89.

McGowan, John P. *Representation and Revelation: Victorian Realism from Carlyle to Yeats.* Columbia: Univ. of Missouri Press, 1986.

Mackail, J. W. *The Life of William Morris.* 2 vols. 1899. Rpt., London: Longmans, Green & Co., 1922.

McMaster, Juliet. *Dickens the Designer.* London: Macmillan, 1987.

———. "George Eliot's Language of the Sense." In *George Eliot: A Centenary Tribute,* edited by Gordon S. Haight and Rosemary T. VanArsdel. Totowa, N.J.: Barnes & Noble, 1982. Pp. 11–27.

———. *Thackeray: The Major Novels.* Toronto: Univ. of Toronto Press, 1971.

———. *Trollope's Palliser Novels.* New York: Oxford Univ. Press, 1978.

McMaster, R. D. *Trollope and the Law.* New York: St. Martin's Press, 1986.

———. "Women in *The Way We Live Now.*" *English Studies in Canada* 7 (1981): 68–80.

Maidment, Brian. "Readers Fair and Foul: John Ruskin and the Periodical Press." *The Victorian Periodical Press: Samplings and Soundings,* edited by Joanne Shattock and Michael Wolff. Toronto: Leicester Univ. Press and Univ. of Toronto Press, 1982. Pp. 29–58.

Mancoff, Debra. *The Arthurian Revival in Victorian Painting.* New York and London: Garland, 1990.

Mann, Karen B. *The Language That Makes George Eliot's Fiction.* Baltimore: Johns Hopkins Univ. Press, 1983.

Manning, Sylvia Bank. *Dickens as Satirist.* New Haven: Yale Univ. Press, 1971.

Marcus, Steven. *Dickens: From Pickwick to Dombey.* New York: Basic Books, 1965.

Martin, Carol A. "Contemporary Critics and Judaism in *Daniel Deronda.*" *Victorian Periodicals Review* 21 (1988): 90–107.

Martin, Graham. "'Daniel Deronda': George Eliot and Political Change." In *Critical Essays on George Eliot,* edited by Barbara Hardy. New York: Barnes & Noble, 1970. Pp. 133–50.

Martin, Loy D. *Browning's Dramatic Monologues and the Post-Romantic Subject.* Baltimore and London: Johns Hopkins Univ. Press, 1985.

Martin, Wallace. *Recent Theories of Narrative.* Ithaca, N.Y., and London: Cornell Univ. Press, 1986.

Maurer, Oscar. "William Morris and the Poetry of Escape." In *Nineteenth-Century Studies,* edited by Herbert Davis, William C. DeVane, and R. C. Bald. 1940. Rpt., Folcroft, Pa.: Folcroft Press, 1969. Pp. 247–76.

Measures, Joyce Elaine. *Meredith's Diana of the Crossways: Revisions and Reconsiderations.* Ann Arbor, Mich.: University Microfilms, 1966.

Meisel, Martin. *Realizations: Narrative, Pictorial, and Theatrical Arts in Nineteenth-Century England.* Princeton: Princeton Univ. Press, 1983.

Meisel, Perry. *Thomas Hardy: The Return of the Repressed.* New Haven: Yale Univ. Press, 1972.

Menaghan, John M. "Embodied Truth: *The Ring and the Book* Reconsidered." *University of Toronto Quarterly* 52 (1983): 263–76.

Meredith, George. *Diana of the Crossways.* London: *Fortnightly Review,* June–December 1884.

Miller, D. A. "The Novel as Usual: Trollope's *Barchester Towers.*" In *Sex, Politics, and Science in the Nineteenth-Century Novel,* edited by Ruth Bernard Yeazell. Baltimore: Johns Hopkins Univ. Press, 1986. Pp. 1–38.

Miller, J. Hillis. *Charles Dickens: The World of His Novels.* Cambridge: Harvard Univ. Press, 1965.

———. *Fiction and Repetition.* Cambridge: Harvard Univ. Press, 1982.

———. *The Linguistic Moment.* Princeton: Princeton Univ. Press, 1985.

———. *Thomas Hardy: Distance and Desire.* Cambridge: Harvard Univ. Press, 1970.

Millgate, Michael. *Thomas Hardy: A Biography.* New York: Random House, 1982.

Morris, May. Introductions. *The Collected Works of William Morris.* 24 vols. New York: Russell & Russell, 1966.

———. *William Morris: Artist, Writer, Socialist.* 2 vols. 1936. Rpt., New York: Russell & Russell, 1966.

Morris, William. *The Earthly Paradise.* 3 vols. London: F. S. Ellis, 1868–70.

———. *The Pilgrims of Hope.* London: *Commonweal,* March 1885–3 July 1886.

Moser, Thomas C., ed. *Joseph Conrad's Lord Jim.* New York: W. W. Norton, 1960.

Moynahan, Julian. "Dealings with the Firm of Dombey and Son: Firmness versus Wetness." In *Dickens and the Twentieth Century,* edited by John Gross and Gabriel Pearson. 1962. Rpt., London: Routledge & Kegan Paul, 1966. Pp. 121–31.

Muendel, Renate. *George Meredith.* Boston: Twayne, 1986.

Murray, Isabel. "*Pilgrims of Hope:* Aspects of the Poetry of Morris and Chesterton." *Chesterton Review* 4 (1977–78): 7–36.

Murray, Janet Horowitz. *Courtship and the English Novel.* New York: Garland, 1987.

Myers, William. *The Teaching of George Eliot.* Totowa, N.J.: Barnes & Noble, 1984.

Najder, Zdzislaw. *Joseph Conrad: A Chronicle,* translated by Halina Carroll-Najder. New Brunswick, N.J.: Rutgers Univ. Press, 1983.

Newton, K. M. *George Eliot: Romantic Humanist.* Totowa, N.J.: Barnes & Noble, 1981.

Oberg, Charlotte H. *A Pagan Prophet: William Morris.* Charlottesville: Univ. Press of Virginia, 1978.

Oliver, E. J. *Coventry Patmore.* New York: Sheed & Ward, 1956.

Orel, Harold. *Thomas Hardy's Epic-Drama: A Study of The Dynasts.* Lawrence: Univ. of Kansas Press, 1963.

———. "What *The Dynasts* Meant to Hardy." *Victorian Poetry* 17 (1979): 109–23.

Page, Frederick. *Patmore: A Study in Poetry.* London: Oxford Univ. Press, 1933.

Page, Norman. Preface. *Jude the Obscure,* by Thomas Hardy, edited by Norman Page. New York: W. W. Norton, 1978.

Parins, James W. "Poetic Calculus: Patmore's Parabolic Vocabulary." *Victorians Institute Journal* 6 (1977): 49–66.

Paris, Bernard J. *Experiments in Life: George Eliot's Quest for Values.* Detroit: Wayne State Univ. Press, 1965.

[Pater, Walter.] Review of *The Earthly Paradise,* parts 1 and 2. *Westminster Review* 90 (October 1868): 300–12. Rpt. in *William Morris: The Critical Heritage,* edited by Peter Faulkner. London: Routledge & Kegan Paul, 1973. Pp. 79–92.

[Patmore, Coventry.] *The Angel in the House: The Betrothal.* London: J. W. Parker & Son, 1854.

———. *The Angel in the House: The Espousals.* London: J. W. Parker & Son, 1856.

Patmore, Coventry. *Faithful for Ever.* London: J. W. Parker, 1860.

———. *The Poems of Coventry Patmore,* edited by Frederick Page. London: Oxford Univ. Press, 1949.

———. *The Victories of Love. Macmillan's Magazine,* October–December 1861.

———. *The Victories of Love.* London and Cambridge: Macmillan, 1863.

Patmore, Derek. *The Life and Times of Coventry Patmore.* London: Constable, 1949.

Pattison, Robert. *Tennyson and Tradition.* Cambridge: Harvard Univ. Press, 1979.

Peckham, Morse. "Afterword: Reflections on Historical Modes in the Nineteenth Century." In *Victorian Poetry,* edited by Malcolm Bradbury and David Palmer. Stratford-upon-Avon Studies, no. 15. London: Edward Arnold, 1972. Pp. 277–300.

Perkin, Harold. *The Origins of Modern English Society, 1780–1880.* London: Routledge & Kegan Paul, 1969.

Peters, Katherine. *Thackeray's Universe: Shifting Worlds of Imagination and Reality.* New York: Oxford Univ. Press, 1987.

Polhemus, Robert M. *The Changing World of Anthony Trollope.* Berkeley: Univ. of California Press, 1968.

———. *Comic Faith: The Great Tradition from Austen to Joyce.* Chicago: Univ. of Chicago Press, 1980.

Pollard, Arthur. *Anthony Trollope.* London: Routledge & Kegan Paul, 1978.

Pollard, Graham. "Serial Fiction." *New Paths in Book Collecting: Essays by Various Hands,* edited by John Carter. London: Constable, 1934. Pp. 245–77.

Poston, Lawrence. "Setting and Theme in *Romola.*" *Nineteenth-Century Fiction* 21 (1966): 225–33.

Pritchett, V. S. *George Meredith and English Comedy.* New York: Random House, 1969.

Purdy, Richard Little. *Thomas Hardy: A Bibliographical Study.* Oxford: Clarendon Press, 1954.

———, and Michael Millgate. *The Collected Letters of Thomas Hardy.* Vol. 2: *1893–1901.* Oxford: Clarendon Press, 1980.

Qualls, Barry V. *The Secular Pilgrims of Victorian Fiction: The Novel as Book of Life.* Cambridge: Cambridge Univ. Press, 1982.

Raval, Suresh. "Narrative and Authority in *Lord Jim:* Conrad's Art of Failure." *ELH* 48 (1981): 387–410.

Rawlins, Jack P. *Thackeray's Novels: A Fiction That Is True.* Berkeley: Univ. of California Press, 1974.

Ray, Gordon. *Thackeray: The Age of Wisdom, 1847–1863.* New York: McGraw-Hill, 1958.

Redinger, Ruby V. *George Eliot: The Emergent Self.* New York: Knopf, 1975.

Reed, John R. "Tennyson's Narrative on Narration." *Victorian Poetry* 24 (1986): 189–205.

Ricks, Christopher. "The Pink Toads in *Lord Jim.*" *Essays in Criticism* 31 (1981): 142–44.

———. *Tennyson.* New York: Collier, 1972.

———, ed. *The Poems of Tennyson.* 1969. Rpt., New York: W. W. Norton, 1972.

Rosen, Charles. "Romantic Originals." *New York Review of Books,* 17 December 1987, pp. 22, 24–31.

Rosenberg, John D. *The Fall of Camelot: A Study of Tennyson's "Idylls of the King."* Cambridge: Harvard Univ. Press, 1973.

Roussel, Royal. *The Metaphysics of Darkness: A Study in the Unity and Development of Conrad's Fiction.* Baltimore: Johns Hopkins Univ. Press, 1971.

Russell, Norman. *The Novelist and Mammon: Literary Responses to the World of Commerce in the Nineteenth Century.* Oxford: Clarendon Press, 1986.

Ryals, Clyde de L. *From the Great Deep: Essays on Idylls of the King.* Athens: Ohio Univ. Press, 1967.

Sacks, Sheldon. *Fiction and the Shape of Belief.* Berkeley: Univ. of California Press, 1964.

Sadleir, Michael. *Trollope: A Commentary.* London: Oxford Univ. Press, 1927.

Sadoff, Dianne F. *Monsters of Affection: Dickens, Eliot, and Brontë on Fatherhood.* Baltimore: Johns Hopkins Univ. Press, 1982.

Saldivar, Ramon. "*Jude the Obscure:* Reading and the Spirit of the Law." *ELH* 50 (1983): 607–25.

Schivelbusch, Wolfgang. *The Railway Journey: The Industrialization of Time and Space in the Nineteenth Century.* 2d English ed. Berkeley: Univ. of California Press, 1986.

Schmidt, Barbara Quinn. "Novelists, Publishers, and Fiction in Middle-Class Magazines: 1860–1880." *Victorian Periodicals Review* 17 (1984): 142–53.

Schulz, Max F. *Paradise Preserved: Recreations of Eden in Eighteenth- and Nineteenth-Century England.* Cambridge: Cambridge Univ. Press, 1985.

Schwartz, Barry N. "*Jude the Obscure* in the Age of Anxiety." *Studies in English Literature* 10 (1970): 793–804.

Schwarz, Daniel R. *Conrad: Almayer's Folly to Under Western Eyes.* Ithaca, N.Y.: Cornell Univ. Press, 1980.

Sedgwick, Eve Kosofsky. "The Beast in the Closet: James and the Writing of Homosexual Panic." In *Sex, Politics, and Science in the Nineteenth-Century Novel,* edited by Ruth Bernard Yeazell. Baltimore: Johns Hopkins Univ. Press, 1986. Pp. 148–86.

Seidel, Michael. "Isolation and Narrative Power: A Meditation on Conrad at the Boundaries." *Criticism* 27 (1985): 73–95.

Shaw, W. David. *The Lucid Veil: Poetic Truth in the Victorian Age.* Madison: Univ. of Wisconsin Press, 1987.

Sherry, Norman, ed. *Conrad: The Critical Heritage.* London: Routledge & Kegan Paul, 1973.

Showalter, Elaine. *A Literature of Their Own: British Women Novelists from Brontë to Lessing.* Princeton, N.J.: Princeton Univ. Press, 1977.

Shuttleworth, Sally. *George Eliot and Nineteenth-Century Science: The Make-Believe of a Beginning.* Cambridge: Cambridge Univ. Press, 1984.

Silver, Carole. *The Romance of William Morris.* Athens: Ohio Univ. Press, 1982.

Skilton, David. *Anthony Trollope and His Contemporaries.* New York: St. Martin's Press, 1972.

Slakey, Roger L. "Melmotte's Death: A Prism of Meaning in *The Way We Live Now.*" *ELH* 34 (1967): 248–59.

Slinn, E. Warwick. *Browning and the Fictions of Identity.* Totowa, N.J.: Barnes & Noble, 1982.

Smalley, Donald, ed. *Trollope: The Critical Heritage.* London: Routledge & Kegan Paul, 1969.

Smith, Grahame. *The Novel and Society: Defoe to George Eliot.* Totowa, N.J.: Barnes & Noble, 1984.

Solimine, Joseph, Jr. "The *Idylls of the King:* The Rise, Decline, and Fall of the State." *Personalist* 50 (1969): 105–16.

Southerington, F. R. *Hardy's Vision of Man.* New York: Barnes & Noble, 1971.

Srebrnik, Patricia T. *Alexander Strahan, Victorian Publisher.* Ann Arbor: Univ. of Michigan Press, 1986.

Staines, David. *Tennyson's Camelot: The Idylls of the King and Its Medieval Sources.* Waterloo, Ontario: Wilfred Laurier Univ. Press, 1982.

Stephen, Sir James Fitzjames. Review of *A Tale of Two Cities. Saturday Review,* 17 December 1859, pp. 741–43. Rpt. in *The Dickens Critics,* edited by George H. Ford and Lauriat Lane, Jr. Ithaca, N.Y.: Cornell Univ. Press, 1961. Pp. 38–48.

Stevenson, Lionel. *The Ordeal of George Meredith.* New York: Charles Scribner's Sons, 1953.

Stone, Donald D. *Novelists in a Changing World: Meredith, James, and the Transformation of English Fiction in the 1880's.* Cambridge: Harvard Univ. Press, 1972.

————. *The Romantic Impulse in Victorian Fiction.* Cambridge: Harvard Univ. Press, 1980.

Stone, Harry. *Dickens and the Invisible World: Fairy Tales, Fantasy, and Novel-Making.* Bloomington: Indiana Univ. Press, 1979.

Sudrann, Jean. "*Daniel Deronda* and the Landscape of Exile." *ELH* 37 (1970): 433–55.

Sullivan, Mary Rose. *Browning's Voices in The Ring and the Book: A Study of Method and Meaning.* Toronto: Univ. of Toronto Press, 1969.

Sullivan, William J. "The Sketch of the Three Masks in *Romola.*" *Victorian Newsletter* 41 (1972): 9–13.

Sulloway, Frank J. "The Metaphor and the Rock." *New York Review of Books,* 28 May 1987, pp. 37–40.

Sunstroem, David. "Order and Disorder in *Jude the Obscure.*" *English Literature in Transition* 24 (1981): 6–15.

Super, R. H. "Was *The Way We Live Now* a Commercial Success?" *Nineteenth-Century Fiction* 39 (1984): 202–10.

Sutherland, John A. "The Commercial Success of *The Way We Live Now:* Some New Evidence." *Nineteenth-Century Fiction* 40 (1986): 460–67.

——. *Thackeray at Work.* London: Univ. of London, Athlone Press, 1974.

——. "Trollope at Work on *The Way We Live Now.*" *Nineteenth-Century Fiction* 37 (1982): 472–93.

Swann, Brian. "George Eliot's Ecumenical Jew, or, The Novel as Outdoor Temple." *Novel* 8 (1974): 39–50.

Tanner, Tony. *Adultery in the Novel: Contract and Transgression.* Baltimore: Johns Hopkins Univ. Press, 1979.

——. "Butterflies and Beetles—Conrad's Two Truths." In *Twentieth Century Interpretations of Lord Jim,* edited by Robert E. Kuehn. Englewood Cliffs, N.J.: Prentice-Hall, 1969. Pp. 53–67.

Teets, Bruce E. "Joseph Conrad and Poststructuralism." *English Literature in Transition* 3 (1985): 95–107.

Tennebaum, Elizabeth Brody. "'And the Woman is Dead Now': A Reconsideration of Conrad's Stein." *Studies in the Novel* (North Texas State Univ.) 10 (1978): 335–45.

Tennyson, Alfred. *Gareth and Lynette Etc.* London: Strahan, 1872.

——. *The Holy Grail and Other Poems.* London: Strahan, 1870.

——. *Idylls of the King.* London: Edward Moxon, 1859.

——. "The Last Tournament." *Contemporary Review* 19 (December 1871), 1–22.

——. *Poems.* Vol. 2. London: Edward Moxon, 1842.

——. *Tiresias and Other Poems.* London: Macmillan, 1885.

——. *The Works of Tennyson in Six Volumes.* London: Strahan, 1873.

Thackeray, William Makepeace. *The Newcomes.* London: Bradbury and Evans, 1853–55.

Thomas, Donald. *Robert Browning: A Life within Life.* New York: Viking, 1983.

Thompson, E. P. *William Morris: Romantic to Revolutionary.* 1955. Rpt., New York: Pantheon, 1977.

Tillotson, Geoffrey, and Donald Hawes, eds. *Thackeray: The Critical Heritage.* London: Routledge & Kegan Paul, 1968.

Tillotson, Kathleen. *Novels of the Eighteen-Forties.* 1954. Rpt., London: Oxford Univ. Press, 1956.

——. "Tennyson's Serial Poem." In *Mid-Victorian Studies,* by Geoffrey and Kathleen Tillotson. London: Univ. of London, Athlone Press, 1965. Pp. 80–109.

Timko, Michael. "Splendid Impressions and Picturesque Means: Dickens, Carlyle, and the French Revolution." *Dickens Studies Annual* 12 (1983): 177–95.

Tobin, Patricia D. *Time and the Novel: The Genealogical Imperative.* Princeton: Princeton Univ. Press, 1978.

Torgovnick, Marianna. *Closure in the Novel.* Princeton: Princeton Univ. Press, 1981.

Toulmin, Stephen, and June Goodfield. *The Discovery of Time.* 1965. Rpt., Chicago: Univ. of Chicago Press, 1977.

Tracy, Robert. *Trollope's Later Novels.* Berkeley: Univ. of California Press, 1978.

Trodd, Anthea. Introduction. *The Moonstone,* by Wilkie Collins. Oxford: Oxford Univ. Press, 1982.

Trollope, Anthony. *The Prime Minister.* London: Chapman & Hall, 1875–76.

————. *The Way We Live Now.* London: Chapman & Hall, 1874–75.

Tucker, Herbert F., Jr. *Browning's Beginnings: The Act of Disclosure.* Minneapolis: Univ. of Minnesota Press, 1980.

Turner, Paul. *Tennyson.* London: Routledge & Kegan Paul, 1976.

Uglow, Jennifer. Notes. *The Prime Minister,* by Anthony Trollope, edited by Jennifer Uglow. New York: Oxford Univ. Press, 1983.

Vann, J. Don. *Victorian Novels in Serial.* New York: MLA, 1985.

Vargish, Thomas. *The Providential Aesthetic in Victorian Fiction.* Charlottesville: Univ. Press of Virginia, 1985.

Vigar, Penelope. *The Novels of Thomas Hardy: Illusion and Reality.* London: Univ. of London, Athlone Press, 1974.

Wain, John. Introduction. *The Dynasts,* by Thomas Hardy. New York: St. Martin's Press, 1965.

Wall, Stephen. "Trollope, Satire, and *The Way We Live Now.*" *Essays in Criticism* 37 (1987): 43–61.

Watt, Ian. *Conrad in the Nineteenth Century.* Berkeley: Univ. of California Press, 1979.

Weinig, Sister Mary Anthony. *Coventry Patmore.* Boston: Twayne, 1981.

Weissman, Judith. "*Tess of the D'Urbervilles:* A Demystification of the Eternal Triangle of Tennyson's *Idylls of the King.*" *Colby Library Quarterly* 11 (1975): 189–97.

Wellesley Index to Victorian Periodicals, 1824–1900, edited by Walter E. Houghton, Esther Rhoads Houghton, and Jean Harris Slingerland. Toronto: Univ. of Toronto Press, 1966–1987.

Welsh, Alexander. *The City of Dickens.* 1971. Rpt., Cambridge: Harvard Univ. Press, 1986.

————. *George Eliot and Blackmail.* Cambridge: Harvard Univ. Press, 1985.

Wickens, G. Glen. "Hardy's Inconsistent Spirits and the Philosophic Form of *The Dynasts.*" In *The Poetry of Thomas Hardy,* edited by Patricia Clements and Juliet Grindle. Totowa, N.J.: Barnes & Noble, 1980. Pp. 101–18.

Wiener, Joel H. "Edmund Yates: The Gossip as Editor." In *Innovators and Preachers: The Role of the Editor in Victorian England,* edited by Joel H. Wiener. Westport, Conn.: Greenwood Press, 1985. Pp. 259–74.

Wiles, R. M. *Serial Publication in England before 1750.* Cambridge: Cambridge Univ. Press, 1957.

Wilkenfeld, R. B. "Tennyson's Camelot: The Kingdom of Folly." *University of Toronto Quarterly* 37 (1968): 281–94.

Williams, Ioan, ed. *Meredith: The Critical Heritage.* London: Routledge & Kegan Paul, 1971.

Williams, Raymond. Introduction. *Dombey and Son,* by Charles Dickens. New York: Penguin, 1970. Pp. 11–34.

Wilson, Keith. "'Flower of Man's Intelligence': World and Overworld in *The Dynasts.*" *Victorian Poetry* 17 (1979): 124–33.

Wilt, Judith. *Ghosts of the Gothic: Austen, Eliot, and Lawrence.* Princeton, N.J.: Princeton Univ. Press, 1980.

———. *The Readable People of George Meredith.* Princeton, N.J.: Princeton Univ. Press, 1975.

Witemeyer, Hugh. *George Eliot and the Visual Arts.* New Haven, Conn.: Yale Univ. Press, 1979.

Wolff, Michael. "Victorian Reviewers and Cultural Responsibility." In *1859: Entering an Age of Crisis,* edited by Philip Appleman, William A. Madden, and Michael Wolff. Bloomington: Indiana Univ. Press, 1959. Pp. 269–89.

Wolff, Robert Lee. "The Way Things Were: The Hundredth Anniversary of a Classic: Anthony Trollope's *The Way We Live Now.*" *Harvard Magazine* 77 (1975): 44–50.

Wood, James Playsted. *Magazines in the United States.* 2d ed. 1943. Rpt., New York: Ronald Press, 1971.

Woodfield, Malcolm. "Victorian Weekly Reviews and Reviewing after 1860: R. H. Hutton and the *Spectator.*" In *Yearbook of English Studies* 16 (Literary Periodicals Special Number, edited by C. J. Rawson and Jenny Mezciems). London: Modern Humanities Research Association, 1986. Pp. 74–91.

Woolford, John. "Periodicals and the Practice of Literary Criticism, 1855– 64." *The Victorian Periodical Press: Samplings and Soundings,* edited by Joanne Shattock and Michael Wolff. Toronto: Leicester Univ. Press and Univ. of Toronto Press, 1982. Pp. 109–42.

Wright, Andrew. *Anthony Trollope: Dream and Art.* Chicago: Univ. of Chicago Press, 1983.

Wright, Walter F. *The Shaping of The Dynasts: A Study in Thomas Hardy.* Lincoln: Univ. of Nebraska Press, 1967.

Yelin, Louise. "Strategies for Survival: Florence and Edith in *Dombey and Son.*" *Victorian Studies* 22 (1979): 297–319.

Zietlow, Paul. "The Ascending Concerns of *The Ring and the Book:* Reality, Moral Vision, and Salvation." *Studies in Philology* 84 (1987): 194–218.

Zwinger, Lynda. "The Fear of the Father: Dombey and Daughter." *Nineteenth-Century Fiction* 39 (1985): 420–40.

Index